Exploring Western Civilization

1600 to the PRESENT

A WORKTEXT FOR THE ACTIVE STUDENT

Revised Edition

THOMAS J. KEHOE

HAROLD E. DAMEROW

JOSE M. DUVALL

KENDALL/HUNT PUBLISHING COMPANY
4050 Westmark Drive   Dubuque, Iowa 52002

Cover photos

Left—Louis XIV, 1643–1715.
Courtesy of The Metropolitan Museum of Art, Rogers Fund, 1920.

Right—Nikita Khrushchev, 1894–1971 (in front of picture of Vladimir Lenin, 1870–1924).
Courtesy of The Library of Congress. USN&WR Collection.

Copyright © 1994, 1999 by Thomas J. Kehoe, Harold E. Damerow and Jose M. Duvall

Revised Printing

ISBN 0-7872-6302-8

Printed in the United States of America
10 9 8 7 6 5 4

CONTENTS

EXPANDED CONTENTS

FOR EACH SUBCHAPTER*

---

 * Each subchapter (numbers 1 through 15) corresponds to approximately one week of subject matter in a one semester course lasting fifteen weeks.

LIST OF MAPS

PREFACE

"The present is part of a chain of events that links the past and the future. Since we cannot explore the future, it is only by studying the past that we can try to understand the present and, maybe, discern a glimmer of what is to come." These lines were taken from the Preface of Volume One, Exploring Western Civilization to 1648: A Worktext for the Active Student. They apply equally well as the opening for the revised edition of Volume Two, Exploring Western Civilization: 1600 to the Present.

The authors are pleased that there is a second edition of Volume Two. Dr. Thomas J. Kehoe and Prof. Jose M. Duvall welcome the addition of Dr. Harold E. Damerow to the team which is doing the revisions. This makes for the identical authorship of both volumes.

The authors once again want to emphasize that we have created a **worktext.** We have combined the features of a textbook, book of readings, and study guide. We want you, the student, to write in the margins, answer the sidebar questions, and take the various self-tests provided at the end of each chapter. There is a list of names and concepts that serve as a source for identification questions on a test. There are multiple choice questions similar to those which might be included on an objective type of examination. There are thought and full-length essay questions that you might want to answer both in your head and as writing samples.

Our worktext is written by three community college professors for all undergraduate students, but especially for those attending community colleges. We have kept the text simple without being simplistic. More and more students come to college without having taken a Western Civilization course in high school. Many of our adult students last took such a history course more than twenty years earlier. There is a need to familiarize contemporary students with the broad patterns of Western civilization before they delve into the sometimes overly encyclopedic standard texts.

Volume Two covers the Modern Period of history from the end of the wars of religion to the wars of the twentieth century. The end of the Thirty Years War in 1648 is usually considered to be the beginning of the modern European State System. Out of their feudal and medieval beginnings, a half dozen or so European states formed the core of that system: Portugal; Spain; the United Provinces of the Netherlands; France; England; the Hapsburg Empire of Austria and Hungary; Prussia and, after 1871, Germany; Russia; and, after 1860,

Italy. Some of these States established colonies and created empires in the Americas, Asia, and Africa. Technological innovation, associated with the Industrial Revolution, gave Europeans the military superiority required for their global dominance. Rivalries between these States led to great wars: the wars of the French Revolution and Napoleon, World War I, and World War II. But this contentious state system also produced governments limited by the rule of law, demands for the respect of human rights, democratic elections to choose political leaders, and social welfare legislation to benefit the poor. Since World War II, the great powers have been replaced by two superpowers: the United States and the Soviet Union. With end of the Cold War and the collapse of the Soviet Union with its ideology of communism in 1991, only one superpower remains.

The emergence of the European Union with a single currency creates new possibilities for a Europe that had almost destroyed itself in two world wars. This new Europe, while still linked to the United States through the North Atlantic Treaty Organization, is also in competition with the U.S. While powerful again, Europe is no longer the center of the globe as it had been for three hundred years. European colonialism is a thing of the past and the state system has truly become global. Resurgent Japan, Communist China, nuclear India, fundamentalist Iran, and many newly industrialized countries of what used to be called the Third World have truly, and for the first time, begun to create a global civilization with one hundred and eighty sovereign member states of the United Nations. Western Civilization has helped to fuel a new world civilization of the twenty-first century. This is the story which we will tell in Volume Two, Exploring Western Civilization: 1600 to the Present: A Worktext for the Active Student.

So write in the margins, tear out our multiple-choice tests, discuss the challenging issues presented, and above all enjoy the excitement of history. What a wondrous creature is mankind: what marvelous deeds and what villainous depravities, what sublime insights and what sordid immoralities. Mass murderers, empire builders, generals, scientists, and poets: all of us part of the human condition.

Acknowledgements

The authors would like to thank our spouses for their support and patience:

Toni Damerow
George B. Duvall
Jane C. Kehoe

Without their encouragement and considerable understanding, the completion of this work would have been impossible.

INTRODUCTION

Volume One, <u>Exploring Western Civilization to 1648: A Worktext for the Active Student</u>, by Thomas J. Kehoe, Harold Damerow, and Jose Marie Duvall ended with the Reformation Period and the resulting Wars of Religion. The Thirty Years war, in what was then called the Holy Roman Empire, and which is today called Germany, lasted from 1618 to 1648. The forces of Catholicism and of the Empire failed to wipe out the Protestants and the princes who championed Protestantism. The result was the end of Christian unity within Western Christendom and the permanent division of Europe into sectarian States.

Catholic France entered the war on the side of the Protestants, not because its kings favored Protestantism, but because dynastic rivalries made the French kings bitter enemies of the Hapsburgs. Keeping the Holy Roman Empire weak and disunited benefited the rising power of the Bourbon dynasty of France.

The result of the Thirty Years War was the creation, de facto, of the European State System. That system remained dominant in the world for the next three hundred years, until the end of World War II in 1945 and, in a significantly modified way, continued to function even at the end of the twentieth century. The coming of age of the European State System in 1648 is often used by historians to mark the beginning of the Modern Period of History.

Volume Two, <u>Exploring Western Civilization: 1600 to the Present: A Worktext for the Active Student</u>, covers this modern period of history. The Treaties of Westphalia marked the beginning of the modern state system. The Thirty Years War devastated the territories of the Holy Roman Empire, ended the last chance of centralization within that Empire, and definitively established the religious and political divisions of Europe for the next three hundred years. France and its Bourbon dynasty replaced the Hapsburg dynasty, with its two branches on the thrones of Spain and Austria, as the greatest power and dynasty on the European continent. The Hapsburg family, rulers of Spain, the Netherlands, Austria, diverse Italian possessions, and the Holy Roman Empire, had suffered a decisive defeat. The Spanish branch of that family had already lost its bid for dominance in Europe. The United Provinces of the Netherlands had their independence confirmed by the Treaty of Westphalia, as had the Swiss Confederation. The Holy Roman Empire became a weak confederation of more than 300 independent principalities, weakly united under an emperor who was elected by eight ecclesiastical and temporal princes. Despite their defeat, the Austrian branch of the

Hapsburg family survived until 1917. They remained the elective emperors of the Holy Roman Empire until 1806, when Napoleon mercifully ended the first Thousand Year Reich. They even gained a new power base, and great power status, when Leopold II took Hungary away from the slowly declining Ottoman Empire.

A Broader Look at History

Before we begin to look at the details of Modern European History, another look at the material already covered may be in order. It was during the Renaissance, that historians began to classify history into distinct periods. The Renaissance thinkers divided history into three periods: the Classical Period, the Dark Ages, and their own time, which they labeled the Rebirth. We know that the Dark Ages were never as dark as they seemed to the men of the Renaissance. Contemporary historians have given up this threefold division of time, but we have kept the basic idea.

History before 1648, for our purposes here, may be broadly divided into seven periods: 1. Natural History from the Big Bang to the Evolution of Humanity; 2. The Paleolithic; 3. The Neolithic; 4. The Earliest Civilizations: Sumerians and Egyptians; 5. Classical Civilization: Greeks and Romans: 1200 BC - 500 AD; 6. The Middle Ages: 500 - 1500 AD; 7. The Early Modern Period: 1350 - 1648 AD

1. Natural History from the Big Bang to the Evolution of Humanity. The Big Bang is supposed to have begun the physical universe some 15 billion years ago. Since then, the universe has evolved to its current shape of billions of galaxies, one of which is our own Milky Way galaxy. Our solar system is one of millions of stars within this galaxy and our planet is the third from our sun. Our solar system is about 4.6 billion years old. By about 4 million years ago, upright walking ancestors of mankind were living on earth. Their appearance and their use of tools begin the Paleolithic Period of Human History.

2. The Paleolithic. The Paleolithic or the Old Stone Age began when upright walking hominids began to shape stones into tools about 2 million years ago. Several species of hominids are found in the fossil record until about 200,000 years ago when our own species made its appearance. By the time of the Cro-Magnon culture, 20,000 years ago, all other hominid species had become extinct. The last of our human competitors were the Neanderthal Men.

Throughout the Paleolithic, hominids were foragers, scavengers, and hunters living, like other animals, off the bounty of nature. It is only after the last Ice Age, which ended about 12,000 years ago, that human beings entered a new stage of cultural development when they developed agriculture.

3. The Neolithic. The Neolithic or New Stone Age is also called the Age of Agriculture. About 12,000 years ago, human beings began the domestication of various animals and plants. People living in the highlands of modern-day Iran appear to have been the first to have begun the deliberate growing of grass seeds to harvest various grains. By 8000 BC, a sizable agricultural town had formed at Jericho. Primitive, village-based agricultural communities had developed throughout the Near East by 3500 BC.

Agricultural settlement spread throughout the world. Farmers came to replace hunters wherever suitable farming conditions could be found. The Paleolithic way of life survived only in deserts, rain forests, arctic regions, and other inhospitable places. Agriculture came to different parts of the world at different times and appears to have been independently developed.

In many ways, the Age of Agriculture continues to this day. We all continue to depend on agriculture as the primary basis for our food supply. In many parts of the world, including much of Africa and Asia, village agriculture remains at the core of what are called traditional societies. The way of life and the methods of agricultural production have little changed in these traditional village communities for thousands of years. But even in the remotest parts of the world, modern civilization with its methods of industrial production, including the mechanization of agriculture, is creating change. Modernization is in the process of transforming the entire planet.

4. The Earliest Civilizations: Sumerians and Egyptians. The two earliest civilizations on earth are those of the Sumerians and the Egyptians. Both were riverine civiliza-

tions, that is, they depended on rivers for their prosperity. The Sumerians were located in modern-day Iraq, at the mouth of the Tigris and Euphrates rivers, in what the Greeks called the land between the rivers, Mesopotamia. There, about 3500 BC, an irrigation system was developed which increased food production more than 200-fold over the preceding slash and hoe methods that depended solely on natural rainfall. The Sumerians were the first people to develop city-states, organized temple worship, a writing system, social class divisions, hereditary kingship, organized warfare, and small empires. Their pioneering innovations were soon copied by other peoples throughout the Fertile Crescent.

Independent of the Mesopotamian civilization, the Egyptians created their kingdom centered on the Nile about 3000 BC. The pharaoh was both high priest and king. He was believed to be a living god, who rejoined the immortal gods after death. The pyramids of the Old Kingdom period were built about 2700 BC. They were splendid tombs to house the mummified remains and artifacts of these great rulers. The Egyptians, too, developed irrigation agriculture, a writing system, and magnificent artwork.

Other primary civilizations developed elsewhere in the world: the Indus River civilization and the Chinese civilization. The history of civilization is a history of trade, cultural exchange, and warfare. Through warfare, ever larger empires were established. Proud city-states were conquered, destroyed, rebuilt, destroyed again, occupied by invaders, and rebuilt. Civilization is the history of the rise and fall of cities. These cities were centers of wealth, power, technologies, art, and writing.

An independent Egyptian civilization came to an end by 1100 BC when the New Kingdom or Egyptian Empire went into decline. Egypt was conquered by the Assyrians, Persians, Greeks, and Romans. It became the rich province in someone else's empire.

The Mesopotamian civilization lasted until 550 BC, when the New Babylonian Empire or Chaldean Empire was conquered by the Persians.

5. Classical Civilization: Greeks and Romans: 1200 BC - 500 AD. About 1200 BC, a major migration of Indo-European peoples flooded the Aegean and Middle East. Aryans, Persians, and Greeks were related peoples who settled in India, Iran, and Greece and founded new civilizations in these areas.

Hellenic (Greek) civilization began about 800 BC, had its golden century from 500 to 400 BC, declined, and was taken over by Philip of Macedon in 338 BC The Hellenistic period followed under the leadership of Alexander the Great, who conquered the entire civilized world from India to Egypt. Three Hellenistic kingdoms followed: Ptolomaic Egypt, Seleucid Syria, and Antigonid Macedonia.

In the Western Mediterranean, Rome had come to dominate the Italian peninsula by 264 BC. Its struggles for dominance of the Western Medi-terranean with Carthage began in that year and were essentially won by 200 BC. Then began the contest for the Eastern Mediterranean that was completed in 31 BC when Ptolomaic Egypt, the last of the great Hellenistic kingdoms, fell to Octavian, who, in 27 BC, became Caesar Augustus, the first of the Roman Emperors.

The Romans conquered the Greeks militarily, but were themselves conquered culturally by the more advanced Greek civilization. Greco-Roman civilization is an appropriate name for the next five centuries of the Roman Empire.

Caesar Augustus founded the Principate, which, for a time, provided stable, one-person rule. After 180 AD, the Principate was followed by the Third Century Decline. That decline had been arrested through the formation of the Autocracy when the center of the empire shifted from Rome to Constantinople in the Greek-speaking East and when Christianity replaced paganism as the official religion of the Roman Empire.

6. The Middle Ages: 500 - 1500 AD. The Germanic invasions of the Roman Empire, during the fifth century, brought the Roman Empire to an end in the West. The last of the Western emperors, Romulus Augustulus, was deposed in 476 AD.

The triumph of Christianity really marks the end of the Classical Age. The fact that the Roman Empire in the West fell to relatively uncivilized Germanic tribesmen shortly after that triumph is simply a further mark of the end of an age. The old, pagan Roman Empire was dead even before the Visigoths, Ostrogoths, Vandals, Franks, Saxons, Angles, Burgundians, and Lombards gave it the coup de grâce.

By 700 AD, three successor states had developed in what had once been the Roman Empire encircling the entire Mediterranean Sea. These three were the Byzantine Empire with its Greek Orthodox Christian Church; the Islamic Empire spanning from Syria to Spain with Islam as the official religion of the state; and the Frankish kingdom in the West with the Roman Catholic Christian Church as dominant.

Our historical perspective narrowed at this point in the previous volume to focus on this Frankish kingdom. While the most backward of the three successor states of Rome, it is the core out of which Western Civilization developed.

700 to 900 AD is the period of the great Carolingian leaders of the Frankish kingdom: Charles Martel, Pepin, Charlemagne, and Louis the Pious. After 843 AD, the kingdom was divided into three pieces and is buffeted by the ninth century invasions of Vikings, Magyars, and Muslims. By 900 AD, we are truly in the Dark Ages. A new stability is found at a very low level. Feudalism and manorialism provide the basis on which the modern European civilization was founded.

900 to 1100 AD is the period of the Early Middle Ages. Urban life has almost disappeared. Literacy flickers in a few monasteries. This is a primitive age, indeed. 1100 to 1300 AD is the period of the High Middle Ages. Town life returns, universities are founded, a new middle class of burghers joins the nobility and clergy as a political force. The majority of the population, as always in history until the Industrial Revolution, are peasants. The medieval synthesis breaks down during the period of 1300 to 1500 AD.

The Papacy undergoes its period of trials: the Avignon Papacy, the Great Schism, the Conciliar Movement, the Renaissance Papacy, and then the Reformation. The feudal monarchies of France and England fight their Hundred Years War, which keeps both busy with each other, weakens each, and helps to destroy the old feudal nobility of warriors. But perhaps most important in undermining the Middle Ages is the Black Death. This natural disaster killed one third to one-half of the population of Europe during the fourteenth century.

7. The Early Modern Period: 1350 - 1648 AD. This period is discussed in Chapter 1. There begins the material that is the focus of the present volume: the Modern Age.

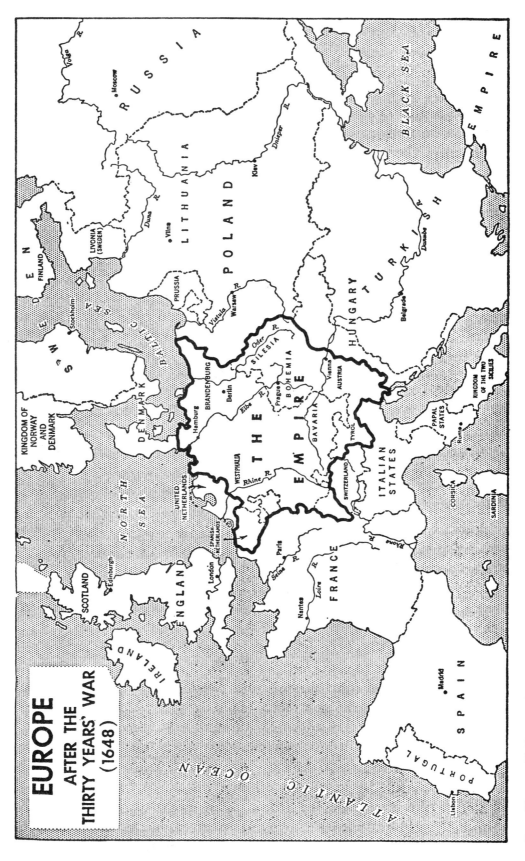

EUROPE
AFTER THE
THIRTY YEARS' WAR
(1648)

RUSSIA

Volga R.

Moscow

LITHUANIA

Vilna

Duna R.

Dnieper R.

Kiev

POLAND

FINLAND

LIVONIA
(SWEDEN)

S W E D E N

PRUSSIA

Vistula R.

Warsaw

Stockholm

B A L T I C   S E A

HUNGARY

T U R K I S H   E M P I R E

Danube R.

Belgrade

B L A C K   S E A

KINGDOM OF
NORWAY
AND
DENMARK

DENMARK

BRANDENBURG

Hamburg

Berlin

Elbe R.

Oder R.

SILESIA

BOHEMIA

Prague

Vienna

AUSTRIA

T H E

E M P I R E

BAVARIA

TYROL

SWITZERLAND

ITALIAN
STATES

Rome

PAPAL
STATES

KINGDOM
OF THE TWO
SICILIES

CORSICA

SARDINIA

N O R T H   S E A

WESTPHALIA

Rhine R.

UNITED
NETHERLANDS

SPANISH
NETHERLANDS

Paris

Seine R.

FRANCE

Loire R.

Nantes

Rhône R.

Po R.

SCOTLAND

Edinburgh

ENGLAND

London

IRELAND

A T L A N T I C   O C E A N

SPAIN

Madrid

PORTUGAL

Lisbon

From *Western Civilization Since 1500*, Second Edition by Walther Kirchner. Copyright (c) 1958, 1966 by Barnes & Noble, Inc. Copyright (c) 1975 by Walther Kirchner. Reprinted by permission of HarperCollins Publishers, Inc.

Chapter I

THE DAWN OF

MODERN EUROPE

Figure 1.1 **Thirty Years' War** (1618 - 1648). Engraving. This conflict was one of the bloodiest and ugliest wars of religion fought on the European continent. Catholics and Protestants slaughtered each other while at the same time raping, looting, and despoiling the countryside. (Courtesy of The Library of Congress)

1

The Modern European State System

UNDERSTANDING The Early Modern Period

The Modern Age did not spring into being unexpectedly in the seventeenth century. It has its antecedents. There is an Early Modern Period, roughly from 1350 to 1648. This time period overlapped with the ending of the Middle Ages. During this time, six major historical movements helped to shape the Modern Age. These movements were: 1. The Renaissance; 2. The Voyages of Discovery; 3. The formation of a Capitalistic Global Economy; 4. The Reformation; 5. The Creation of the Modern, Centralized State, initially ruled by an absolute monarchy; and 6. The Formation of the European State System. These movements helped to transform the Middle Ages into our own Modern Age.

List the major historical movements that helped to shape the Early Modern Period.

The Renaissance

The Renaissance began in Northern Italy and may be dated from the beginning of the Black Death in 1343 to the Council of Trent in 1555. The Renaissance was itself a continuation of trends begun during the High

Describe three causes of the Renaissance.

What were the effects of the Renaissance?

What initiated the Voyages of Discovery?

Middle Ages. The Renaissance had been made possible by the growth of medieval towns into rich, independent republics, like Venice, Florence, and Genoa. A new secular spirit replaced the otherworldly orientation of the Middle Ages. The commercial spirit of the Italian city-states opened up new opportunities for ambitious, talented, and ruthless individuals. Humanism replaced scholasticism as the dominant philosophy. The search for salvation took second place to the desire for profit and fame. The Renaissance produced a burst of human creativity comparable only to the Golden Age of Classical Greece in the fifth century before Christ. Indeed, the Renaissance sought to imitate the Classical Age. It looked at the time after the fall of Rome as the Dark Ages. But the Renaissance was not only antiquarian; it was also creative. In art, architecture, literature, and science new techniques were tried. Leonardo da Vinci was not only a great artist but a great scientist as well. Machiavelli's prince foreshadowed the absolute monarchs of the seventeenth century. A miniature state system existed in Northern Italy before it came to Europe in 1648, and to the world after 1945.

The Voyages of Discovery

Without the new spirit of the Renaissance, it is doubtful that the Voyages of Discovery would have taken place. The Portuguese began the exploration of the coast of Africa in the fifteenth century. Prince Henry the Navigator established a school for sea captains and helped finance these early expeditions. The fall of the Byzantine Empire in 1453 closed the overland routes to Asia to European commerce. When the Ottoman Turks conquered the second capital of the

Roman Empire, Constantinople, they interrupted the profitable trade in spices and other commodities. The decline of Venice and other North Italian cities may be dated from 1453. The centers of commerce and prosperity began to shift toward the Atlantic seaboard.

Portuguese successes fanned the jealousies of the newly formed Spanish kingdom. Christopher Columbus, a Genoese sea captain and adventurer, persuaded Ferdinand of Aragon and Isabella of Castile, joint rulers of Spain, to stake him for a high risk adventure to find India by sailing West across the Atlantic. We all know the results of Columbus' voyages. In 1492, he unexpectedly discovered a new continent, the Americas. Within fifty years, the Spaniards had destroyed the Aztec Empire of Mexico and the Inca Empire of Peru. They created a vast empire in the Americas. Tons of gold and silver were shipped from the new world to the old. This wealth helped to strengthen the Spanish monarchy, financed its wars for dominance in Europe, and, ironically, helped to undermine the Spanish middle class. Religious bigotry, as evidenced by the ouster of the Jews and Moslems from Spain beginning in 1492, contributed to the ultimate failure of Spanish ambitions. Nonetheless, the Portuguese and the Spaniards began the Europeanization of the globe. By 1914, almost the entire planet was under the colonial domination of a handful of European states.

After Portugal and Spain led the way, other European states entered the race for exploration, trade, and colonization. The Dutch, English, and French came to challenge the front-runners and created their own colonial empires. The rivalry between France and England for colonies abroad and power within Europe forms a major part of modern

Why did Ferdinand and Isabella support the efforts of Columbus?

What were the consequences of the Spanish entry into the Americas for the Amerindians?

What happened internally in Spain as a result of the influx of gold and silver from the Americas?

history and is discussed in the following chapters.

What credit instruments developed as a capitalistic global economy expanded?

The Formation of a Capitalistic Global Economy

The growth of trade and commerce depended on the development of a monetary system. Gold and silver coins are a useful medium of exchange, but even more valuable can be letters of credit, promissory notes, and exchange rates between currencies. Credit and borrowing are important methods whereby trade can be financed. Modern banking has its roots in banking house of the Medicis in Florence. The Italian city-states invented double-entry bookkeeping. The creation of the joint stock company with limited liability made the Voyages of Discovery profitable. Central governments are forever hungry for money and what taxes cannot raise must be secured by borrowing. War, especially, increases the demand for money to finance its expenditures.

What made trade and commerce so essential to a central government's policies? Explain

The financial capital of Europe has shifted from Florence, to Amsterdam, to London, to New York. Since the Catholic Church during the Middle Ages condemned usury, that is the charging of interest for money lent, much of the middle class converted to Protestantism. Max Weber, a twentieth-century German sociologist, wrote a famous book linking the rise of capitalism to the Protestant ethic.

The Reformation

The Reformation began on October 31, 1517 when an Augustinian monk and theology professor named Martin Luther posted 95 theses for a disputation on the cathedral door of the small university town of Wittenberg in Saxony, Germany. It is rare that a major historical movement has such a definite date as its beginning. Luther's actions unleashed a firestorm that permanently altered history. He helped to shatter the unity of Western Christendom. The ideal of the Middle Ages had been one universal empire and one universal church. The Holy Roman Empire was a pale shadow of a universal empire, but it kept a dream alive. The Roman Catholic Church, however, was a true universal church, at least within Western Europe. For a time the Popes had indeed been the mightiest rulers of Europe. And while their power declined after 1300, the Catholic Church was rich and powerful in all European dominions. The popes in Rome had become captivated by the Renaissance spirit of the age. They were often men of the world, patrons of the arts, and crafty princes seeking to unify Italy under papal control.

In many ways, Luther was a reactionary. He looked backwards toward primitive Christianity. He discarded ecclesiastical authority and sought salvation by faith alone. Only the Bible served as his authority. God would speak to the individual believer directly through the Bible. He rejected the elaborate Gothic cathedral of medieval Catholic theology as crafted by St. Thomas Aquinas. Pope, bishops, monasteries, saints, relics, seven sacraments, and even the high mass could all be eliminated. The true Christian needed only his Faith and his Bible. God, in his mercy, would do the rest.

Luther turned away from the secularism of the Renaissance; he was certainly no humanist. And yet, the Protestant Reformation was, in its own way, as individualistic as the Renaissance. More than the Renaissance, it shattered the claims of authority.

What was the Reformation?

What made the Reformation a major historical movement?

Who was Martin Luther? What did he do that was so unusual?

What are two essential beliefs for a Lutheran?

Why and how did the Reformation shatter the unity of Christendom? Discuss.

Luther's "Here I stand. I can do no other."[1] is a radical assertion of individual rights.

The Reformation, which followed Luther's pronouncements, shattered the unity of Christendom and helped to fragment Europe into the shards of the modern state system. Religious divisions led to bitter wars of religion. But Catholic orthodoxy failed to wipe out the Protestant heresy. The Hapsburg dynasty in the person of Emperor Charles V and later King Philip II of Spain could not restore religious unity. Dynastic ambitions combined with religious passions to create the religious and political divisions of modern Europe.

Explain why the German kingdoms were not considered states.

The Creation of the Modern, Centralized State

While the ideal of the Middle Ages had been a universal empire, the political reality had been a patchwork of free towns, ecclesiastical principalities, and various feudal territories ruled by lords using many different titles, all under the nominal authority of a king. In the feudal hierarchy, the Holy Roman Emperor and the Roman Pontiff enjoyed ceremonial precedence over all others: kings, feudal lords, and ecclesiastical princes. Since the fall of the Roman Empire, there had always been a number of distinct Germanic kingdoms. But these kingdoms were not "states" in the modern sense since they lacked an effective centralized administrative structure. And while students in medieval universities had usually grouped themselves together by "nations," even though the common language of the educated was Latin, there was as yet no nationalism in the modern sense. Nationalism was not born until the French Revolution of 1789. The modern, centralized, bureaucratic state developed gradually out of the feudal and dynastic states of the early modern period.

The formation of the modern state is linked to the transformation of feudal monarchy into absolute monarchy. Absolute monarchs managed, for the first time since the fall of the Roman Empire, to exercise direct control over all parts of their kingdom. To become absolute rulers, these kings had to break the independent power of the feudal nobility, the church within their country, the free cities, and all other self-governing corporate bodies. Local autonomy had to be replaced with centralized control. Local law had to be subordinated to the king's law. In order to govern a large kingdom from one central location, it became necessary to build a central administration. Absolute monarchy required a corps of bureaucrats to do the central government's bidding. It also needed a centralized taxing system and a powerful military directly under the ruler's control. The central government had to acquire a monopoly of the legitimate use of force. Local military power had to be broken because it might be used to defy the king's will.

The Church also had to be brought under the control of the government. Its possessions were too vast; its church courts too extensive; its influence too deep. Its highest officials had to be loyal to the king; they could not be allowed to preach sedition or treason. In both Protestant and Catholic countries, the newly emerging absolute monarchs gained control over their "national" churches. In return for surrendering political control to the monarchy, the churches gained the king's protection. The 1648 Treaty of Westphalia established the principle that the religion of the ruler would become the religion of all his subjects. During the formative

What were some of the requirements for an absolute monarch to establish control over the government?

Why did the Church have to be under the control of the central government?

Explain how mercantilism is intertwined with absolutism.

period of the modern state, religious toleration was not considered to be a virtue. Absolute monarchs also tried to gain control over the economy within their state. Mercantilism is the economic theory linked to absolutism.

Absolute monarchy attempted to become all-powerful within its territory and over its subjects. The logical extreme of absolute monarchy is the formation of the totalitarian state of the twentieth century. But while each ruler sought supremacy within his territory, he or, rarely, she was equally fierce in defending the independence of his (or her) state against all others. Sovereignty became the new operative word to describe states. The central governments of modern states are sovereign, both internally and externally. It is these sovereign states which make up the state system.

Have there been attempts at establishing a world state or world empire? If so, what states have tried to do so? When?

The Formation of the European State System

The state system is a by-product of the existence of several sovereign states. This statement may seem trivial, but there are important consequences given this factual condition. Potentially any given sovereign state may seek to become all-powerful. If that state succeeded in its ambitions, then the state system would come to an end. We would have, once again or for the first time depending which historical perspective one adopts, a single universal, world state or world empire. In European history, several sovereign states have at various times attempted to gain dominance over all the others. Since 1648, France tried twice to become dominant (under Louis XIV and again under Napoleon), Germany tried twice (in 1914 and again in 1939), and the Soviet

THE DAWN OF MODERN EUROPE

Union may have had that goal after 1945. The point to stress is that all these attempts have failed. The power and aggressiveness of any single sovereign state can be checked by the combined weight of the other states. As long as each sovereign state guards its own survival and independence, it may be impossible for any single state or group of states to succeed in its objectives. The state system itself generates a dynamic for its persistence. This dynamic is called the balance of power.

Since the formation of the modern state system, the absolute monarchs, and the central governments which have succeeded them in more recent times, have learned to play the balance of power game to maintain the system and their own independence. Through alliances and coalitions, the major powers of Europe have maintained their existence through three centuries.

Explain why modern states and rulers have entered into coalitions and alliances.

The Cast of Characters: The Major States of the European State System in 1648

What countries were republics in seventeenth century Europe?

The modern history of Europe has been dominated by a dozen or so states. Listing these states in the order of their importance during the seventeenth and eighteenth century, we come up with the following: France, England, Spain, Austria-Hungary, Prussia, Russia, United Provinces of the Netherlands, Sweden, and Portugal. Most of these states functioned as monarchies during most of this time period. The exceptions were the Netherlands and, briefly from 1649 to 1660, England which were republics. To a much greater degree than most students can appreciate today, the history of each of these states is linked to the ruling family, or dynasty, which governed these kingdoms. People, that is the common people, did not yet

Did the common people have a voice in government? Explain why or why not?

Identify the major ruling dynasties of the seventeenth century and tell which country each ruled.

How were the Hapsburgs different from other dynasties?

matter. Most people were peasants, illiterate and often living in the legal condition known as serfdom. There were peasant uprisings here and there, but even those did not alter the underlying patterns of monarchy and aristocratic land ownership.

The Protestant Reformation, Catholic Counter Reformation, and the major wars of religion had already taken place by 1648. France had become the most powerful country on the European continent and was ruled by the Bourbon dynasty. England was ruled by the Stuart dynasty, which in 1648 was losing its civil war with Parliament under the leadership of Oliver Cromwell. Separate branches of the Hapsburg dynasty ruled Spain and Austria. The Hapsburgs had dominated Europe during much of the sixteenth century. The wars of religion weakened the Hapsburg power in both branches of the family. In addition to their hereditary lands, the Austrian Hapsburgs were also the Holy Roman Emperors. The Holy Roman Empire, discussed above, was made up of over 300 separate feudal states and included most of what is today called Germany. While the Hapsburgs were the most powerful family within the Holy Roman Empire, they had to contest with other dynastic families of which the Hohenzollerns became their chief rivals. The Hohenzollern family were the rulers of Brandenburg, which after 1701 became the Kingdom of Prussia.

Russia was ruled by the Romanov dynasty. The seven United Provinces of the Netherlands were a republic without a king, although the most important province, Holland, had a hereditary leader known as the Stadtholder. The House of Orange held that position. Sweden was ruled by the Vasa, and Portugal was under the Braganza dynasty in 1648. We shall now proceed with a more detailed account of the history of the West.

The Thirty Years' War

Our exploration of Western Civilization in modern times begins with a look at Germany. In the seventeenth century there was no national state called Germany. Instead there was a political conglomeration known as the Holy Roman Empire, which had existed since at least 962. Since 1438 it had been customary to elect members of the Hapsburg family or dynasty as Holy Roman Emperors. In 1600, the electors were seven princes or churchmen from different parts of the Holy Roman Empire. Their number was changed to eight in 1648. While the emperors traditionally claimed jurisdiction over Italy and Burgundy as well as Germany, the area they actually controlled more closely resembled present-day Germany, Austria, and the Czech Republic. In fact, their control of Germany was much less certain than the control of their kingly counterparts over England or France. The emperor representing the Empire as a whole, and the princes who were the various dukes, counts, and bishops who ruled its components, struggled continuously over who should exercise more political power. The emperor wished to create a strong, more centralized nation-state after the model of France or England, but the princes preferred decentralization and local autonomy.

To complicate matters further, the seventeenth-century Holy Roman Empire was also deeply divided along religious lines. The 1555 Peace of Augsburg had attempted to settle the religious disputes in Germany by allowing each prince to determine whether his particular territory was to be

Describe the process of selecting the Holy Roman Emperor. Do you think this was a prestigious position?

How did the seventeenth century Empire differ from countries like England or France?

What were the religious divisions within the Holy Roman Empire by 1618? Why were these divisions important?

Catholic or Lutheran. It also sought to prohibit Catholic churchmen, who became Lutheran after 1552, from transforming Catholic property into Lutheran territory. By 1618, when the Thirty Years' War began, the Holy Roman Empire had a significant number of Calvinists, who were not included under the Peace of Augsburg. More territories of the Catholic Church had become Protestant possessions.

List the four phases of the Thirty Years' War.

The Phases of the War

Historians usually divide the Thirty Years' War into four phases. The first phase is the BOHEMIAN PHASE (1618-1625). The Kingdom of Bohemia (part of the present-day Czech Republic) was ruled by the Hapsburg Ferdinand of Styria, who would soon become Ferdinand II (1619-37), the Holy Roman Emperor. Ferdinand attempted to force Catholicism upon his Protestant Czech subjects. They revolted and in 1618 tossed two Hapsburg ambassadors out the window of a Prague castle. Though they fell some 50 feet, they landed in a dung heap and lived. The event is known as the DEFENESTRATION (the act of throwing out of a window) OF PRAGUE. In place of Ferdinand, the Czechs chose Frederick V, the Elector of the Palatinate, as their king. Frederick was also the leader of a Protestant Union, designed to defend the gains Protestantism had made throughout the Empire. From the start, the war had an international dimension. The Bohemians received money from the Dutch and the forces of Transylvania harassed the Emperor from the rear. Ferdinand received troops from Bavaria, within the Empire, and from Spain, outside the Empire, and money from the Pope. In 1620, Ferdinand's forces

Describe the events of the Bohemian Phase.

defeated the Bohemians at the battle of the White Mountain near Prague. Frederick became known as the Winter King (since he was king only for a short period in 1619 and 1620). He was pushed out of not only Bohemia, but his own Electorate of the Palatinate as well.

The next phase of the war is the DANISH PHASE (1625-29). The king of Denmark, Christian IV (1588-1648),* intervened on behalf of the Protestants. He most likely hoped to gain some northern bishoprics for himself or his son. The Emperor commissioned Albert of Wallenstein (1583-1634) to raise an army on his behalf. The campaign ended in disaster for the Danes. Christian was beaten by Wallenstein and other imperial generals. The overconfident Emperor issued, in 1629, the Edict of Restitution, which restored to the Catholic Church all property secularized since 1552 and forbade Calvinist worship. The Protestant princes of the Holy Roman Empire were alarmed and quickly found new allies outside Germany.

The next phase, the SWEDISH PHASE of the war, lasted from 1630 to 1635. The Swedish king, Gustav II Adolph or Gustavus Adolphus (1611-1632) wanted to rescue the German Lutherans and to protect his Baltic interests from possible imperial intrusion. He received financial aid from the French, who did not want to see the Empire ruled by a strong monarch. Gustavus Adolphus was a superb general, with an army seasoned by previous battles with Russia and Poland. He defeated an imperial army at Breitenfeld in 1631, and the following year won a major

Describe the causes and effects of the Danish phase.

What were the major events of the Swedish phase?

---

* For monarchs and popes, the dates shown after their names represent the years of their reigns; dates after the names of other persons represent their life spans.

What was Cardinal Richelieu's main goal when he supplied funds and troops to the Protestant cause? Was he successful in his endeavors?

What happened to the population, cities, and land in Europe as a result of the French-Swedish Phase?

victory at Lutzen. However, Gustavus Adolphus lost his life at Lutzen, while Wallenstein, who had begun to negotiate peace independently of the Emperor, was assassinated on February 25, 1634. In September of that year the Swedes, without Gustavus Adolphus, were badly defeated at Nordlingen. It looked as if there might be a reconciliation between Ferdinand II and the princes of the Empire. The Emperor even agreed to annul the Edict of Restitution and made peace with the Saxons, who had been allies of the Swedes.

The German principalities in 1635 were ready to make peace, but peace did not come. By this time, the war had become an international struggle involving the French, the Swedes, the Spanish, and the Dutch, as well as the Germans. Each of these powers had its own agenda. The chief French minister was Cardinal Richelieu (1585-1642). Although a Cardinal of the Catholic Church, he decided not only to supply funds, but also troops for the Protestant cause. His major objective was to weaken the Hapsburgs, whose territories bordered France on the east (Ferdinand II of the Holy Roman Empire) and on the south (Philip IV of Spain).

In 1635 the fourth phase of the war began, the FRENCH-SWEDISH PHASE, which lasted until the making of peace in 1648. Much of this phase was spent in looting the cities and the countryside. The French and Swedish armies managed to maintain the upper hand. There was much loss of civilian life. Some have estimated that for the whole war the cities lost one third of their population, while the population in the countryside was reduced by two-fifths. If correct, this would represent an overall decrease in population from perhaps 21 to 13 million.

The Peace of Westphalia

The 1648 Peace of Westphalia, which ended the Thirty Years' War, is considered by many historians to be a turning point in modern Western civilization. After 1648, political rather than religious considerations predominate in international relations. In most areas of Europe, the division between Catholic and Protestant stabilized. The Hapsburg Holy Roman Empire and Hapsburg Spain were on the losing side in the conflict. Germany would not become a united, modern nation-state until the latter half of the nineteenth century. France was free to establish itself as the dominant power on the European continent.

The Peace of Westphalia permitted the 300-odd principalities of the Holy Roman Empire to conduct their own foreign diplomacy and to make treaties. The Empire, which could not raise taxes or declare war without the consent of the principalities, was destroyed as an effective political entity for modern times. The Hapsburg rulers (Ferdinand III was Holy Roman Emperor from 1637 to 1657) henceforth concentrated their attention on Austria and other hereditary holdings. Each prince within the Holy Roman Empire could determine the religion of his territory, whether it might be Catholic, Lutheran, or Calvinist. Dissatisfied individuals were free to migrate to other territories. Church territories confiscated by Protestants after 1552 remained Protestant.

In early 1648, the independence of the Dutch from Spain was recognized. The French and Spanish did not make peace until the 1659 Treaty of the Pyrenees. Both Holland and the Swiss Cantons were recognized as independent of the Holy Roman Empire.

Who won the Thirty Years' War? Who lost the Thirty Years' War?

Describe the terms and conditions of the Peace of Westphalia.

The French and the Swedes received some border territories of the Holy Roman Empire. Sweden was left in a dominant position in the Baltic, France in most of continental Europe.

Figure 1.2 **Louis XIV** (r.1643-1715). France's paramount absolutist monarch is portrayed in brocaded royal splendor. His silk hose and high heels were the fashion rage for the aristocracy. (Courtesy of the Library of Congress)

THE DAWN OF MODERN EUROPE

2

The Age of Absolutism

France

ABSOLUTISM, in the political sense, is an arrangement whereby the ruler of a state exercises authority without any effective checks upon him or her. Louis XIV (1643-1715) of France is one of the best examples of absolutism in early modern times. He is famous for reputedly making the statement: *L'état, c'est moi*[2] - most often translated as: "I am the State." Many absolutist kings justified their power by claiming that they received their authority from God. These kings, often called divine-right monarchs, rejected the sharing of power with legislatures or courts.

**Define absolutism.
What makes a king an absolutist ruler?**

Background

To understand how Louis was able to make such a claim and become the epitome of absolutism, we need to look briefly at seventeenth-century France. Louis' grandfather, King Henry IV (1589-1610), was the first Bourbon king of France. His accession to the throne marked the end of the religious wars that had preoccupied France for 30 years. Henry, a Protestant Huguenot, converted to Catholicism for political reasons, supposedly saying: "Paris is well worth a Mass."[3] After becoming a Catholic, Henry was recognized in Paris and the rest of

What did Henry IV achieve?

What roles did Cardinals Richelieu and Mazarin play?

How did the Frondes influence Louis XIV?

northern France. In 1598, seeking to heal the country from the wounds of the civil war, he issued the Edict of Nantes. This proclamation granted religious toleration to the Huguenots and also gave them the right to have private armies and fortified towns as a guarantee of their religious rights and freedom. In 1610, Henry IV, while riding through Paris in his carriage, was stabbed to death by a mad monk. Despite Henry's efforts, France had not achieved political stability.

Louis XIII (1610 - 1643), the son of Henry IV, took the throne when he was only nine years old. The Queen Mother, Marie de' Medici, led a court coalition in governing. Gradually power fell into the hands of Cardinal Richelieu, who acted as the chief minister of Louis XIII. The cardinal, not a particularly religious person, was more interested in political power. He pushed Catholic France into the Thirty Years War (1618-1648) on the side of the German Protestants, in order to weaken the Holy Roman Emperor and enhance the power of his own king.

In 1642 Richelieu died leaving his protégé, Cardinal Mazarin (1602-1661), to replace him. Ambitious and totally unscrupulous, Mazarin is rumored to have bedded the queen mother to enhance the security of his position. The following year, Louis XIV (1643-1715) came to the throne at the age of five.

When the Thirty Years War ended in 1648, a civil disturbance, known as the FRONDE, broke out. The rebellion was led by the nobles, but for a time had the support of the law courts (parlements), newly unemployed soldiers, and the bourgeoisie (middle class). Barricades were erected and there was fighting in the streets of Paris. There were several Frondes in the early years of Louis XIV, and they must have been truly frightening experiences for the young king. Louis kept in mind the fate of his grandfather and the personal experience of the upheaval of rebellion. We can understand Louis's passion for control when, upon Mazarin's death in 1661, he personally assumed the powers of governance, at the age of 23.

Why did the building of the palace of Versailles enhance the reputation of Louis XIV?

Policies of Louis XIV

Louis XIV removed his court from Paris, the scene of the disturbances of his youth, by building a magnificent palace at Versailles. It reflected the Baroque style of architecture. The Baroque with its dynamic lines and emotional intensity had grown out of the Catholic Reformation and was fashionable in Italy and other Catholic countries from around 1600 to 1750. As adopted by the architect Louis Le Vau (1612-70) and the landscape architect André Le Nôtre (1613-1700) to Versailles it resulted in an extravagant ornateness and elegance suitable to the Sun King.

Why did Louis XIV encourage the nobility to come to Versailles?

Versailles was luxurious in every sense. There was the Hall of Mirrors (mirrors were an expensive item at the time) and many formal gardens, which "required" 1,400 fountains for decoration. Ten thousand noblemen, servants, and bureaucrats lived there. The king was waited on by the highest nobles of the land, who considered it an honor to hold even the sleeve of his nightshirt as Louis got dressed in the morning. Such preoccupations left little time to plot new Frondes.

Louis used bureaucrats, called *intendants*, who were personally loyal to him to administer most of the country. His chief minister, Colbert, pursued a policy of MER-

What were the economic and religious policies of Louis XIV?

CANTILISM, a form of state intervention in the economic system designed to increase the financial resources available to the state. The idea was to have more money come into the country through the sale of exports than left the country to pay for imports. The production of goods, such as woolens destined for export, was strictly regulated to ensure quality. Subsidies were given for the production of certain goods, such as silk, and French trading companies were created to increase the amount of exports.

In religious matters, Louis XIV sought to weaken the Pope's power within France. But the staunchly Catholic king could not tolerate "heretics" within his land. In 1685, he revoked the Edict of Nantes. Henceforth, Protestants were to enjoy no civil rights and their children were to be obliged to become Catholics. Many Huguenots, perhaps as many as 200,000, fled France for the Protestant countries of Europe and for America. Ironically, France lost the skills of many middle-class Protestants because of the intolerance of a king who, as we saw, was interested in state-sponsored economic development.

The Wars of Louis XIV

What is meant by a "balance of power"?

Between 1667 and 1713, Louis fought a series of aggressive wars designed to increase vastly French possessions and bring great glory to him as the "Sun King." He failed in these aims — very largely because of the operation of BALANCE OF POWER principles. During much of modern European history, a balance of power was maintained to prevent any one nation from dominating Europe. When a large power threatened to obtain supremacy, several major states would create a coalition of powers to frustrate the efforts of the aggressor.

In 1667, Louis launched the WAR OF DEVOLUTION (1667-1668) against the Spanish Netherlands to the north. He claimed rights of inheritance through his wife, who was the daughter of the Spanish king, Philip IV. Louis's actions were especially threatening to Holland, which counted on the Spanish Netherlands to serve as a buffer between itself and France. Holland formed an alliance with England and Sweden to thwart Louis. The war ended with the Treaty of Aix-la-Chapelle in which France received twelve fortified towns along its border with the Spanish Netherlands, much less than Louis XIV claimed.

Louis's next war was a war of revenge against the Dutch that began in 1672 with the direct French invasion of Holland. This SECOND DUTCH WAR lasted till 1678. The Dutch resisted by opening the dikes, by finding a new leader, William, from the revered House of Orange, and by forming alliances with Austria, Spain, Brandenburg, and Denmark. By the Treaty of Nimwegen, France had to accept Dutch territorial integrity, though it did gain Franche-Comté from Spain and some ten additional border towns.

The WAR OF THE LEAGUE OF AUGSBURG lasted from 1688 to 1697. It was truly a world war, since England and France fought each other in the colonies as well as in Europe. In America, this war was called King William's War. William of Orange had become William III, King of England, as a result of the Glorious Revolution. He used England's resources in his continued struggle against France. Joining Holland and England were such other countries as Spain, Austria, and Savoy. At the conclusion of almost a decade of fighting, the Treaty of Ryswick left most possessions in the same

Why did Holland oppose Louis XIV from the start?

List the wars of Louis XIV.

What were the provisions of the Peace of Utrecht?

Was Louis XIV a success at war?

hands as after the 1678 Treaty of Nimwegen, though France did keep Strasbourg.

The WAR OF THE SPANISH SUCCESSION, 1702-1713, was more decisive. A major aim of Louis XIV was to set up a situation that would unite Spain with France. The last of the Spanish Hapsburgs, Charles II, had died and left the Spanish throne to Philip of Anjou, the grandson of Louis XIV. For Louis this meant that the "Pyrenees exist no longer."[4] As usual, other powers formed a grand alliance against Louis to prevent him from upsetting the balance of power in Europe. Included in this alliance were England, Holland, most of the small principalities of the Holy Roman Empire, Austria, and Prussia. This long war, known as Queen Anne's War in North America, was concluded by the Peace of Utrecht (1713-14), which provided:

- ◆ Philip could become the King of Spain (as Philip V).
- ◆ But Spain and France could never be united.
- ◆ Austria gained the Spanish Netherlands and most Spanish territories in Italy. Spain also ceded Sicily (later exchanged for Sardinia) to Savoy.
- ◆ England gained Gibraltar, Minorca, Newfoundland, Nova Scotia, and recognition of her rights to the Hudson Bay territory.

This War of the Spanish Succession was the last of Louis XIV's aggressions. His wars had produced poverty, starvation, and general misery for France and put the country into severe financial straits. The domestic reputation of the "Sun King" was severely damaged. Certainly these wars contributed to setting the stage for the French Revolution that was to occur later in the century. Spain, who had been France's ally, kept its American possessions. But Spain increasingly became a bit player in European affairs.

Russia

Peter the Great

After a chaotic period known as the Time of Troubles (1604-1613), Russia gained a new ruling family, the Romanovs. One of the most effective Romanov rulers was Peter the Great who came to the throne in 1682 and gained full control of the government by 1689. He ruled in absolutist fashion until his death in 1725. Peter brought many important changes to Russia. In 1697-1698 he visited Western Europe, particularly Holland and England. There he had an opportunity to inspect workplaces, shipyards, and forts. He was very interested in Western technology and in recruiting Westerners for work in Russia.

Peter is famed for his program of westernizing Russia. He vigorously encouraged western dress and discouraged such Russian customs as wearing a beard. His economic policies adopted to the Russian scene the mercantilism fashionable in contemporary France. State ownership or regulation of enterprises was fostered. In religious matters, he created a Holy Synod, which he controlled, to replace the Patriarch as head of the Russian Orthodox Church. To speed the process of westernization, he moved the capital from the inland city of Moscow to a new city, St. Petersburg, on the Baltic Sea. Much closer to the heartland of Europe, St. Petersburg served as Peter's "window on the West."

How did Peter the Great attempt to westernize Russia?

Discuss the other policies of Peter the Great.

How did Catherine the Great gain her throne?

Peter had gained the territory along the Baltic, where he built his new capital, in the Great Northern War with Sweden that lasted from 1700 to 1721. He also gained Azov, a trading port, in a war against the Ottoman Empire.

All these moves had a profound impact on Russian development. Peter was not only czar (caesar), but also the first Russian ruler to call himself emperor. He reinforced the autocratic tendencies in Russian history, but he also made Russia an important and lasting player on the European scene. When Peter's own son, Alexis, threatened (as the future emperor) to undo his father's work, Peter put him to death rather than risk the reversal of his innovations!

Catherine the Great

How enlightened was Catherine the Great?

The eighteenth-century Russian ruler who proved to be the worthiest successor to Peter the Great was actually a German-born princess, Catherine the Great. She ruled as Catherine II from 1762 to 1796.

To obtain the throne, Catherine connived with a group of nobles (among them her lover) to depose and probably murder her husband, Peter III. She cultivated the thinkers of the French Enlightenment, including Voltaire and Diderot. While she did, in fact, inaugurate such legal reforms as restricting the use of torture and permitting greater religious toleration, her regime grew increasingly repressive. This was especially true after putting down a serf revolt led by Emelian Pugachev in 1773-1775. During Catherine's reign the position of the serfs continued to deteriorate to the point where they could be sold by their masters in much the fashion of slaves in the Americas.

In foreign policy, Catherine is credited with securing for Russia a firm hold on the north shore of the Black Sea, including the Crimea, through a series of wars against the Turks. She also gained for Russia the right to intervene in the internal affairs of the Ottoman Empire to protect the interests of its Christian population. This right provided a pretext for future Russian aggression against the Turks.

In the west, she participated in the three partitions of Poland at the end of the eighteenth century, gaining control of many ethnic Byleorussians and Ukrainians. More details about these partitions are provided later.

Did Catherine the Great have a successful foreign policy? Explain.

Prussia

Origins

An especially important development in early modern Europe was the rise of Prussia to the status of a major power. In 1525 Prussia was surrounded almost entirely by Poland. Bounded on the north by the Baltic Sea, it had been for centuries in the possession of a crusading order called the Teutonic Knights. With the coming of the Reformation, Prussia had become a secular duchy under the rule of Albert, a member of the German Hohenzollern family.

In 1618 Prussia had been inherited by another branch of the Hohenzollerns, which also ruled the far more important Electorate of Brandenburg within the Holy Roman Empire. Brandenburg was an Electorate because its ruler was an "Elector" who had

What was the relationship between Prussia and Brandenburg?

What did Frederick William, the Great Elector, do?

the right to vote for who would become the Holy Roman Emperor. It was separated from the Duchy of Prussia, or East Prussia, by Royal Prussia, which was a part of Poland. This was to prove unfortunate for the Poles!

The first of the great Prussian leaders was Frederick William, the Great Elector, who ruled from 1640 to 1688. Having witnessed the devastation of the Thirty Years War, Frederick William lavished resources on building up his military. By the time he died, Prussia had a professional army of 30,000. Frederick William was also an able administrator, encouraging agriculture and industry. He welcomed the Huguenots who left France upon the revocation of the Edict of Nantes.

How did the Elector Frederick III become King?

His son began his rule as Elector Frederick III in 1688. During the War of the Spanish Succession, he agreed to give military support to the Holy Roman Emperor. In return, he gained the right to call himself "King in Prussia," which was outside the domains of the Holy Roman Emperor. So in 1701, Elector Frederick III gained the additional, and much more prestigious, title of King Frederick I. It was not long before there was simply a "King of Prussia" rather than a "King in Prussia."

The son of King Frederick I was King Frederick William I, who ruled from 1713 to 1740. He is best known for doubling the size of the Prussian army—from approximately 40,000 troops to 83,000 troops. He made his army one of the best-disciplined in Europe. He was mad about tall soldiers and collected a special unit of troops over six feet tall, drawn from all over Europe.

Frederick the Great

Speculate on why Frederick II, disregarding the Pragmatic Sanction, grabbed Silesia.

King Frederick William I was also an uncultured barbarian. When his son Frederick ran away from home and was recaptured, the king disciplined the boy by forcing him to witness the execution of his best friend, who had participated in the escape!

The young man, who loved poetry and music, became Frederick II (1740-1786), better known as Frederick the Great. He became the vigorous, devoted monarch that his father had desired. The Prussian monarchs who have been discussed thus far, built up the army, but made little actual combat use of it. Not so with Frederick II, who assumed the throne the same year that a woman, Maria Theresa, became the ruler of Austria.

The PRAGMATIC SANCTION, which was initiated by her father, the Emperor Charles VI, in 1713, should have allowed Maria Theresa to inherit *all* of the Hapsburg territories. By the Pragmatic Sanction, Prussia, along with the other major states of Europe, was committed to recognizing the indivisibility of Austrian domains. Frederick, however, grabbed Silesia, a province close to Poland, from Austria in the War of the Austrian Succession (1740-1748). This new acquisition doubled the population of his state. Maria Theresa strove to regain Silesia during the Seven Years' War (1756-1763) discussed later. In the end, Frederick, though almost defeated by several major powers, kept Silesia and his throne.

What were the consequences?

After 1763, Frederick devoted his greatest energies to peacefully rebuilding his kingdom. He liked to call himself the "first servant of the state."[5] He started new industries; he reformed the judicial system; he

Why weren't the partitions of Poland violations of balance of power rules?

Which countries participated in <u>each</u> of the partitions?

drained swamps and introduced new crops like turnips.

The Partitions of Poland

Frederick the Great also found the energy for another major acquisition. This was the Polish territory that separated Brandenburg from Prussia. He did this by arranging the First Partition of Poland, in 1772. This time, instead of a major war in Europe, he negotiated a deal with both Russia and Austria. Each took a chunk of Poland in order to maintain the balance of power among them. Poland was no match for the combined forces of Prussia, Russia, and Austria. After Frederick II died, there was a Second Partition of Poland in 1793. Additional territories were taken by Russia and Prussia. An unsuccessful Polish revolt followed, leading to a Third Partition of Poland in 1795. The participants in the Third Partition were Prussia, Russia, and Austria. The result was the complete absorption of Poland, which was not to re-emerge as a sovereign state until 1918!

Louis XIV of France and Peter the Great of Russia are seventeenth-century monarchs who personify the absolutist tradition. They made no pretense at enlightened concern for the liberties of their subjects. Catherine the Great of Russia and Frederick the Great of Prussia, who ruled in the eighteenth century, are sometimes called Enlightened Despots. They were concerned with legal reforms and constitutional issues; they avoided making claims of divine-right monarchy.

The European Impact Overseas

How did Spain organize its American colonies?

The Americas

By 1700, the Spanish Empire was still the largest in the world. The Spanish Empire had originally claimed all of the Americas and had been divided into two viceroyalties: New Spain (the territory north of Panama including Mexico) and Peru (from Panama south). Later the separate viceroyalties of New Granada and La Plata were carved out of Peru. But other European powers had entered the race for colonies throughout the world and in the Americas. The Portuguese had acquired the huge landmass known as Brazil in South America as a result of the Treaty of Tordesillas in 1494 that divided the New World between Spain and themselves. The English and French muscled in and were in the process of contesting for supremacy of North America. The English were establishing their thirteen North American colonies stretching from New Hampshire to Georgia on the Atlantic seaboard. The French were entrenched in Quebec and seeking to expand down the Ohio and Mississippi rivers to Louisiana. The West Indies was a major area of rivalry between Spain, France, and Britain. The West Indies raised tobacco, cotton, coffee, and especially sugar. The European demand for these products made this area particularly profitable.

Throughout the Americas, the plantation system of agriculture had come to predominate in most of the European colonies. Slaves imported from Africa provided most

What other European powers entered the race to colonize the Americas?

What difficulties did the Spanish experience using Amerindian labor?

of the agricultural labor on these plantations. Here, too, the Spaniards had set the patterns which others followed.

The Spaniards granted large estates, plantations, or *latifundia* to Spanish noblemen within the provinces of their Empire. A Spanish institution, the *encomienda*, was adapted to colonial rule. The lord of the *encomienda* or manor was entitled to services and payments from the Indians, who were treated like serfs had been during the feudal period of history in Europe. The Spanish lord was expected to christianize his Indian serfs. In practice, the *encomienda* system and a form of conscript labor known as the *repartimiento* became methods of forced labor in which the Indians were frequently worked to death. Any pretense of Christian values was lost to the profit motives of the large landowners and the Spanish crown.

In addition, the American Indians were susceptible to European diseases, such as smallpox, measles, and syphilis, which killed many more. Furthermore many Indians escaped from these intolerable conditions into the jungles and countryside with which they were more familiar than the colonial overlords. These factors created a "labor problem" for the Spaniards and other European powers that adopted their plantation system.

How did the Spanish empire solve its labor problem in America?

The answer to this "labor problem" was the importation of slaves from Africa. Except for French Canada (Quebec), where the fur trade predominated, and the British New England colonies, which were settled by religious and political refugees, slavery became the economic underpinning of all the European colonies in the Americas.

The Slave Trade

The Portuguese were the first Europeans to engage in the Atlantic slave trade. The British and French quickly followed. Slave trading had been practiced by the Africans along the Atlantic coast long before the coming of the Europeans. Most of the slaves sold in the Atlantic trade were war captives. A triangular trade developed. Ships sailed from Europe to Africa with merchandise, including gunpowder and gin, to be exchanged for African slaves, who were then taken across the Atlantic to the colonies. There the slaves were exchanged for colonial produce, especially sugar, which was brought back to Europe to complete the third leg of the triangle.

The horrors of the transatlantic passage are well known. Slaves were jammed into the ships with inadequate food, sanitation, and breathing space. It has been estimated that there was a death rate during the crossing as high as twenty percent. What is less well known are the huge numbers of slaves imported to the Americas. A conservative estimate is that, between the fifteenth and nineteenth centuries, eleven to twelve million slaves were removed from Africa.

Mercantilism

In early modern times, the slave trade and the whole colonial system were part of a larger state policy now known as mercantilism. Mercantilism involved state intervention in the economy in order to increase national wealth. This wealth could then be used for financing war and other state activities. The gold and silver bullion imported

Describe the slave trade. What moral judgments would you apply to this trade?

Define mercantilism.

Why did the mercantilists want colonies?

Examine the strategies commonly used by mercantilist governments.

by Spain from its colonies financed Spanish imperial armies. Countries such as Britain and France did not have colonies with extensive gold and silver mines. But the colonies could be used as part of a favorable balance of trade scheme. The idea was to make sure that more gold and silver entered the country, to pay for goods exported, than left the country to pay for goods imported. Colonies were ideal captive markets for the export of finished products at prices higher than free markets would bear, and also for the import of raw materials at comparatively low prices. Some companies were given trading monopolies. The British East India Company's activities in India are a good example. Mercantilism also demanded that goods be shipped across the oceans in only the mother country's sailing vessels. Government licensed monopolies of all kinds were an integral part of mercantilism. This was a form of state-sponsored trade and commerce.

Government subsidies to goods intended for export and customs barriers to raise the prices of goods intended for import were standard mercantile practices. In England, for example, the effort was made to grow grapes in Scotland so that wine would not have to be imported from elsewhere. In France, Jean Baptiste Colbert encouraged and subsidized many industries particularly those making luxury items for export. He strictly regulated the quality of these products to maintain the market for these lucrative export items. French perfumes, china, tapestries, and fancy clothing (*haute couture*) continue to have high reputations and high prices. They still earn France a great deal of foreign exchange.

The critics of mercantilism at the end of the eighteenth century scorned the notion that there was only a fixed amount of wealth in the world or that it was measurable by the amount of gold and silver in a country's treasury. They criticized the inefficiencies in production which mercantilism produced. Laissez-faire economists advocated unregulated trade, free competition, and open markets.

What criticisms of mercantilism can you offer?

The Seven Years' War

Ever since the Voyages of Discovery, conflicts within the European state system have also been reflected in colonial rivalries overseas. The ascendancy of France and Great Britain in European affairs over Spain, Portugal, and the Netherlands is reflected in the fortunes of their respective colonial empires. France and Great Britain, in particular, were bitter colonial rivals in North America and in Asia. Wars in Europe had their counterparts in the colonial world. In North America, these two countries fought several wars to achieve supremacy over the other.

This colonial rivalry between France and Britain come to overshadow the older rivalry between the Bourbons of France and the Hapsburgs of Spain and Austria. During the War of the Austrian Succession, France was allied with Prussia against Maria Therese of Austria, whereas Britain supported Austria. Between 1748 and 1756, a DIPLOMATIC REVOLUTION took place in Europe. The French reconciled themselves with their traditional Hapsburg enemy and made an alliance with Austria against Prussia. This, in turn, led the British to support Prussia. What remained constant was that Britain and France were enemies.

The SEVEN YEARS' WAR, or the FRENCH AND INDIAN WAR as it is known

Explain the Diplomatic Revolution.

What did the major European powers gain or lose as a result of the Seven Years' War?

from the American perspective, lasted from 1756 to 1763. During this period the French and British also fought each other for predominance in India. On all three fronts—European, American, and Asian—the British won. Prussia, Britain's ally in Europe, survived the assaults by Russia, Austria, and France through a great deal of luck and British financial subsidies. Frederick the Great kept Silesia. In America, the British defeated the French decisively and took over Quebec, the rest of French Canada, and the French territories east of the Mississippi. Spain received Louisiana from France, but ceded Florida to Britain. The French kept control of Haiti and some other West Indies territories. The British also defeated the French in India, receiving Bengal, and thereby gained a green light to dominate that large subcontinent. Britain also acquired Senegal in Africa, an important slave trading post. Britain emerged in 1763 with a worldwide colonial empire and the largest navy in the world. It kept that position until after World War II.

Explain the long-term consequences of this war.

An ironic consequence of the English triumph in North America was the perception among the people of the thirteen original British colonies that English military assistance was no longer essential to their survival. The colonists became increasingly disturbed by the mercantilist regulations and increased taxes imposed by the mother country. 1763 marks the beginning of the power struggle between the colonials and the British, which led to the American Revolution in 1775.

3

From the Scientific Revolution to the Enlightenment

The Scientific Revolution

The American Revolution of 1776 and the French Revolution of 1789 were encouraged by intellectual developments, as well as by political, economic, and social changes. Many leaders of these revolutions were imbued with the spirit of "The Enlightenment," which helped to justify challenges to the established order. Enlightened thinking, in turn, was indebted to persons and events associated with the Scientific Revolution and with the Glorious Revolution in England.

Before Copernicus, what was the prevailing view of the universe?

Astronomy

Just as Columbus's "discovery" of the Americas changed the European map of the earth, so also Copernicus's publication in 1543 of his book *On the Revolutions of the Heavenly Spheres* changed the intellectual map of the heavens for Europeans. The old view of the universe was dependent on the ideas of Aristotle (4th century B.C.) and Ptolemy (2nd century A.D.). According to these Greek thinkers, the earth was the center of the universe. The planets and stars moved around the earth in hierarchical

What authorities could be cited to support this view?

How does the heliocentric theory of the universe differ from the geocentric theory?

How did Copernicus, Brahe, and Kepler contribute to the development of the heliocentric theory?

spheres. The geocentric notion, that the earth was the center of the universe, fitted in well with Christian theology. Humans and the earth they inhabited were so important that God sent his only Son to save mankind.

Nicholas COPERNICUS (1473-1543), a Polish cleric, proposed that not the earth but the sun is the center of the universe. Copernicus believed that he could account more simply for the movement of the planets if he placed the sun at the center of the universe. The earth and the other planets revolved around the sun. The earth also rotated daily on its axis. His was a heliocentric rather than a geocentric cosmos. Copernicus started a revolution in scientific thinking. But he still held many traditional cosmological notions. For instance, he thought heavenly bodies moved in perfect circles.

The Danish astronomer, Tycho BRAHE (1546-1601), added to the body of scientific knowledge by tracking the movement of the planets with great accuracy without a telescope. Though Brahe refused to accept the heliocentric theory, his assistant, Johannes KEPLER (1571-1630), did. Kepler used Brahe's observations and his own knowledge of mathematics to demonstrate that the movement of the planets around the sun took place in elliptical rather than simple circular orbits. Kepler not only used mathematics to demonstrate laws of planetary motion, but he mathematically proved the correctness of the Copernican idea that the sun is the center of our universe.

The man who did the most to popularize the heliocentric theory was GALILEO Galilei (1564-1642). Galileo was a mathematics professor both at Pisa and later at Padua in Italy. When he heard about the newly invented telescope, he constructed one for himself. He used this telescope to discover that the moon has mountains and valleys, and to confirm the correctness of the heliocentric theory.

In 1632 he published the *Dialogue Concerning the Two Chief World Systems.* The book, which discussed the Ptolemaic and Copernican systems, was heavily weighted in favor of Copernicus. Galileo was put on trial by the Catholic Inquisition. He was condemned to life imprisonment on suspicion of heresy. This action certainly demonstrated that in this period the Catholic Church and the Christian Churches generally were hostile to scientific theories that challenged an earth-centered universe. The practical consequences were somewhat different. The publicity of the trial facilitated the wide distribution of the *Dialogue* throughout Europe. Galileo's sentence was lessened to a type of house arrest. He was able to continue his studies and even to have new work published in Holland outside the reach of the Inquisition.

Galileo not only contributed to a new astronomy, but also to a new physics. He developed a notion of inertia that included bodies in motion as well as at rest. He changed notions of gravity by showing that a heavier object does not fall to earth at greater speed than a light body. His work helped to destroy the hold of Aristotelian physics and to emphasize the importance of mathematics and observation in science.

Explain what brought Galileo fame.

Evaluate the significance of Galileo's contributions to science.

Sir Isaac Newton

An Englishman, Isaac NEWTON (1642-1727), had the greatest impact on the Scientific Revolution. Newton's most important work is the *Mathematical Principles of Natural Philosophy (Philosophiae Naturalis Principia Mathematica).* In the *Principia,* he

Why might Newton deserve more acclaim than his predecessors?

propounded three laws of motion. The first law deals with inertia, the second with attraction, and the famous third law with gravity. The law of gravity states that "every piece of matter attracts every other piece with a force proportional to the product of their masses and inversely proportional to the square of the distance between them."[6]

It is hard for us to grasp the importance of Newton. His laws apply the same physics to all commonly observed movement, ranging for example, from an apple falling from a tree to the planets moving around the sun. Stating physical laws mathematically permits scientific verification. Most significantly, his achievement inspired his successors in the physical and the social sciences to seek other universally applicable laws that could be stated in precise mathematical terms. This quest for universal, mathematically formulated laws has persisted down to our own time.

The Scientific Societies

What were the best known scientific societies in England and France?

Scientific societies were formed in several countries. In 1662, King Charles II of England founded the Royal Society of London. In France, Colbert, Louis XIV's minister, founded the Royal Academy of Sciences in 1666. Scientific periodicals began to be published. Thinkers recognized that the scientific method of discovery is unique and very different from the philosophical inquiry of an Aristotle or the scholastic method of a Thomas Aquinas. The two men most associated with the development of the scientific method in the seventeenth century are Francis Bacon, an Englishman, and René Descartes, a Frenchman.

Bacon and Descartes

Francis BACON (1561-1626) had a distinguished public career, even serving as Lord Chancellor of England. He was not a great scientist, but he did stress the importance of experimentation and inductive reasoning in science. In 1620, he published the *Novum Organum* (*The New Organon*). The new method he stressed was inductive thinking. The scientist observes particulars, such as individual trees, and from the observation of these particulars proceeds to make a generalization, perhaps about the nature of trees in general. In contrast, Aristotle, and the Scholastics who followed his method, had most often used deductive reasoning. Starting with a generalization, possibly that trees are rooted in the ground, they would reach a conclusion about a particular, such as the maple tree in my back yard, which is indeed rooted in the ground. Looking from a different perspective, Bacon wanted people to put aside their preconceived judgments. He thought that, rather than deduce from the already known, open-minded scientists should make fresh observations and experiments. He encouraged the empirical or experimental approach to knowledge.

There was, however, a weakness in Bacon's approach. He tended to underestimate the importance in science of mathematics, which is abstract and deductive. René DESCARTES (1596-1650) compensated for this Baconian deficiency. Descartes, an accomplished mathematician, created coordinate geometry. He believed that each particle of matter in the universe could be defined in mathematical terms, that is by length, width, and depth!

Descartes is most famous for the statement *cogito ergo sum*[7] (I think, therefore I

How did Bacon contribute to the development of scientific methodology?

How did Descartes influence scientific method?

Explain why systematic doubt may be useful in science.

am). This statement must be understood in the context of his approach to knowledge. As a foundation for the new science, he wanted to arrive at knowledge that was certain and undoubted. So he adopted the method of systematic doubt. He doubted all that it was possible to doubt, including belief in the physical world. He supposed that some evil being had set out to deceive him about reality. But he concluded that since he was thinking, he could not be deceived about his own existence. He then proceeded, deductively, to re-establish the universe. Descartes' stress on mathematics and his doubt about what our senses tell us to be true are useful stratagems even for contemporary science.

Who were Vesalius and Harvey?

There were also developments in the life sciences. VESALIUS (1514-1564) used dissection to lay the foundations of modern anatomy. William HARVEY (1578-1657) discovered how the blood circulated throughout the body using the heart as a pump.

Who was the last Tudor monarch of England?

The English Revolutions

The First Stuarts

Who was the first Stuart king of England?

Another type of revolution occurred on the religious and political scene in England that influenced the Enlightenment. In 1603, the first Stuart king of England, James I (1603-1625), came to the throne. His predecessor had been Elizabeth I (1558-1603), the last of the Tudors. Elizabeth and her father, Henry VIII (1507-1547), had been powerful monarchs, but they had also known how to get along with the English Parliament. This was not so with James I. He came from Scotland and the English parliamentary tradition was foreign to him. When he became king of England, he was already serving as King James VI of Scotland.

In spirit, James was an absolutist unwilling to share power with Parliament. He had actually written a book, *The True Law of Free Monarchy*, defending divine-right monarchy (the idea that kings get their authority from God rather than from the people or the constitution). James continually struggled with Parliament over funds to run the government. The legislature was reluctant to grant new taxes, especially to a monarch it did not trust. The king was willing to raise funds (e.g., through special import duties) without Parliament's permission. He also displeased many in Parliament by favoring an alliance with Spain and by pursuing anti-Puritan religious policies.

Thus there was much political tension even before Charles I, the son of James I, ascended the throne in 1625. Charles managed to alienate large segments of the English public. He garrisoned troops in the homes of private citizens. He taxed without the consent of Parliament. He imprisoned those who dared to criticize him. He resorted to ruling without Parliament from 1629-1640, to avoid making concessions to his adversaries.

It was the very complicated religious issue that led to the undoing of Charles. In England, the state religion was Anglican. But there were several varieties within Anglicanism, ranging from low to high. High Anglicanism was, in ceremonials, very similar to Catholicism. Catholics were a minority who had little political influence. Much more influential were a variety of Calvinists, some of whom were more moderate Presbyterians, while others were more radical Puritans,

Why is James I and James VI the same Stuart king?

What is divine right monarchy?

Explain James I's difficulties with Parliament.

What was the religious situation in England, Scotland, and Ireland?

Describe the grievances the Scots and the English parliament had against Charles I.

such as the Levellers, who wanted universal manhood suffrage, and the Diggers, who advocated the abolition of private property. In Scotland, the state religion was Presbyterian. In Ireland, while the majority of native Celts were Catholic, Anglicans and especially Scotch Presbyterians were encouraged to settle in the Ulster "plantation" to foster elements more loyal to the Crown.

Elizabeth I had tried to blur many religious differences by fostering a Church of England (the Anglican Church) which had room for many varieties of Protestants. Charles I, in contrast, sharpened religious differences by encouraging the head of the English Church, William Laud (1573-1645), Archbishop of Canterbury, to force all church members to adhere to the ceremonials and structure of High Anglicanism. Laud first rooted out non-conformists from the church in England and then he sought to force the same Anglican conformity (especially the use of bishops) upon the Scotch Presbyterians.

In 1637 the Scots began a rebellion. By 1640, after an eleven-year break, Charles felt obliged to call the English Parliament into session. He needed new sources of revenue The new Parliament voiced pent-up grievances, and Charles dismissed it again after less than a month. Later in the year, even more desperate for funds, he called another Parliament into session. This one became known as the Long Parliament, since it lasted (on and off) for twenty years—until 1660.

Cromwell

By August of 1642 a full-fledged civil war had developed, since King and Parliament could not agree on the structure of either the Church or the state. The king's supporters were called the CAVALIERS, while the supporters of the Parliament were known as the ROUNDHEADS (because of their short haircuts). A leading figure in what became the New Model Army of Parliament was Oliver Cromwell (1599-1658). Cromwell was instrumental in the defeat of the King, who was captured in 1646. When the King participated in a new uprising in 1648 with his newfound allies, the Scots, Cromwell not only defeated Charles once more, but also decided that the King could not be trusted. There was understandably much disagreement in Parliament over the question of what to do with the King. To settle the matter, Cromwell had a Colonel Pride (d. 1658) exclude from Parliament all except a group of some sixty "Independents" who were favorable to Cromwell and his army. It was this "Rump" Parliament which established the court that condemned Charles to death. He was beheaded on January 30, 1649.

Cromwell was a success in military matters and foreign policy. In Ireland he put down Irish rebels and slaughtered them freely to compensate for an earlier Catholic slaughter of Protestants. Moreover he placed a large Scotch Protestant population in northern Ireland to replace the Catholics he forcibly exiled. He also put down a Scotch revolt, occasioned by the execution of their Stuart King. These actions paved the way for the later union of England and Scotland and, some would argue, for the recent troubles in Northern Ireland.

Oliver Cromwell was less successful when it came to creating a viable, constitutional government. From 1649-1660, England had a republican form of government, called the Commonwealth. At the start the principal holders of power were Cromwell, his army,

What part did Oliver Cromwell play in the defeat of Charles I?

Evaluate the policies followed by Cromwell after he achieved power.

What were the Commonwealth and the Protectorate?

and the Rump Parliament. Cromwell quarreled with the Parliament and in 1653 dismissed it. From 1653 till his death in 1658, he governed the "Protectorate" of England as Lord Protector. Although he made attempts at fashioning various types of parliamentary bodies, the reality was that England was under a military dictatorship. Cromwell's son and successor, Richard, was not as forceful as his father. After conflict between the officers of the army and members of Parliament, a newly elected Parliament invited Charles II, son of the slain Charles I, to restore the Stuart monarchy.

Was Charles II a successful monarch? Explain.

The Stuart Restoration

The reign of Charles II lasted from 1660 to 1685. The atmosphere in England was much more relaxed than it had been under the rigorously puritanical rule of Cromwell. Charles had several mistresses and liked gambling and horseracing. He was concerned to get along with Parliament and the English populace, lest the fate of his father befall him also. Charles, who was pro-French and pro-Catholic, did not formally convert to Catholicism until his deathbed. By the Treaty of Dover (1670), he secretly received subsidies from the French king, Louis XIV (1643-1715), in exchange for supporting French policy.

Charles did encounter difficulties with Parliament over religious issues. In 1672 Charles issued a Declaration of Indulgence, which would grant religious toleration to both Catholics and Nonconforming Protestants. The response of Parliament was to pass the Test Act (1673), which required all office holders to receive communion in the Anglican rite. This legislation was a special blow to the brother of Charles II, James, who had converted to Catholicism. After 1681, Charles actually ruled without Parliament to avoid legislative moves to exclude his brother from succession to the throne.

James II (1685-1689) took the throne with little opposition. But his Catholic leanings quickly proved to be his undoing. Despite the Test Act, he appointed Catholics to high government positions. He issued another Declaration of Indulgence (1687) allowing Catholics and Nonconformists freedom of worship and the right to hold public office. He unsuccessfully sought the conviction of seven bishops who refused to have his declaration read from the pulpits. To many English citizens, it appeared that the king wished to restore "popery," which they detested.

The Glorious Revolution

The final blow came in June 1688 when James had a male heir by his second wife, who was also Catholic. It appeared that a Catholic succession was assured. James also had two Protestant daughters, Mary (the eldest) and Anne, by his first wife who had been Protestant. But males had preference over females in determining succession to the royal throne. By late June, a group of prominent leaders, representing both Whig and Tory parties, had invited Mary, the Protestant daughter of James, and her Dutch husband, William of Orange, to invade England. To assure himself of English resources in his struggle against Louis XIV of France, William agreed. When the actual invasion took place in November, there was minimal opposition. There was more substantial fighting later in Ireland at the Battle of the

Why were the English frightened by the religious policy of James II?

Compare the Glorious Revolution with the Civil War of the 1640's.

What were the immediate results of the Glorious Revolution?

Why is the Glorious Revolution significant?

Boyne (1690), where William of Orange defeated James II, the last Stuart king of England. In 1689 William and Mary jointly ascended the throne of England as William III and Mary II.

Mary died in 1694 and William in 1702. The 1701 Act of Settlement was meant to insure a Protestant succession. By its terms, Mary's sister, Anne, ruled from 1702 to 1714. During her reign, in 1707, the Act of Union was passed which united England and Scotland into one kingdom, Great Britain, with one parliament. In 1714, George I (1714-1727), also Protestant and the heir of Sophia of Hanover who was a granddaughter of James I, ascended the throne. The 1689 Bill of Rights had already provided that the English monarch could not be a Catholic. This same Bill of Rights had generally strengthened the powers of Parliament. Indeed, a chief effect of the Glorious Revolution was to assure Parliamentary Supremacy over the monarch in England. John Locke helped to popularize the idea that the Glorious Revolution protected such individual liberties as life, liberty, and property against arbitrary government interference. The English Revolution served as a prelude to what became parliamentary democracy. Also, the ideas generated by the revolution were influential not only in England, but in the West generally, and very specifically in the United States.

Hobbes and Locke

The revolution in England had a major impact on the development of political thinking. The most noted defender of absolute power was Thomas Hobbes (1588-1679). In his *Leviathan*, Hobbes argued that in their natural state, outside society, human beings are at war with one another. Because of this unrelenting struggle, life is "nasty, brutish, and short."[8] For the sake of self-preservation, humans enter into a social contract. They form a commonwealth, in which each person surrenders his right to govern himself or herself. All rights are surrendered to a sovereign ruler who has almost absolute power.[9] The ruler's only obligation is to preserve the lives of his subjects. He can tax, seize property, etc., without limitation. To question the authority of the sovereign was to risk chaos.

The force of this argument, and the influence it attained, made it necessary for those who supported the political movement against James II to rebut Hobbes. John Locke (1632-1704) provided a distinguished rebuttal that was to influence generations on both sides of the Atlantic. Locke also contributed to modern philosophy, with his *Essay Concerning Human Understanding*. In the *Essay* he argues that all human knowledge derives from sense experience. There are no such things as innate ideas with which we are born. The mind at birth is a tabula rasa, like a blank sheet of paper. This idea that all knowledge comes from our senses was to have a profound effect upon subsequent philosophers.

In 1690, Locke's *Two Treatises of Civil Government* were published. The *Treatises* served to justify the Glorious Revolution, although they were undoubtedly written before the events of 1688-1689, and should be seen as tracts not merely justifying but actually urging revolution.

The *Second Treatise* is an answer to Hobbes' *Leviathan*. In it Locke maintains that humans, in the state of nature prior to the establishment of society, could lead happy lives governed by the natural law or reason. Reason would show that individuals

What is life like in the state of nature according to Hobbes?

Why did Locke write his *Two Treatises of Civil Government*?

How do Locke's views differ from those of Hobbes?

What is the purpose of government according to Locke?

had certain rights, especially rights to life, liberty, and property. But there were certain inconveniences, particularly in maintaining property against the avarice of others. The remedy was the establishment of a social contract whereby people agreed first to form a society and later, as a society, to form a government.

Unlike Hobbes, Locke did not believe one surrendered all rights to government for the sake of self-preservation. Rather, the individual entering society retained the fundamental natural rights of life, liberty, and property. Government existed for the sake of preserving these rights. Should the government or ruler fail to preserve these individual rights, or arbitrarily act contrary to individual rights, there was a right of revolution.

There is much more to Locke than can be discussed here. He has a concept of checks and balances among branches of government, and he insists on the prerogatives, even the supremacy, of the legislature. His notion of property was to influence economists as well as political scientists. Locke argues that originally the fruits of nature were equally available to all humans. Private property arose through the use of human labor. He says:

> Whatsoever then he removes out of the state that nature hath provided and left it, he hath mixed his labor with, ...[and] thereby makes it his property.[10]

This labor could take the form of plucking wild fruit or of cultivating the land. In the latter case we have real property. This is the labor theory of value that was later to influence Adam Smith and Karl Marx. But Locke is not a socialist. He says God gave property to the use of the "industrious and rational."[11] This means that even in the state of nature some will have more than others, since they are smarter and work harder.

There are, however, natural limits on accumulation. No one should appropriate as his property more than he can use. For example, there is no right to accumulate unlimited amounts of fruits, grains, etc., which are perishable. When humans enter into society, by common consent they set a store of value on some article that is accepted as money. Money is imperishable. With the invention of money, there is the opportunity to accumulate possessions without any natural limits.

Not surprisingly, Locke accepts the unlimited accumulation of property as socially beneficial. He argues that even the poorest in England benefit from the improved estates of property holders, whereas the same amount of land left unimproved in America, is of much less social benefit to the Amerindian population. Locke is a man of his times. He argues in favor of the wealthy landholders,[12] who helped make the Glorious Revolution. True, he is a democrat in so far as he insists that government, and taxation in particular, must rest on the consent of the governed, who are presumably property holders. Lockean political thought provides an equality of opportunity, rather than an equality of actual possessions.

Explain Locke's theory of property.

What are the implications of his theory for the poor?

To what extent was Locke a democrat?

The Enlightenment

The new thinking engendered by the Scientific Revolution and the English Revolution helped to bring on the eighteenth century Enlightenment. It was an optimistic age of reason that challenged religious and political traditions. Enlightenment thought

What were the origins of the Enlightenment?

owed much to the Scientific Revolution. The new astronomy had cast doubt upon the scriptural version of the origins of the universe. Newton's laws served to inspire others who would look for similar laws in the affairs of humankind. Cartesian doubt was quickly applied to the existing religious and political authorities. The Glorious Revolution had demonstrated that limits could be placed on government authority, with a simultaneous increase in individual freedom. Locke had provided a rationale for curbing royal authority.

Discuss the ideas of Rousseau.

The French Philosophes

The Enlightenment was an especially strong force in France where the leaders of the movement were known as *philosophes*, or philosophers. From today's perspective, they would be considered media types rather than serious philosophers. The most celebrated of the French philosophes was François Marie Arouet (1694-1778), better known as VOLTAIRE. Voltaire spent almost a year in the Bastille prison and some three years in exile in England. He was influenced by English intellectual currents which he, in turn, helped to popularize in France. Much of his most famous book, *Candide* (1759), which is a satire, is directed against the evils caused by religion. Voltaire was adamantly opposed to religious persecution. His saying, *écrasez l'infâme*[13] (crush the infamous thing), constituted a direct attack on the Catholic Church, which he viewed as a source of superstition and as a hindrance to progress through reason. Voltaire was a deist. He believed in a God who resembled a watchmaker. God made the world like a watch with precise movements. Once the world was started, there was no further need for God's intervention. This

What is a deist?

deistic view is opposed to the theistic God, found in Judeo-Christian belief, who intervenes in human affairs and reveals his will. For Voltaire, Christianity and all other organized religions were merely human creations that perpetuated clerical power.

The *Encyclopédie* or *Encyclopedia,* edited by Denis DIDEROT (1713-1784), fostered skepticism concerning both the established religious and political orders. The first volume of the *Encyclopédie* was published in 1751. Its attacks on the Church reflected its deistic and rationalistic bent. Leading writers of the day, such as Voltaire, Turgot, Montesquieu, and Rousseau contributed articles.

The writings of Montesquieu and Rousseau in particular contributed to the undermining of political authority. Charles Louis de Secondat, Baron de la Brède et de MONTESQUIEU, lived from 1689 to 1755. His best-known writings are the *Persian Letters*, a satire on French society, and *The Spirit of the Laws*, which had an influence on the Founding Fathers in the United States.

In this last work, Montesquieu advocated the separation of powers of government as a means of protecting individual liberty. He suggested the English Constitution as a model for such a separation. The executive power would be exercised by the king, the legislative power by parliament, and the judicial power by the judges. The actual British constitution in 1748, when *The Spirit of the Laws* was published, made parliament supreme over the other branches of government. Though Montesquieu's separation of powers theory misinterpreted the existing English form of government, it still had a great impact on the Constitution of the United States written later in the century.

Montesquieu also emphasized the importance of climate, custom, and geography

How did Diderot influence the Enlightenment?

What were Montesquieu's political ideas? Why are they important?

What was the theme of Rousseau's *Émile?*

Compare Rousseau to Locke.

in shaping the political institutions of different countries. He believed, for example, that the great plains of Asia fostered despotism, whereas the natural boundaries that made European nations smaller, fostered greater liberty. Today, he would be accused of ethnocentrism, but at least he recognized that establishing particular forms of government would not have the same results everywhere.

Montesquieu was a very respected aristocrat who had served as a judge at Bordeaux. Jean-Jacques ROUSSEAU (1712-1778), who was born in Geneva, was a very different character. Rousseau's father was a watchmaker and dance master who abandoned Jean-Jacques at the age of ten. Rousseau, himself, had five children out of wedlock with Thérèse Le Vasseur, whom he later married. Though Rousseau sent all five children to an orphanage, he wrote *Émile*, a noted book on child rearing. A major theme of *Émile* is that humans are essentially good and that children should be reared to encourage their natural goodness while protecting them from the corrupting influences of society. It is not hard to understand why Rousseau is considered to be the spiritual father of the Romantic Movement of the nineteenth century.

Rousseau wrote several works on politics. The most famous of these is *The Social Contract*, published in 1762. One of the problems tackled in this work is how the individual in society can be free. Rousseau, influenced by Hobbes, accepts the notion of a social contract. Unlike Locke, Rousseau holds that once an individual has entered into society he gives up all natural rights. He says:

> These articles of association, rightly understood, are reducible to a single one, namely the total alienation by each

associate of himself and all his rights to the whole community.[14]

Whatever rights one has, one gets from the Sovereign. So far, this sounds very Hobbesian. How is it possible to have individual liberty? But Rousseau has an important twist. He introduces the principle of popular sovereignty by which the people themselves are the sovereign. They make the laws. Thus the individual as part of the body politic has made the law which he must obey. Freedom consists in obedience to a law he has helped to make. What if the individual would disobey the law made by all in the general interest? Rousseau answers:

> ...whoever refuses to obey the general will shall be constrained to do so by the whole body, which means nothing other than that he shall be forced to be free.[15]

Many are uneasy with this association of force and liberty. Much depends on what is meant by "general will" and how it is to be discovered. Most often Rousseau seems to mean what most would call the "public interest." The general will is what is best for the whole society. It is not the selfish, private will of the individual. Nor is it the wishes of particular factions or interest groups. Law, according to Rousseau, should not apply to particular individuals or groups only, but to all in the same way.

At times the general will and the will of the majority are identical, but Rousseau admits that this is not always so. Rousseau proposes that there should be a Lawgiver or Legislator whose function is to propose laws that are in the general interest. While the consent of the majority is still needed, and the Lawgiver is not permitted executive functions; nevertheless, it is hard to reconcile the Lawgiver with modern notions of popular sovereignty and democracy.

What does Rousseau mean by saying that a person can be "forced to be free"?

How is the general will to be determined?

Consider whether Rousseau is a defender of democracy or of dictatorship.

Name some Enlightenment thinkers who were not French. Describe their contributions.

Even more chilling is Rousseau's demand that citizens adhere to the dogmas of a civil religion in order to give moral support to the social contract and the law. He prescribed the banishment of adherents to religions (such as Catholicism) that had dogmas at odds with those of the civil religion. It is not hard to find justification for various forms of totalitarianism in Rousseau. Maxmilian Robespierre, a leader in the Terror of the French Revolution, claimed himself to be a follower of Rousseau!

The Enlightenment Outside France

The Enlightenment spirit impacted many countries and persons. An Italian, Cesare Beccaria (1738-1794) from Milan, helped to bring about a more enlightened attitude towards criminals. In his book, *On Crimes and Punishments* (1764), he argued that punishments for crime need not be so severe as to be barbaric. Penalties should serve to insure good social order and for this purpose the sureness of punishment was more important than its harshness. He opposed the use of torture and the death penalty.

In the United States, such leaders as Benjamin Franklin and Thomas Jefferson were familiar with the ideas of the *Philosophes*. In England, one of the Enlightenment writers was Mary Wollstonecraft (1759-1797) She published *A Vindication Of The Rights Of Women*, in which she vehemently rejected male domination of women. She argued forcefully for equal education of women, for their right to representation in government, and for other rights. Today she is seen as one of the founders of the women's movement.

The Scottish Enlightenment

There was also a Scottish Enlightenment. David HUME (1711-1776) and Adam SMITH (1723-1790) are its best-known representatives. Hume was a skeptic who challenged the belief in the existence of God and even in causality. He argued that the relation we assume between cause and effect is based on habit rather than reason. He was unwilling to admit that, since event B had followed event A in the past, A was necessarily the cause of B, or that event B would follow event A in the future.

Who was David Hume?

Smith is particularly important because of his influence on later generations of economists and statesmen. If Wollstonecraft wanted women to be free from the domination of men, Smith wanted producers and traders to be free of government regulation. In the *Wealth of Nations*, he contrasted the prevailing mercantile system of his time with a "system of natural liberty"[16] — what now would be called "free enterprise." Smith hoped to discover laws of political economy comparable to the laws Newton had discovered in the field of physics.

Has Adam Smith influenced the U.S.? Explain.

Smith argued that government activities should be limited to protection from foreign invasion, the administration of justice, and the undertaking of unprofitable enterprises (such as schools), which are needed for the public good. People are motivated basically by self-interest. Left to their own devices, they will make the most efficient use of available resources in order to maximize profit.

What are the functions of government according to Smith?

The real wealth of a nation consists of the goods and services produced by private enterprise, not in the amount of gold and silver gained by government balance-of-trade policies. Smith perceived that ignorant gov-

In what does wealth really consist? What is the best way to increase the real wealth of a nation?

ernment officials were led astray by grasping merchants. These latter sought monopolies that increased their own wealth, by making goods scarcer and thus more expensive for the ordinary consumer. If government kept hands off, each individual pursing his own interests would direct his labor so that, "led by an invisible hand,"[17] the greatest possible gain for the whole society was realized.

To many, the fall of states such as the Soviet Union, which had a government-mandated economic structure, appears to be a vindication of Smith. Whether or not this is true, Smith's continuing ideological influence is obvious.

Common Threads in the Enlightenment

Why is the Enlightenment often associated with reason?

Many people and events can be seen as producers of the Enlightenment. There are, however, some similarities in thought and attitude worth pondering. The emphasis on using reason rather than faith or feeling is certainly a common thread. Descartes was willing to doubt all beliefs—even belief in his own existence. He also embraced the logic of mathematics as an aid to understanding the universe. Newton used mathematics to propose physical laws that were universally applicable. Gravity applied in the heavens as well as on earth. He inspired others to search for similar laws in the natural and social sciences. Such laws lessened the need to assert direct divine intervention to explain individual events.

Locke applied reason to justify revolution and thoroughly rejected the idea of divine-right monarchy. There is also a fundamental optimism in Locke that will be characteristic of later Enlightenment thinkers. He rejects the pessimism of Hobbes.

Locke believes the government should and can be made to protect the liberties and properties, as well as the lives of the governed. If the human mind is a <u>tabula</u> <u>rasa</u> at birth as he suggests, then altering the experiences of individuals can alter society.

Voltaire thought that society could change for the better. That is why he wished to crush the Catholic Church, which he saw as a supporter of superstitions hindering progress. Smith is profoundly optimistic when he argues that selfish individuals pursuing their own interests will produce for the greater social good. His "invisible hand" substituted rationally derived economic laws for the intervention of government or the deity. In the next chapter we will see how ideas such as these helped to start the French Revolution

Many Enlightened thinkers of the eighteenth century were optimists. Consider whether their optimism has been validated by the events of the twentieth century.

Figure 1.3 **Marble Sculpture of Voltaire** (1694-1778) by Joseph Rosset. Witty, major prose writer of the French Enlightenment, an advocate of religious toleration, he was famous for his attacks on religious bigotry. (Courtesy of The Metropolitan Museum of Art, Bequest of Annie C. Kane, 1926)

NOTES

[1]Martin Luther at the Diet of Worms in 1521 allegedly made this statement. Quoted in Willem Berends, Prophecy in the Reformation Tradition (Internet, <http://www.pastornet.net.au/rtc/prophecy.htm>, 31 December 1998).

[2]R. R. Palmer and Joel Colton, A History of the Modern World to 1815. 7th. ed. (New York: McGraw-Hill, 1992), vol. 1, p. 184.

[3]Palmer, v. 1, p. 138.

[4]Palmer, v. 1, p. 193.

[5]Quoted in Department of Government University of Queensland, GT802 Administrative History, "Topic 11: Prussia to the 19th Century" (Internet, <http://www.library.uq.edu.au/eres/gt802/1996/topic_11.html>, 31 December 1998).

[6]Grolier's Academic American Encyclopedia, 1992, "Newton, Sir Isaac," by J. A. Schuster.

[7]Palmer, v. 1, p. 291.

[8]Thomas Hobbes, Leviathan (Oxford: Basil Blackwell, 1946), p. 82.

[9]The ruler cannot force a person to kill himself. This would be contrary to the human instinct for self-preservation.

[10]John Locke, Two Treatises of Government (New York: Hafner, 1947), p. 134.

[11]Locke, p. 137.

[12]The landholders often belonged to the Whig party.

[13]Palmer, v. 1, p. 321.

[14]Jean-Jacques Rousseau, The Social Contract, trans. Maurice Cranston (Baltimore: Penguin, 1968), p.60.

[15]Rousseau, p.64.

[16]Adam Smith, The Wealth of Nations (New York: Modern Library, 1937 [1776], p. 651.

[17]Smith, p. 423.

Figure 1.4 **John Locke** (1632-1704). A staunch advocate of the natural rights of life, liberty, and property, English philosopher John Locke argued that the people had the right to violent revolution if the monarch or legislature abused their trust. Later revolutions in America and France were influenced by his ideas. (Courtesy of The Library of Congress)

JOHN LOCKE

Two Treatises of Government *

Considered a genius by the philosophes, John Locke's (1632-1704) political philosophy greatly contributed to the French and American Revolutions. Locke, a medical doctor by vocation, became a political theorist by virtue of his alliance with a Whig politician, the Earl of Shaftesbury, who opposed the Stuart king, Charles II of England. When the Earl was forced to flee to Holland, Locke joined him where he found the time to write *The Second Treatise of Government* to justify the, still to occur, Glorious Revolution. Locke was extremely opposed to the absolutist style of monarchy associated with the Stuart kings. During his exile Locke was an adviser to William of Orange, prince and stadtholder of the United Provinces of the Netherlands. Locke returned to England with William's wife, Mary (Protestant daughter of James II, who had succeeded his brother, Charles II, on the throne). There he saw Parliament enact the English Bill of Rights establishing England's first constitutional monarchy in 1689. As a consequence of the Glorious Revolution, William and Mary ascended the English throne. The Revolution was supported by Locke's political theories that you will find on the next several pages. His brilliant work was published in 1690, after the Revolution. Locke's ideas became a blueprint for later revolutionaries, for example, Thomas Jefferson, who were looking for grounds to justify acts of rebellion. We have provided sidebar comments to aid you in your understanding Locke's seventeenth-century style of writing.

Of the ends of Political Society and Government

If Man in the state of Nature be so free, as has been said; if he be absolute Lord of his own Person and Possessions, equal to the greatest, and subject to no body, why will he part

For Locke, the state of nature is the period before the formation of a society.

*John Locke, Two Treatises of Government. 5th ed. (London: A. Bettesworth, J. Pemberton, and E. Symon, 1728). All selections are from *The Second Treatise of Government*.

Individuals enjoy the natural rights of life, liberty, and property. It is to protect these rights that fearful individuals form a society.

with this Freedom? Why will he give up this Empire, and subject himself to the Dominion and Control of any other Power? To which 'tis obvious to answer, That tho in the state of Nature he hath such a Right, yet the Enjoyment of it is very uncertain, and constantly exposed to the Invasion of others. For all being Kings as much as he, every Man his equal, and the greater part no strict Observers of Equity and Justice, the Enjoyment of the Property he has in this state, is very unsafe, very unsecure. This makes him willing to quit this Condition, which however free, is full of Fears and continual Dangers: And 'tis not without Reason, that he seeks out, and is willing to join in Society with others, who are already united, or have mind to unite, for the mutual Preservation of their Lives, Liberties and Estates, which I call by the general Name, Property.

The chief purpose of government is to protect property rights.

The great and chief End therefore, of Mens uniting into commonwealths, and putting themselves under Government, is the Preservation of their Property. To which in the state of Nature there are many things wanting.

First, There wants an established, settled, known Law...

Secondly, In the state of Nature there wants a known...judge, with Authority to determine all Differences according to the established Law. For every one in that state being both Judge and Executioner of the Law of Nature, Men being partial to themselves, Passion and Revenge is very apt to carry them too far.

Thirdly, In the state of Nature there often wants Power to back and support the Sentence when right, and to give it due Execution.

Often Locke's term "legislative" can be updated to "legislature."

Of the Extent of the Legislative Power.

The great end of Men's entering into Society, being the Enjoyment of their Properties in the Peace and Safety, and the great instrument and means of that being the Laws established in that Society; the first and fundamental positive Law of all Common-wealths, is the establishing of the Legislative Power; as the first and fundamental natural Law, which is to govern even the Legislative it self, is the preservation of the Society, and (as far as will consist with the public good) of every Person in it. This Legislative is not only the Supreme Power of the Commonwealth, but sacred and unalterable in the hands where the Community have once placed it; nor can any Edict of any body else...have the force and obligation of a Law, which has not its sanction from that Legislative, which the Publick has chosen and appointed. For without this, the Law could not have that which is absolutely necessary to its being a Law, the consent of the Society, over whom no body can have a Power to make Laws, but by their own Consent, and by Authority received from them; and therefore all the Obedience, which by most solemn Ties any one can be obliged to pay, ultimately terminates in this Supreme Power...Nor can any Oaths to any foreign Power whatsoever, or any domestic subordinate Power, discharge any Member of the Society from his Obedience to the Legislative, acting pursuant to their Trust; nor oblige him to any Obedience contrary to the Laws so enacted, or farther than they do allow; it being ridiculous to imagine one can be tied ultimately to obey any Power in the Society, which is not the Supreme.

Tho the Legislative, whether placed in one or more, whether it be always in being, or only by intervals, tho it be the Supreme Power in every Commonwealth; yet...It is not, nor can possibly be, absolutely Arbitrary over the Lives and Fortunes of the People. For it being but the joint Power of every Member of the Society, given up to that Person or Assembly which is Legislator; it can be no more than those Persons had in a state of Nature, before they entered into Society, and gave up to the Community. For no body can transfer to another more Power, than he has in himself; and no body has an absolute arbitrary Power over himself, or over any other, to destroy his own Life, or take away the Life or Property of an-

Note that much of this section is devoted to advocating "legislative supremacy" over other government officials.

Even legislative power is limited.

other. A man, as has been proved, cannot subject himself to the arbitrary Power of another; and having in the state of Nature no arbitrary Power over the Life, Liberty, or Possession of another, but only so much as the Law of Nature gave him for the Preservation of himself, and the rest of Mankind; this is all he doth, or can give up to the Commonwealth, and by it to the Legislative Power, so that the Legislative can have no more than this. Their Power in the utmost bounds of it, is limited to the publick Good of the Society. It is a Power that hath no other end but Preservation, and therefore can never have a right to destroy, enslave, or designedly to impoverish the Subjects.

The Obligations of the Law of Nature cease not in Society, but only in many cases are drawn closer, and have by human Laws know Penalties annexed to them, to enforce their Observation. Thus the Law of Nature stands as an eternal Rule to all Men, Legislators as well as others. The Rules that they make for other Mens Actions must, as well as their own, and other Mens Actions, be conformable to the Law of Nature, i. e. to the Will of God, of which that is a Declaration; and the fundamental Law of Nature being the preservation of Mankind, no human Sanction can be good, or valid against it.

Absolute, Arbitrary Power, or governing without Settled Standing Laws, can neither of them consist with the Ends of Society and Government, which Men would not quit the freedom of the State of Nature for, and tie themselves up under, were it not to preserve their Lives, Liberties and Fortunes; and by stated Rules of Right and Property to secure their Peace and Quiet. It cannot be supposed that they should intend, had they a Power so to do, to give to any one, or more, an absolute Arbitrary Power over their Persons and Estates, and put a Force into the Magistrate's Hand to execute his unlimited Will arbitrarily upon them. This were to put themselves into a worse Condition than the State of Nature, wherein, they had a Liberty to defend their Right against the Injuries of others, and were upon equal Terms of Force to

Legislative power is limited to the public good and must conform to the natural law (right reason).

maintain it, whether invaded by a single Man, or many in Combination.

The Supreme Power cannot take from any Man any part of his Property without his own Consent. For the preservation of Property being the End of Government, and that for which Men enter into Society, it necessarily supposes and requires, that the People should have Property, without which they must be supposed to lose that, by entering into Society, which was the End for which they entered into it; too gross an Absurdity for any Man to own. Men therefore in Society having Property, they have such a Right to the Goods, which by the Law of the Community are theirs, that no body hath a Right to take Substance, or any part of it, from them, without their own Consent; without this they have no Property at all. For I have truly no Property in that which another can by Right take from me when he pleases, against my consent. Hence it is a mistake, to think that the Supreme or Legislative Power or any Commonwealth, can do what it will, and dispose of the Estates of the Subject arbitrarily, or take any part of them at pleasure. This is not much to be feared in Governments where the Legislative consists, wholly or in part, in Assemblies which are variable, whose Members, upon the Dissolution of the Assembly, are Subjects under the common Laws of their Country, equally with the rest. But the Governments where the Legislative is in one lasting Assembly, always in Being, or in one Man, as in absolute Monarchies, there is danger still, that they will think themselves to have a distinct Interest from the rest of the Community; and so will be apt to increase their own Riches and Power, by taking what they think fit from the People. For a Man's Property is not at all secure, tho there be good and equitable Laws to set the Bounds of it, between him and his fellow Subjects, if he who commands those Subjects, have Power to take from any private Man, what part he pleases of his Property, and use and dispose of it as he thinks good.

There should be no taking of property or taxation without consent.

Absolute monarchs may think they have an interest distinct from the rest of the community. Thus they have a greater incentive to take property without the consent of the majority.

'Tis true, Governments cannot be supported without great Charge, and 'tis fit every one who enjoys his Share of the Protection, should pay out of his Estate his Proportion for the Maintenance of it. But still it must be with his own Consent, i.e. the Consent of the Majority, giving it either by themselves, or their Representatives chosen by them. For if any one shall claim a Power to lay and levy Taxes on the People, by his own Authority, and without such consent of the People, he thereby invades the Fundamental Law of Property, and subverts the End of Government. For what Property have I in that which another may be right take when he pleases to himself?

Of the Dissolution of Government.

Besides this overturning from without, Governments are dissolved from within.

The Legislative power embodies the will of the majority.

First, When the Legislative is altered. Civil Society being a state of Peace, amongst those who are of it, from whom the state of War is excluded by the Umpirage, which they have provided in their Legislative, for the ending all Differences that may arise amongst any of them; 'tis in their Legislative that the Members of a Commonwealth are untied, and combined together into one coherent living Body. This is the Soul that gives Form, Life, and Unity to the Commonwealth: From hence the several Members have their mutual Influence, Sympathy, and Connection: And therefore when the Legislative is broken, or dissolved, Dissolution and Death follows. For the Essence and Union of the Society consisting in having one Will, the Legislative, when once established by the Majority, has the declaring, and as it were keeping of that Will. The Constitution of the Legislative is the first and fundamental Act of the Society, whereby provision is made for the continuation of their Union, under the Direction of Persons, and Bonds of Laws, made by Persons authorized thereunto, by the Consent and Appointment of the People; without which no one Man, or number of Men, amongst them, can have Authority of making Laws, that shall be binding to the rest. When any one or more shall take upon them to make Laws, whom the People have not appointed so to do, they make Laws without Authority, which the People are not therefore bound to obey; by which means they come again to be out of Subjection, and may constitute to themselves a new Legislative, as they think best, being in full liberty to resist the Force of those, who without Authority would impose any thing upon them. Every one is at the disposer of his own Will, when those who had by the Delegation of the Society, the declaring of the publick Will, are excluded from it and others usurp the Place, who have no such Authority of Delegation.

This being usually brought about by such in the Commonwealth, who misuse the Power they have; it is hard to consider it aright, and know at whose door to lay it, without knowing for Form of Government in which it happens. Let us suppose then the Legislative placed in the Concurrence of three distinct Persons:

1. A single hereditary Person, having the constant, supreme, executive Power, and with it the Power of convoking and dissolving the other two within certain Periods of time.
2. An Assembly of hereditary Nobility.
3. An Assembly of Representatives chosen *pro tempore*, by the People. Such a Form of Government supposed, it is evident,

First, That when such a single Person, or Prince, sets up his own arbitrary Will in place of the Laws, which are the Will of the Society, declared by the Legislative, then the Legislative is changed. For that being in effect the Legislative, whose Rules and Laws are put in execution, and required to be obeyed; when other Laws are set up, and other Rules pretended, and inforced, than what the Legislative, constituted by the Society, have enacted, 'tis plain, that the Legislative is changed. Whoever introduces new Laws, not being thereunto authorized by the fundamental Appointment of the Society, of subverts the old, disowns and over-

Only law made by those appointed by the people must be obeyed.

If the Prince arbitrarily changes rules or laws made by the legislative power, the Prince need not be obeyed.

turns the Power by which they made, and so sets up a new Legislative.

Secondly, When the Prince hinders the Legislative from assembling in its due time, or from acting freely, pursuant to those Ends for which it was constituted, the Legislative is altered. For 'tis not a certain number of Men, no, nor their meeting, unless they have also freedom of debating, and leisure of perfecting, what is for the Good of the Society, wherein the Legislative consists; when these are taken away or altered, so as to deprive the Society of the due Exercise of their Power, the Legislative is truly altered. For it is not Names, that constitute Governments, but the Use and Exercise of those Powers, that were intended to accompany them; so that he, who takes away the Freedom, or hinders the acting of the Legislative in its due Seasons, in effect takes away the Legislative, and puts an end to the Government.

Thirdly, When by the arbitrary Power of the Prince, the Electors, or ways of Election are altered, without the Consent, and contrary to the common Interest of the People, there also the Legislative is altered. For if others, than those whom the Society hath authorized thereunto, do choose, or in another way than what the Society hath prescribed, those chosen are not the Legislative appointed by the People.

Fourthly, The Delivery also of the People into the Subjection of a foreign Power, either by the Prince, or by the Legislative, is certainly a Change of the Legislative, and so a Dissolution of the Government. For the End why People entered into Society, being to be preserved one entire, free, independent Society, to be governed by its own Laws; this is lost, whenever they are given up into the Power of another.

There is another way whereby Governments are dissolved, and that is, when the Legislative, or the Prince either of them act contrary their Trust.

The Prince may not prevent the legislature from meeting to enact law.

First, The Legislative acts against the Trust reposed in them, when they endeavor to invade the Property of the Subject, and to make themselves, or any part of the community, Masters, or arbitrary Disposers of the Lives, Liberties, or Fortunes of the People.

The reason why Men enter into Society, is the Preservation of their Property; and the End why they choose and authorize a Legislative, is, that they may be laws made, and Rules set, as Guards and Fences to the Properties of all the Members of the Society, to limit the Power and moderate the Dominion of every Part and Member of the Society. For since it can never be supposed to be the Will of the Society, that the Legislative should have a Power to destroy that, which every one designs to secure, by entering into Society, and for which the People submitted themselves to Legislators of their own making; whenever the Legislators endeavor to take away, and destroy the Property of the People, or to reduce them to Slavery under arbitrary Power, they put themselves into a state of War with the People, who are thereupon absolved from any farther Obedience, and are left to the common Refuge, which God hath provided for all Men, against Force and Violence. Whensoever therefore the Legislative shall transgress this fundamental Rule of Society; and either by Ambition, Fear, Folly or Corruption, endeavor to grasp themselves, or put into the hands of any other, an absolute Power over the Lives, Liberties, and Estates of the People; by this breach of Trust they forfeit the Power the People had put into their hands, for quite contrary Ends, and it devolves to the People, who have a Right to Resume their original Liberty, and, by the Establishment of a new Legislative, (such as they shall think fit) provide for their own Safety and Security, which is the End for which they are in Society. What I have said here, concerning the Legislative holds true also concerning the supreme Executor, who having a double Trust put in him, both to have a part in the Legislative, and the supreme Execution of the Law, acts against both, when he goes about to set up his own arbitrary Will, as the Law of the Society.

There is a right to replace the legislature which has acted contrary to the people's trust.

There is a similar right to replace a chief executive who has acted arbitrarily, contrary to the trust given by the people.

Here, 'tis like, the common Question will be made, Who shall be judge, whether the Prince or Legislative act contrary to their Trust? This, perhaps, ill affected and factious Men may spread amongst the People, when the Prince only makes use of his due Prerogative. To this I reply; The People shall be judge: for who shall be judge whether his Trustee or Deputy acts well, and according to the Trust reposed in him, but he who deputes him, and must, by having deputed him, have still a Power to discard him, when he fails in this Trust? If this be reasonable in particular Cases of private Men, why should it be otherwise in that of the greatest moment, where the Welfare of Millions is concerned, and also where the evil, if not prevented, is greater, and the Redress very difficult, dear, and dangerous?

There is a right to violent revolution, if the Prince acts contrary to his obligations.

If a Controversy arise betwixt a Prince and some of the People, in a Matter, where the law is silent, or doubtful, and the thing be of great, consequence, I should think the proper Umpire, in such a Case, should be the Body of the People. For in Cases where the Prince hath a Trust reposed in him, and is dispensed from the common ordinary Rules of the Law; there, if any Men find themselves aggrieved, and think the Prince acts contrary to, or beyond that Trust, who so proper to judge as the Body of the People, (who at first lodged that Trust in him) how far they meant it should extend? But if the Prince, or whoever they be in the Administration, decline that way of Determination, the Appeal then lies no where but to Heaven. Force between either Persons, who have no known Superior on Earth, or which permits no Appeal to a Judge on Earth, being properly a state of War, wherein the Appeal lies only to Heaven: and in that State the injured Party must judge for himself, when he will think fit to make use of that Appeal, and put himself upon it.

Questions for Critical Thinking and Discussion

1. Pretend you are a seventeenth-century Lockean theorist. Argue for or against the abolition of absolutism.

2. Why does Locke feel the Legislature is the Supreme Power?

3. How do Locke's ideas find their way into the United States' system of government?

4. Pretend you are urging a change in government via violent revolution. Argue from Locke's point of view.

5. Compare and contrast the political thought of Locke and Rousseau. Look at the information on Rousseau given earlier in this chapter.

6. Explain why individuals form a society, according to John Locke.

7. Under what conditions are people bound to obey the laws?

8. At what point may the people replace the legislature or the monarch?

9. What are natural rights? Do they really exist?

Figure 1.5 **The First Lecture in Experimental Philosophy**. London. 1748. From the examples of Bacon, Galileo, and Newton, educated people, using the scientific method, made strides in the application and advancement of science. Note the telescope on the

Self-Test

Part I: Identification

Can you identify each of the following? Tell who, what, when, where, why, and/or how for each term.

1. Early Modern Period
2. Prince Henry the Navigator
3. Ferdinand and Isabella
4. Reformation
5. Martin Luther
6. Thirty Years' War
7. Great Elector
8. Divine-Right Monarchy
9. Mercantilism
10. "Sun King"
11. Fronde
12. Peace of Utrecht
13. Enlightened despot
14. Voltaire
15. *Two Treatises on Government*
16. Absolutism
17. Frederick II
18. The Restoration
19. Huguenots
20. Glorious Revolution
21. William III and Mary II
22. English Bill of Rights
23. Act of Settlement
24. *The Social Contract*
25. Philosophe
26. Triangular Trade
27. *Encomienda*
28. Seven Years' War
29. Edict of Nantes
30. *A Vindication of the Rights of Women*
31. Nicholas Copernicus
32. "Invisible hand"
33. Peace of Westphalia
34. Holy Roman Emperor
35. Romanov Dynasty
36. Intendants
37. Ottoman Empire
38. *Leviathan*
39. Peter the Great
40. Catherine the Great
41. William Harvey
42. *The Spirit of the Laws*
43. Great Northern War
44. Enlightenment
45. Scientific Revolution
46. *Encyclopedia*
47. Heliocentric theory
48. Jean-Jacques Rousseau
49. Tycho Brahe
50. *On the Revolutions of Heavenly Spheres*
51. Isaac Newton
52. Galileo Galilei
53. Francis Bacon
54. *Wealth of Nations*
55. David Hume
56. Pragmatic Sanction
57. Cromwellian Commonwealth
58. "I think, therefore I am."
59. Cavaliers

Part II: Multiple Choice Questions

Circle the best response from the ones available.

1. Major historical movements that helped shape the Early Modern period included each of the following EXCEPT:

    a. the Renaissance.
    b. the Voyages of Discovery.
    c. the Industrial Revolution.
    d. the Reformation.

2. Modern Banking has its roots in the banking house of :

    a. DaVincis.
    b. Medicis.
    c. Rockefellers.
    d. Biondes.

3. The Spanish destroyed:

    a. the Aztec Empire of Mexico.
    b. the Inca Empire of Peru.
    c. both of the above.
    d. none of the above.

4. Absolute monarchs needed:

    a. a central administration.
    b. a centralized taxing system.
    c. a powerful military.
    d. all of the above.

5. The list of states and associated ruling families given below is correct EXCEPT for:

    a. Prussia—Hapsburgs.
    b. Russia—Romanovs.
    c. Portugal—Braganzas.
    d. Sweden—Vasas.

6. The Protestant Reformer who is alleged to have said: "Here I Stand. I can do no other." was:

   a. Martin Luther.   c. John Knox.
   b. John Calvin.   d. Ignatius Loyola.

7. The supporters of Charles I of England were known as:

   a. Roundheads   c. Cavaliers
   b. Squareheads   d. Independents

8. The Peace of Westphalia (1648) had all of the following effects EXCEPT:

   a. France and Sweden were solidly defeated by a coalition led by the Holy Roman Emperor.
   b. The principalities of the Holy Roman Empire were permitted to conduct their own foreign diplomacy.
   c. The Holy Roman Empire was destroyed as an effective political entity.
   d. Each prince within the Holy Roman Empire could decide the religion of his territory.

9. As a result of the Seven Years' War:

   a. England surrendered Bengal in India.
   b. France retained Haiti.
   c. Britain received Louisiana.
   d. Spain received Paris.

10. Which one of the following responses places English rulers in their correct chronological order?:

    a. James II, Charles I, Cromwell, William III and Mary II.
    b. Cromwell, Charles II, James II, William III and Mary II.
    c. William III and Mary II, Anne, Charles II, James II.
    d. Charles II, James II, Cromwell, William III and Mary II.

11. Which of the following principles would NOT be consistent with Adam Smith?

    a. Self-interest.
    b. Free enterprise.
    c. Extensive government regulation of business.
    d. "Invisible hand."

12. The Glorious Revolution (1688) resulted in:

   a. the execution of Charles I of England by a court of the "Rump" Parliament.
   b. the defeat of Charles II by William of Orange at the Battle of Boyne.
   c. the restoration of the Stuart monarchy to the throne of England.
   d. an invitation to William and Mary by Parliament to assume the throne of England.

13. The following authors and their respective works are correctly matched EXCEPT:

   a. Hobbes — An Essay Concerning Human Understanding.
   b. Rousseau — Émile.
   c. Montesquieu — The Spirit of the Laws.
   d. Voltaire — Candide.

14. What ruler in the 17th century best exemplified absolutism?

   a. Louis XIII.   c. William III.
   b. Louis XIV.   d. Philip V.

15. Which of the following was NOT true of René Descartes?

   a. His writings directly attacked the Catholic Church.
   b. He emphasized the importance of arriving at knowledge that is certain.
   c. He believed each particle of matter could be defined in mathematical terms.
   d. He doubted all that it is possible to doubt, including belief in the physical world.

16. What policy or policies did Peter the Great use to westernize Russia?

   a. He built a new capital, St. Petersburg, on the Baltic Sea.
   b. State ownership of enterprises was encouraged.
   c. He cut off the beards of his nobles.
   d. All of the above.

17. Enlightened despots differed from divine-right monarchs in that:

   a. they did not believe in enhancing the image of their nation-state.
   b. they did not pursue aggressive territorial wars.
   c. they were concerned with legal reforms.

    d. they believed in the principle of popular sovereignty.

18. The Scientific Revolution originated with the publication of:

    a. <u>The New Organon</u>.
    b. <u>Mathematical Principles of Natural Philosophy</u>.
    c. <u>On the Revolutions of the Heavenly Spheres</u>.
    d. <u>Dialogue Concerning the Two Chief World Systems</u>.

19. Which of the following was NOT employed by mercantilist governments?

    a. Building up gold and silver bullion to increase the national treasury.
    b. Importing more goods than were exported.
    c. Subsidizing goods destined for export.
    d. Establishing colonies to trade with the mother country.

20. The philosophe Jean-Jacques Rousseau is best known for:

    a. separation of powers with a system of checks and balances of government theory.
    b. compilation of a 26-volume encyclopedia.
    c. his idea that the individual's natural rights were retained in society.
    d. his theory of popular sovereignty.

21. Which of the following was NOT a war of Louis XIV?

    a. Great Northern War.
    b. War of the League of Augsburg.
    c. War of Devolution.
    d. War of the Spanish Succession.

22. The name of the Russian ruling dynasty in the 18th century was:

    a. Hapsburg.   c. Smirnoff.
    b. Hohenzollern.   d. Romanov.

23. The English Bill of Rights was enacted as a result of:

    a. Cromwell's edict to Parliament.
    b. Glorious Revolution.
    c. The Restoration of Charles II to the British throne.
    d. The execution of Henry IV by the "Rump" Parliament.

24. Which one of the following philosophes was well known for his/her satirical attacks on the Catholic Church?

    a. Diderot.   c. Montesquieu.
    b. Rousseau.   d. Voltaire.

25. Catherine the Great was responsible for all of the following EXCEPT:

    a. Freeing the serfs.
    b. Participating in three partitions of Poland.
    c. Cultivating the philosophes Diderot and Voltaire.
    d. Inaugurating legal reforms.

26. Johann Kepler was one of the first 17th-century scientists to:

    a. Discover the mountains and valleys of the moon.
    b. Use mathematics to prove the heliocentric theory.
    c. Build an observatory.
    d. Believe in the geocentric theory.

27. All of the following scientists are connected with the heliocentric theory EXCEPT:

    a. Harvey.   c. Galileo.
    b. Kepler.   d. Newton.

28. James II was unable to get along with Parliament because:

    a. He had very stern Puritanical leanings.
    b. He gambled and liked horse racing.
    c. He appointed Catholics to high government positions.
    d. He showed signs of mental instability.

29. Frederick the Great of Prussia seized:

    a. Hanover.   c. Baden.
    b. Gibraltar.   d. Silesia.

30. According to medieval thought, the center of the universe was the

    a. Sun.   c. Venus.
    b. Earth.   d. Heaven.

Part III: Review and Thought Questions

1. Describe the development of the centralized state that helped to make absolute monarchy possible.

2. Why are the development of banking and the Voyages of Discovery linked?

3. How might the Reformation have contributed to the development of individualism and capitalism?

4. Explain this statement: "The state system is a by-product of the existence of several sovereign states."

5. Explain the tensions between the Holy Roman Emperor and the ruling princes. Who elected the Holy Roman Emperor?

6. Why did the Holy Roman Emperor and his Catholic supporters fail in their efforts to dominate in the Thirty Years' War?

7. Why is the period of 1660-1685 known as The Restoration in British history?

8. How do Enlightened Despots differ from absolutist monarchs?

9. Give some of the more important effects of Louis XIV's wars upon France.

10. What nations successfully devoured Poland in the 18th century? Why were they successful?

11. Why are dynasties important to history? What do the dynasties of the Bourbons, Romanovs, Hapsburgs, and Hohenzollerns have to do with the Age of Absolutism and Enlightened Despots?

12. What strategies did Peter the Great use to westernize Russia?

13. Discuss the strategies used by mercantilist governments with their respective colonial empires. Give examples.

14. Contrast the Europeans' treatment of the Amerindians with their treatment of the African slaves. Were their goals similar or different?

15. What policies did Charles I pursue that turned Parliament against him? How was it possible for Parliament to sentence Charles I to death?

16. Why is the Glorious Revolution also known as "The Bloodless Revolution"? What made it so different from the Civil War of the Cromwellian Commonwealth?

17. What was the big accomplishment of Queen Anne's reign?

18. Explain how John Locke's political theories promoted democracy in England and in the colonies.

19. Discuss how John Locke gave sanction to the right of revolution.

20. How did Jean-Jacques Rousseau suggest that humans might live in society and yet enjoy individual freedom?

21. Why is Sir Isaac Newton important in the history of science?

22. Evaluate Galileo Galilei's contributions both as a scientist and as a writer.

Figure 1.6 **Medallion of Oliver Cromwell** (1599-1658) on Wedgewood Pottery. English 18th Century. Staunch Puritan advocate, Commander-in-Chief of the New Model Army, and Lord Protector of the Commonwealth, Cromwell successfully led the opposition to the Stuart King Charles I during the English Civil War. (Courtesy of the Metropolitan Museum of Art, Gift of James Hazen Hyde, 1948)

Part V: Full-Length Essays

1. List and explain the major historical movements of the Early Modern Period that helped to shape the Modern Age.

2. Describe, in some detail, each of the stages of the Thirty Years' War.

3. Discuss the effects of the Thirty Years' War. Include your evaluation of the Treaty of Westphalia.

4. Explain why René Descartes and Francis Bacon are considered to be the forerunners of scientific thought. Who else made important contributions to the Scientific Revolution?

5. Evaluate the effects of the Scientific Revolution on the Enlightenment.

6. Discuss the ideas and works of the Voltaire, Montesquieu, Rousseau, and Smith.

7. How do the ideas of Rousseau differ from those of Hobbes and Locke?

8. Compare and contrast mercantilist and free enterprise policies.

9. Summarize English history from the reign of James I to the Glorious Revolution.

Figure 2.1 **The Burning of Moscow**. September 14, 1812. The Retreat of Napoleon. After the Battle of Borodino, the Russians drew Napoleon and his troops into Moscow, which they then set ablaze. Napoleon was forced to retreat, but it was a month too late, for the deadly Russian winter had commenced. With the combination of the scorched earth policy and the hit and run tactics of the Russian Cossacks, only a remnant of Napoleon's Grand Army straggled back to their homeland. (Courtesy of The Library of Congress)

Chapter II

THE AGE OF

REVOLUTIONS

Figure 2.2 **The Fall of the Bastille.** Paris. July 14, 1789. The seizure of this infamous prison fortress by the working-class of Paris is commemo-

Figure 2.3 **Marie Antoinette** (1755-1793). Charged with treason and other heinous crimes against the French people, this former queen of France was tried by the Revolutionary Tribunal and decapitated during the Reign of Terror. (Courtesy of The Library of Congress)

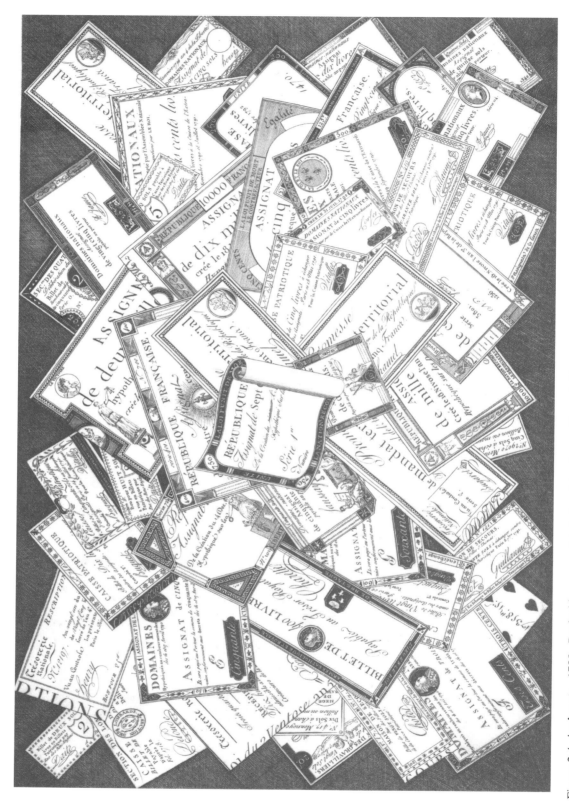

Figure 2.4 **Assignats.** 1789. Backed by expropriated church lands as collateral, this paper money was circulated by the revolutionary National Assembly. It was used to pay government expenses and in a short time became totally worthless. (Courtesy of The Library of Congress)

4

The French Revolution

UNDERSTANDING Revolution

A "revolution" can be several things. It can be the violent overthrow of a government. It can also be a major change in technology, or in the political and/or social order. The events described in this chapter can justly be described as "revolutions".

This first section portrays the French Revolution that began in 1789. In rapid succession, it proceeded through its various phases: the National Assembly, the Legislative Assembly, the National Convention, and the Directory. The early part of the revolution was moderate. A constitutional monarchy was established in 1791. But King Louis XVI was guillotined in 1793, and a Reign of Terror was unleashed by Maximilian Robespierre. The Thermidorean Reaction set in by 1794 after Robespierre's death. Then the republican Directory assumed control in 1795 and Napoleon began his rise to power. By 1799, France was a consulate with Napoleon Bonaparte as its First Consul. The absolute monarchy of Louis XIV and the *Ancien Regime* under his weak successors had been replaced by a new absolutism, that of Napoleon.

Discuss the meaning of the term "revolution." Why can the events in France from 1789-99 be justly described as a revolution?

Was France politically stable after 1799? Explain.

Napoleon spread the upheaval experienced by France to most of Europe in his relentless drive for conquest and glory. When the Napoleonic Wars ended in 1815, the Congress of Vienna sought to restore as much of the old political and social order as possible. Ultimately, it failed. The Revolutions of 1830 and 1848 showed how shaky the foundations of the old order were. France was the great beacon of change for the period. 1830 saw the removal of the Bourbons from the French throne to which they had been restored in 1815. 1848 marked the end of the French monarchy altogether. It was briefly followed by a Second Republic and then a Second Empire under another member of the Bonaparte family.

Discuss non-political revolutions that you have read about or are now witnessing.

The events of 1830 and 1848 were very much influenced by another kind of revolution, the Industrial Revolution. This revolution began in England in the eighteenth century. By the middle of the nineteenth century, it had spread from England and Scotland to France, the Low Countries, and Germany. The steam engine and coal drove the first phase. In its second phase, the Industrial Revolution moved toward oil and the internal combustion engine, diesel engines, and turbines. Steel replaced iron as the metal of choice. Railroads and ocean liners were revolutionizing transportation. By the end of the nineteenth century, the telegraph, telephone, and electricity were transforming human societies.

Origins of the French Revolution

One of the defining moments of modern European history is the French Revolution, which began in 1789. Many factors have been cited as causes of the French Revolution. Yet there is no general consensus among historians. Certainly the IDEAS OF THE ENLIGHTENMENT created a climate of public opinion that favored political reform. The French monarchy had no constitution or social contract, as Rousseau suggested in his writings; nor was there a separation of powers as a check against arbitrary government, as Montesquieu had suggested.

The AMERICAN REVOLUTION had also contributed to setting the stage for the French Revolution. The society established by the former English colonies looked from afar like an ideal embodiment of the noble ideas of the Philosophes. Just as important, France had financed its support of the American cause by taking out high interest loans, which weakened an already shaky government financial structure. French finances are discussed in more detail below.

There were many SOCIAL GRIEVANCES. This was true for the peasantry who paid the bulk of taxes, which the privileged nobles and clergy avoided. The peasants also suffered under the remnants of feudalism, which gave the nobles the right to hunt in the fields of the farmers and to collect a variety of fees from the peasants, who were no longer serfs. The middle class or bourgeoisie also resented the political assertiveness of the nobility. While the nobility had increased their power since the death of Louis XIV (1715), they still sought a more significant role in government. In fact, France suffered from the WEAK LEADERSHIP OF THE KING. Louis XVI, who came to the throne in 1774, had conciliated the nobles by recalling the parlements, or law courts, which his father had abolished in 1770. Louis XVI was well-meaning, but insecure. He frequently changed his mind depending on the vigor of the opposition and who spoke to him last.

How did the Enlightenment help to bring about the French Revolution?

What were some of the other causes of the French revolution?

The Financial Crisis

Describe the efforts of the French government to resolve the financial crisis.

The immediate cause of the French Revolution was a fiscal crisis. The French government, because of its poor credit, had to pay 10% on the loans it took to help the American revolutionaries. The English, in contrast, were able to borrow at 3 or 4% to fight the same revolutionaries. By the 1780's, interest payments made up half of the royal budget and there was a chronic budget deficit.

The problem was not that France was a poor country. Rather, government revenues were insufficient to meet outlays. Most of the taxes were collected from the commoners by the very inefficient method of using private tax farmers or collectors. In seeking a solution to the problem, Louis XVI tried and dismissed several finance ministers. One of these officials, Charles de Calonne, proposed a new tax, which would be levied on all landed property without exception. The trick was to get the nobles to agree to be taxed. The new tax could have been registered as a decree with the thirteen regional parlements, or law courts, the most prestigious of which was the Parlement of Paris. But these parlements had the right of remonstrance; that is, they had the right to object to laws registered with them. Since the parlements favored the nobles, they were hardly likely to accept decrees designed to initiate the taxation of the nobility. To avoid the opposition of the parlements, Calonne convinced the king to call an Assembly of Notables in 1787. The assembled nobles refused to accept the new tax. Rather, they insisted that there should be a check or audit on the monarch's own accounts. The king dismissed Calonne and decided to submit the new tax proposal to the

Why was the Assembly of Notables called? Did it succeed?

Parlement of Paris. The Parlement did not register the proposal, suggesting instead that it would be necessary to call the Estates General to get new taxes approved.

Did the Parlement of Paris help or hinder the king?

The Calling of the Estates General

The Estates General had met occasionally in France since 1302. It was the closest thing the French had to a legislature. Yet it was an advisory rather than a true law-making body. Within the Estates General were three separate Estates. The First Estate represented the clergy, the Second—the nobility, and the Third—the commoners (in practice the middle-class bourgeoisie, rather than the peasants). At the last Estates General, which had met in 1614, the commoners squabbled badly with the other estates.

Louis's initial reaction to the Parlement's ruling was to disband it and send its members into exile. When the heat of public scorn became too great, Louis relented and agreed to convene the Estates General in May 1789. Since the last Estates General had been called over a century earlier, there were many procedural questions to be settled. The actual election procedures were relatively democratic. Members of the nobility and clergy, including ordinary parish priests, could vote directly for representatives to their respective estates. All male commoners over 25 whose names appeared on the tax rolls could vote at least indirectly for representatives to the Third Estate. The Third Estate was to be entitled to 600 representatives—double the number permitted to each of the other estates. A much more controversial matter was how the representatives, once elected, would cast their votes. Traditionally each estate voted separately. The

What groups made up the Estates General?

Why did so much controversy arise in 1789 when the Estates General was called?

Was the Abbé Sieyès a typical member of the clergy? Explain.

Parlement of Paris, and ultimately the king, favored this tradition. But the result would be to favor the nobility in the Second Estate. The clergy in the First Estate were expected to side with the nobility. Thus, the lawyers and officials who had been elected as representatives of the commoners in the Third• Estate were likely to be outvoted two to one. The members of the Third Estate had no intention of permitting this to happen. Their opposition to subordinating the Third Estate to the privileged classes had been strengthened by the publication of a pamphlet, by the Abbé Sieyès, entitled *What Is the Third Estate?* This pamphlet, published in January 1789, argued that the Third Estate, though it had been treated as nothing, was in reality "everything," because it represented the useful, working people of France.

The Beginnings of the Revolution

What was the Tennis Court Oath?

On June 17, 1789, the commoners of the Third Estate, joined by a few clergy, finally declared themselves to represent the whole country as the "National Assembly" of France. Finding themselves locked out of their regular meeting place on June 20th,[1] they moved to an indoor tennis court and took the famous Tennis Court Oath, vowing not to dissolve until France had a constitution. These actions were revolutionary! The commoners had acted without any authorization. The king at first resisted, declaring these actions invalid, and sought to maintain the three distinct estates. But he relented in the face of determined resistance from the commoners, who were joined in the National Assembly by some nobles and even more clergy. On June 27th, the king ordered the rest of the clergy and nobility to join the commoners in the National Assembly.

The events at Versailles occasioned the rise of violence and mob action in various parts of France. A notable incident was the STORMING OF THE BASTILLE, a prison in the heart of Paris. On July 14, 1789, a mob, searching for weapons was fired upon and 98 of its members were killed. After the governor of the prison was persuaded to surrender, he and several of his troops were killed in revenge; their heads were cut off, placed on pikes (long spears), and paraded through the streets of Paris. Bastille Day, commemorating the prison's fall, is an important national holiday in France.

There was also violence in the countryside. Rumors spread that the nobles had hired thugs to attack the peasants and devastate their crops. Groups of peasants armed themselves and attacked the manor houses. Sometimes they burned the chateaus; at other times they simply destroyed the records of the fees and dues they owed their lords. These rural riots became known as the GREAT FEAR. The army wasn't called out, because it was considered to be too unreliable. One response to the threat of mob action was the creation of a National Guard to keep order. In Paris, the Marquis de Lafayette became commander of the guard.

In October, a group of Parisians, composed largely of women, marched from Paris to Versailles. Complaining of the price of bread, they were disturbed by rumors that the king intended some negative reaction to the work of the Assembly. At Versailles, the crowd demanded that the king return with them to Paris. The king, encouraged by Lafayette, yielded to their demands. Escorted by the women and the National Guard, the king marched back to Paris and took up

How did the National Assembly come about?

Explain the Great Fear.

How was Louis XVI persuaded to return to Paris with the women protesters?

Indicate some of the accomplishments of the National Assembly.

residence in the Tuileries Palace in Paris. The National Assembly also moved from Versailles to Paris. The net result was to make the government much more susceptible to the influence of the Parisian mob or whoever could excite that mob.

Achievements of the National Assembly

The National Assembly had a number of achievements. During the night of August 4, 1789, in response to the Great Fear, various clerical and noble members of the Assembly rose and repudiated feudal dues and other special privileges. By the end of the night, feudalism in France was abolished.

On August 26, 1789 the National Assembly issued the Declaration of the Rights of Man and the Citizen. The Declaration lists such rights as freedom of speech, and equality of all before the law, while making the nation itself the sovereign.

Dealing with the National Debt

How did the National Assembly deal with the debt problem?

A chief cause of the Revolution had been the inability of the government to pay its debts. The resistance of the nobility to new taxation had forced the calling of the Estates General. Its successor, the National Assembly (which began to be called the Constituent Assembly because it had the task of writing a constitution for France) dealt with the debt problem by confiscating the land of the Catholic Church. The state would sell the land to pay off its debts. Even before selling the land, the former Church property was used as collateral to issue bonds, known as "assignats," to meet government expenses. These assignats soon began to circulate as money, and successive governments could not resist the temptation to issue more and more assignats to meet expenses. In the final stages of the revolution, the assignats had lost perhaps as much as 99 percent of their value.

The Church lands had been used to pay the expenses of the clergy. The National Assembly now undertook to pay salaries to the clergy. In turn, the Church became a department of the state and the clergy became state employees. This scheme was formalized in the Civil Constitution of the Clergy issued in 1790. Priests and bishops were to be elected by members of district and departmental assemblies, respectively. This meant that non-Catholics could participate in the election of Catholic clergy, a right not to be available to the Pope. The Pope simply would be given the names of those elected. Under these circumstances, the sharp opposition of Pope Pius VI was not surprising. The struggle intensified when, in November 1790, the clergy were obliged to swear an oath of allegiance to this constitution. Only half the clergy would take the oath, and only seven of these oath takers were bishops. Those who took the oath were known as "juring" (swearing) clergy; those who refused to take the oath were known as the "nonjuring" clergy. These events had fateful implications for the Revolution. It became difficult to be a good Catholic and a good revolutionary at the same time. In the more conservative countryside, the balance was definitely tipped in favor of the Catholic Church, and the Revolution lost important support.

What was the Civil Constitution of the Clergy?

Why was the Pope opposed to the Civil Constitution?

Who were the nonjuring clergy?

How did there come to be a Legislative Assembly ?

How democratic was the Constitution of 1791?

Reforming the State

The National Assembly reorganized the French state so that the 26 provinces were replaced by 83 departments of approximately equal size. The departments were given new names, with the intent of weakening the historical ties to the old provinces. Local government officials were to be elected rather than appointed. The most significant political reform was establishing a written constitution for France, which severely limited the power of the king. Under the Constitution of 1791, the king shared power with a newly created Legislative Assembly. Not only was the king to be a constitutional monarch, with limited power (in contrast to the divine-right monarch exemplified by Louis XIV), but he was to be a rather weak monarch at that. He was granted a mere three-year suspensive veto over acts of the Legislative Assembly. These restrictions on the king were in part due to the influence of the writings of the philosophes. But the extremely negative attitude of the king towards the revolution also helped to bring about the restrictions. The king preferred the nonjuring clergy for his sacraments. In June 1791 he actually attempted to flee the country, leaving behind a written note rejecting the Revolution. He was captured near the border, brought back to Paris, and forced to embrace his role as constitutional monarch.

Louis the XVI was not the only person facing restrictions under the new constitution. While all citizens had civil rights, the constitution distinguished between "active" and "passive" citizens. Only active citizens could vote. To qualify as an active citizen, one had to be an adult male, at least twenty-six years old, and had to pay direct taxes equivalent to at least three days of local labor. These active citizens did not vote directly for representatives to the Legislative Assembly. Instead they voted for "electors" with even higher property-holding qualifications. These electors, in turn, chose the deputies to the Legislative Assembly. This was not popular democracy as currently understood!

The Legislative Assembly

The Legislative Assembly, the new one-house legislature created by the Constitution of 1791, met for the first time on October 1, 1791. There were high hopes for calm and the restoration of stability. However, the new government had several things going against it. The king's hostility was already evident in his attempt to flee the country. The former National Assembly, seeking to avoid any appearance of a conflict of interest, had voted that none of its members could serve in the new assembly. This meant that the new legislature was deprived of seasoned leadership.

The leadership of the Legislative Assembly was in the hands of a relatively moderate faction known as the Girondins, so called because of the region in France where many of their members had originated. Their major opponents were known as the Jacobins, so called because they met at the former Jacobin monastery in Paris. The Jacobins were the more radical party that favored replacing the monarchy with a republic. They also had an advantage because they were more tightly organized than the Girondins.

What occasioned the downfall of the Legislative Assembly was military loss. On

What factors worked against the success of the new Legislative Assembly?

Describe the chief factions within the Legislative Assembly.

What was the importance of the Brunswick Manifesto?

April 20, 1792, the French, led by the Girondins, declared war on Austria. The Prussians soon joined the Austrian side. The Girondins hoped to strengthen their influence by uniting the country in war. The Austrian royal family was concerned with the fate of the French queen, Marie Antoinette, who was the daughter of Maria Theresa of Austria and the aunt of Austria's then ruling Emperor Francis II. European rulers were generally concerned about events in France. They did not want their subjects to follow the revolutionary example of the French people. Émigré French nobles had done their utmost to stir up fear of the revolution abroad.

Initially, the war went against the ill-prepared French forces. These losses were followed by a statement from the Prussian general, the Duke of Brunswick, who commanded the anti-French forces. The Brunswick Manifesto of July 25th declared that a severe punishment would be visited upon Paris, if any harm was done to the French king or queen. It did not take great imagination for the Parisians to figure out on which side the king and queen were really on. Egged on by the Jacobins, a mob stormed the Tuileries palace where the king was staying.

Why was the National Convention created?

While the king took refuge with the Legislative Assembly, his Swiss guards, and even household servants were massacred. The municipal government of Paris was replaced by a Paris Commune under the domination of the Jacobins, and the king and his family were turned over to the Commune to be imprisoned. A National Convention was elected by universal manhood suffrage (all adult male citizens could vote). This National Convention was to have two primary tasks. One task was to decide the fate of the king. The other was to draw up a new constitution replacing the government of the failed Legislative Assembly.

The National Convention

What were some of the chief factions within the National Convention?

The National Convention first met on September 20, 1792, and was to last until October 26, 1795. At the start of the Convention, the Girondist delegates occupied the political right. The middle formed the Plain and the left made up the Mountain, so called because of their fondness for occupying the uppermost seats in the meeting hall. Most of the members of the Mountain came from the ranks of the Jacobins. The Mountain men, or *Montagnards* in French, were supported outside the Convention by the working class people known as "sans-culottes" because they wore long workers' trousers rather than the fancier *culottes,* or knee breeches, preferred by the middle and aristocratic classes.

What was the fate of Louis XVI?

In December 1792, Louis XVI was put on trial before the National Convention. There was enough evidence of his collaboration with France's enemies for him to be unanimously found guilty on January 15, 1793. However, the decision to execute him immediately was made by a bare majority of one. He was guillotined on January 21, 1793.

France had become a republic, but one without a constitution. While the debate over the constitution was in process, a Committee of Public Safety (eventually including 12 members) was formed and charged with conducting the government. A Committee of General Security was also created to oversee the political police who were charged with rooting out internal enemies.

The Military Situation

The new government had enough enemies, both internal and external. A region

What were the causes of the revolt in the Vendée?

Which foreign nations opposed France?

Why did the *levée en masse* succeed?

in western France along the coast, known as the Vendée, rose in counter-revolution. The peasants of the region had become disaffected. They were egged on by the clergy who had not supported the Civil Constitution and for whom the revolutionaries were "heretics." When the draft was introduced to raise forces to fight on the eastern frontiers, the Vendée broke out in a royalist rebellion in March 1793. The revolt spread to include all of Anjou, Britttany, and Poitou, as well as such major cities as Marseilles and Toulon. External enemies included not only Austria and Prussia, but in February 1793 a First Coalition had been formed, adding Great Britain, Holland, Spain, Sardinia, and Naples to the list of opponents of France.

Militarily, the National Convention enjoyed some successes. A *levée en masse* or draft of the entire adult male population was made in August 1793. Fourteen armies were organized and put into the field. What these raw troops lacked in training, they made up in patriotic fervor. Traditional European armies were made up largely of professional soldiers motivated more by the pay they received than by the idea of serving their country. Such forces were quite limited against the new French troops. By the spring of 1794, French armies had gained control of the Austrian Netherlands (modern Belgium) and the entire left bank of the Rhine. The Vendée had at least been contained.

The Reign of Terror

There was a struggle within the Convention between the Girondins and the Jacobins. The Jacobins, with the aid of the Paris Commune, arranged the arrest of 31 Girondist deputies on June 2, 1793. This opened the way for domination of the Convention by the Jacobin radicals, who comprised the Mountain. The period of radical rule, which lasted about a year, has come to be known as the Reign of Terror because of the bloody way in which the regime dealt with its enemies. The Montagnard leadership included Maximilien Robespierre, Georges Danton, Antoine St. Just, Georges Couthon, and Lazare Carnot. Of these, only Carnot survived the Revolution. Robespierre became the leading figure in the Terror. Thoroughly committed to democracy, he believed in the intelligence and good sense of the common people. He was personally untainted by corruption and dedicated to the establishment of a republic of virtue modeled on Rousseau's *Social Contract*.

Robespierre was also thoroughly ruthless, willing to issue orders and use special revolutionary tribunals to exterminate all those, friend or foe, who might stand in his way. He eliminated the journalist Jacques Hébert, who proposed a cult of reason in opposition to Robespierre's less extreme deistic cult of the Supreme Being. He also had Danton and other fellow Jacobins, who were perceived to be too moderate, guillotined. Marie Antoinette, charged correctly with having secretly aided Austria's invasion of France, was also guillotined. Exactly how many were killed in the Terror is not clear. But an estimate of thirty to forty thousand is reasonable. This is especially true if one considers the killing that took place outside Paris in the Vendée and other regions where there was opposition to the regime. The Terror did not end until fellow members of the Convention, fearful that they were next on Robespierre's list, had him seized on July 27, 1794, and executed along with Couthon and St. Just the next day.

What was the Reign of Terror?

Who were the leaders of the Reign of Terror?

Describe the character and activity of Robespierre.

Describe the political and social changes that accompanied the Thermidorean Reaction.

The Thermidorean Reaction

Since July 27th was the 9th of Thermidor in the Revolutionary calendar, the events that followed are often called the Thermidorean Reaction. The remaining Jacobin leaders were sent into exile, and the Convention fell under the control of the moderates. Fancy dress and the pleasures of the theater and the ballroom returned to style. The Constitution of 1793, which was never implemented, had quite democratically provided for a republic with universal male suffrage. The Constitution of 1795, which replaced it, still maintained a republic, but it was less democratic. While it gave most adult males the right to vote, they voted only for "electors." The electors, who had to have a yearly income equaling at least 100 days of labor, actually voted for those who were to hold office. This Constitution, with its system of indirect election, clearly favored the propertied classes over the working-class sans-culottes. To prevent royalist sympathizers from winning the coming election, a provision was added that initially two-thirds of the seats in the two-house legislature were to be reserved for members of the National Convention. This last provision provoked a serious disturbance in Paris, which was put down with a "whiff of grape-shot"[2] (cannon fire) by a young general by the name of Napoleon Bonaparte.

What occasioned Napoleon's "whiff of grapeshot"?

The Directory

The government under the Constitution of 1795 was known as the Directory after the name of the executive branch. This was a plural executive composed of five Directors. It shared power with a legislature consisting of two houses. The Council of Ancients, a 250-member body, derived its name from the fact that the delegates had to be elders over forty. The second house, the Council of Five Hundred, had the power to actually initiate legislation. The Directory faced a number of problems. There was the continued fighting with foreign powers. Russia had joined Great Britain and other powers to form a Second Coalition against the French in 1798. Inflation was also a difficult problem. In 1796, the *assignats* were replaced by a new form of paper currency known as *mandats*. These also quickly depreciated, to about one tenth of their value, and the following year a metallic currency was adopted. Financial difficulties continued, however, when two-thirds of the national debt was effectively repudiated by the Directory.

The biggest obstacle to the success of the Directory was the lack of public respect engendered by the government's failure to adhere to the provisions of the Constitution. The elections to the legislative council in 1797 resulted in a large block of royalist deputies. The members who had been part of the old National Convention, and had voted to kill Louis XVI, feared that they would be endangered as regicides (king killers) in any restored monarchy. Rumors circulated of a rightist *coup d'état*. Rather than take the risk, three of the Directors called in troops. They nullified the election of the rightist deputies, and ousted the two other Directors for royalist sympathies. While the Directors justified their actions in the name of saving the Revolution, the reality was that they had acted unconstitutionally and were becoming ever more dependent on the army. Other purges, both of unwelcome rightists and

Describe the problems besetting the Directory.

What was the Directory's most important failure?

How did the Directory end?

Who participated in the *coup d'état* of Brumaire?

leftists, followed. The end of the Directory came when Napoleon Bonaparte entered into a conspiracy with two of the Directors, Abbé Sieyès and Pierre Roger Ducos. On November 9, 1799, they used military force to break up the Directory and, on the following day, they drove uncooperative legislators out of the Council of Five Hundred. The excuse was an alleged Jacobin plot; the reality was the *coup d'état* of Brumaire (using the Revolutionary calendar) that made France a military dictatorship called the Consulate. Napoleon Bonaparte served as First Consul.

With the ascent of Napoleon to power, we come to the end of the French Revolution. Was the Revolution a good or a bad thing? Historians and political thinkers do not agree on the answer to this question. Certainly the revolution destroyed the privileges of the aristocracy of the Old Regime. It did so at the cost of great turmoil and bloodshed. It also gave rise to the military dictatorship of Napoleon Bonaparte, with the consequent spread of turmoil and death throughout Europe. At the same time, the revolution spread nationalism and the ideals of liberty, equality, and fraternity. It was a step towards more democratic societies in Europe.

5

Napoleon and the Congress of Vienna

Napoleon Bonaparte

What was the background of the Bonaparte family?

Napoleon Bonaparte was born on August 15, 1769 in Corsica, off the west coast of Italy. Corsica had become a French possession only the year before. The Bonaparte (or Buonaparte to use the original spelling) family was of Italian origin. His father, Charles, was from the petty nobility, but had little wealth. He did obtain a scholarship for his son to attend French military school. When his schooling was completed, Napoleon was commissioned a second lieutenant in the artillery in 1785.

Describe Napoleon's early career.

Under the Old Regime Napoleon's chances for advancement would have been rather limited, but the Revolution opened up new opportunities. In 1793, he gained a reputation as a competent artillery officer during the siege of Toulon, whose royalist leaders were collaborating with the British. He became identified with the Jacobins and was briefly imprisoned after the overthrow of Robespierre. After successfully squashing the Paris insurrection against the Convention (October 1795), he was rewarded by the Directory with the post of commander of the Army of the Interior. In March 1796, he took command of the army in Italy, where he conducted a brilliant campaign. A result was

What were the results of Napoleon's Italian campaign?

Contrast the results of the Egyptian campaign with the Italian campaign. What did Napoleon gain from his campaign in Egypt?

the Treaty of Campo Formio (October 17, 1797) between France and Austria, which Napoleon personally negotiated. By this treaty, Austria gave up the Austrian Netherlands (Belgium) and the Ionian Islands (in the Adriatic Sea) to France. Austria also recognized a French-dominated Cisalpine Republic in northern Italy.

The next project the Directory had in mind for Napoleon was the invasion of England. Realizing that such an invasion was not likely to succeed, given the overwhelming superiority of British naval forces, Napoleon persuaded the Directors to instead threaten England's hold on India by seizing Egypt. Successfully evading the British fleet, he crossed the Mediterranean to Africa and captured Alexandria and Cairo. However, the British commander, Lord Nelson, found the French fleet at Abukir Bay and smashed it. The whole project generated much favorable publicity for Napoleon, even though there was no practical way of getting his army back to France. While the French public was still enthralled by his feats of glory, Napoleon deserted his army in Egypt, returned to France, and participated in the *coup d'état* of Brumaire (November 9, 1799), which resulted in the establishment of the Consulate.

From Consulate to Empire

Napoleon quickly took control of the reins of government. In December 1799, the Constitution of the Year VII was put to a plebiscite (popular vote on a policy issue) and won by an overwhelming majority (3,011,107 yeses compared to only 1,567 noes). Napoleon was elected First Consul for a term of ten years and given the power to appoint two other Consuls to assist him. Popular participation was very indirect. The people elected notables from whom, after other filtering elections, members of the legislative bodies were chosen.

Napoleon went to work on several important reforms. One of his projects was to reach a settlement with the Pope and thereby restore the support of devout Catholics for the Revolution and especially for Napoleon. The result of his efforts was the Concordat of 1801 between Napoleon and the recently elected Pope Pius VII. The Pope gave up claims to the Church lands seized during the Revolution, and in turn the bishops and priests were to receive salaries from the state. The pope regained control of the clergy. He received the right to discipline clergy and depose bishops. Napoleon could nominate bishops and archbishops, but these had to be confirmed by the Pope. Catholicism was not restored as the state religion; rather, it was merely recognized as the religion of the majority of the French. Freedom of religion was maintained. Indeed, the Protestant clergy were also to receive state salaries.

Bonaparte also strengthened the state by establishing the Bank of France in 1800 to increase the availability of credit. He balanced the budget, and centralized the collection of taxes to insure a consistent cash flow. He also gave the central government in Paris greater influence on the educational system. Thus gaining for himself greater control over youthful minds.

Napoleon considered his revision of the legal system to be one of his most important reforms. The Code Napoleon was actually a series of codes promulgated at different times and heavily influenced by the Roman law code of Justinian. The best known of Napoleon's codes is the Civil Code

Explain the terms of the Concordat of 1801.

What were some of Napoleon's economic reforms?

What was the Code Napoleon?

What were some of the positive aspects of the Code Napoleon?

What were the negative aspects of this Code?

How did Napoleon manipulate public opinion?

of 1804. The code had much to recommend it, and it has been copied in the laws of many countries. The code provided a uniform system of law for the entire country. It recognized the equality of all citizens before the law, retained the abolition of feudal obligations and privileged classes, and guaranteed freedom of religion. But it also favored husbands in the family and employers in the workshop. Women were to obey their husbands and the wife's property was placed at the disposal of the husband, who had greater freedom, as head of the family, in deciding the disposition of his own estate. Children could be imprisoned for up to six months on the request of their father. The word of an employer was more important than that of a worker in a court of law. The workers did not have the right to form labor unions. Other codes also reflected an increased authoritarianism. For example, after the Revolution, criminal proceedings were changed to recognize the presumption of innocence. Napoleon's codes restored the presumption of the defendant's guilt until proven otherwise.

Napoleon's regime was in many respects the first modern police state. Newspapers suppressed information considered detrimental to the regime. The minister of police, Joseph Fouché, was notorious for his excessive brutality during the Terror. In 1802, Napoleon arranged another plebiscite to determine if he should be made consul for life. The usual overwhelming majority was obtained in favor of the proposal.

The Consulate was not good enough for Napoleon, and in 1804, he found the opportunity to make himself Emperor. In February a plot against Napoleon's life was discovered. The conspiracy was quickly squashed, and the accomplices were killed or fled. The Duke of Enghien, a Bourbon prince from the house of Condé, who was an alleged conspirator, was seized in the territory of Baden and brought to France, where he was speedily tried and executed without benefit of judicial niceties. From Bonaparte's viewpoint any adverse publicity was more than offset by the gains. His shedding of Bourbon blood allayed the suspicions of regicide Republicans. More importantly, he used the pretext of the assassination attempt to justify gaining a hereditary title for himself. He maintained that if, when he died, there was an assured succession, there would be less incentive for attempts on his life. He decided to take the title of Emperor because of its grandeur and because the title of king was too closely associated with the deposed Bourbons. He crowned himself Emperor on December 2, 1804 in a ceremony in Notre Dame Cathedral in Paris.

Later the childless Napoleon entered into a fittingly imperial marriage. At the time of his coronation, Napoleon had been married to Josephine, a commoner, who then became Empress. Anxious for an heir, he divorced Josephine and, in April 1810, he married a Hapsburg princess, Marie Louise, the daughter of the Austrian Emperor. The previous July, Austria had suffered a devastating defeat at the hands of Napoleon in the Battle of Wagram. Giving the hand of the eighteen-year-old princess in matrimony to the victor helped to ensure at least a temporary respite!

Military Success

The royal wedding was an affirmation of the successes of Napoleon. He was an outstanding general who was, of course, skilled in the use of artillery. He also carefully planned his campaigns, moving quickly

What did Napoleon gain by killing Condé?

Why did he become Emperor?

Why did the Austrians consent to the marriage of the Hapsburg princess Marie Louise to Napoleon?

Describe Napoleon's military tactics.

What were some of Napoleon's military successes?

to his preferred position using forced marches. He habitually lived off the land, avoiding slow-moving supply trains, which would have held him back. A favorite tactic was to concentrate his forces at one point and overwhelm the enemy's forces, before there was time for the enemy to bring sufficient troops together to match the numbers Napoleon had amassed.

Bonaparte had consistently defeated the great continental European powers. The 1809 Battle of Wagram had represented at least the fifth major defeat for the Austrians against French forces since 1797. By the time of the October 1809 Treaty of Schönbrünn, Austria had lost 32,000 square miles and over 3 million people. It lost control of Illyria and Galicia.

Napoleon enjoyed similar successes in dealing with the Prussians and Russians. The Russians suffered major defeats at Austerlitz in December 1805 and at Friedland in June 1807. The Prussians were beaten at Jena and Auerstadt in October 1806. Austerlitz, one of Napoleon's greatest military victories, is still studied for its brilliance at military academies.

Remaking the Map of Europe

In June of 1807 Czar Alexander I of Russia and Napoleon met on a raft in the Nieman River to make peace. The resulting Treaties of Tilsit (1807) divided Europe into French and Russian spheres of influence and gave Napoleon a potential Russian ally against England. Prussia suffered major losses. It was forced to accept the creation of a Duchy of Warsaw out of the territories Prussia had gained from the partitions of Poland, and then the formation of a Kingdom of Westphalia, which included most of Prussia's territory west of the Elbe River. These two new states were clearly French dependencies.

The result of these successes was the formation of what Napoleon himself termed the "Grand Empire." In 1812, the Grand Empire included first of all a very expanded France. Holland and the Austrian Netherlands had become part of the French Empire, as well as Nice, Savoy, Genoa, and the Papal States. France even included the Illyrian Province along the Adriatic Sea, a territory that shared borders with the Austrian and Ottoman Empires. Included in the Grand Empire were a second group of states that were not formally a part of France, but were clearly under Napoleon's control. These included the two newly created states, the Duchy of Warsaw and the Kingdom of Westphalia, as well as Spain, a newly formed Kingdom of Italy, a Kingdom of Naples, Switzerland, and the western German states comprising the Confederation of the Rhine. The Confederation of the Rhine was created by Napoleon in 1806 as a replacement for the Holy Roman Empire, in which Austria had been the leading state. The new Confederation had fewer principalities than the old Holy Roman Empire, was not associated with Austria, and was under the protection of Napoleon. All the satellite states of the Grand Empire had to support French policy and supply troops to Napoleon. A third grouping of states were those allied with France. These included Austria, Prussia, and the Kingdom of Denmark and Norway. This third group retained their own rulers. The territories within the French Empire itself were administered using the structure of departments that grew out of the Revolution. The satellite states under Napoleon's control were assigned rulers. Napoleon cheerfully

How did Napoleon remake the map of Europe?

List the various states which were a part of the Grand Empire. Which states were allied with Napoleon's Empire?

Why was the Battle of Trafalgar so important?

appointed brothers, sisters, and close relatives, whom he could depend on to follow his orders.

What Napoleon Could Not Solve

Trafalgar

For all his achievements, there were several problems which Napoleon could not solve and that ultimately were fatal to his empire. Because of France's continued occupation of Belgium and Napoleon's commercial ambitions, England remained at war with France, except for a brief period after the 1802 Treaty of Amiens. Napoleon never had sufficient naval forces to overcome the English. Without naval superiority, he lacked the ability to invade England successfully and make use of his mighty armies. The decisive naval engagement took place at Trafalgar, off the southwest coast of Spain, on October 21, 1805. There Lord Horatio Nelson, the British commander, with 27 ships defeated a combined French and Spanish fleet of 33 ships. The battle cost Nelson his life, but not a single British ship was lost. The enemy lost 17 ships. The British were to dominate the seas for the rest of the century!

What was the Continental System?

The Continental System

After Trafalgar, Napoleon needed some way of beating the British. His solution was an economic blockade. In 1806, Napoleon introduced what became known as the Continental System. It forbade the importation of British goods in all countries of

Europe under his control, or allied with him. He prohibited not only direct British trade, but also trade by neutrals carrying British products. He hoped to ruin English markets and eventually cause mass unemployment, forcing the English to sue for peace. While the British suffered some dislocation, and there were in fact riots, they were able to compensate by finding new markets in South America and in other parts of the world. Besides, from the beginning, there was widespread smuggling, causing Napoleon to take ever more desperate measures and increasing discontent with French rule. As the interests of the merchants in the dependent states were subordinated to French mercantile interests through unfavorable tariffs, resistance to the Continental System stiffened on the European Continent.

How much were the British harmed by the Continental System?

The Peninsular War

Portugal, a traditional ally of the English, had refused to join the Continental System. In 1807, Napoleon persuaded Charles IV, the Bourbon ruler of Spain, which had become a French satellite, to permit French troops to cross through Spain in order to conquer Portugal. In May 1808, once his soldiers were in Spain, Napoleon took advantage of the situation to force the abdication of Charles IV and of his son, Ferdinand VII. Bonaparte then had his brother, Joseph, installed on the Spanish throne. The Spanish reacted against the occupying French army by resorting to guerrilla warfare. They were aided by the British who sent Sir Arthur Wellesley (1769-1852), later the Duke of Wellington, to Portugal. Wellesley began a push against the French from the west. The warfare continued until, in 1813, French

What caused the Peninsular War?

Why did Napoleon invade Russia?

What military tactics did the Russians use?

troops were pushed out of the whole of the Iberian Peninsula (Portugal and Spain). Upwards of 300,000 to 400,000 French troops were kept penned down on the peninsula for much of this war, which was a grave drain on Napoleon's resources and certainly contributed to his ultimate defeat.

The Invasion of Russia

The 1807 Treaty of Tilsit seemed to make Russia and France into allied masters of Europe. Indeed, Russia did subsequently declare war on England and join the Continental System. But the Czar's pursuit of the war against Britain was not very forceful. Russia was more interested in fighting Turkey, and the French and Russian emperors were in reality rivals who distrusted one another. In December 1810, Russia withdrew from the Continental System and began to prepare for war with France—even going so far as to enter into an anti-French alliance with England.

The first blow was actually struck by Napoleon. In June 1812, he crossed into Russia with a force that eventually numbered over 600,000 men. Only about a third of these were French, the rest were supplied by Napoleon's allies. The Russians chose to retreat and burn the crops that would have supported Napoleon's army. Bonaparte, who kept his supply trains light, had difficulty feeding his army by living off the land. Also, Napoleon's usual tactics failed him. He could not mass his forces for a decisive blow against an enemy who did not want to stand and fight. The Russians engaged in an indecisive battle at Borodino, not far from Moscow. While the Russians lost perhaps 50,000 troops, and the French 30,000, the Russian forces were able to withdraw in good order. The Russians let Napoleon enter Moscow unopposed on September 14, 1812. Then, within hours, Moscow was ablaze. The Russians had set the mostly wooden structures of their capital on fire to deny Napoleon their use. Nor would Czar Alexander agree to peace terms. Finally, on October 19th, with the severe Russian winter approaching and without adequate food supplies, a frustrated Napoleon was forced to order his troops to retreat. As the soldiers of the invading force withdrew, they were frozen, starved, and cut down by the Russian troops menacing their perimeter. When what had been Napoleon's Grand Army finally got out of Russia at the end of December, there were less than 100,000 badly disorganized troops left.

Defeat and Exile

Napoleon hurried back to Paris ahead of his troops and promptly raised a new army of about 250,000 men. But of course, these were raw recruits—not the seasoned veterans he had left behind in Russia. Another coalition was formed to oppose him. This Sixth Coalition included England, Prussia, Russia, Sweden, and later Austria. The decisive battle, the Battle of the Nations, was fought at Leipzig on October 16-19, 1813. Outnumbered two to one, Napoleon was defeated and forced back into France. The following March 1814, the allies took Paris and Napoleon finally abdicated in April. He was exiled to the island of Elba, off the coast of Italy, supposedly to be the island's sovereign. In the meantime, the Bourbons were restored to the throne in France in the person

What was the result of the Russian campaign?

What led to Napoleon's defeat at Leipzig? Who opposed him?

What was the Hundred Days?

Who participated in the Battle of Waterloo?

Was Napoleon a great man? Explain.

of Louis XVIII, a younger brother of the guillotined Louis XVI. An ever-restless Napoleon took advantage of dissatisfaction with the restored Bourbons to escape from Elba and land at Cannes in Southern France on March 1, 1815. The troops sent to arrest him went over to his side. The Bourbon monarch was forced to flee France as Napoleon entered Paris on March 20th. The short imperial restoration that followed is known as the Hundred Days. On June 18, 1815, Napoleon attacked the regrouped allied forces at Waterloo, in what is now Belgium. The French forces (72,000) were defeated by the numerically superior forces of Britain's Duke of Wellington (68,000) and Prussia's General Blucher (90,000). Napoleon once again abdicated and surrendered to the British. Louis XVIII was restored to Paris.

This time, Napoleon was exiled to the rocky island of St. Helena, off the Atlantic coast of South America, under secure British guard. There he wrote his romanticized memoirs, helping to create the Napoleonic legend. He died there, most likely of stomach cancer, on May 5, 1821.

Objectively, Napoleon Bonaparte was self-interested and ruthless. His ambition cost hundreds of thousands of lives. Yet his exploits captured the imagination of succeeding generations. He certainly had a profound impact on France; to this day, his laws form the basis of its legal system. The legend of Napoleon aided a nephew in gaining control of France in the second half of the nineteenth century. Napoleon also helped to spread the ideals of the French Revolution beyond France to the rest of Europe.

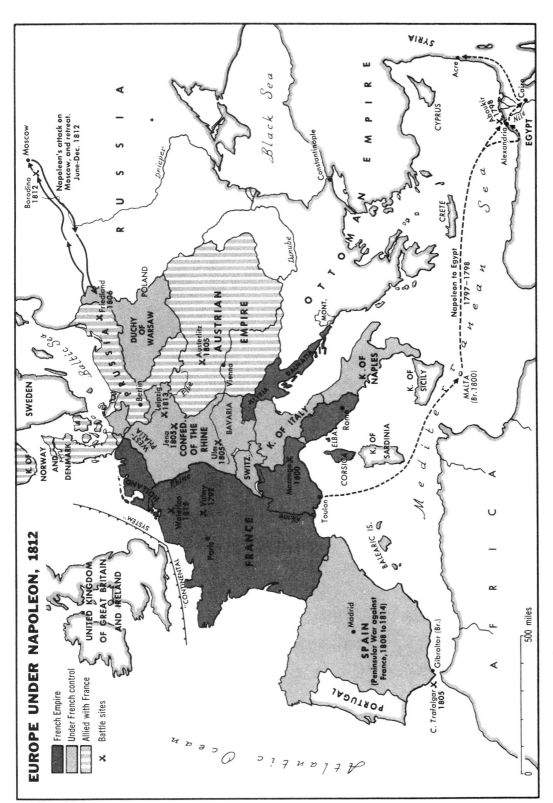

From *History of Western Civilization: A Handbook*, 6th edition by William H. McNeill. Copyright 1986 by University of Chicago Press. Reprinted by permission.

DONNÉ
PAR S. M. L'EMPEREUR ET ROI
AU PRINCE
ARCHI-CHANCELIER DE L'EMPIRE

Figure 2.5 **Napoleon I on a Gobelins Tapestry after a painting by Francois Gerard**. The great national hero of France is shown in his ermine robes as an imposing ruler. (Courtesy of The Metropolitan Museum of Art, Purchase 1943, Joseph Pulitzer Bequest

The Congress of Vienna

Purpose

The peace conference, which followed the Napoleonic Wars, was known as the Congress of Vienna. It took place in Vienna, the capital of the Austrian Empire, from September 1814 to June 1815. The statesmen gathered there faced the problem of how to restructure Europe after the major upheavals caused by the French conquests. Another problem was how to protect against possible future French aggression. The victors at Versailles in 1919, after the conclusion of World War I, faced similar problems with regard to Germany. Most historians think the statesmen at Vienna did pretty well compared to those at Versailles. After Napoleon I's second exile in 1815, there was no general European war until 1914. After Germany's Kaiser William II abdicated in November 1918, another world war started as soon as September 1939!

Participants

While every European state except Turkey came to Vienna, there were only a few important decision makers. Prince Klemens von Metternich (1773-1859), the Austrian foreign minister, was a realist diplomat with a consuming ego. He was concerned with preserving and furthering the interests of the multinational Austrian Empire. To achieve his objectives, Metternich had to resist appeasing the nationalistic impulses

Why did the delegates meet at the Congress of Vienna?

Who led the delegations from Austria, Britain, Russia, Prussia, and France?

Discuss the character and aims of Metternich.

unleashed by the French Revolution. Given the ethnic diversity of the Austrian Empire, accepting the legitimacy of national self-determination would doom the very existence of the Empire. Metternich was not only concerned to check future French aggression, but also to limit the influence of Russia in Central Europe.

Russia was represented by the Czar himself, Alexander I, who ruled from 1801 to 1825. His interest in religious mysticism made him appear to be flaky to some of the less devout attendees. Prussia was represented by its state chancellor, Karl von Hardenberg (1750-1822), who followed his king's policy of deference to Russia in most matters. England's foreign secretary at the Congress was Robert Stewart, Viscount Castlereagh (1769-1822). He had coordinated the final coalition against Napoleon and, given England's lack of ambition on the European continent, could play a mediating role in the clash of great power interests.

Why would some describe Talleyrand as a "survivor"?

France was fortunate in having Charles Maurice de Talleyrand (1754-1838) as its foreign minister. Talleyrand was the archetype of the survivor. He had been a bishop under the Old Regime and a member of the National Assembly. He had served as foreign minister under the Directory, under Napoleon, and under the restored Bourbon king, Louis XVIII. Later he even managed to serve the Orleanist monarch, Louis Philippe, who replaced the Bourbons. He was a cunning, effective opportunist. One example of his opportunism occurred at Vienna. The Russian Czar Alexander wanted to create a Kingdom of Poland, with the Czar as king. This Poland would include territories that the Russians, Austrians, and Prussians had gained in the eighteenth-century partitions of Poland. Prussia was willing to go along with Russia, as long as Prussia in turn received the entire Kingdom of Saxony. Metternich was sternly opposed to the aggrandizement of Russia and Prussia, who were Austria's rivals. Castlereagh backed Metternich. For a time it seemed as if there was a standoff among the four major-power victors. But in January 1815, Talleyrand had France enter into a secret alliance with Austria and England. This alliance provided that each of these nations would support the other, if they were attacked by Russia or Prussia. When news of the treaty leaked out, the Russians and Prussians quickly backed down. Russia got a Poland of considerably reduced size (about the extent of Napoleon's Grand Duchy of Warsaw), and Prussia had to settle for two-fifths of Saxony. From Talleyrand's point of view, what was important was that France had played a major role in determining the outcome. From that point on, France was a regular participant in big power negotiations.

How was the dispute over Poland resolved?

Principles

The major players at the Congress were guided by several principles: balance of power, compensation, and legitimacy.

In international affairs, a BALANCE OF POWER exists when no major power can dominate the other powers in the system. This is attained by making sure that there are enough large powers around to band together to counterbalance the force of any ambitious aggressor. At the Congress, the emphasis was on preventing France from once again dominating Europe. On France's northern border, a new Kingdom of the Netherlands was created. It consisted of Holland together with the former Austrian Netherlands, under a ruler from the house of Orange. In the east, Prussia was given territories along the left

What was done to strengthen the balance of power as a check to French ambitions?

What steps did the Congress take to restore "legitimate" rulers?

What territories did Austria, Russia, Prussia, and England receive at Vienna?

bank of the Rhine to check traditional French ambitions. Along France's southeastern border, the Kingdom of Sardinia-Piedmont was enlarged.

LEGITIMACY meant restoring the ruling families from pre-Revolutionary days. The Bourbons were restored to Spain, the Two Sicilies, and France. France was treated very leniently. Before Napoleon's escape from Elba, it was not even fined. After Napoleon's Hundred Days, the French received, by terms of the second Treaty of Paris, some punishment for their cooperation in Napoleon's attempt at restoring his empire. France had to pay a fine of 700 million francs, accept minor losses of territory, and live with a 150,000 troop army of occupation until 1818. France was treated generously to insure the acceptance of the Bourbons by its people. Many other rulers were also restored. The pope regained the Papal States.

In the former Holy Roman Empire legitimacy was not applied. Instead of reestablishing hundreds of small states, the Napoleonic precedent was followed. A German Confederation of 39 states under the leadership of Austria was established.

COMPENSATION meant that when one of the major victors gave up territory, it received other territory in return. Some states also compensated themselves with territory for the resources they lost in the years of fighting the French. Austria gave up the Austrian Netherlands to the new Kingdom of the Netherlands, but it more than compensated itself by acquisitions in the south. Austria received Venetia, as well as Lombardy, and Hapsburg princes were given the duchies of Parma, Modena, and Tuscany. Austria also gained the Illyrian provinces on the other side of the Adriatic Sea. Russia not only got most of Poland, but kept Finland and Bessarabia as well. Prussia's gains in the

Rhineland and Saxony have already been mentioned. Sweden got Norway as compensation for the loss of Finland. England had little interest in territory on the continent of Europe, though it did receive Helgoland in the North Sea. Other new English possessions included the Cape of Good Hope in southern Africa, Ceylon, Malta, and the Ionian Islands.

What was the Quadruple Alliance?

The Congress System

Preserving the Peace

A Quadruple Alliance had been formed even before Napoleon's first exile. After the Hundred Days there was a renewal of the Quadruple Alliance, to insure France's adherence to the terms of the second Treaty of Paris. England, Austria, Prussia, and Russia were the signatories. They each agreed to provide sixty thousand troops to use against treaty violators and to hold future meetings to discuss their common interests.

In addition to the Quadruple Alliance, there was a broader and fuzzier HOLY ALLIANCE, drawn up at the instigation of Czar Alexander I. It was initially signed by the rulers of Austria, Prussia, and Russia. The sovereigns agreed to adhere to the principles of the Christian religion in dealing with each other and with their subjects. The rest of the rulers of Europe were invited to join. All but three agreed to do so, lest they needlessly give offense to the Czar. The three decliners were: the British regent, who dreamed up a constitutional impediment to his signing; the Turkish sultan, who was not

How did Europe react to the Czar Alexander's proposal for a Holy Alliance?

What was the Congress System?

What was England's objection to the implementation of the Congress System?

a Christian; and the Pope, who thought he was already in possession of Christian truth.

A Period of Reaction

The political trends following the end of the Napoleonic Wars in 1815 were conservative and, indeed, reactionary. The stress was on attaining stability in international affairs and suppressing internal revolutions. The liberalism and nationalism fostered by the previous era were looked upon with deep suspicion by those in power.

The Quadruple Alliance had provided for periodic meetings of those enforcing the Treaty of Paris. These conferences are collectively known as the CONGRESS SYSTEM. The first of these meetings, the Congress of Aix-la-Chapelle, occurred in 1818. It arranged for the withdrawal of the occupation army from France and permitted France to join the other four major powers in what was now the Quintuple Alliance. Congresses met at Troppau in 1820, and at Laibach in 1821, to consider rebellions in Spain and the Two Sicilies. The Troppau Protocol authorized intervention in the internal affairs of states by the sending of troops to put down revolutions. The Austrians, with the support of Russia and Prussia, sent forces to crush the rebellion in Naples (capital of the Kingdom of the Two Sicilies). Neither France nor England agreed with these moves. England, in particular, objected to interference in the internal affairs of other nations. When France was authorized at the Congress of Verona in 1822 to send troops to crush the Spanish Revolt, all hope of Britain's continued adherence to the Congress System ended. England was not only opposed to intervening in internal affairs, but also feared that attempts might be made to restore royal Spanish rule to the newly independent South American countries, which were British trading partners. The Holy Alliance, which England had not signed, did not cease. Indeed it provided cover, especially for Austria, Prussia, and Russia, to act together in crushing other revolts. There also persisted a broader concept of a Concert of Europe that led the major European powers to consult intermittently, thereby attempting to avoid direct clashes with one another.

What was the Concert of Europe? Is there any equivalent today?

From *Western Civilization Since 1500*, Second Edition by Walther Kirchner. Copyright (c) 1958, 1966 by Barnes & Noble, Inc. Copyright (c) 1975 by Walther Kirchner. Reprinted by permission of HarperCollins Publishers, Inc.

Figure 2.6 **The Congress of Vienna** (1814-15). Painting by J. B. Isabey (1767-1855). The Congress of Vienna's most significant achievement was a European peace that lasted from 1815 to the onset of World War I in 1914. Prince Klemens von Metternich of Austria, the Congress' chief statesman, stands sixth from the left; France's representative Maurice de Talleyrand is seated with his arm on the table. (Courtesy of The Library of Congress)

6

From the Industrial Revolution to the Revolutions of 1848

The Industrial Revolution

Economic developments that began in Britain around 1750 have led to the mechanization of the manufacturing process, a huge increase in the amount of goods produced per worker, and the increased urbanization of society. These changes are often referred to as "The Industrial Revolution."

However, the term "revolution" needs to be used with some caution. Radical, but not necessarily rapid, changes characterized the industrialization of England which took about a century, until 1850. Some parts of the world—principally the underdeveloped countries of the Third World—are still experiencing the first stages of industrialization today.

Changes in Agriculture and Population

Several factors influenced the push to industrialize. In the English case, agricultural change was an important prerequisite for industrialization. Thanks to the revolutions of the seventeenth century, large landowners dominated parliament. In an effort to increase their incomes, these landowners

What was the Industrial Revolution?

Where did it first occur?

Is the use of the term "revolution" justified?

Did the mercantilist emphasis on accumulating gold and silver help industrialization? What other factors were important?

Describe some of the inventions that helped make the manufacture of textiles an outstanding example of industrialization.

passed several laws enclosing or fencing in lands that had formerly been open fields or common lands for villagers. As large land-owners assumed ownership of these fields, they experimented with new methods of stock breeding and uses of fertilizers. Many of the small farmers who were driven off the land provided surplus labor for the industrial revolution. Total food production greatly increased, thanks to the new methods and the economies of scale permitted by the enlarged farms. As food production increased, the population increased, encouraging even more food production. The populations of England, Ireland, and Scotland combined probably tripled from about 10 million to 30 million in the period from 1750 to 1850.

The Importance of Commerce and Capital

In 1776, Adam Smith had spoken disparagingly of the "mercantile system" and the tools of mercantilism. But England's thriving commerce and established colonies supported the process of industrialization. The accumulation of gold and silver helped to provide the capital for buying new machines. Colonial and other trading links helped to insure the raw materials and markets needed for developing industries.

New Advances in the Textile Industry

Credit should also be given to the entrepreneurial (risk taking) drive and inventiveness of those who helped develop new industries. Developments in the cotton textile industry illustrate the new spirit. British hand labor could not compete with Asian workers in the production of cotton cloth. Instead, the English captured the world market for cottons by mechanizing the production of cotton cloth. John Kay, in 1733, invented the flying shuttle, which made it possible for one person to weave a double width of cloth. James Hargreave's spinning jenny (1765) increased the output of yarn. In 1769, Richard Arkwright used a water frame for multiple spinning of many threads to any thickness desired. Edmund Cartwright, in 1787, invented a steam-driven power loom. The invention of the cotton gin in 1793 by Eli Whitney, an American, increased the supply of raw cotton to feed these machines. By 1820, cotton textiles made up half of all British exports. It should be noted that the much older woolen industry was mechanized much more slowly and did not enjoy the same gains in quantity produced.

Other Advances in Technology

The steam engine played an important role in industrialization. Before its use became widespread, factories were often located near sources of water power. Around 1712, Thomas Newcomen developed a steam engine used for pumping water out of mines. Significant improvements in steam engines, making them practical to use in factories and with a wide variety of applications, was achieved by the Scottish engineer, James Watt. By the 1780's, Watt's engines were widely used in England and abroad. In the first half of the nineteenth century, steam engines saw use in improving transportation—first in steamboats (by 1807) and later in locomotives (by 1825). Between 1850 and 1890, Britain's railroads expanded from 6,635 to over 20,000 miles. The use of steam increased the demand for coal and iron.

Why was the steam engine important?

What were some of the other technological advances that accompanied the Industrial Revolution?

Although the Industrial Revolution developed over several decades from textile manufacturing to mining to transportation, industries clamored for iron with fewer impurities to give machines strength, precision, and durability. Fortunately for Great Britain, they were endowed with the natural resources of coal and iron ore and the entrepreneurship of innovative ironmasters. Abraham Darby (c. 1678-1717) discovered a process for smelting pig iron using coke instead of charcoal. Henry Cort's (1740-1800) puddling process made a cheaper, more workable iron. Then John Wilkinson (1728-1808) built one of the world's first iron bridges in Britain in addition to creating precision cylinders for cannons. His name is still a household word for razor blades and cutlery.

The process of technological innovation continued in the second half of the nineteenth century. The invention of the Bessemer Process (after the Englishman Henry Bessemer) in the 1850's made possible the mass production of steel, while allowing the construction of new types of machines, bridges, and buildings. The telephone (1876), the electric light bulb (1878-9), and the automobile (powered by an internal-combustion engine in 1885) followed.

When did industrialization occur in Belgium, France, and Germany?

The Spread of Industrialization

Belgium, with its rich coal deposits, began to industrialize in the 1820's, France began industrialization in the 1830's, and the quickening tempo in the 1840's contributed to the Revolution of 1848. Germany, led by Prussia, industrialized rapidly after the Customs Union or Zollverein of 1834 had established a large free trade zone. By 1871, when it was unified, mineral-rich Germany had easily surpassed France. The United States industrialized in the second half of the nineteenth century. It had vast mineral wealth, a good supply of labor fed by continuing immigration, and business interests in firm political control after the Civil War. By 1900, the U.S. had surpassed England in producing iron and coal and in consuming raw cotton!

When did the United States industrialize?

The Factory System

The organization of work was changed by the reliance on power-driven machines in the production process. The textile industry was the earliest example. Before industrialization, the cottage or domestic system predominated in the making of clothes. An employer provided the yarn and looms to spinners and weavers, who worked at home. The employer later collected and sold the products of the cottage or "putting-out" system.

In the new textile industry, machines that required large, complex buildings doomed the work-at-home system. Sizable groups of workers were brought together, often in one place. Organizing the flow of work through the factory in a series of steps resulted in the imposition of discipline and close supervision upon the workers. Human needs and activities were subordinated and shaped to meet the needs of the machines, whereas in the previous rural environment workers often set their own pace and standards of performance.

How did the factory system differ from earlier ways of organizing work?

Why did many factory owners prefer to employ women and children rather than adult men?

Poor Working Conditions

Women and children were less resistant to the harsh discipline required of early factory workers than adult males. Consequently, many of the male workers displaced by economic change found themselves at home, while their wives and children went out to work. In England, where we have the reports of parliamentary commissions, the working conditions were horrible by modern standards. Fourteen-hour workdays were common. Working class children began factory toil at the age of five or six. Floggings and other physical abuse were common for minor work infractions. Safety conditions were poor, and it was not uncommon for workers to fall into their machines and suffer grave injuries. The conditions at the coal mines appear to have been worse than in the factories. The mines were cramped and wet. It was common for the men to work naked, despite the presence of women hurriers (coal carriers).

Describe working conditions in the factories and mines.

The Growth of Cities

The development of factories led to the growth of industrial cities. In nineteenth century England, the Midlands and the north, where coal and iron were located, saw a vast rise in population. Manchester was the first of these industrial cities. It grew from 25,000 in 1772 to 455,000 in 1851. All over Britain, the Industrial Revolution brought town growth. In 1801, there were 106 towns of 5,000 or more population. By 1851, there were 265 such towns, and by 1891 the figure had more than doubled again to 622 towns. Workers lived in close quarters near their

Explain how industrialization stimulated the growth of cities.

factories, and at times whole families lived in a single room. Because sanitary conditions were extremely poor, there were frequent outbreaks of typhoid, cholera, and other diseases. Tuberculosis was common. Charles Dickens described these poor conditions in his novel *Hard Times*:

> It was a town of red brick, or of brick that would have been red if the smoke and ashes had allowed it; but as matters stood, it was a town of unnatural red and black like the painted face of a savage. It was a town of machinery and tall chimneys, out of which interminable serpents of smoke trailed themselves for ever and ever, and never got uncoiled. It had a black canal in it, and a river that ran purple with ill-smelling dye, and vast piles of building full of windows where there was a rattling and a trembling all day long, and where the piston of the steam-engine worked monotonously up and down, like the head of an elephant in a state of melancholy madness.[3]

Reforms

This has been a very dismal picture of the social conditions attending industrialization. It should be remembered, however, that industrialization ultimately brought an increase in the standard of living for all classes. Many who, at the time, moved from the rural areas to the new cities also enjoyed a rise in their standard of living.

In any case, reforms did eventually better the conditions of the workers. In England, the first child labor act, passed in 1802, was ineffective because of the lack of en-

What problems accompanied this urban growth?

Describe some of the more important reform measures passed to alleviate the suffering that accompanied industrialization.

What might be some of the gains resulting from industrialization for the average person?

forcement. The first effective child labor law was the Factory Act of 1833, which prohibited the use of children under nine in textile mills and restricted child laborers under thirteen to a 48-hour week and nine hours a day. The Reform Bill of 1832 extended the right to vote to about an eighth of adult males. By 1884, about three-fourths of adult males in Britain could vote. The extension of the political suffrage was a way to contain worker dissatisfaction with economic conditions. Labor laws were passed and voting rights extended in much of the industrialized West. These served to blunt the appeal of such movements as socialism and communism.

Socialism

What is socialism?

Various socialist ideologies were developed in response to the harsh social conditions commonly experienced in economies undergoing industrialization. Socialism is a political philosophy advocating that people collectively own the means of producing and distributing goods. Collective ownership by the people may be achieved through a group or, more frequently, through the state. The aim is to replace competition for profit with cooperation to insure social justice. In practice, the emphasis is on the transfer of benefits from capitalists to workers. Some socialists believed that their goals could be achieved through moral persuasion. These are often called the utopian socialists, because their theories were seen by critics as unrealistic and visionary. They included Henri Comte de Saint-Simon (1760-1825), Charles Fourier (1772-1837), and Robert

Owen (1771-1858). Fourier envisioned an idealized society, a phalanstery, based on cooperative farming. Experiments based on Fourier's concepts were started in Red Bank, New Jersey and Brook Farm, Massachusetts. Owen desired cooperative communities of a more industrialized character. He founded a model community at New Harmony, Indiana. All of these attempts at social improvement were short-lived.

Another variety of socialists were the anarchists, who believed that the abolition of government was a precondition for social justice. Pierre Joseph Proudhon (1809-1865) and Mikhail Bakunin (1814-1876) were nineteenth century socialist anarchists.

The most influential of the socialists who advocated violent revolution was Karl Marx (1818-1883). Together with his friend and collaborator, Frederick Engels (1820-1895), he laid the foundations of Communist or Marxist theory, which was to change the course of nineteenth and twentieth century history.

Karl Marx was born in the Prussian Rhineland (Trier) of Jewish parents, who had converted to Christianity for career considerations. In 1841, he received a doctorate in philosophy. Because of his radical views, he was not permitted to pursue an academic career. He worked for a time as a journalist and lived variously in the German states, Brussels, and Paris. Marx was an enthusiastic supporter of the revolutions of 1848. After these revolutions failed, he moved in 1849 to London, where he spent the rest of his life in poverty, receiving financial assistance from Engels. His many writings include *The Communist Manifesto* (1848) and *Capital* (the first volume was published in 1867).

Distinguish the utopian socialists from the anarchists. Name some members from each camp.

Give a brief biography of Karl Marx.

Explain dialectical materialism.

Marxist Theory

Marx embraced DIALECTICAL MATERIALISM. He borrowed from the German idealist philosopher, Georg W. F. Hegel the notion of the dialectic, that change comes from the clash of opposites. Both Hegel and Marx applied this notion to history. Throughout history the conflict between a thesis (a concept or thing) and its opposite, the antithesis, gives rise to a synthesis in which the two are reconciled and become a new thesis. While Hegel was an idealist, Marx was a materialist. According to Marx economic forces drive history. As his friend Engels put it:

> *all* past history . . . was the history of class struggles; . . . these warring classes of society are always the products of the modes of production and exchange - in a word, of the *economic* conditions of their time; . . . the economic structure of society always furnishes the real basis, starting from which we can alone work out the ultimate explanation of the whole superstructure of juridical and political institutions as well as the religious, philosophical, and other ideas of a given historical period.[4]

What is economic determinism?

Marx was a materialist then, in the sense that he believed the methods or means of production determined social structure and even prevailing ideologies. This focus on economic causation is sometimes called ECONOMIC DETERMINISM.

Another basic Marxist notion is that of CLASS STRUGGLE. Social class is determined in reiation to the means of production. Those who own the means of production form the ruling class and exploit the other classes in society. Classes have varied in history. There have been masters and slaves, patricians and plebeians, lords and serfs. In industrialized society, the fundamental class division is between the capitalists or bourgeoisie, who own the factories and mines, and the workers or proletariat, who earn their living using the machines and other tools supplied by the capitalists.

Explain class struggle.

To explain how the capitalists exploited the workers, Marx developed the theory of surplus value. Accepting the ideas of Adam Smith and David Ricardo, Marx believed that the value of a product is determined by the labor put into it. What the worker actually receives is a subsistence wage—just enough to support his or her continued living. The difference between the price or value of the good produced and the wage paid to the worker is what Marx calls SURPLUS VALUE. Marx contends that the worker is exploited because his or her labor has created the surplus value, the source of the capitalist's profits.

Define surplus value.

Church and state are tools of capitalist exploitation. The executive branch of government is merely "a committee for managing the common affairs of the whole bourgeoisie."[5] Similarly, religion is "the opium of the people,"[6] which prevents the proletariat from looking at the real cause of their suffering, abuse by the bourgeoisie.

According to Marx, the class struggle would inevitably intensify. Competition with big capitalists would drive under small businessmen and shopkeepers, the so-called petty bourgeoisie, into the ranks of the proletariat. Greed for profits would lead to periodic overproduction; economic crises would develop as production halts. Fewer and fewer capitalists would face the swelled ranks of the proletariat. The workers, aware of their misery, would rise up, seize control of the

Why does Marx think revolution is inevitable?

What happens after the proletariat seizes power?

state and form a DICTATORSHIP OF THE PROLETARIAT. The workers would then use the state machinery to smash the bourgeoisie.

Gradually, there would evolve a CLASSLESS SOCIETY in which the state would wither away. Since government is only a means by which the ruling class dominates other classes, there would be no need for a state. This would be true communism, with collective ownership of the means of production. The workers would cease to be alienated from what they produce and would continue to work for the sake of self-fulfillment. In this new paradise on earth, the new rule of society would be: "From each according to his ability, to each according to his needs!"[7]

Offer criticisms of Marxist thought.

Marxism has been criticized on many grounds. Its collapse in Russia and other parts of Eastern Europe is seen by many as decisive proof of the insufficiency of the theory. Certainly the optimism about what would happen after the overthrow of the capitalists seems entirely unwarranted on the basis of historical experience.

For Marx, economics determined everything in society. Yet religion and nationalism are forces that today, as in the past, seem to motivate people's actions, regardless of adverse economic consequences. Friction between workers and owners has not disappeared. But government does not function simply to guarantee the dominance of the capitalists, as Marx described. The enfranchisement of the masses in advanced industrial nations has led to political systems that more often seek to balance the conflicting interests of management and labor.

The Revolutions of 1830

France

This chapter began with the 1789 revolution in France. Two major revolutions in France in the nineteenth century also shook Europe: one in 1830 and another in 1848. To understand the events of 1830 it is well to look back to France after the Congress of Vienna. When the Bourbons were restored in 1815, France enjoyed a moderate regime. Louis XVIII issued a Charter providing a two-house legislature elected through a system of restricted suffrage. The right wing, known as the *Ultras,* was led by Louis's brother, Charles, the Count of Artois. When Louis died in 1824, Charles came to the throne as Charles X (1824-1830). He and his fellow Ultra Royalists acted as if they would restore the type of society existing under the Old Regime, prior to the Revolution. An indemnity was voted for those nobles who lost their land in the Revolution; and the influence of the Catholic clergy increased. In the elections of 1830, the liberal opponents of the King were victorious in the Chamber of Deputies, the lower house. They voted no confidence in the royalist government. The king's response was to issue the July Ordinances (on the 26th) without seeking legislative approval. If these ordinances had been implemented, the recently elected Chamber would have been dissolved. A new Chamber would have been elected under voting rules excluding much of the middle class.

The popular reaction was swift. On July 27th, barricades were thrown up in Paris by groups of workers and intellectuals who wished to overthrow the king and establish a

Why do you think Louis XVIII fared better as king than Louis XVI?

How did Charles X seek to advance the policies of the Ultras?

What events led Charles X to abdicate?

republic. Charles X abdicated and fled to England. The middle-class liberals who had led the opposition in the Chamber of Deputies preferred a constitutional monarchy to a republic. With the help of Talleyrand and Lafayette, they placed Louis Philippe of the house of Orleans (related to the Bourbons) on the throne of France. Louis Philippe (1830-1848), making sure he appealed to this bourgeois constituency, adopted the tri-color flag of the revolution and went around Paris wearing the forerunner of a business suit and carrying an umbrella. He scrupulously honored the constitution. There was no appearance of kingly absolutism in his dress or his pronouncements.

Other Countries

How did Louis Philippe conciliate the bourgeoisie?

The July 1830 revolution in France inspired revolution in other countries. The most successful of these was in the southern part of the Kingdom of the Netherlands. The old Austrian Netherlands revolted against the Dutch northerners and became the independent state of Belgium. The insurrectionists objected to the mandatory use of the Dutch language and to the regulation of Catholic schools and the creation of rival secular secondary schools. The Russians considered sending their troops to put down the Belgium revolt. Neither France nor Britain wanted to see Russian troops penetrate so far west. Instead, France and England recognized the independence of a *neutral* Belgium and forced the Dutch king to accept the territorial loss.

The Poles revolted against the new Russian Czar, Nicholas I (1825-1855). The czar crushed the Poles and eliminated the nominally separate Polish state that the czars had ruled since the Congress of Vienna.

Polish lands in Russian hands became an integral part of Russia. Similarly, ineffectual revolutions in Italy and Germany were put down.

In England, the example of the French Revolution across the Channel led to passage of the Reform Bill of 1832, which was seen as a way of avoiding possible revolution. The House of Lords agreed to the measure rather than see the king create new lords who would vote to approve the Bill. The Reform Act eliminated most "rotten boroughs" that had lost population over the years, and it transferred seats to underrepresented industrial cities. While the number of voters was doubled, England hardly became a mass democracy. The estimated size of the all-male electorate, after the reform, was 813,000 or one in thirty.

The Revolutions of 1848

1848 was the year of revolution in Europe. There were almost fifty revolutions in Europe during the year. The first of these revolutions occurred on January 12th in Palermo against Ferdinand II (1830-1859), King of the Two Sicilies. The revolution that caught the attention of the rest of Europe and inspired others was that which began in France on February 22nd, against Louis Philippe.

France

France had several problems. There were food shortages, rising prices, and widespread unemployment in the now industrialized country. The government itself was

Contrast developments in Belgium and Poland in 1830.

What did the British Reform Bill of 1832 accomplish?

What problems prompted the 1848 revolution in France?

noted for its corruption and its restricted franchise. Approximately one man in thirty could vote. François Guizot, the king's first minister, insisted that voting should be restricted to men of substantial property. Unrelenting in the face of opposition, Louis Philippe and his minister stoutly resisted pressures for change. Though political rallies of the type commonly used in the United States were forbidden by law, the cause of electoral reform was pushed at political banquets. In the winter of 1847, there had been a series of banquets throughout France, with a large one scheduled for February 22, 1848, in Paris. The Guizot government banned the dinner on the day it was scheduled. This action prompted the revolt. The National Guard refused to disperse the crowds; the workers took up paving stones from the streets and began to erect barricades. Guizot was dismissed on the 23rd, and the king, who abdicated on February 24th, went into exile in England.

Discuss the makeup of the Provisional Government.

A ten-man provisional government was formed, headed by Alphonse de Lamartine (1790-1869). Lamartine was a poet turned politician who favored what might be termed moderate republicanism. He wanted a republican form of government with extensive political rights for the average person. The majority of the Provisional Government were moderate republicans. There was a smaller three-person faction, led by Louis Blanc, the socialist, which was further to the left. Blanc and his followers favored a more radical republic that would emphasize social rights, especially the right of wage earners to work in the newly industrialized nation.

As a carrot for Blanc, the Provisional Government established National Workshops that seemed to mimic the producer's cooperatives, run by workers, that Blanc envisioned. But they put in charge of these workshops an admitted anti-socialist who had no intention of cooperating in the implementation of Blanc's vision. The workshops simply became welfare projects, providing pay and little real work to the Parisian masses. The numbers enrolled in the National Workshops jumped from 10,000 in March to about 120,000 in June.

In April 1848, elections were held throughout France for a Constituent or National Assembly that was to write a new republican constitution. This Assembly was elected by universal manhood suffrage. Suddenly the electorate, which under the Orleanist Monarchy had been about 200,000, had risen to nine million. Nobody had fully anticipated what the outcome would be. The result of this election was that the country regions outside Paris found a voice. That voice was much more conservative than in the city! When the Assembly met in May, it replaced the Provisional Government with a five-person executive board headed by Lamartine. No socialists were included in the new executive. Some workers responded by trying to dissolve the Constituent Assembly, but the National Guard supported the Assembly. There was bloodshed during the June Days Riots from June 23-26th. These riots were a response to the dissolution of the National Workshops. To regain control of the streets, martial law was proclaimed under General Louis Cavaignac (1802-1857). The army won. Some ten thousand were killed or wounded, and eleven thousand were captured and deported to the colonies. This example of class warfare deeply frightened the rest of France and sent shudders throughout Europe.

In December 1848, elections were held for a President of the Second Republic, using universal manhood suffrage. The man elected had the advantage of good name recognition and symbolized the restoration

What were the National Workshops?

Why did the June Days occur?

How did Louis Napoleon gain power?

of effective government. He was Louis Napoleon, the nephew of Napoleon Bonaparte. He beat his nearest opponent, General Cavaignac, in a landslide of 5,317,345 votes to 1,879,298. By December 1852, the first president of the Second Republic had succeeded in establishing, by plebiscite, still another form of government—the Second Empire.

Germany

What was the Frankfurt Assembly? What problems confronted it?

Nationalism and liberalism were leading factors in bringing revolutions to Germany and Italy in 1848. Neither area was as yet united into a single nation. The largest German states were Austria and Prussia. From May 1848 to June 1849, liberals from all over Germany, without the official authorization of their governments, met in the FRANKFURT ASSEMBLY to try to find a constitutional basis for a united German nation. One of the major problems was to decide whether the ruler of this united state would come from the Austrian Hapsburgs or the Prussian Hohenzollerns. Another concern was what were to be the boundaries of such a state. How much of the multinational Austrian Empire should be included? Or should Austria be completely excluded, and the lead given to the Prussian monarch? Or what about the inclusion of Schleswig, with a mixed German and Danish population but ruled by the Danish monarch? It is not surprising that this body, without any military armies at its disposal, was long on talk and short on effective action. The delegates had to drop the idea of including Austria, when the Austrians made it clear they were opposed to all forms of nationalism—including the German variety. In April 1849, the Prussian King refused the throne of a united

German empire, saying he had no wish to pick a crown from the gutter. Most of the delegates simply left, and those who remained were dispersed in June by the Prussian army.

Prussia

In Prussia itself, demonstrations occurred in Berlin in March 1848. When fighting broke out between the demonstrators and the army, King Frederick William IV (1848-1861) was persuaded to withdraw his troops from Berlin. He remained in the city and felt humiliated by the crowd. In May, an assembly was elected to draw up a constitution for Prussia, but by November Frederick William got up enough courage to call the troops back to Berlin. The constitutional assembly was dissolved in December, and the King issued a constitution on his own. Though the new constitution was fairly liberal, he modified it the following year to give decisive electoral advantage to property holders.

Austria

Austria was the state in Europe that, with its many non-German peoples, had the most to fear from nationalism. The Austrians experienced revolts among the north Italians, the Czechs, and the Hungarians. The Hungarians, led by Louis Kossuth (1802-1894), were the most successful. They achieved independence for a time, until, facing simultaneous attacks from Austrian and Russian armies, the Hungarians were forced to surrender in August 1849.

Compare the 1848 revolutions in Prussia and Austria.

How well did the revolutionaries do in Italy?

Italy

While there were numerous revolts in Italy, little was achieved in the face of determined foreign opposition to a united Italy. The Austrians delivered decisive blows in Lombardy and Venetia, and they defeated King Charles Albert of Sardinia, who tried to lead the unification movement. A short-lived Roman Republic was established in February 1849. The French troops of Louis Napoleon, who wanted to gain favor among French Catholics, crushed the republic in July. The pope, who had been in exile, returned to Rome. The French stayed in Rome as protectors of the pope until 1870.

What consequences did the revolutions of 1848 have?

Though by the end of 1849 the revolutions that swept Europe in 1848 were failures, many historians agree that there were some consequences from these revolts. Universal manhood suffrage was retained in France and became an ideal throughout Europe. The force of nationalism was, if anything, quickened. Germany and Italy did attain national unification, under conservative leadership, in the second half of the century. Indeed, political leaders after 1849 displayed a realistic respect for force and national self-interest. The idealism, represented by Alexander I's Holy Alliance, was notably absent.

NOTES

[1]The commoners believed they were locked out to prevent further, unauthorized activity. Other explanations have been offered, including preparing the meeting hall for a scheduled royal function.

[2]Thomas Carlyle, <u>The French Revolution,</u> 2 vols. (New York: John W. Lovell), II: Book 20, Ch. 7.

[3] Charles Dickens, <u>Hard Times</u> (New York: The Heritage Press, 1966 [originally published in 1854], p.23.

[4]Frederick Engels, "Socialism: Utopian and Scientific," in <u>Karl Marx and Frederick Engels: Selected Works</u> (New York: International Publishers, 1968), p. 415.

[5]Karl Marx and Frederick Engels, "Manifesto of the Communist Party", in <u>Karl Marx and Frederick Engels: Selected Works</u> (New York: International Publishers, 1968), p. 37.

[6]Karl Marx as quoted in T. B. Bottomore, ed., <u>Karl Marx; Selected Writings in Sociology & Social Philosophy</u> (New York: Mc Graw-Hill, 1964), p.27.

[7]Karl Marx, "Critique of the Gotha Programme," in *Karl* <u>Marx and Frederick Engels: Selected Works</u> (New York: International Publishers, 1968), p. 325.

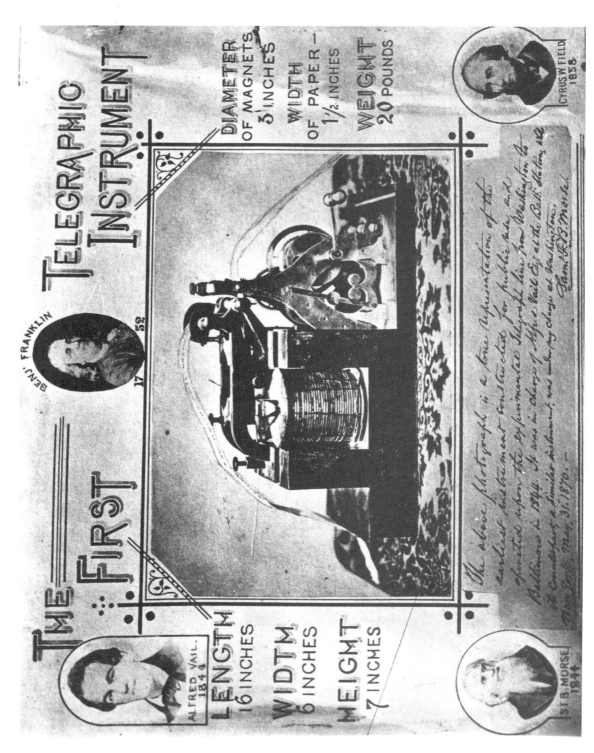

Figure 2.7 **The First Telegraphic Instrument.** Using Samuel F. B. Morse's (1791-1872) invention of the telegraph, the first public telegraph line was initiated between Washington and Baltimore in 1844. It was one of a series of inventions in communications before the portable

KARL MARX AND FREDERICK ENGELS
MANIFESTO OF
*THE COMMUNIST PARTY**

Considered to be the father of communist ideology, Karl Marx (1818-1883) changed the course of history, but not in his lifetime. The revolution he urges in *The Communist Manifesto* (1848) inspired Lenin's takeover in Russia almost 70 years later. His influence on Western civilization cannot be minimized, for his activist approach truly changed billions of lives. Think of Cuba, Communist China, and the former Eastern European countries!

Remember the Industrial Revolution with its long hours and abysmal, unsafe working conditions inflicted on many workers (proletarians) by their capitalist (bourgeoisie) factory owners. As a result of this exploitation, Marx and life-long friend and collaborator Friedrich Engels (1820-1895) urge the proletarians to rise up — yes, revolt — against their masters. They want to abolish the central characteristic of capitalism: the ownership of private property. Along with this dictum, they advocate the violent *overthrow* of the government, which they claim is controlled by capitalists for their own advantage. By establishing this workers' paradise, the workers will now control the factories, the coal mines, the steel mills (the means of production) as well as the government. All class frictions and jealousies will be eliminated. As a result of the elimination of the "evil" capitalists, Marx and Engels envision a new society that transforms the worker into a truly free human being where each gives according to his ability and each receives according to his need. The *Manifesto* ends with the cry: "WORKING MEN OF ALL COUNTRIES, UNITE!"

A spectre is haunting Europe—the spectre of Communism. All the powers of old Europe have entered into a holy alliance to exorcise this spectre; Pope and Czar, Metternich and Guizot, French Radicals and German police-spies.

The Austrian and French chief ministers, Metternich and Guizot, were both driven from office in the revolutions of 1848.

---

*From Karl Marx and Frederick Engels, *Manifesto of the Communist Party*, trans. by Samuel Moore, notes by Frederick Engels (London: William Reeves, 1888 [first published in 1848]).

Where is the party in opposition that has not been decried as communistic by its opponents in power? Where the opposition that has not hurled back the branding reproach of Communism, against the more advanced opposition parties, as well as against its reactionary adversaries?

Two things result from this fact.

I. Communism is already acknowledged by all European Powers to be itself a Power.

II. It is high time that Communists should openly, in the face of the whole world, publish their views, their aims, their tendencies, and meet this nursery tale of the Spectre of Communism with a Manifesto of the party itself.

A manifesto is a proclamation; a public announcement of objectives, views, etc.

To this end, Communists of various nationalities have assembled in London, and sketched the following manifesto, to be published in the English, French, German, Italian, Flemish and Danish languages.

I

BOURGEOIS AND PROLETARIANS[*]

The history of all hitherto existing society is the history of class struggles.

Note that Marx and Engels begin their analysis with _classes_ rather than individuals. Locke, in contrast, stresses the rights of _individuals_.

Freeman and slave, patrician and plebian, lord and serf, guild-master[†] and journeyman, in a word; oppressor and oppressed, stood in constant opposition to one another, carried on an uninterrupted, now hidden, now open fight, a fight that each time ended, either in a revolutionary re-constitution of society at large, or in the common ruin of the contending classes.

---

[*]By bourgeoisie is meant the class of modern Capitalists, owners of the means of social production and employers of wage-labor, By proletariat, the class of modern wage-laborers who, having no means of production of their own, are reduced to selling their labour-power in order to live.

[†]Guild-master, that is a full member of a guild, a master within, not a head of, a guild.

In the early epochs of history, we find almost everywhere a complicated arrangement of society into various orders, a manifold graduation of social rank. In ancient Rome we have patricians, knights, plebians, slaves; in the middle ages, feudal lords, vassals, guild-masters, journeymen, apprentices, serfs; in almost all of these classes, again, subordinate gradations.

The modern bourgeois society that has sprouted from the ruins of feudal society, has not done away with class antagonisms. It has but established new classes, new conditions of oppression, new forms of struggle in place of the old ones.

Our epoch, the epoch of the bourgeoisie, possesses, however, this distinctive feature; it has simplified the class antagonisms. Society as a whole is more and more splitting up into two great hostile camps, into two great classes directly facing each other: Bourgeoisie and Proletariat.

From the serfs of the middle ages sprang the chartered burghers of the earliest towns. From these burgesses the first elements of the bourgeoisie were developed.

The discovery of America, the rounding of the Cape, opened up fresh ground for the rising bourgeoisie. The East-Indian and Chinese markets, the colonization of America, trade with the colonies, the increase in the means of exchange and in commodities, generally, gave to commerce, to navigation, to industry, an impulse never before known, and thereby, to the revolutionary element in the tottering feudal society, a rapid development.

The feudal system of industry, under which industrial production was monopolized by closed guilds, now no longer sufficed for the growing wants of the new markets. The manufacturing system took its place. The guild-masters were pushed on one side by the manufacturing middle-class; division of labour between the different corporate guilds vanished in the face of division of labour in each single workshop.

Meantime the markets kept ever growing, the demand, ever rising. Even manufacture no longer sufficed. Thereupon, steam and machin-

The previous periods of history were complicated by the existence of several conflicting classes in society. In the modern epoch class antagonism are simplified by the establishment of two principal classes, the bourgeoisie and the proletariat.

The burghers were the town dwellers of medieval times. These were often merchants from which the middle class later developed.

As the markets grew so did demand. To meet demand machinery replaced hand-crafted production. Industrialization created the modern bourgeoisie led by industrial millionaires.

The modern bourgeois class is the product of changes in the modes, or means, of production and exchange. Marx thought that changes in the means of production also were responsible for the development of the proletariat. Marx was an economic determinist. He was convinced that the way in which goods and services are produced determines class structure and the rest of the social structure.

ery revolutionized industrial production. The place of manufacture was taken by the giant, Modern Industry, the place of the industrial middle-class, by industrial millionaires, the leaders of whole industrial armies, the modern bourgeoisie.

Modern industry has established the world market, for which the discovery of America paved the way. This market has given an immense development to commerce, to navigation, to communication by land. This development has, in its turn, reacted on the extension of industry; and in proportion as industry, commerce, navigation, railways extended, in the same proportion the bourgeoisie developed, increased its capital, and pushed into the background every class handed down from the Middle Ages.

We see, therefore, how the modern bourgeoisie is itself the product of a long course of development, of a series of revolutions in the modes of production and of exchange.

Each step in the development of the bourgeoisie was accompanied by a corresponding political advance of that class. An oppressed class under the sway of the feudal nobility, an armed and self-governing association in the medieval commune,* here independent urban republic (as in Italy and Germany), there taxable "third estate" of the monarchy (as in France), afterwards, in the period of manufacture proper, serving either the semi-feudal or the absolute monarchy as a counterpoise against the nobility, and, in fact, corner stone of the great monarchies in general, the bourgeoisie has at last, since the establishment of Modern Industry and of the world-market, con-

*"Commune" was the name taken, in France, by the nascent towns even before they had conquered from their feudal lords and masters, local self-government and political rights as the "Third Estate." Generally speaking, for the economical development of the bourgeoisie, England is here taken as the typical country, for its political development, France.

quered for itself, in the modern representative State, exclusive political sway. The executive of the modern State is but a committee for managing the common affairs of the whole bourgeoisie.

The bourgeoisie, historically, has played a most revolutionary part.

The bourgeoisie, wherever it has got the upper hand, has put an end to all feudal, patriarchal, idyllic relations. It has pitilessly torn asunder the motley feudal ties that bound man to his "natural superiors," and has left remaining no other nexus between man and man than naked self-interest, than callous "cash payment." It has drowned the most heavenly ecstasies of religious fervor, of chivalrous enthusiasm, of philistine sentimentalism, in the icy water of egotistical calculation. It has resolved personal worth into exchange value, and in place of the numberless indefeasible chartered freedoms, has set up that single, unconscionable freedom—Free Trade. In one word, for exploitation, veiled by religious and political illusions, it has substituted naked, shameless, direct, brutal exploitation.

The bourgeoisie has stripped of its halo every occupation hitherto honored and looked up to with reverent awe. It has converted the physician, the lawyer, the priest, the poet, the man of science, into its paid wage-labourers.

The bourgeoisie has torn away from the family its sentimental veil, and has reduced the family relation to a mere money relation.

The bourgeoisie has disclosed how it came to pass that the brutal display of vigor in the Middle Ages, which Reactionists so much admire, found its fitting complement in the most slothful indolence. It has been the first to show what man's activity can bring about. It has accomplished wonders far surpassing Egyptian pyramids, Roman aqueducts, and Gothic cathedrals; it has conducted expeditions that put in the shade all former Exoduses of nations and crusades.

The bourgeoisie cannot exist without constantly revolutionizing the instruments of production, and thereby the relations of production, and with them the whole relations of society. Conservation of the old modes of pro-

The state is an instrument of the bourgeoisie, the ruling class.

Past feudal ties, which bound superiors to subordinates, have been replaced by cash payments. The cash nexus reveals exploitive relationships formerly cloaked by religious or political illusions.

Even such professions as physician, lawyer, and priest have been reduced to the status of paid wage-laborers.

The bourgeoisie are constantly changing production techniques. As the instruments of production change, so also do the societal relations dependent on the relations of production. Society is in a constant state of revolutionary change in the capitalist era.

The bourgeoisie has forced changes in the production of goods and services throughout the world. Raw materials, needed for manufacture, are drawn from many parts of the world. Local and national self-sufficiency have been replaced by global inter-dependence.

duction in unaltered form, was, on the contrary, the first condition of existence for all earlier industrial classes. Constant revolutionizing of production, uninterrupted disturbance of all social conditions, everlasting uncertainty and agitation distinguish the bourgeois epoch from all earlier ones. All fixed, fast-frozen relations, with their train of ancient and venerable prejudices and opinions, are swept away, all newly-formed ones become antiquated before they can ossify. All that is solid melts into air, all that is holy is profaned, and man is at last compelled to face with sober senses, his real conditions of life, and his relations with his kind.

The need of a constantly expanding market for its products chases the bourgeoisie over the whole surface of the globe. It must nestle everywhere, settle everywhere, establish connections everywhere.

The bourgeoisie has through its exploitation of the world-market given a cosmopolitan character to production and consumption in every country. To the great chagrin of Reactionists, it has drawn from under the feet of industry the national ground on which it stood. All old-established national industries have been destroyed or are daily being destroyed. They are dislodged by new industries, whose introduction becomes a life and death question for all civilized nations, by industries that no longer work up indigenous raw material, but raw material drawn from the remotest zones; industries whose products are consumed, not only at home, but in every quarter of the globe. In place of the old wants, satisfied by the productions of the country, we find new wants, requiring for their satisfaction the products of distant lands and climes. In place of the old local and national seclusion and self-sufficiency, we have intercourse in every direction, universal inter-dependence of nations. And as in material, so also in intellectual production. The intellectual creations of individual nations become common property. National one-sidedness and narrow-mindedness become more and more impossible, and from the numerous national and local literatures, there arises a world-literature.

The bourgeoisie, by the rapid improvement of all instruments of production, by the immensely facilitated means of communication, draws all, even the most barbarian nations into civilization. The cheap prices of its commodities are the heavy artillery with which it batters down all Chinese walls, with which it forces the barbarians' intensely obstinate hatred of foreigners to capitulate. It compels all nations, on pain of extinction, to adopt the bourgeois mode of production; it compels them to introduce what it calls civilization into their midst, i. e., to become bourgeois themselves. In a word, it creates a world after its own image.

The bourgeoisie has subjected the country to the rule of the towns. It has created enormous cities, has greatly increased the urban population as compared with the rural, and has thus rescued a considerable part of the population from the idiocy of rural life. Just as it has made the country dependent on the towns, so it has made barbarian and semibarbarian countries dependent on the civilized ones, nations of peasants on nations of bourgeois, the East on the West.

The bourgeoisie keeps more and more doing away with the scattered state of the population, of the means of production, and of property. It has agglomerated population, centralized means of production, and has concentrated property in a few hands. The necessary consequence of this was political centralization. Independent, or but loosely connected provinces, with separate interests, laws, governments and systems of taxation, became lumped together into one nation, with one government, one code of laws, one national class-interest, one frontier and one customs-tariff.

The bourgeoisie, during its rule of scarce one hundred years, has created more massive and more colossal productive forces than have all preceding generations together. Subjection of Nature's forces to man, machinery, application of chemistry to industry and agriculture, steam-navigation, railways, electric telegraphs, clearing of whole continents for cultivation, canalization of rivers, whole populations conjured out of the ground—what earlier century

The bourgeoisie with their cheap, mass-produced goods force the less-civilized nations to adopt their methods—"to become bourgeois themselves."

The "idiocy" of rural life is scorned. The bourgeoisie is seen as subjecting the countryside to the urban centers, the barbarian nations to the civilized ones.

The bourgeoisie has concentrated property along with political control in a few hands—in an increasingly centralized state.

had even a presentiment that such productive forces slumbered in the lap of social labour?

We see then: the means of production and of exchange on whose foundations the bourgeoisie built itself up, were generated in feudal society. At a certain stage in the development of these means of production and of exchange, the conditions under which feudal society produced and exchanged, the feudal organization of agriculture and manufacturing industry, in one word, the feudal relations of property became no longer compatible with the already developed productive forces; they became so many fetters. They had to be burst asunder; they were burst asunder.

Into their places stepped free competition, accompanied by a social and political constitution adapted to it, and by the economical and political sway of the bourgeois class.

At a certain stage in feudal society, changes in the means of production and exchange were no longer compatible with the feudal social structure which made the nobility the ruling class. When this occurred, the developed productive forces burst apart the existing feudal social structure, permitting the bourgeois class to gain economic and political domination.

A similar movement is going on before our own eyes. Modern bourgeois society with its relations of production, of exchange and of property, a society that has conjured up such gigantic means of production and of exchange, is like the sorcerer, who is no longer able to control the powers of the nether world whom he has called up by his spells. For many a decade past the history of industry and commerce is but the history of the revolt of modern productive forces against modern conditions of production, against the property relations that are the condition for the existence of the bourgeoisie and of its rule. It is enough to mention the commercial crises that by their periodical return put on trial, each time more threateningly, the existence of the entire bourgeois society. In these crises a great part not only of the existing products, but also of the previously created productive forces, are periodically destroyed. In these crises there breaks out an epidemic that, in all earlier epochs, would have seemed an absurdity—the epidemic of over-production. Society suddenly finds itself put back into a state of momentary barbarism; it appears as if a famine, a universal war of devastation had cut off the supply of every means of subsistence; industry and commerce seem to be destroyed; and why? Because there is too much civilization, too much means of subsistence, too

A similar movement is occurring in our own time. Changes in the forces of production are threatening the established social structure. This is especially seen in the periodic crises brought about by epidemics of over-production. These crises threaten the existence of the whole bourgeois society.

much industry, too much commerce. The productive forces at the disposal of society no longer tend to further the development of the conditions of bourgeois property; on the contrary, they have become too powerful for these conditions, by which they are fettered, and so soon as they overcome these fetters, they bring disorder into the whole of bourgeois society, endangering the existence of bourgeois property. The conditions of bourgeois society are too narrow to comprise the wealth created by them. And how does the bourgeoisie get over these crises? On the one hand by enforced destruction of a mass of productive forces; on the other, by the conquest of new markets, and by the more thorough exploitation of the old ones. That is to say, by paving the way for more extensive and more destructive crises, and by diminishing the means whereby crises are prevented.

The weapons with which the bourgeoisie felled feudalism to the ground are now turned against the bourgeoisie itself.

But not only has the bourgeoisie forged the weapons that bring death to itself; it has also called into existence the men who are to wield those weapons—the modern working-class—the proletarians.

In proportion as the bourgeoisie, i. e., capital, is developed, in the same proportion is the proletariat, the modern working-class, developed, a class of labourers, who live only so long as they find work, and who find work only so long as their labour increases capital. These labourers, who must sell themselves piecemeal, are a commodity, like every other article of commerce, and are consequently exposed to all the vicissitudes of competition, to all the fluctuations of the market.

Owing to the extensive use of machinery and to division of labour, the work of the proletarians has lost all individual character, and, consequently, all charm for the workman. He becomes an appendage of the machine, and it is only the most simple, most monotonous, and most easily acquired knack that is required of him. Hence, the cost of production of a workman is restricted, almost entirely, to the means of subsistence that he requires for his mainte-

The developing forces of production will overcome the fetters placed on them by the conditions of bourgeois property.

Just as the bourgeoisie struck down feudalism, the proletariat will strike down capitalism.

The proletariat, the workers, are forced by the bourgeoisie to sell their labor as a commodity, subject to the fluctuations of the market.

The work of the wage laborer has lost its individuality, for the worker is only an attachment to the machine.

The worker is only paid enough to subsist, that is to continue living and to have children who can also become part of the labor supply.

Due to the organization of large numbers of workers in the factory, the laborer is enslaved by the system, which includes the machine, the foremen, and the factory owner.

Labor is exploited by its age and sex within the factory system. The laborer is also at the mercy of the landlord, the merchant, and other components of the bourgeois class.

The lower ranks of the middle class fade into the proletariat, who become the majority of society.

nance, and for the propagation of his race. But the price of a commodity, and also of labour, is equal to its cost of production. In proportion, therefore, as the repulsiveness of the work increases, the wage decreases. Nay more, in proportion as the use of machinery and division of labour increases, in the same proportion the burden of toil also increases, whether by prolongation of the working hours, by increase of the work enacted in a given time, or by increased speed of the machinery etc.

Modern industry has converted the little workshop of the patriarchal master into the great factory of the industrial capitalist. Masses of labourers, crowded into the factory, are organized like soldiers. As privates of the industrial army they are placed under the command of a perfect hierarchy of officers and sergeants. Not only are they the slaves of the bourgeois class, and of the bourgeois State, they are daily and hourly enslaved by the machine, by the over-looker, and, above all, by the individual bourgeois manufacturer himself. The more openly this despotism proclaims gain to be its end and aim, the more petty, the more hateful and the more embittering it is.

The less the skill and exertion or strength implied in manual labour, in other words, the more modern industry becomes developed, the more is the labour of men superseded by that of women. Differences of age and sex have no longer any distinctive social validity for the working class. All are instruments of labour, more or less expensive to use, according to their age and sex.

No sooner is the exploitation of the labourer by the manufacturer so far at an end, that he receives his wages in cash, than he is set upon by the other portions of the bourgeoisie, the landlord, the shopkeeper, the pawnbroker, etc.

The lower strata of the Middle class—the small tradespeople, shopkeepers, and retired tradesmen generally, the handicraftsmen and peasants—all these sink gradually into the proletariat, partly because their diminutive capital does not suffice for the scale on which Modern Industry is carried on, and is swamped in the competition with the large capitalists, partly because their specialized skill is rendered worthless by new methods of production. Thus the proletariat is recruited from all classes of the population.

All previous historical movements were movements of minorities, or in the interest of minorities. The proletarian movement is the self-conscious, independent movement of the immense majority, in the interest of the immense majority. The proletariat, the lowest stratum of our present society, cannot stir, cannot raise itself up, without the whole superincumbent strata of official society being sprung into the air.

Though not in substance, yet in form, the struggle of the proletariat with the bourgeoisie is at first a national struggle. The proletariat of each country must, of course, first of all settle matters with its own bourgeoisie.

In depicting the most general phases of the development of the proletariat, we traced the more or less veiled civil war, raging within existing society, up to the point where that war breaks out into open revolution, and where the violent overthrow of the bourgeoisie, lays the foundation for the sway of the proletariat.

We have seen above, that the first step in the revolution by the working class, is to raise the proletariat to the position of ruling class, to win the battle of democracy.

The proletariat will use its political supremacy, to wrest, by degrees, all capital from the bourgeoisie, to centralize all instruments of production in the hands of the State, i. e., of the proletariat organized as the ruling class; and to increase the total of productive forces as rapidly as possible.

Of course, in the beginning, this cannot be effected except by means of despotic inroads on the rights of property, and on the conditions of bourgeois production, by means of measures, therefore, which appear economically insufficient and untenable, but which, in the course of the movement, outstrip themselves, necessitate further inroads upon the old social order, and are unavoidable as a means of entirely revolutionizing the mode of production.

These measures will of course be different in different countries.

The struggle between the bourgeoisie and the proletariat breaks out into open, violent revolution. The proletariat, having overthrown the bourgeoisie, becomes the new ruling class. The workers use the state as their instrument for democratic change. All the means of production are centralized in the hands of the state. Productive forces and the social structure are reorganized as rapidly as possible by means that are necessarily despotic.

Notice that some of the items in the communist program, such as a graduated income tax and free public school education for all, appear to be far less radical today than in 1848.

The use of repressive political power by the proletariat is a temporary thing.

Marx and Engels believe that once the bourgeoisie are eliminated class antagonisms will disappear

Nevertheless in the most advanced countries the following will be pretty generally applicable:

1. Abolition of property in land and application of all rents of land to public purposes.

2. A heavy progressive or graduated income tax.

3. Abolition of all right of inheritance.

4. Confiscation of the property of all emigrants and rebels.

5. Centralization of credit in the hands of the State, by means of a national bank with State capital and an exclusive monopoly.

6. Centralization of the means of communication and transport in the hands of the State.

7. Extension of factories and instruments of production owned by the State, the bringing into cultivation of waste lands, and the improvement of the soil generally in accordance with a common plan.

8. Equal liability of all to labour. Establishment of industrial armies, especially for agriculture.

9. Combination of agriculture with manufacturing industries; gradual abolition of the distinction between town and country, by a more equable distribution of population over the country.

10. Free education for all children in public schools. Abolition of children's factory labour in its present form. Combination of education with industrial production, etc., etc.

When, in the course, of development, class distinctions have disappeared, and all production has been concentrated in the hands of a vast association of the whole nation, the public power will lose its political character. Political power, properly so called, is merely the organized power of one class for suppressing another. If the proletariat during its contest with the bourgeoisie is compelled, by the force of circumstances, to organize itself as a class, if, by means of a revolution, makes itself ruling class, and, as such, sweeps away by force the old conditions of production, then it will, along with these conditions, have swept away the conditions for the existence of class antagonisms, and of classes generally, and will thereby have abolished its own supremacy as a class.

In place of the old bourgeois society, with its classes and class antagonisms, we shall have an association, in which the free development of each is the condition for the free development of all.

In short, the Communists everywhere support every revolutionary movement against the existing social and political order of things.

In all these movements they bring to the front, as the leading question in each, the property question, no matter what its degree of development at the time.

Finally, they labour everywhere for the union and agreement of the democratic parties of all countries.

The Communists disdain to conceal their views and aims. They openly declare that their ends can be attained only by the forcible overthrow of all existing social conditions. Let the ruling classes tremble at a Communist revolution. The proletarians have nothing to lose but their chains. They have a world to win.

WORKING MEN OF ALL COUNTRIES, UNITE!

There will no longer be a ruling class needing government as an instrument to repress other classes. These passages suggest the Marxist doctrines of the gradual development of a "classless society" and the "withering" away of the state as a consequence of the dictatorship of the proletariat. At that point the free development of the individual will be compatible with the free development of society.

The *Manifesto* ends with a ringing cry for violent revolution.

Questions for Critical Thinking and Discussion

1. How does Marx explain progress and change in *The Manifesto*?

2. Explain Marx's emphasis on the plight of the proletariat as a result of the Industrial Revolution.

3. Outline the deeds and achievements of the bourgeoisie in the course of history.

4. Argue from Marx's point of view why and how the proletariat is exploited by the bourgeoisie.

5. Why must the proletariat violently overthrow the bourgeoisie? Do they have other alternatives?

6. Why are the bourgeoisie their "own grave-diggers" Are they still digging their own grave today in their search for markets for their manufactured goods?

7. What is Marx's argument for the abolition of private property?

8. Outline the measures the proletariat should pursue once they are the ruling class.

9. If you met both Locke and Marx in a time warp, what would each one tell you about the property you own on this planet?

10. Marx and Engels have given an economic interpretation to history. How do they envision the political system to function in their workers' paradise?

Self-Test

Part I: Identification

Can you identify each of the following? Tell who, what, when, where, why, and/or how for each term.

1. Estates General
2. Third Estate
3. National Assembly
4. Tennis Court Oath
5. Storming of the Bastille
6. Great Fear
7. King Louis XVI
8. Declaration of the Rights of Man and the Citizen
9. Assignats
10. Civil Constitution of the Clergy (1790)
11. Legislative Assembly
12. Girondins
13. Jacobins
14. National Convention
15. Sans-culottes
16. Committee of Public Safety
17. Levée en masse
18. Reign of Terror
19. Maximilien Robespierre
20. Thermidorean Reaction
21. The Directory
22. Consulate
23. First Consul
24. Concordat of 1801
25. Code Napoleon
26. The Continental System
27. Peninsular War
28. Hundred Days
29. Enclosure Acts
30. Flying shuttle
31. Richard Arkwright
32. James Watt
33. Bessemer Process
34. Zollverein
35. *Hard Times*
36. Factory system
37. Francois Guizot
38. Socialism
39. Utopian socialists
40. Socialist anarchists
41. Karl Marx
42. *The Communist Manifesto*
43. Dialectical Materialism
44. Class Struggle
45. Surplus Value
46. Dictatorship of the Proletariat
47. Congress of Vienna
48. Louis XVIII
49. Compensation
50. Balance of power
51. Legitimacy
52. Quadruple Alliance
53. Holy Alliance
54. The Congress System
55. *Ultras*
56. Charles X
57. July Ordinances
58. Louis Philippe
59. Reform Bill of 1832 (England)
60. "Rotten boroughs"
61. National Workshops
62. June Days
63. Louis Blanc
64. Second Republic
65. Second Empire
66. Louis Napoleon
67. Frankfurt Assembly

Part II: Multiple Choice Questions

Circle the best response from the ones available.

1. Which was NOT a cause of the French Revolution?

    a. Ideas of the Enlightenment.
    b. France's strong financial position.
    c. Weak leadership of the king.
    d. Excessive taxation of the peasants.

2. One of the chief failures of the National Assembly was:

    a. its appointment of Napoleon Bonaparte as First Consul.
    b. its resolution to permit Charles X to serve as monarch.
    c. its vote that none of its members could serve in the new Legislative Assembly.
    d. its determination to execute dedicated revolutionaries, such as Robespierre.

3. The Third Estate was composed of :

    a. the clergy.
    b. the nobility.
    c. the revolutionary tribunal.
    d. commoners.

4. Some of the National Assembly's achievements were:

    a. Issuing assignats to meet government expenses.
    b. Creating 83 departments of approximately equal size.
    c. Enacting the Civil Constitution of the Clergy.
    d. All of the above.

5. All the following are correctly matched EXCEPT:

    a. Committee of Public Safety — supporters of the Girondists.
    b. *Sans culottes* — urban laborers who wore long trousers.
    c. Jacobins — radical republican revolutionary group.
    d. *Émigrés* — royalist supporters who fled France.

6. Louis XVI was made a constitutional monarch under the:

    a. Constitution of 1791.
    b. National Convention.
    c. National Assembly.
    d. Constitution of 1793.

7. The Reign of Terror's ax fell on all of the following EXCEPT:

    a. Hebert.
    b. Abbé Sieyès.
    c. Robespierre.
    d. Marie Antoinette.

8. Under Napoleon Bonaparte, France became a military dictatorship called:

    a. The Directory.
    b. The Consulate.
    c. The Committee of Public Safety.
    d. The Code Napoleon.

9. The National Assembly's first act was:

    a. The Reign of Terror.
    b. Storming of the Bastille.
    c. The Tennis Court Oath.
    d. Executing Louis XVI.

10. The controversy over voting in the Estates General was based on:

    a. the likelihood of the First Estate to be outvoted 2 to 1.
    b. the fact that all adult males age 25 could vote for the Second Estate only.
    c. the past practice of each estate voting separately.
    d. the king had veto power over each estate.

11. Which of the following statements is NOT true about The Civil Constitution of the Clergy?

    a. Clergy were given back their rights to Church land and monasteries.
    b. Clergy had to swear an oath of allegiance to the Constitution.
    c. Bishops and priests were to be elected.
    d. Clergy were official state employees.

12. All of the following are reforms of Napoleon EXCEPT:

    a. Opening of careers to talent.
    b. Establishing a uniform code of law.
    c. Inaugurating the Bank of France.
    d. Permitting women to have the same rights as men.

13. Napoleon's failures included all of the following EXCEPT the:

    a. Battle of Austerlitz.
    b. Continental System.
    c. Battle of Trafalgar.
    d. Peninsular War.

14. Napoleon's successes as a commanding officer were due to his ability to:

    a. Concentrate his forces at one point and overwhelm the enemy's forces.
    b. Plan campaigns carefully.
    c. Live off the land.
    d. All of the above.

15. Napoleon Bonaparte became First Consul as a result of :

    a. a "whiff of brandy."
    b. winning the Battle of Borodino.
    c. outwitting the British in the Egyptian campaign.
    d. the coup d'état of Brumaire.

16. By the terms of the Concordat of 1801:

    a. Napoleon established the Continental System.
    b. Napoleon placed his brother Joseph on the throne of Spain.
    c. Catholicism was recognized as the religion of the majority of the French people.
    d. Bishops and priests received their salaries from the Church.

17. "The Hundred Days" was:

    a. Napoleon's invasion of Russia.
    b. Three months of the reign of Louis XVIII.
    c. The period between the Battle of Waterloo and Napoleon's exile to St. Helena.
    d. The period between Napoleon's fleeing Elba and the Battle of Waterloo.

18. Which of the following events are in the correct chronological order?

    a. Fall of the Bastille, the Reign of Terror, the Thermidorean Reaction, the Directory.
    b. Tennis Court Oath, Great Fear, National Assembly, Calling of the Estates General.
    c. The Reign of Terror, the execution of Louis XVI, the reign of Louis XVIII, Great Fear.
    d. Tennis Court Oath, Legislative Assembly, Great Fear, the fall of the Bastille.

19. Which one of the following peace settlements lasted without a major European war for almost 100 years?

    a. Treaty of Utrecht.
    b. Congress of Verona.
    c. Congress of Vienna.
    d. Peace of Westphalia.

20. The major powers were guided by which one of the following principles at the 1815 peace settlement:

    a. Balance of power.
    b. Legitimacy.
    c. Compensation.
    d. All of the above.

21. Which one of the major participants in the 1815 peace settlements is incorrectly matched with his country?

    a. Viscount Castlereagh — Great Britain.
    b. Czar Alexander — Russia.
    c. Metternich — Prussia.
    d. Talleyrand — France.

22. The Quadruple Alliance includes the following countries as signatories:

    a. England, Austria, Prussia, Russia.
    b. England, Austria, Prussia, France.
    c. France, Austria, Prussia, Russia.
    d. Austria, Russia, Prussia, Poland.

23. As a result of the Congress of Vienna, all of the following changes occurred EXCEPT:

    a. German Confederation of 39 states under the leadership of Austria was established.
    b. Russia obtained most of Poland.
    c. Prussia obtained two-fifths of Saxony.
    d. France played a minor role in determining the outcome of the Congress.

24. Which of the following statements is true about the Holy Alliance?

    a. Signatories agreed to provide troops to use against treaty violators.
    b. Bourbons were restored to the thrones of Spain, the Two Sicilies, and France.
    c. Signatories agreed to adhere to Christian principles in their dealings with each other.
    d. The Alliance was formed to ensure France's compliance to the terms of the second Treaty of Paris.

25. Which of the following is NOT true of the peace settlement worked out at Vienna?

    a. When one of the victors gave up territory, it received other territory in return.
    b. Balance of power principle prevented India from dominating the European continent.
    c. Legitimate rulers were restored to their thrones in many of the states of Europe.
    d. All of the above.

26. Which of the following was NOT an effect of the Industrial Revolution:

    a. Unhealthy sanitary conditions.
    b. Families living in close quarters.
    c. Children of eight working in the factories.
    d. None of the above.

27. The Industrial Revolution occurred in England as a result of all of the following EXCEPT:

    a. Advances in agriculture.
    b. Inventions in the textile industry.
    c. Ideology borrowed from Karl Marx.

d. Enclosure Acts.

28. All of the following inventors are correctly matched with their inventions EXCEPT:

  a. Bessemer —method of processing steel.
  b. Whitney — spinning jenny.
  c. Cartwright — power loom.
  d. Watt — steam engine.

29. All of the following resulted from the effects of the Enclosure Acts EXCEPT:

  a. Experimentation with the use of fertilizer.
  b. Increase in the economic advantages of the small farmer.
  c. Increase in the availability of labor.
  d. Increase in the size of farms.

30. Socialism is a political philosophy that advocates:

  a. Transfer of benefits from workers to capitalists.
  b. Collective ownership of the means of production.
  c. Free enterprise.
  d. All of the above.

31. Which one of the following was NOT a utopian socialist?:

  a. John Stuart Mill.
  b. Robert Owen.
  c. Charles Fourier.
  d. Henri de Saint-Simon.

32. Karl Marx's ideology includes all but ONE of the following:

  a. surplus value.
  b. class struggle.
  c. economic interpretation of history.
  d. dictatorship of the bourgeoisie.

33. Which country did NOT have a revolution in 1830?

  a. France.   c. Poland.
  b. England.   d. Kingdom of the Netherlands.

34. The Reform Bill of 1832 in England did all of the following EXCEPT:

    a. Created new members of the House of Lords.
    b. Doubled the size of the all-male electorate to 1 in 30.
    c. Eliminated "rotten boroughs."
    d. Transferred seats to underrepresented industrial cities.

35. In 1848 a revolution occurred in:

    a. France.
    b. Prussia.
    c. Austria.
    d. All of the above.

Part III: Review and Thought Questions

1. Explain what ideas of the philosophes contributed to the French Revolution.

2. How did the American Revolution set the stage for the French Revolution?

3. Explain the controversy over voting separately by Estates.

4. How did the National Assembly come into being? Why is the Tennis Court Oath considered to be the first revolutionary act?

5. Why was the violence in the countryside traumatic? What happened to the records of feudal dues?

6. Evaluate the renouncing of special privileges by the nobility the night of August 4, 1789.

7. Why was the Declaration of the Rights of Man and the Citizen a significant achievement of the National Assembly?

8. For what purpose did the Constituent Assembly issue assignats?

9. Discuss the changes enacted by the Civil Constitution of the Clergy. Was the ordinary Catholic supportive of the Civil Constitution?

10. How did the National Assembly reorganize the French government? In what ways did the Constitution of 1791 restrict the power of the king?

11. In what ways did the King show contempt for revolutionary ideals?

12. Evaluate the difference between direct and indirect democracy as practiced in the Constitution of 1791.

13. What was the Legislative Assembly's major blunder? If the blunder had not occurred, do you think the Revolution would have taken a different course?

14. Give the reasons for the downfall of the Legislative Assembly. What was the major concern of the Austrian and Prussian nobility about the events in France?

15. Who were the sans-culottes? What was their significance?

16. Why was Citizen Capet (Louis XVI) guillotined? Would you have voted for his execution?

17. What was the importance of the *levée en masse*? Why were the newly drafted recruits successful in the field against traditional European armies?

18. Why was the period of radical rule known as the Reign of Terror?

19. How did Robespierre's philosophy relate to Rousseau's Social Contract? Why was this radical leader of a republic of virtue guillotined?

20. Explain the makeup of the Directory under the Constitution of 1795. Why was the Directory a failure?

21. How was Napoleon able to rise to power? Why and how was Napoleon able to be elected First Consul?

22. Explain why Napoleon's Egyptian campaign was both a success and a failure.

23. Evaluate the terms of the Concordat of 1801. What rights did the Pope regain? What rights were lost to the Pope?

24. What territories did the Grand Empire include? Do you feel Napoleon should have established a United States of Europe?

25. What was the outcome of the Battle of Trafalgar? Where did it take place?

26. Evaluate the effects of the Continental System.

27. What made the invasion of Russia such a disastrous defeat for Napoleon?

28. Discuss the problems facing the statesmen assembled in Vienna 1814 to 1815. Why was the settlement at the Congress of Vienna such a significant achievement for international peace?

29. Describe the changes in eighteenth-century agriculture that helped make the Industrial Revolution possible.

30. What were the consequences of the factory system on urbanization, workers' safety and health?

31. Can you explain the following Marxian concepts: dialectical materialism, economic determinism, class struggle, surplus value, dictatorship of the proletariat?

32. How did the *Ultras* come to power in France? Why was Charles X overthrown? Why was Louis Philippe acceptable to the bourgeoisie?

33. Trace the evolution of the 1848 Revolution in France. How was it possible for the French to overwhelmingly vote for the Second Empire?

34. How did the English Reform Act of 1832 avoid revolution? Explain its provisions.

35. Discuss the problems considered by the Frankfurt Assembly. What was the final blow to a united German empire?

36. Why did the Austrian empire have the most to fear from nationalistic influences?

37. What were some of the consequences of the Revolutions of 1848 in Europe? Give examples.

Part IV: Full-Length Essays

1. Describe the major stages of the French Revolution. Be sure to discuss events and personalities of importance in each stage.

2. Evaluate Napoleon's legacy and his place in history.

3. Explain how the peace settlement at Vienna in 1815 set the stage for almost 100 years of international peace.

4. Describe the causes, personalities with their inventions, and the effects of the Industrial Revolution.

5. Compare and contrast utopian socialism with Marxist ideology.

6. Describe Marxist ideology as expressed in *The Communist Manifesto.*

7. Take the French Revolution out of history. Write a two- page summary of what you think would have happened in France during that time period without the Revolution.

8. Compare and contrast the Revolutions of 1830 and 1848 in France.

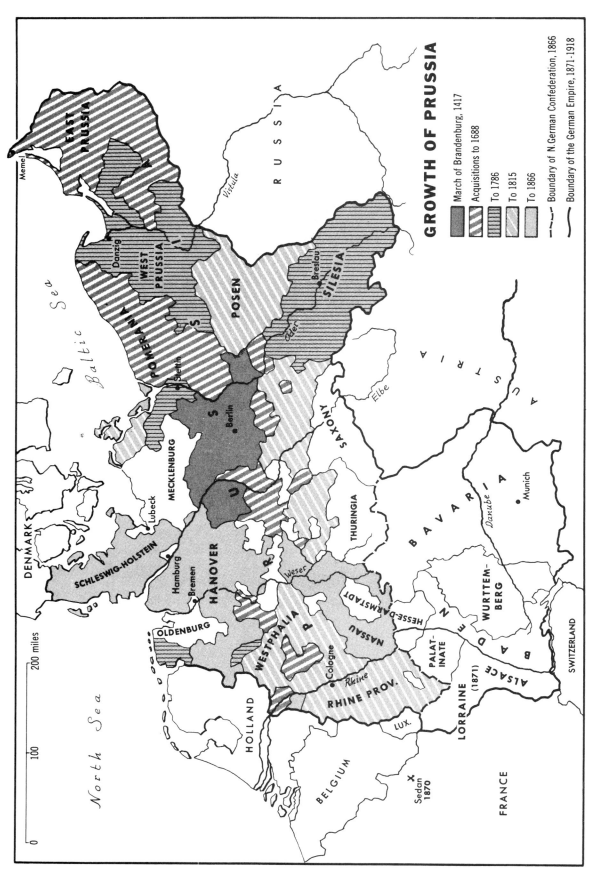

GROWTH OF PRUSSIA

- ◼ March of Brandenburg, 1417
- ▨ Acquisitions to 1688
- ▦ To 1786
- ▨ To 1815
- ▨ To 1866
- - - Boundary of N. German Confederation, 1866
- —— Boundary of the German Empire, 1871-1918

North Sea

Baltic Sea

DENMARK

SCHLESWIG-HOLSTEIN

Lubeck

MECKLENBURG

OLDENBURG

Hamburg
Bremen

HANOVER

Weser

Memel

EAST PRUSSIA

Danzig

WEST PRUSSIA

POMERANIA

Stettin

Oder

Vistula

RUSSIA

POSEN

BERLIN

Berlin

SILESIA

Breslau

SAXONY

Elbe

AUSTRIA

HOLLAND

WESTPHALIA

BRANDENBURG

Cologne

Rhine

RHINE PROV.

NASSAU

HESSE-DARMSTADT

THURINGIA

BAVARIA

Munich

Danube

BELGIUM

LUX.

PALAT-
INATE

WÜRTTEM-
BERG

BADEN

SWITZERLAND

LORRAINE
(1871)

ALSACE

FRANCE

Sedan
1870

0   100   200 miles

From *History of Western Civilization: A Handbook*, 6th edition by William H. McNeill. Copyright 1986 by University of Chicago Press. Reprinted by permission.

Chapter III

THE AGE OF

NATIONALISM

AND IMPERIALISM

Figure 3.1 **Count Camillo di Cavour** (1810-1861). President of the Council of Ministers of the King of Sardinia. On steel by John Sartain after a photograph. This shrewd diplomat, acting on behalf of the King of Sardinia, was able to perform an almost impossible task—the unification of petty Italian states into the Kingdom of Italy. (Courtesy of The Library of Congress)

Figure 3.2 **Count Otto von Bismarck** (1815-1898). Devising three wars to achieve a unified Germany led by Prussia, this architect of German unification upset the balance of power in Europe. Under Bismarck, Germany became a strong military and economic power—a nation to take into account. (Courtesy of The Library of Congress)

THE UNIFICATION OF ITALY

Kingdom of Sardinia at the time of the Congress of Vienna, 1815

Territories acquired, 1859–1860

Territories acquired, 1860–1870

From *The Age of Nationalism and Reform, 1850-1890*, Second Edition by Norman Rich. Copyright (c) 1977, 1970 b
W.W. Norton & Company, Inc. Reprinted by permission of W.W. Norton & Company, Inc.

7

The Unification Of Italy And Germany

UNDERSTANDING Nationalism

What is nationalism?

Nationalism is a political idea that makes loyalty to the nation a fundamental value. The nation, whether existing or hoped for, is composed of people joined together by bonds of common language, culture, history, or, in some instances, experience of domination by others. Modern nationalism has its origins in the French Revolution and its aftermath. Nationalism helped to explain the success of the French revolutionary armies against various European coalitions. Nationalism also spread to those peoples impacted by the force of French arms. Thus in 1807-08, Johann Gottlieb Fichte (1762-1814) delivered his *Addresses to the German Nation,* urging the expelling of Napoleon from German territories. Another early German nationalist, who is often linked to Romanticism, was the philosopher Johann Gottfried von Herder (1744-1803). Herder was a cultural nationalist rather than a political nationalist. Ridiculing those German writers who aped the style of other peoples, he believed that every nation possessed a distinct folk spirit that has been developing over

Give some examples of the German proponents of nationalism in the late eighteenth and early nineteenth centuries.

How did nationalism in the second half of the nineteenth century differ from that of the first part of the century?

centuries. Individuals find their best natural expression through the use of their own distinctive national symbols. Before 1850, nationalism was often tied to liberalism. Giuseppe Mazzini (1805-1872) exemplified this link in his Young Italy movement, which sought to unify Italy through the creation of a republic based on popular support. Mazzini was active in the failed revolutions of 1848-49. Italy and Germany were to gain national unity in the last half of the nineteenth century through leaders who were considerably less hospitable to liberalism. Blood and iron rather than constitutional conventions produced their unification.

The nineteenth century was also an age of imperialism encouraged by national rivalries. European powers engaged in their second wave of colonialism. During the century, most of Africa was colonized with the British grabbing the largest number of colonies, followed by the French, Germans, Belgians, and Italians. The Portuguese hung on to their colonies from the first wave of European colonization, as did the Spaniards. As we will see in the last part of this chapter, almost the entire globe came to be under European domination.

Describe the political divisions of Italy prior to unification.

The Unification of Italy

The unification of Italy and Germany, in the last half of the nineteenth century, decisively changed the balance of power in Europe and the course of world history. Italy at mid-century was split into several parts. In the north, Austria had Lombardy and Venetia. To the west was the rival Kingdom of Sardinia-Piedmont, consisting of the mainland territories of Piedmont, Nice, and Savoy, plus the island of Sardinia. The Kingdom was ruled by King Victor Emmanuel II (1849-1861) from the Savoy dynasty. He was the only ruler from a native Italian family. South of Lombardy were the duchies of Parma, Modena, and Tuscany. In the middle of Italy, along both coasts, were the Papal States ruled by the Pope. South of the Papal States was the Kingdom of the Two Sicilies, consisting of Sicily and the mainland section forming the bottom half of the Italian boot.

Risorgimento

The groundwork for Italian unification was laid by a literary and political movement known as *Risorgimento,* or resurgence, which sought the resurrection of the Italian nation. A key figure in this movement was Giuseppe Mazzini (1805-1872), who began as a member of a secret revolutionary society, the Carbonari. Mazzini founded a new movement, Young Italy, which sought to create a unified Italian republic through a series of popular referendums. He encouraged national revolutions among other groups, such as the Irish and the Poles, and was a leader in the short-lived Roman Republic of 1849.

Giuseppe Garibaldi (1807-1882) was a disciple of Mazzini and a very able military leader. After participating with Mazzini in an abortive republican uprising against the King of Sardinia in 1834, Garibaldi gained fame for military exploits in South America. He returned to Italy in 1848 and fought first against the Austrians and then against the French. He put up a gallant but hopeless struggle to maintain the Roman Republic of 1849.

What was the *Risorgimento?*

Discuss the politics of Mazzini and Garibaldi.

How did Cavour differ from Mazzini?

The most successful leader of the *Risorgimento* movement was Camillo di Cavour (1810-1861). He was from a prominent Piedmontese family and a successful entrepreneur. In 1847, Cavour founded a liberal newspaper, *Il Risorgimento*. While Cavour favored constitutionalism and opposition to Austria, unlike Mazzini and Garibaldi he was not a republican. He favored the achievement of Italian unity under the royal house of Savoy. In 1852, he became prime minister of the Kingdom of Sardinia-Piedmont. The failure of the revolutions of 1848 and 1849 tended to discredit the schemes of Mazzini and Garibaldi and gave Cavour the opportunity to take the lead in seeking Italian unification.

Strategy

What reforms did Cavour introduce in Sardinia?

Cavour began by strengthening the Sardinian economy. He patronized the construction of highways, canals, docks, and railroads. He concluded trade treaties to increase commerce, reformed the credit system, and sought to limit the influence of the church. These efforts were calculated to make Sardinia a model state that its Italian neighbors would want to join.

Cavour realized that he would need the help of a major power to fight Austria, whose Italian possessions constituted the biggest obstacle to Italian unification. He had Sardinia join the side of Britain, France, and Turkey against Russia in the Crimean War (1853-56). The war did not involve any issues of national interest for Sardinia, but attendance at the peace conference following the war gave Cavour an opportunity to call big power attention to the issue of Italian unity.

The French Connection

Cavour determined that Sardinia would form an alliance with France against Austria. He saw the use of French troops as the best hope of pushing Austria out of the Italian peninsula. He succeeded in negotiating with Emperor Napoleon III (Louis Napoleon) the Pact of Plombières in July 1858. France agreed to join Sardinia in a war against Austria, providing the blame for starting the war could be put on Austria. If the war were won, Sardinia would get the Austrian possessions of Lombardy and Venetia. In turn, France would get Nice and Savoy from Sardinia. Italy would be reorganized as a confederation, with the Pope as President.

Louis Napoleon consented to such an agreement, not only to get Nice and Savoy which were on the French side of the Alps and long coveted by France, but for other reasons as well. The Bonaparte family was of Italian (Corsican) origin, and Louis Napoleon had been linked as a young man to the Italian unification movement. In attacking reactionary Austria, he could endear himself to French liberals at home. He may also have been persuaded by the Italian nationalist, Felice Orsini 1819-1858), who threw a bomb at Napoleon in January of 1858 for his failure to do more for the cause of Italian unity.

By encouraging revolutionaries and deserters in Austria's Italian territories and rejecting a related Austrian ultimatum, Cavour provoked Austria into an attack on Sardinia on April 29, 1859. This was the excuse France needed to join Sardinia in a war against Austria. Major battles were fought at Magenta (June 4, 1859) and Solferino (June 24, 1859). While both battles brought Austrian retreats, they were bloodier

What was Cavour's strategy to get Austria out of Italy?

Why did Napoleon III join in the fight against Austria?

Why did Napoleon III pull out of the war against Austria before all the goals had been met?

What territories had Sardinia gained before Garibaldi attacked the Kingdom of the Two Sicilies?

and less decisive than Napoleon III would have liked. Moreover, revolts in the central Italian states by people wanting to join Sardinia meant that Sardinia might actually grow to be a rival of France. Most menacing for France, Prussia and other German states were threatening to come to the aid of Austria. These factors led Napoleon III, without consulting his Sardinian allies, to sign an agreement with the Austrian Emperor, Francis Joseph (1848-1916), at Villafranca in July. The agreement gave most of Lombardy to France, who could then cede it to Sardinia. Austria kept Venetia, and the states of central Italy were restored to their former rulers.

The failure to obtain Venetia as agreed at Plombièrs so angered Cavour that he resigned as premier (he returned to office in January 1860). Sardinia did get Lombardy from France. The French did not dare to claim Nice and Savoy. The central Italian states of Romagna (which had been part of the Papal States), Parma, Modena, and Tuscany resisted restoration of their rulers and voted to join Sardinia. Napoleon and the returned Cavour negotiated an agreement whereby France acquiesced in the annexation of these states by Sardinia in return for finally receiving Nice and Savoy.

The Role of Garibaldi

The next episode in the story of Italian unification is truly extraordinary and romantic. Giuseppe Garibaldi, who fought the Austrians and French in 1848-1849, had returned to fight the Austrians in the war of 1859. Learning of the proposed giveaway of Nice (his birthplace) and Savoy to France, Garibaldi organized an army to protect these territories from the French. Cavour, fearing the consequences of antagonizing the French, diverted Garibaldi by finding him another mission. A revolt had broken out against Francis II (1859-1861), the King of the Two Sicilies. Cavour secretly persuaded Garibaldi to use his volunteers to support this revolt. Publicly, Cavour distanced himself from the scheme. Garibaldi's army of a thousand Red Shirts landed at Marsala in Sicily on May 11, 1860. Enjoying rapid success, Garibaldi captured Palermo, the capital of Sicily by the end of May. In late August, he crossed over to the mainland. Naples, the mainland capital, fell on September 7, 1860. Thousands had deserted from the royal Sicilian army to join Garibaldi. His attractive personality brought many other volunteers.

Cavour became concerned about Garibaldi's successes. He feared that Garibaldi might become a rival to the Sardinian King, Victor Emmanuel II, or provoke intervention by either the French or Austrians. He hastily had a Sardinian army attack the Papal States, defeating the Pope's forces. This Sardinian army joined Garibaldi for the final sweep against the Bourbon King of the Two Sicilies. Garibaldi nobly honored his previous pledge to support the Sardinian monarch. On March 17, 1861, the Kingdom of Italy was proclaimed, with Victor Emmanuel II as King. Cavour was not to serve the new country long. He died on June 6, 1861.

Completing the Kingdom of Italy

The only significant parts of the Italian peninsula not initially included in the new kingdom were Venetia, which was under the control of the Austrians, and Rome, which was under the Pope, who was still backed by French troops. In 1866, Italy joined Prussia in a war against Austria.

Evaluate Garibaldi's success.

When and how was the Kingdom of Italy created?

How did Italy acquire Venetia and Rome?

When the Prussians won, Italy's reward was Venetia. When, in 1870, French troops withdrew from Rome so they could be used to defend France against Prussia; Italian forces seized Rome, which became the capital of the kingdom. Italian unity had at last been obtained—more by diplomacy and astute timing than by military greatness.

The Unification of Germany

Background

Who deserves most credit for unifying Italy?

The Revolutions of 1848-49 had failed to create a constitutionally united Germany. The Prussian monarch, Frederick William IV, had refused the crown offered by the Frankfurt Assembly. He did come up with his own scheme for the unification of Germany, which involved the creation of a Prussian Union. Austria was unwilling to accept a united Germany dominated by Prussia. The Austrians forced a meeting at Olmütz in November 1850 at which the Prussians backed down and agreed to give up the Prussian Union. Prussian historians came to see this meeting as the Humiliation of Olmütz. The Prussians were considerably more successful in the operation of the Zollverein, a German customs union established in 1834 to foster freer trade. By 1854 only five German states, including Austria, were not in the Zollverein. Prussia's economic dominance in Germany was assured.

Political dominance was attained for Prussia by Otto von Bismarck (1815-1898), who became minister president of Prussia in 1862. On his father's side he was from the Prussian nobility, or Junkers. Bismarck was an extreme conservative who had held several diplomatic posts. He became prime minister at a time of constitutional crisis. William I (1861-1888) who had served as regent since 1858, became King of Prussia in 1861 upon his brother's death. The new king was at odds with the lower house of the legislature over funding for the military. The king wanted to build up his armed forces. For this he needed new taxes. The parliament refused to vote the new taxes. Bismarck decided to collect them anyhow, without parliamentary authorization. A loyal army backed the tax collectors, and the dutiful Prussian citizens paid their taxes. The liberal opposition in parliament was not prepared for an actual attempt at revolt. The king, with Bismarck's help, got his strengthened army.

A strong army was important to Bismarck, who is famed for making a speech in which he said that the great questions of the day would be decided by "blood and iron"[1] rather than by speeches or the votes of majorities. Bismarck consciously rejected liberal constitutionalism as exemplified by the Frankfurt Assembly. Following realist politics, he believed force was the best guarantee of success. He also had occasion to say that "the main thing is to make history, not to write it."[2] Bismarck was a conservative man of action willing to use force when necessary. He determined that war was the best route to German unification. Through war he would exclude Austria, Prussia's only serious rival for leadership in a united Germany. He would also use a war against France to arouse German patriotism and gain the support of the smaller German states, especially the Catholic states in the south, who were suspicious of Protestant Prussia.

Discuss the background and character of Bismarck.

Why did the Prussian king need Bismarck?

The Danish War of 1864

What was the background to the Danish War of 1864?

Schleswig and Holstein were two duchies that were personal possessions of the Danish king, but were not an integral part of Denmark. In fact, Holstein, the southernmost duchy, was actually a part of the German Confederation. The population of the two duchies was a mixture of German and Danish-speaking peoples. German national feeling made the integration of these duchies into Denmark extremely difficult. Indeed an international treaty that specifically forbade their inclusion in Denmark had been signed in 1852.

In 1863, the Danes got a new constitution that seemed to anticipate the incorporation of Schleswig as a part of Denmark. This provoked an angry nationalistic response among Germans. There was a demand that the German Confederation go to war to take the two duchies from the Danish king by force. However, Bismarck did not want to act through the German Confederation, which was dominated by Austria. Instead, he persuaded Austria to join Prussia in an ultimatum demanding the rescinding of the Danish constitution. When their demand was not met (as Bismarck had anticipated), the two powers attacked and overwhelmed Denmark. By the Convention of Gastein, signed August 14, 1865, Austria and Prussia agreed to maintain joint sovereignty over the two duchies. Prussia was to administer Schleswig, the northernmost territory, and Austria was to administer Holstein, which was right below it. Since Austria was separated from Holstein by Prussian territory, it would be easy enough, at some future time, for Prussia to make Austria's role in Holstein untenable.

What were the terms of the Convention of Gastein?

The Austro-Prussian War of 1866

Bismarck had set Austria up for a future war to determine which country would lead a united Germany. Bismarck took care to isolate Austria diplomatically from the major Continental powers. He had already gained the favor of the Russians in 1863 by supporting them during a Polish revolt. Austria had supported the rebels. In October 1865, Bismarck met with Napoleon III of France. He gained Napoleon's assurance of neutrality in return for a vague promise of territory along the Rhine. In April 1866, Bismarck concluded an alliance with Italy. If war broke out within three months, Italy was to join Prussia in battle against Austria. As a reward, Italy was promised Venetia.

With Austria effectively isolated, Bismarck was ready for war. In June 1866, when Austria sought to reorganize Holstein, Bismarck found his pretext. He declared that Austria had violated the Convention of Gastein and sent Prussian troops into Holstein. Austria persuaded most of the German Confederation to join in a war against Prussia. Everyone had miscalculated the strength of the refurbished Prussian army. With new weapons, breech-loading needle guns (the Austrians were still using muzzle loaders), new tactics, and an effective rail system for the transportation of troops and supplies, victory became a cinch for the Prussians, who won a decisive victory at Sadowa on July 3, 1866. Peace came so quickly that it is often called the Seven Weeks' War. Bismarck's terms were relatively lenient. He did not want to jeopardize a future relationship with Austria, or prolong the war so as to give France or Russia the opportunity to intervene. Austria was excluded from Germany. The German states north of the Main River

How did Bismarck setup Austria?

Why did the Austrians lose the Austro-Prussian War of 1866?

What was the outcome of the Austro-Prussian War of 1866?

were organized into a North German Confederation, with the King of Prussia as President and represented by a Chancellor (Bismarck). There was to be a two-chamber legislature, with the lower house, or Reichstag, elected by universal male suffrage. Prussia directly annexed the territories of Schleswig, Holstein, Hanover, Hesse-Cassel, Nassau and the city of Frankfurt. The Catholic southern German states were to remain free, but agreed to join militarily with Prussia in the event of a war with France. Italy, which had lost on land and sea against Austria, got Venetia as promised.

The Franco-Prussian War of 1870-71

What grievances did the French have against the Prussians?

France did not get any compensation for Prussian gains in the Austro-Prussian War, as it had hoped. Even France's request for territories was used by Bismarck to first frighten the southern German states, and later England. A new source of friction between France and Prussia arose in 1868. A revolt had broken out in Spain, and the Spanish throne was offered to Prince Leopold of Hohenzollern-Sigmaringen (1835-1905), a distant relative of the Prussian king on the Catholic side of the family. The French, not surprisingly, were opposed to Prince Leopold's candidacy. They did not want to see a Hohenzollern ruler to their south in Spain, while having a Hohenzollern ruler to their east in the expanded Prussia. Bismarck supported the Hohenzollern candidacy for some of the same reasons France opposed it. At the very least, in the event of a Franco-Prussian war, several French regiments would have to be left for security along the Spanish border.

Much to Bismarck's chagrin, it appeared that the French would prevail with the

Prussian king, William I. They had appealed to William as head of the family to get Leopold to withdraw for the sake of peace. William agreed and got Leopold's father to withdraw his son's candidacy. The French ambassador, Vincent Benedetti (1817-1900), visited the Prussian king at a health spa, Bad Ems, and pushed further. The ambassador asked the king to write what was in effect a letter of apology stating that he would never agree to the renewal of a Hohenzollern candidacy for the throne of Spain. The king refused to write the letter and refused to see Benedetti again. He sent a telegram to Bismarck, who was in Berlin, explaining what had happened. Bismarck edited the telegram to make it appear that there had been a very curt and insulting exchange between the king and the ambassador. He then released the edited version of the EMS DISPATCH to the press. This action had the desired effect. Both German and French national honor was now at stake. A few days later, on July 15, 1870, France declared war on Prussia.

Prussia fought an isolated France. Bismarck released to the English press a document showing Napoleon's desire for Belgium during the Austro-Prussian War of 1866. Austria was still trying to recoup from the same war. Italy saw an opportunity to get Rome, which was still protected by French troops. The southern German states joined Prussia in the attack. Several German armies invaded France. When a French force became trapped at Metz, a second French army moved to relieve it. Instead, the second army was surrounded at Sedan. On September 2, 1870 that army surrendered. Emperor Napoleon III himself was captured. Paris was not taken until January 28, 1871.

In contrast with the lenient treatment of the Austrians after the Austro-Prussian War, the French were treated much more

Was William I as militant as Bismarck?

What was the Ems Dispatch?

Contrast the victorious Prussia's treatment of France with its treatment of Austria.

harshly. Even before the surrender of Paris, the Hall of Mirrors at Versailles, a French national monument, was used on January 18, 1871 as the site for proclaiming a new German Empire, with William I of Prussia as Emperor. The new state included northern Germany and southern Germany, with the notable exception of Austria. At last, Germany had been united on Prussian terms. The constitutional arrangement for the German Empire mirrored those first used in the North German Confederation. There was a parliament with a lower house, or Reichstag, elected by universal male suffrage. The empire's ministers were responsible to the emperor, rather than the parliament. Since the emperor was the hereditary Prussian king, the constitution assured Prussian dominance in German affairs, and the strength of the new state magnified Prussian influence on a global basis. France had to give up Alsace and Lorraine to Germany, pay an indemnity of five billion francs, and sustain a German army of occupation until the fine was paid.

What, for the historian, was the most important consequence of the unification of Germany and of Italy?

Consequences

The unifications of Italy and Germany truly changed the course of history. Both Italy and Germany had political, imperial, and economic ambitions that upset the status quo. France was bitter after the Franco-Prussian War and obsessed with revenge. When Bismarck departed the political scene in 1890, German foreign policy fell into much less capable hands. There developed a pair of rival alliance systems setting the stage for World War I. The balance of both political and economic power in Europe was altered. The two world wars of this century can be tied to the rise of a united Germany. Today, Germany is the most important economic power in Europe and is very likely to be the dominant economic force in a united Europe of the future.

There were indirect consequences of unification. The Austrian Empire changed dramatically after Austria's defeat in the Austro-Prussian War of 1866. In 1867, the Dual Monarchy of Austria-Hungary was created. The Hungarians, especially the Magyars, attained control over internal affairs within Hungary. The Germans were dominant within the Austrian part of the empire. Hungary and Austria had a common foreign policy and a common ruler. In France, the monarchists could not agree among themselves on who should replace the discredited Napoleon III. The consequence of this disagreement was the birth of the Third French Republic by default.

The Papacy was also deeply affected by these events. The Pope, who had lost Rome and all temporal power, considered himself to be a prisoner in the Vatican (the papal court). It was not until the signing of the Lateran Treaty with Mussolini in 1929 that the Pope regained sovereignty over territory in Italy. The Vatican City State recognized in 1929 was a small enclave in Rome, in contrast to the Papal States, which had their origins in the Donation of King Pepin in the eighth century, and which had eventually extended clear across the central portion of the Italian peninsula. It is an interesting coincidence that in the very year, 1870, that the Pope lost Rome, he reaffirmed his spiritual authority with the declaration of papal infallibility at the First Vatican Council.

How did Austria change as a result of the Austro-Prussian War?

What was the impact on the Papacy?

Figure 3.3 **Surrender of Napoleon III on September 2, 1870.** With his army surrounded at Sedan, France's Napoleon III surrenders his sword to Count Otto von Bismarck and General Helmuth von Moltke (1800-1891). This Franco-Prussian War of 1870-71 caused the lasting enmity of France against a

8

Domestic Politics and Cultural Trends in Europe before World War I

DOMESTIC POLITICS

Who was Disraeli? What policies did he favor?

Great Britain: 1850-1914

Britain in the latter part of the nineteenth century was dominated by two political parties. The leader of the Conservative Party (formerly the Tories) was Benjamin Disraeli (1804-1881). Disraeli was an ardent defender of British imperial interests and the continued union of Ireland with England and Scotland. He served as prime minister in 1868, and from 1874 to 1880. The Liberal Party (formerly the Whigs) was led by William Gladstone (1809-1898). Gladstone was a moralist bent on reforms. Unlike Disraeli, Gladstone had supported the repeal of the Corn Laws in 1846, which resulted in cheaper grain for the masses but hurt the interests of the landed gentry. He was prime minister in the periods 1868-1874, 1884-1885, 1886, 1892-1894. Much of Gladstone's time in office was preoccupied with electoral reform and obtaining home rule for Ireland.

What party did Gladstone lead? What were his preoccupations?

What measures were taken to extend voting privileges?

How were Parliament and education reformed?

Earlier mention was made of the Reform Bill of 1832, which got rid of many rotten boroughs. The act only extended the suffrage to an eighth of the adult male population. After the Liberals had failed, it was the Conservatives, under Disraeli, who succeeded in getting the Second Reform Bill passed in 1867. The Conservatives hoped to enlarge their base of voters. The act added about a million eligible voters. Over a third of adult males could vote, including most home owners and city workers.

In 1884, under Gladstone, another reform measure extended the franchise to an additional two million males, including most agricultural workers. In 1885 election districts were redistributed to more closely conform to actual population. It was not until 1918 that the right to vote in Britain was extended to women over thirty (the age was lowered to twenty-one in 1928). A vigorous women's suffrage movement and the important role women played on the home front in World War I were factors in getting women the right to vote.

Another important change in the English political structure took place with the passage of the Parliament Act of 1911. The act was proposed because the House of Lords had been resisting progressive income and inheritance taxes. The threat that the king would create enough new lords to guarantee approval, induced the lords to approve the act. This legislation provided that the House of Lords would have no power to amend or reject a money bill and could only delay other public bills for a period of two years. With the passage of the Parliament Act and the granting of the suffrage to women, England was more fully a democracy and a model of parliamentary government for the world.

Educational reforms followed electoral reforms. Free elementary education for children ages five to ten became mandatory with the passage of the Elementary Education Act of 1870. Later, children were required to stay in school until they are sixteen. The Education Act of 1902 recognized responsibility to provide free secondary education. The English also have "public" schools, but these are elite schools for the upper strata of society.

England was considerably less successful in solving the so-called "Irish Question." The Irish had many grievances. In 1801, as a reaction to the United Irish revolt of 1798, the British insisted that the Irish give up their separate parliament and accept incorporation into the United Kingdom. Because of the great potato famine of 1845-47, a million Irish died and another million emigrated. The British, given their anti-Irish Catholic and pro free enterprise prejudices, were quite hesitant to give relief. The Liberals under Gladstone were more sympathetic. There was also an uprising of the Fenian Brotherhood in 1867 to urge the reformers on. In 1869, Irish Catholics were freed from the obligation to provide financial support for the Anglican Church of Ireland. In 1870, provision was made that evicted tenants should be compensated for the improvements they made on the landlord's property. But the Irish agitated for more, particularly for HOME RULE, or the right to have a separate Irish parliament. Charles Stewart Parnell (1846-1891) and other Irish representatives in the British House of Commons began a campaign of parliamentary obstruction to force the passage of a measure creating an Irish parliament. Gladstone attempted in 1886 to pass a Home Rule bill, but the measure was defeated. Several other attempts at a Home Rule bill were also

What grievances did the Irish Catholics have against the English?

What was Home Rule?

Why did many of the inhabitants of Ulster object to Home Rule?

defeated. It was not until 1914, on the eve of World War I, that a Home Rule measure was finally passed in the British parliament. When the Protestant Ulstermen made clear their vehement objections, implementation of the measure was postponed for the duration of the war. With the Easter Rising of 1916 and subsequent events, demands for Home Rule were replaced with demands for independence—which was obtained in successive stages for most of Ireland, with the exception of Ulster.

France: 1850-1914

What were some of the accomplishments of Napoleon III's rule?

Louis Napoleon had been elected president of the Second French Republic in 1848. In December of 1851, he arranged for a plebiscite that gave the president the power to draw up a new constitution. Napoleon's new constitution provided for the establishment of the Second French Empire. He became Napoleon III (supposedly Napoleon Bonaparte's son, who never ruled, had the right to the title of "Napoleon II"). The Second Empire lasted from 1852-1870.

The French Empire of the 1850's was authoritarian rather than democratic. Napoleon III undertook an extensive building program in and around Paris. He found in Baron Georges Haussman (1809-1891) a city planner who could complete a massive public works program—building wide boulevards, railroad stations, etc. Not so incidentally, the widened roads made it much more difficult for revolutionaries to construct barricades as had happened in 1789, 1830, and 1848. He also created a mortgage bank, the Crédit Mobilier, to encourage large industrial undertakings. Napoleon negotiated a lowering of tariff barriers to make French enterprises more competitive. This was not particularly popular, and to gain new support he liberalized his regime in the 1860's, giving more budgetary control to the legislature.

Napoleon generally lacked foreign policy shrewdness. His contributions to unifying Italy gained little for France. During the American Civil War, he sent French troops to Mexico to support a Hapsburg (Archduke Maximilian) as Emperor of Mexico. When the Civil War ended, the U.S. forced him to withdraw the troops, leaving Maximilian to be killed by the Mexicans. Indeed, his foreign policy ultimately did in Napoleon III. As we saw, his defeat in the Franco-Prussian War led to the collapse of the Second Empire in 1870.

The Second French Empire was replaced by the Third French Republic. The sentiment for a republic was strong in Paris, but not in the countryside. When a constitutional assembly met, the majority were monarchists. Since the assembly was split among Orleanist and Bourbon supporters, the republic was the result of the failure of the monarchists to reach an agreement.

It was only over time that the republic built up real support. One of the incidents that helped the republicans was the BOULANGER CRISIS. Georges Boulanger (1837-1891) was a popular general who attracted the support of the monarchists and frightened the republicans, who thought they saw another Napoleon on the rise. The republican government dismissed him from the army. He then ran for political office and won several elections. On January 27, 1889, he won an election in Paris and the expectation among supporters and enemies was that he would use the momentum to initiate a coup. Instead he spent the night with his mistress. When he heard he might be arrested

Describe Louis Napoleon's major weakness.

What was the Boulanger Crisis? How did it help the Third French Republic?

What was the Dreyfus Affair?

for treason, he fled to Belgium. Two years later, he committed suicide at the grave of his mistress. The whole affair was a disaster that served to discredit the monarchists and the military.

The Catholic Church, another anti-republican body in France, as well as the military lost prestige in the DREYFUS AFFAIR. Alfred Dreyfus (1859-1935) was a Jewish army captain who served on the French general staff. He was falsely accused of spying for Germany. In late 1894 he was tried and convicted of treason. Stripped of his rank, he was sent to Devil's Island in French Guiana for life imprisonment.

After Dreyfus's imprisonment, the leaks to the Germans continued and evidence began to point the finger at another man, Major Ferdinand Esterhazy, who was in financial distress. It was with great difficulty that the case was reopened and Esterhazy brought to trial in 1898. Despite the preponderance of evidence against him, Esterhazy was acquitted and the dignity of the military preserved. In reaction to the acquittal, Émile Zola (1849-1902), a novelist, published an open letter to the president of the republic on January 13, 1898. In the letter, he exposed those on the army's general staff who were involved in the cover up. Each paragraph naming those responsible began with the French phrase *J'accuse*, "I accuse." Zola had to flee to England to avoid imprisonment. Then it was discovered that a document used to obtain Dreyfus's conviction was a forgery. The forger admitted his guilt. Under these circumstances, Dreyfus was retried by court-martial in 1899 and again found guilty. The army did not want to lose face and admit its mistake. Dreyfus was granted a presidential pardon the same year. In 1906, the court-martial was finally voided by order of a higher court, and Dreyfus was returned to the

What role did Émile Zola play in the Affair?

army with the rank of major. But it was not until 1995 that the army publicly admitted the innocence of Dreyfus.

The whole affair discredited the army, the anti-Semites, the Catholics, and the monarchists who were among the anti-Dreyfusards. The affair contributed to the movement for the separation of church and state, which was achieved in December of 1905 by a French law renouncing the Concordat of 1801 that Napoleon I had signed with the pope.

How did the Dreyfus Affair affect church/state relations?

Russia: 1850-1914

Russia experienced significant military defeats and attempts at internal reform in the period prior to World War I. The Crimean War of 1853-56 was one in a series of struggles between Russia and the Ottoman Empire. What was unusual in this case was that Turkey found allies in two of the leading states of western Europe: Britain and France. Neither side conducted brilliant military campaigns. This was the war in which the militarily disastrous *Charge of the Light Brigade* was immortalized by Lord Tennyson. Russia's opponents won, and Russian ambitions in the Balkans and the Black Sea area were checked for a while.

A new czar, Alexander II (1855-1881), came to the throne in 1855. With the defeat in war, he was more open to domestic reform than his predecessors had been. A major accomplishment was the freeing of the serfs on March 3, 1861. Russia's agricultural land was divided between the landed nobility and the former serfs, who got about half the land. The land did not go directly to individual peasants. Rather it became the collective

What was Alexander II's greatest reform?

What problems remained after freeing the serfs?

Did Nicholas II create a democracy? Explain.

property of the village, or *mir*. Installment payments for the land had to be made by the village to the government, which had compensated the former noble owners. Because of his indebtedness, the peasant was not free to simply walk away from the village. Nevertheless, 20 million peasants had been legally freed from their masters. Vast labor reserves would become available for the modernization and industrialization of Russia. The judiciary was reformed; and the zemstvos, elected institutions of local government with limited powers, were introduced.

The reforms did not produce a western-style democracy. More radical demands by intellectuals were rejected, and the radicals were suppressed. The would-be reformers turned to terrorism. After several unsuccessful attempts, they assassinated Czar Alexander II, on March 13, 1881. Alexander III (1881-1894) was more conservative than his father. Industrial development, however, actually accelerated under Count Sergei Witte (1849-1915), the minister of finance from 1892-1903.

The last Russian czar was Nicholas II (1894-1917). It was partly to distract attention from internal problems that Nicholas became embroiled in the Russo-Japanese War of 1904-05. The war was a major victory for the Japanese. It set off widespread violence in Russia. The agitation accelerated after a group of peaceful protesters marching before the czar's palace in St. Petersburg were shot on Bloody Sunday, January 22, 1905. Sailors mutinied and a general strike was called. The Revolution of 1905 forced Czar Nicholas to offer concessions. He allowed the creation of a Duma or legislative assembly. Representatives to the Duma had very limited powers and were elected under a very restricted suffrage. Government ministers were responsible to the czar, rather than to the Duma.

Even so, Nicholas II was rather uncooperative, actually dismissing the first two Dumas. The Duma, as an institution, survived with minimal power. As World War I approached, Russia was a nation with large, unresolved internal problems.

Austria-Hungary: 1867-1914

The defeat of Austria in the Austro-Prussian War led to the creation of the Dual Monarchy of Austria-Hungary in 1867. The Hapsburg monarch, Francis Joseph (1848-1916), was the single ruler of both parts of the empire. There were common imperial ministries for foreign policy, war, and finance, and also a common postal system and a common currency. In other respects, the two parts functioned as separate countries with their own constitutions, parliaments, and government offices for domestic affairs. German was the administrative language of the Austrian section, while Magyar was the administrative language of the Hungarian section.

The fundamental problem with the arrangement was that within Austria German speakers made up less than half the population, while in Hungary Magyar was similarly the mother tongue of about forty-seven percent of the people. The Austrian government tended to be conciliatory, albeit in fits and starts. A diversity of languages was tolerated and, by 1907, universal manhood suffrage was granted. In Hungary, the Magyars took the opposite tactic. They tried to force Magyarization upon the whole populace. Because of this policy of suppressing the use of other languages, the Magyars did not dare permit universal manhood suffrage in their king-

How was the Dual Monarchy of Austria-Hungary supposed to function?

What was the most fundamental problem of Austria-Hungary?

How successful was Austria-Hungary in dealing with its problems?

dom. When World War I came, only about twenty-five percent of the adult males in Hungary had the right to vote. Neither policy satisfied ethnic minorities. The nationalities issue was the greatest problem in both parts of the empire. Czechs, Romanians, Serbs, Croats, and other nationalities wanted independence, which would require the dissolution of the empire. Strangely, Austria-Hungary became interested in expanding in the Balkans at the expense of the dissolving Ottoman Empire. Expansion was seen as one means of distracting people from the internal discontent. In 1908, Austria annexed Bosnia-Herzegovina, which Serbia also desired. This helped set the stage for the chain of events that led to the First World War.

Germany: 1871-1914

The German Empire was guided by Bismarck as Chancellor from 1871 to 1890. The constitution made the emperor and the chancellor, who was responsible to the emperor rather than to the legislature, the driving organs of imperial policy. Nevertheless, Bismarck maneuvered for the support of the lower house of parliament, the Reichstag, which was elected by universal manhood suffrage.

What was the *Kulturkampf*?

In 1871, Bismarck began a series of anti-Catholic measures known as *Kulturkampf*, or cultural struggle. These measures assumed that Catholics, seen as loyal to a now infallible pope, might not be loyal to the new empire. The Jesuits were expelled, and many Catholic bishops were arrested. By 1878, Bismarck had some second thoughts. Catholics might not be such a danger to the state after all. More importantly, he needed the support of conservative Catholics in the

Center Party for new economic and political policies. He adopted a protective tariff, which alienated the Liberals. He outlawed the German Social Democratic Party, a moderate socialist group. As part of his anti-socialist campaign, he initiated extensive social welfare legislation. In the period 1883-1889, workers were given health, accident, and old-age insurance. This was long before laborers in other industrialized nations received comparable benefits. (In the U.S. comprehensive social benefits were only introduced in the 1930's, with the coming of the New Deal.)

In 1888, Emperor William II (1888-1918) came to the throne. He disagreed with Bismarck regarding both the anti-socialist laws and foreign policy. In 1890, William II dismissed Bismarck and, with the help of several less able chancellors, became the chief maker of German public policy. He did try to reach out to the masses, but he was not tolerant of democracy. He stoutly resisted constitutional revisions that would have made the chancellor responsible to the Reichstag. Most importantly, William abandoned Bismarck's policy of isolating France, while also managing to antagonize Britain with his desire for naval equality. These policies directly contributed to the creation of the hostile international environment that precipitated World War I.

How did Bismarck deal with the political left in Germany?

What policy changes did William II introduce?

CULTURAL TRENDS

What was Romanticism?

Romanticism

Romanticism was a cultural movement prominent in the latter part of the eighteenth and the first half of the nineteenth century. In contrast to the rationalism of the Enlightenment, Romanticism stressed feeling, the unique characteristics of the individual, and the importance of genius. Though Romanticism differed from country to country, the proponents of this movement tended to reject deism in favor of revealed religion, and to glory in the achievements of the Middle Ages rather than those of classical Greece and Rome. Praise for nature and nation were characteristic of the Romantics.

Name some Romantics in English literature. What did they write about?

In literature, the English Romantics are represented by the poets William Wordsworth (1770-1850) and Samuel Taylor Coleridge (1772-1834). Together they published *Lyrical Ballads* in 1798. Coleridge is also remembered for the *Rime of the Ancient Mariner*, about a sailor cursed for killing a friendly bird, the albatross; only after he repents is his ship saved. The poem emphasizes reverence for all things God has created. Sir Walter Scott (1771-1832), a Scotsman, is known for his romantic novels. The Waverley series were about Scotland, while *Ivanhoe* glorifies the chivalric ideal of the Middle Ages. Mary Wollstonecraft Shelley (1797-1851), daughter of Mary Wollstonecraft and wife of the romantic poet Percy Shelley, gave us *Frankenstein*.

The most important work of the German writer, Johann Wolfgang von Goethe (1749-1832) is the dramatic poem *Faust*, about a man who sold his soul to the devil in exchange for greater knowledge. Goethe contributed to the Romantic movement with his novel *The Sorrows of Young Werther* (1774). The story, told with great sentimentality, is about a young man in love with someone else's wife. The tension between individual satisfaction and societal requirements leads to his suicide after they part company. The French romantic Victor Hugo (1802-1885) wrote plays, novels, and poetry. His novel, *The Hunchback of Notre Dame*, contrasts the selfless love of the deformed bell ringer Quasimodo for the gypsy Esmeralda with the dishonorable love of a cathedral cleric.

The Romantic movement also found expression in music and painting. Among the musicians associated with Romanticism are the Austrian Franz Schubert (1797-1828) and the French composer Louis Hector Berlioz (1803-1869). Such geniuses as the German Richard Wagner (1813-1883) and the Russian composer Peter Illich Tchaikovsky (1840-1893), whose careers stretch into the late nineteenth century, were also influenced by Romanticism.

The French painter Eugene Delacroix (1798-1863) idealized death and the struggle for freedom. "Ruins of Missolonghi" (Musée des Beaux-Arts, Bordeaux) commemorates the Greek struggle for independence and "Liberty Leading the People" (Louvre, Paris) celebrates the French Revolution of 1830. The Englishman Joseph Mallord William Turner (1775-1851) is famed for his landscapes and seascapes (in profusion at the Tate Gallery, London), which capture subtle

Mention some examples of Romanticism in German and French literature.

Give examples of Romanticism in music and painting.

What are the characteristics of conservatism as a political philosophy?

Was nineteenth century conservatism particularly democratic?

What conservative advocate wrote *Reflections on the French Revolution?*

nuances of light and color in nature. Two of his over 300 paintings are *The Slave Ship* and *Keelmen Heaving Coals by Moonlight.*

Conservatism

Conservatism is a political philosophy that seeks to preserve existing institutions and established beliefs. Believing that the costs of rapid, radical change often outweigh the benefits, conservatives support evolution rather than revolution. The conservatism of the nineteenth century was based on a reaction to the upheaval of the French Revolution. Like romanticism, conservatism rejected the rationalism of the Enlightenment. Individuals and society were seen as too complex to be adequately explained by the theories of the Philosophes.

Conservatives characteristically believed that the only legitimate sources of political authority are God and history. They rejected the notion of a social contract, as found in Locke and Rousseau, to convey political authority. Neither individuals nor the people as a whole give their authority to form a government. Democracy is to be distrusted; society is a delicate organism whose organs should not be cut off or reshaped at the whim of popular votes. The traditions and institutions of society have been created by past generations and should be passed on intact to future generations.

A leading proponent of conservatism was the Anglo-Irish writer and statesman Edmund Burke (1729-1797). His *Reflections on the French Revolution* (1790) blames the Revolution on the mistaken doctrines of the philosophes and on the ambitions of power hungry politicians. Burke denounced the

THE AGE OF NATIONALISM AND IMPERIALISM

tyranny of the multitude and rejected the democratic notion that all votes should count equally. This was Jacobin democracy, which failed to recognize the natural aristocracy of large property owners. According to Burke, preference based on noble birth is "neither unnatural, nor unjust, nor impolitic."[3] He saw the execution of Marie Antoinette as a horrible example of what happens when gallantry and chivalry are gone.

Burke thought people capable of acting wildly and irrationally. Over time, society developed traditions and institutions, such as the church and the monarchy, to contain these passions. The best of these traditions and institutions should be conserved. Change should come only gradually, to allow people time to adjust.

Edmund Burke, at one point in his career, represented the industrial city of Bristol in western England. He rejected the idea that he should follow instructions from the people of the city in deciding how to vote in the House of Commons. In 1774, he actually gave a speech to his constituents saying that, though their wishes would have great weight with him, he reserved the right to use his own mature judgment and enlightened conscience when voting. He saw Parliament not as a congress of representatives from different districts, but as a deliberative body that must be faithful to the interests of the nation as a whole. The ideals were certainly noble, even if they went against the democratic tide that industrialization brought with it. In 1780, Burke chose to stand for a safe seat in quieter Yorkshire, rather than face almost certain defeat in Bristol.

Summarize Burke's arguments against the radicalism of the French Revolution.

Do you agree or disagree with Burke's idea that a legislature ought to be more of a deliberative than a representative body? Explain.

Chapter Three   211

Define liberalism as a political philosophy. Discuss its origins.

Liberalism

Liberalism is a political philosophy that emphasizes individual freedom and well-being. The liberalism of the eighteenth and much of the nineteenth centuries stressed protecting the individual from oppressive government restraints. Early sources of liberalism include the ideas of John Locke, Adam Smith, and the French philosophes, who said that humans have certain rights government should protect. Influential lists of these rights are found in the United States' Bill of Rights (the first ten amendments to the U. S. Constitution passed by Congress in 1789 and ratified by December 1791) and in the Declaration of the Rights of Man and the Citizen (passed by the French National Assembly in 1789). To protect such rights, government must be checked. Adherence to a written constitution, the election of representatives who could give their consent to the laws, and the separation of the powers of government among different branches are all means of safeguarding individual rights from arbitrary government interference.

In what sense were Malthus and Ricardo liberals?

One view of liberalism was found in the classical economics of Thomas Malthus (1766-1834) and David Ricardo (1772-1823). In his essay on the *Principle of Population* (1798 and revised in 1803), Malthus argued that the population would increase geometrically, while the means of subsistence would only increase arithmetically. This Anglican clergyman thought there would be little sense in raising the wages of the poor, since they would only have more children. It would be far better if the poor learned the discipline of sexual abstinence. His friend, David Ricardo, took up the population ideas of Malthus in developing his own notion of an iron law of wages. In his *Principles of Political Economy and Taxation* (1817), Ricardo argued that it did no good to give higher wages to workers. They would only have more children. This would increase the supply of labor further. Consequently, in accord with the laws of supply and demand, wages would come back down as more workers competed for the available jobs. This line of reasoning supported the freedom of capitalists, without government interference, to offer whatever wages market conditions warranted.

Jeremy Bentham (1748-1832) made an interesting attempt to change the Lockean rationale for government, which had been based on the preservation of natural rights. Bentham, who was seeking legal reforms, argued that the basis of law should not be natural rights which are abstractions, but a practical calculus of utility—law ought to provide the greatest happiness for the greatest number of people. This principle made Bentham and his followers far more open to changes supporting the happiness of the majority, than Burke who favored the stability of the established law and institutions.

John Stuart Mill (1806-1873) considered himself to be a utilitarian. Indeed his father, James Mill, had been a close associate of Bentham. In 1859, the younger Mill published an essay, *On Liberty*, in which he argued that government had no right to interfere with the liberty of any person whose actions did not harm another. A dissenter holding opinions unpopular with the majority must be allowed the free expression of his convictions. Mill is also remembered for his work, *The Subjection of Women* (1869), in which he argued that the legal subordination of women to men was wrong, and that women should enjoy complete equality with men, including the right to vote. Mill, how-

What was the iron law of wages?

What were the contributions of John Stuart Mill to liberal thinking?

How do Alexis de Tocqueville and John Stuart Mill differ from present day democrats?

How does the liberalism of Thomas Hill Green differ from earlier liberalism?

ever, could not bring himself to accept the principle of one person, one vote for the uneducated masses. He favored in *Considerations on Representative Government* (1861) a form of plural voting that gave preference to intellectuals over workers.

The Frenchman Alexis de Tocqueville (1805-1859), had recognized earlier, in his *Democracy in America* (1835), that inevitably Europe's old, aristocratic institutions would give way to more democratic ones, as was happening in the United States. De Tocqueville, like John Stuart Mill, who was influenced by his work, feared the possible tyranny of the majority. It was later in the century that the modern liberals found a voice in the English idealist philosopher Thomas Hill Green (1836-1882). Green was one of those who accepted government action in favor of the masses, who had been enfranchised as a consequence of industrialization. Classic liberals, such as Ricardo, did not believe government should interfere in contracts, such as those between employer and employee concerning wages and working conditions. Green and his followers argued that, given his or her fundamental inequality, the employee was not truly free to accept or reject a position offering low wages. Government should step in to protect the mass of the people from the occasional inequities of the market place. The state could play a positive role by championing wage and hour laws, the right to form unions, unemployment insurance, decent housing, etc.

The modern liberalism of the late nineteenth and twentieth centuries found government intervention to be a means of freeing the poor from conditions that prevent their full development as individuals and citizens. In the United States, when one speaks of liberal politics, one means the politics of *modern liberalism*. U.S. conservatives are not only indebted to Edmund Burke, but to such classic or old liberals as John Locke, Adam Smith, and even, some would argue, the likes of David Ricardo.

What do the terms "liberalism" and "conservatism" mean in the context of contemporary American politics?

Socialism

The rise of socialism as an ideology was discussed in Chapter Two. During the second half of the nineteenth century and throughout the twentieth century, socialism remained a powerful belief system that challenged both capitalism and democratic liberalism. It helped to mitigate the evils of the industrial revolution and spurred the growth of democracy based on universal suffrage. Labor unions, which formed throughout the industrialized world, were partially indebted to socialist ideas. In Germany, France, and Great Britain, organized labor formed its own political parties and began to contest for power within the political arena. Those who gave up the revolutionary rhetoric of Karl Marx and concentrated on legislative reforms through the democratic process came to be called revisionists. Revisionist social democratic parties succeeded gradually in improving the working conditions of the industrial proletariat. Only in Russia, and only as a consequence of military defeat in World War I, did Marxism triumph in 1917.

How does the socialism of the revisionists differ from the ideas of Karl Marx?

The Theory of Evolution

The last half of the nineteenth century witnessed profound changes in the intellectual outlook of Europeans. The idea perhaps

What led Darwin to the theory of evolution?

most responsible for stimulating these changes was the theory of evolution developed by Charles Darwin (1809-1882). In the 1830's, Darwin had observed the adaptation of finches on the Galapagos Islands off the Pacific coast of South America. The birds had developed different sized beaks and other characteristics depending on what they ate and on the geographical distance between flocks. In 1859, he published *On the Origin of Species by Means of Natural Selection,* which propounded the theory of evolution. In this book, he argued that there were more organisms born in a species than could survive. This brought a struggle for survival within a species and between different species. There were variations within members of a species that made some better fitted than others to survive in a particular environment. (They might have longer beaks or whatever.) These members survived and passed on the variations to their offspring. Over time, by this process of natural selection there evolved new species, while less adapted species died out. In 1871, Darwin published *The Descent of Man.* He applied evolution to human beings, arguing that humankind descended from anthropoid apes.

Why were Darwin's ideas controversial?

Darwin's ideas were both influential and controversial. Evolution appeared to contradict the biblical account of creation, which had God creating each distinct species within a time period of six days. In fact, the principle of natural selection could be used to explain the development of living organisms without reference to a divine planner. Darwin did not directly enter into battle with the theologians. But his supporters, such as Thomas Huxley (1825-1895), did. Huxley's debate with the Anglican cleric, Bishop Samuel Wilberforce (1805-1873), at Oxford University in 1860 helped to make many more receptive to evolutionary theory and more critical of those who would subordinate science to theology. Huxley continued until his death to be a strong advocate of intellectual freedom and of education in the sciences.

Herbert Spencer (1820-1903) applied evolution to society. Spencer believed in progress and thought that natural selection would allow only the fittest of humans to survive and thus benefit society as a whole. For Spencer, it was important that government not interfere in natural selection by protecting the unvirtuous poor. The ideas of Spencer and others gave rise to a sociological theory known as SOCIAL DARWINISM. According to the Social Darwinists, societies evolved in much the same way as species. The most successful social classes were made up of those most fitted to survive. The poor were biologically inferior. Applied to international relations, Social Darwinism was one of the props for imperialism. Its adherents argued that the West ruled other peoples because of cultural and/or biological superiority. Those who were ruled were seen as less advanced and less fitted in the struggle for survival. The racism of Social Darwinism helped provide the Nazis with a justification for genocide.

What is Social Darwinism?

Who were the masters and slaves according to Nietzsche?

Nietzsche's Attack on Christianity

The implications of the breakdown in traditional Christian ethics, brought by the acceptance of ideas such as evolution, were explored by the German philosopher Friedrich Nietzsche (1844-1900). Nietzsche declared that God is dead in the sense that belief in the God of Christian tradition was no longer feasible. Indeed, Nietzsche specifically attacked the values of Christianity,

Why did Nietzsche think Christianity was a slave religion?

What influence did Nietzsche's ideas have?

which he believed constituted a slave morality.

In any society there are those who dominate over others and who are risk takers and power seekers, and those who are weak, fearful, and insecure. The former are the natural masters, whereas the latter are the natural slaves, according to Nietzsche. While the masters are needed to defend society when it is threatened, they are also feared. The slaves lessen the threat from the strong by having the masters adopt a slave morality, such as Christianity. Christianity makes virtues of submissiveness and friendliness, warm heartedness and patience—the virtues of slaves. The tendency of the strong man to dominate and to appropriate is checked by the guilt such behavior generates among convinced Christians.

Nietzsche would free the masters to follow their own instinctual will to power, which leads them to obtain advantage and to gain ascendancy. He had nothing but contempt for democracy and the dominance of the common herd. Nietzsche thought that by freeing the "blond" beast of prey to follow his instincts, it was possible to see the rise of the superman who would bring human achievement to new heights.

The Nazis later used Nietzsche to justify their own aggression. However, most commentators are agreed that linking Nietzsche to aggressive German nationalism is a distortion of his ideas. Though Nietzsche's ideas are not the easiest to follow, or always consistent with one another, he appears to have welcomed the supermen as great cultural achievers, rather than as the creators of some super empire. What is clear is that Nietzsche's attack on Christianity, and on its predecessor—Judaism, paved the way for the moral relativism that characterizes much of twentieth-century thought.

Who was Sigmund Freud?

Psychoanalysis

Nietzsche and others were aware of the inner drives of humankind, such as the will to power. An Austrian doctor of Jewish origins, however, focused world attention on the unconscious and on instinctual drives. This was Sigmund Freud (1856-1939), the founder of psychoanalysis. According to Freud, the unconscious region of the mind contains ideas and urges which a person is not aware of, because they are repressed from rising to the level of consciousness.

The two most important drives for explaining human behavior are sexual pleasure and aggression. Much of Freud's treatment of his patients centered on the analysis of repressed sexual drives, particularly the Oedipus complex, or desire for sexual union with the parent of the opposite sex. Freud believed it was possible through the process of free association (discussing without censorship whatever comes to the patient's mind) and the interpretation of dreams to examine such repressed drives. By recognizing repressed drives and reorganizing structures for dealing with them, the patient's ego could better deal with reality and mediate between the id (the unconscious where these basic drives are located) and the superego (the conscience which makes a person guilty when he or she gives in to the impulses of the id).

Freud had come up with an alternative to religion for dealing with guilt and finding inner peace. Indeed, he was quite critical of religion, believing that it supported continued childlike dependence on fantasies. Yet, it must be recognized that he is also at odds

Why is the unconscious important in Freud's psychology?

What is meant by "Impressionism"?

with the fundamental assumptions of the Enlightenment. Humans are not seen as fundamentally rational creatures with a natural tendency towards good. Rather, humans are driven by powerful irrational urges that must be suppressed for the sake of civilization.

Impressionism

The term "Impressionism" most often refers to a late nineteenth-century movement in painting that was centered in France. Claude Monet (1840-1926) exhibited a painting entitled *Impression: Sunrise* (1872). A jeering critic of the painting coined the term "Impressionism." The Impressionists painted things not as they were, but as they impressed the senses of the viewer at any given moment under specific environmental conditions. They liked to paint outdoors using bold colors and brushstrokes designed to capture the texture of objects as light played on them at different times of the day. Monet painted a series of haystacks at different hours to show how they appeared in varying conditions of light. He also produced a series of views under changed light of such subjects as the facade of the cathedral at Rouen and the lily pond by his home at Giverny.

Name some Impressionist painters.

Pierre August Renoir (1841-1919) is another founder of Impressionism. His subjects and style varied over time. He is well known for his painting of nude female figures in warm flesh tones. Other painters associated with Impressionism are Edgar Degas (1834-1917), Edouard Manet (1832-1883), Camille Pissaro (1830-1903), and Alfred Sisley (1839-1899). An American woman, Mary Cassatt (1847-1926), displayed her works at several French Impressionist exhibitions. One of these paintings, *A Woman in Black at the Opera,* showed the influence of Japanese prints, which interested both her and her friend, Edgar Degas.

Impressionism was followed by Postimpressionism. Painters such as Paul Cezanne (1839-1906), Paul Gaugin (1848-1903), and Vincent Van Gogh (1853-1890) were greatly influenced by Impressionism, but they moved away from the faithful representation of objects as found in nature. The Postimpressionists were willing to amplify and distort nature in order to give more expression to their personal outlooks. Cezanne's landscapes often reveal elemental forms such as the cube, the pyramid, and the cylinder to which he believed all the forms found in nature could be reduced. Gaugin is well known for his scenes of Tahiti, which depict the beauty of the people and their spirituality. Van Gogh, who was born in Holland, suffered periodic mental depression and took his own life. Many of his paintings, such as the *Starry Night,* or the *Landscape with Olive Trees*, depict a frenzied distortion of nature suggesting passion and mental imbalance.

How did the Postimpressionists differ from the Impressionists?

Who were some Postimpressionists?

COLONIAL EMPIRES IN AFRICA • 1914

DEPENDENT STATES:

- British
- French
- Belgian
- Portuguese
- Italian
- Spanish
- German

EUROPE

ASIA

Mediterranean Sea

Tangier
ER RIFF
Algiers
Tunis
FRENCH MOROCCO
TUNISIA
ALGERIA
Tripoli
Agadir
Alexandria
Suez Canal
Cairo
RIO DE ORO
LIBYA
EGYPT

Nile R.
Red Sea

FRENCH WEST AFRICA

Dakar
SENEGAL
GAMBIA
Niger R.
PORT. GUINEA
DAHOMEY
SIERRA LEONE
GOLD COAST
LIBERIA
NIGERIA
TOGO
CAMEROONS
SP. GUINEA

Omdurman
ANGLO-EGYPTIAN SUDAN
Fashoda
Aduwa
Addis Ababa
ETHIOPIA
ERITREA
FR. SOMALILAND
BR. SOMALILAND
ITALIAN SOMALILAND

EQUATORIAL AFRICA

ATLANTIC OCEAN

Congo R.

CABINDA

UGANDA
BR. EAST AFRICA
BELGIAN CONGO
GER. EAST AFRICA

INDIAN OCEAN

ANGOLA
N. RHODESIA
NYASALAND
Zambesi R.
S. RHODESIA
MOZAMBIQUE
MADAGASCAR

GER. SOUTH-WEST AFRICA
BECHUANALAND PROTECTORATE
TRANSVAAL
SWAZILAND
Johannesburg
NATAL
UNION OF
Kimberley
Ladysmith
SOUTH AFRICA
CAPE COLONY
BASUTOLAND
Capetown
Cape of Good Hope

0   1000 miles

From *The End of the European Era, 1890 to the Present*, Fourth Edition by Felix Gilbert with David Clay Large. Copyright (c) 1991, 1984, 1970 by W.W. Norton & Company, Inc. Reprinted by permission of W.W. Norton & Company, Inc.

9

Imperialism and International Rivalry

IMPERIALISM

Explanations for Imperialism

An aggressive scramble for colonial domination, often called the "new imperialism," broke out among the European powers and the United States after 1870. During this second wave of European imperialism, most of Africa and Asia came under the domination of Western powers.

The first wave of European imperialism began with the Voyages of Discovery and lasted to the American Revolution, roughly from 1450 through 1780. During this first wave, the Americas, North and South, were colonized by the Europeans. The European control of Africa and Asia, however, was relatively minor. Europeans established trading posts, but were unable to establish their colonial domination over the native populations. The spice trade with Asia and the slave trade with Africa did make many sea captains and merchants wealthy and laid the foundations for a global economy.

The American and French Revolutions resulted in the independence of the United States of America, Brazil, and most of the Spanish colonies. European settler populations gained their independence from the

Discuss the waves of European imperialism.

What was the "new imperialism?"

Give examples of advantages Europeans gained from having colonies.

mother country. The conditions of the native peoples, the American Indians and the imported black slaves, did not improve under these new settler governments. The American republics, including the United States, continued to be an offshoot of the European state system and continued to be economically dependent on Europe.

Nonetheless, the French Revolution, Napoleon, and the colonial losses in the Americas resulted in a slowdown of the European drive for colonies. The British did colonize Australia, expanded their hold on India, and began their drive to open up China to Western trade and influence. The Chinese century of humiliation was about to begin. From 1839 to 1842, the British engaged in the Opium War with China to force the Chinese government to permit the importation of opium. Opium was one of the few products which Chinese consumers were interested in buying, once they became addicted, from greedy merchants wishing to trade with China. In 1853, Commodore Perry, acting for the United States, similarly, used naval force to open Japan to trade with the West on terms that were disadvantageous for the Japanese. This slow expansion of European imperialism, largely for purposes of expanding trade, became a torrent after 1870. Many reasons have been given for the renewed growth of imperialism.

The continuing hope for ECONOMIC ADVANTAGE was one of these reasons. The Europeans desired products such as tea, ivory, and rubber. Colonies provided controlled markets for the manufactured goods of industrialized nations. India provided such a market for British textiles.

Economic gain also came from the investment of capital. Countries abroad represented opportunities for investors who wanted higher returns than were available at home. The risks were higher but so were the profits to be made. Some of these risks might be reduced through the proper application of military force against weak governments. Western governments could be persuaded to intervene in the internal affairs of debtor states that failed to repay foreign loans on time and at usurious interest rates. High-risk capital ventures could be made to pay off by seizing the customs collections of the debtor country. Forcing extraterritoriality on weak native governments was another benefit which European merchants might gain through military force. Instead of being subject to the native laws of the country visited, extraterritoriality allowed each European visitor to remain under the laws of his own country. Fraudulent practices and even murder would thus be tried not in the native courts but in special extraterritorial courts run by the foreigners themselves.

John A. Hobson and, later, Vladimir Ilich Lenin wrote books on the economic origins of imperialism. The drift of these works was that laborers in industrialized countries were underpaid, contributing to periodic depressions and the accumulation of surplus capital that could not easily be invested in the depressed home economies. This surplus capital could readily be invested in the country's colonies. This created a strong motive for imperialism and the acquisition of further colonies. Lenin described imperialism as the final stage of capitalism. He sought to link the competition inherent in imperialist capitalism with the origins of World War I.

A problem with Hobson's and Lenin's theories is that they focus on factors which can plausibly apply to one or more cases, but they are certainly not true of all cases of imperialist expansion. In 1914, the British had twenty-five percent of their wealth in-

How did Lenin explain imperialism?

Was he entirely correct? Why?

How did Pan-Slavism influence Russian imperialism?

Give examples of how nationalism encouraged the imperialism of other nations.

vested outside Great Britain, approximately twenty billion dollars! The surplus capital theory of Lenin's would seem to fit the case of English imperialism. But Russia was also an imperialist nation in the nineteenth century, making repeated attempts to take advantage of the declining Ottoman empire. In 1914, Russia was still in the early stages of industrialization, clearly without much capital to invest abroad. Its imperialism cannot be explained by Lenin's surplus capital theory.

To understand imperialist motivations, we have to look beyond economics. NATIONALISM in its various forms seems to be a better candidate as the primary factor in explaining the imperialism of the second half of the nineteenth century. In the case of Russia, nationalism expressed itself in the form of Pan-Slavism (the desire to unify all Slavs). Russia fought the Ottoman Empire to liberate the Slavic population of that empire and to bring the Slavs under Russian control. Nationalism led Russia into World War I. It mobilized its troops against Austria in the name of Slavic solidarity.

National pride motivated other European countries to imperialist expansion as well. Germany and Italy, in particular, as recently united nations were especially nationalistic and sought to catch up with the established powers by seeking their own colonies as a sign of first-class nationhood. France sought new colonies abroad in part to compensate for the humiliations suffered in the Franco-Prussian War. The non-Western nation of Japan, once industrialized, sought an empire to match its new-found strength, even if it meant going to war against China and Russia. Even the United States took a hand at imperialism as a result of the Spanish American War.

STRATEGIC INTERESTS are yet another theory seeking to explain imperialism. The British interest in maintaining a safe route to India is said to explain why Britain involved itself in the Middle East from Egypt to Afghanistan. Control over strategic resources, such as oil, may foster imperialism. Preventing others from gaining control over otherwise useless territory may serve as a motive for new colonial acquisitions. Who knows what national interest may be served by getting there first? Prestige and national honor can be powerful motivating factors.

What prompted British interest in the Middle East?

Many Western colonizers were persuaded that they possessed a CULTURAL SUPERIORITY that gave them the right and the duty to civilize and Christianize non-white colonial peoples. This religious motive dates back to the initial Voyages of Discovery but persisted into the second wave of imperialism. Missionaries were often in the vanguard of colonial exploration. They were quickly followed by the merchants and soldiers. Many missionaries were sincere in their beliefs and brought Western medicine and education in addition to Western forms of spiritual beliefs.

Do you think that European efforts to Christianize non-European peoples was evidence that the Europeans considered themselves to be culturally superior?

In many cases the Western notions of cultural superiority included what we would today recognize as RACISM. An interesting illustration of this point is found in Rudyard Kipling's poem, *The White Man's Burden,* which was written to persuade the United States to take over the Philippines:

> Take up the White man's burden—
> Send forth the best ye breed—
> Go bind your sons to exile
> To serve your captives' need;
> To wait in heavy harness,
> On fluttered folk and wild—
> Your new-caught, sullen peoples,
> Half-devil and half-child.[4]

Analyze Kipling's attitude towards non-White peoples as evidenced by the poem presented on this page.

Was the United States an impe-rialist nation? Is it one today?

Give an example of how techni-cal superiority aided Western imperialism.

Many Filipinos sought their independence after the Spanish American War and fought the United States at the cost of their lives. Not until after World War II did the Philippines finally gain their national independence.

It was Western TECHNOLOGICAL SUPERIORITY that made possible the new imperialism. The coming of the second wave of the Industrial Revolution with steel ships, better cannon, and machine guns gave Europeans a clear technological superiority over Asian and African societies. The West had the firepower to conquer with breech-loading rifles, machine guns, and iron gunboats. It had railroads and steamships to haul off desired commodities or to bring manufactured goods to captive, colonial markets.

Until the nineteenth century, Africans living south of the Sahara desert were able to control the terms of exchange with the white men. Native blacksmiths were quite capable of making muskets. With the introduction of the rifle and the machine gun, the situation changed. Improvements in medicine, such as the use of quinine against malaria, also helped Europeans to penetrate into the interior of Africa and survive.

The non-industrial world could no longer compete with the industrialized, Western world. Until the traditional societies of Africa and Asia became industrialized, they could no longer resist the Western onslaught.

The Partition of Africa

The Portuguese had explored the coast of Africa during their initial Voyages of Discovery. The Dutch and English had followed their examples and a string of trading posts had been established all along the Atlantic coast of Africa. The slave trade, as we have seen, had siphoned up to twelve million Africans off into the New World. The loss of these people and its impact on African development, cultural and economic, can only be imagined.

Despite these ravages, the interior of Africa had remained largely unexplored by Europeans until the nineteenth century. The Victoria Falls in south central Africa on the boarder of the present-day Democratic Republic of the Congo (formerly Zaire), and Zimbabwe were not discovered by Europeans until 1855. David Livingston (1813-1873) was a Scottish missionary who explored the interior of Africa during several expeditions. He discovered the Falls, which are 5,500 feet wide and nearly 350 feet deep.

In 1871, the supposedly lost Livingstone was "found" by a publicity-seeking journalist named Henry M. Stanley (1841-1904), who was working for the *New York Herald*. Stanley's newspaper stories and Livingstone's own best-selling accounts of his travels helped to generate intense public interest in Africa. Livingstone's descriptions of the brutality of the slave trade horrified the British public and helped the anti-slavery movement. Livingstone died in 1873 of malaria.

Stanley went on to make several other explorations of the Congo and developed a scheme of exploiting the resources of Africa. He found a sponsor in King Leopold II (1865-1909) of Belgium. With the king acting as a private individual rather than as the head of the Belgian state, he and Stanley formed the International Congo Association in 1878. Stanley returned to the Congo and had hundreds of chiefs put marks on indecipherable pieces of paper in exchange for

How did the missionary, David Livingstone, influence European expansion in Africa?

Describe Henry M. Stanley's work in Africa.

How did the International Congo Association gain its land? How was the Congo administered?

token payments. The chiefs had no idea that they were signing away tribal lands. An estimated 900,000 square miles were obtained for the Congo Association in this manner.

Using similar tactics, other powers got into the race. Portugal, France, Britain, and Germany began to make their own claims to Africa. A mad scramble for Africa had begun. The fact that King Leopold and Stanley were acting as private individuals further confused the situation. Otto von Bismarck convened the Berlin Conference of 1884-5. While the Berlin Conference was in session, King Leopold succeeded in transforming the International Association of the Congo into the Congo Free State in 1885. (Gross maladministration and brutality created a population decline in the millions. International indignation led to the transformation of the Congo Free State into a Belgian colony in 1908.)

Describe the work of the Berlin Conference.

At the Berlin Conference, it was agreed that each European power must give proper notice of claims to other powers. For a territorial claim to be accepted, there would have to be effective occupation with troops and administrators, not merely claims on paper. What followed was a wild scramble among European powers to establish the effective occupation of African territories so that they could claim the land as their colony.

What initiated the European scramble for Africa?

By 1914, all of Africa had become colonized by the Europeans. The French dominated in North Africa. The British had colonies reaching from Egypt to South Africa and on the Indian Ocean side of Africa, as well as a smattering of colonies on the Atlantic side. The Belgians had the Congo region in the center. Portuguese, Spaniards, Italians, and Germans filled in the rest. Only Ethiopia could be considered a truly inde-

THE AGE OF NATIONALISM AND IMPERIALISM

pendent African county. Liberia, while nominally independent, was really an American protectorate dominated by ex-slaves from the United States. The Union of South Africa was a self-governing while settler colony within the British Commonwealth of Nations. Egypt was also partly self-governing as a British protectorate.

The Boer War

The largest conflict that took place during the European scramble for Africa was the Boer War, which lasted from 1899 to 1902. This was a fight among whites. The Boers, or Afrikaners, were originally Dutch colonists who had settled around the Cape of Good Hope on the tip of Africa in the seventeenth century. When the English annexed the territory after 1815, the Boers moved north to avoid English rule and formed two independent republics: the Transvaal and the Orange Free State.

The discovery of gold in 1886 led a large number of new immigrants, mainly British, to settle in the Transvaal. The Boers, an agricultural people, refused to pass legislation to protect the commercial interests of the new settlers. A raiding party of armed British irregulars from the Cape tried to provoke a revolt in 1895, but the raid was defeated. Three years later, the British sent a huge army of at least 300,000 troops against a Boer force that did not exceed 80,000. The Afrikaners eventually resorted to guerrilla warfare, while the English established concentration camps for Boer women and children. Approximately 20,000 perished in these camps. The Transvaal and the Orange Free State were successfully subjugated. In 1910, these two colonies were joined with the Cape Colony and Natal to form the Union

Who were the Boers?

How did the British treat the Boers or Afrikaners?

What was the impact on the West of the fall of the Byzantine Empire?

of South Africa, as a part of the British Empire. The English conduct of the war was very unpopular among other European states.

Ottoman Decline and Great Power Expansion

In 1453, the Ottoman Turks succeeded finally in conquering the ancient city of Byzantium or Constantinople, which they renamed Istanbul. The Byzantine or Eastern Roman Empire had fallen at last, a thousand years after the Western Roman Empire. Islam had finally triumphed over Orthodox Christianity. Only in Russia did Orthodoxy have the protection of a strong state and Moscow promptly declared itself to be the Third Rome.

The fall of Byzantium profoundly impacted on the West. It disrupted the trade and wealth of the Italian city-states, triggered the Voyages of Discovery, and led to the economic dominance of countries bordering on the Atlantic ocean. Having breached the walls of Byzantium with their cannons, the Ottomans crossed over into Europe and conquered Romania, Bulgaria, Greece, Serbia, Albania, and Hungary. In 1683, the Ottomans were at the gates of Vienna, which the emperor and his court had fled. Only the heroic rescue mission of the Polish King John Sobieski saved the city. This marked the high point of Ottoman power. The Peace of Carlowitz in 1699 marked the end of the Ottoman Empire's ability to wage offensive wars in Europe.

What was the high point of Ottoman penetration of Europe?

Throughout the eighteenth and nineteenth centuries Ottoman power declined. Russia and Austria were its perennial enemies, with France and Britain switching alliances as their own national self-interests dictated. Hungary regained its independence from Turkey, only to become a component of the Austrian empire. The Ottoman Empire's possessions on the Black Sea were nibbled away by the Russian empire.

Large as the Ottoman Empire had been in Europe, it was far more extensive in the Near East and Northern Africa. The Ottoman Turks had become the successors of the vast Islamic Empire stretching from the Persian Gulf to Iraq, Syria, Palestine, Egypt, Libya, Tunisia, and Algeria. The degree of control exercised from the center fluctuated over the centuries. Local governors were often in revolt and semi-independent from the Ottoman caliphs. Nonetheless, nominal authority over these regions was maintained, in some cases, until the end of World War I. Throughout the nineteenth century, France and Great Britain, later joined by Italy and Germany, sought to wrest territory away from the Porte, as the Ottoman Empire was called by European diplomats.

The beginning of this process may be seen in the invasion of Egypt by Napoleon during the French Revolution in 1798. While intended to be a blow against England and seen by Napoleon as a first step toward attacking the British in India, Egypt, in fact, was part of the Ottoman possessions. Napoleon's invasion brought Turkey into the wars against the French until peace was made in 1802. Thereafter Turkey remained on the sidelines in the wars against Napoleon. Russia was its main enemy, steadily encroaching on its territories in Europe. Misgovernment and internal rebellion within the Ottoman state facilitated this process.

Russia emerged from its victory over Napoleon in the War of 1812 as the strongest power on the European continent. It encouraged pan-Slavism in the Balkans, an idea that was also compatible with the growing sense of nationalism engendered by the French Revolution. The Greeks fought a

Describe the extent of the Ottoman Empire in the Near East and North Africa.

Which European countries sought to gain territories at the expense of the Turks?

Name some of the countries that gained independence from the Ottoman Empire in the nineteenth century.

Why did British and Russian interests clash?

When did the Ottoman Empire come to an end?

revolution beginning in 1821 and had their independence internationally recognized by 1827. Greek independence marked the first successful nationalistic revolution of the nineteenth century. Serbian nationalism was equally strong, but formal independence was not gained until 1878. Albania became independent in 1912.

Russian expansion in the Balkans was checked by Austrian ambitions. As the Sick Man of Europe, the Ottoman Empire, decayed, these two rival empires picked up the pieces. When they could not annex territories to themselves outright, they encouraged the independence of states like Greece, Serbia, and Albania. Russian ambitions for the Black Sea, Persia, and Afghanistan were opposed by Great Britain. The British were seeking to protect the flanks of their colonial crown jewel, India. The Crimean War (1853-1856) was waged to check Russian ambitions. Ultimately, rivalries in the Balkans triggered the events leading to World War I.

Egypt remained nominally under Ottoman rule until 1914, but had in fact been under local rule dominated by the Europeans for some time. Ever since Napoleon's invasion of Egypt, that country had been under increasing French and British influence. The Suez Canal was built by a French corporation between 1859 and 1869, but was taken over by the British in 1875. Egypt became a de facto British protectorate in 1882.

In Northern Africa, the Ottoman Empire lost Algeria to French rule in 1830. Tunisia became a French protectorate in 1881. Libya remained part of the Ottoman Empire until 1911 when it was conquered by Italy. The Ottoman territories in the Middle East—Palestine, Syria, and Iraq—were not taken over by Britain and France until after World War I. The Ottoman Empire came to an end after its defeat in World War I. It was replaced by a Turkish Republic led by Kemal Ataturk.

Imperialism in Asia

India

The 1763 Treaty of Paris, which concluded the Seven Years' War, had eliminated the French from most of India. The dominant British continued to expand their influence by pursuing a policy of divide and conquer with respect to the native rulers. By the middle of the nineteenth century the English controlled all of India. They ruled through the British East India Company. The British East India Company had been chartered originally by Queen Elizabeth I as a trading company to compete with the Dutch for the spice trade. By the 1850's, it was simply an administrative agency of the British government exercising control over about three-fifths of India. The other two-fifths were under some 562 native princes, who were clearly subservient to the British government.

The Indians had a number of grievances against the British. Not only were the Indians politically subordinate, but English feelings of racial and social superiority were quite evident. The British attempted to modernize and westernize India. Suttee, or the self-cremation of widows on their husbands' funeral pyres, was forbidden, as was the practice of child marriage. There was talk of abolishing the caste system, which structured Indian society. In May 1857, there occurred a revolt among native Indian troops or "sepoys" in the British Indian Army. The

When did the British come to dominate India?

What grievances did the Indians have against the British?

Discuss the Sepoy rebellion.

immediate cause of the Sepoy Rebellion was the issuing of new rifle cartridges rumored to be greased with cow or pig fat. Cows were sacred to Hindus, while Moslems did not want to touch pork. The British were caught off guard and the revolt spread in the north. Deposed princes, those who had lost land, and others joined the revolt. Atrocities were committed on both sides. Fortunately for the British, the south and the Punjab remained loyal. By July of 1858, the revolt had been broken. In August of 1858, the Crown took direct control from the British East India Company.

How did British policies change after 1857?

Changing their policies after 1857, the British became more tolerant of Indian religious traditions. Subordinate Indian maharajahs were left in place. In 1877, Queen Victoria was made Empress of India. Indian economic subordination to British industrial interests was continued. India was encouraged to become a supplier of such raw materials as cotton, tea, jute, and indigo. Indian industrialization was discouraged, so that the subcontinent would remain a market for British manufactured goods, such as textiles. In 1885, natives organized the Indian National Congress. Its original purpose was to advocate moderate reforms, including the creation of an Indian legislature loyal to the British Crown. In the twentieth century the Congress Party played a more militant role. In 1946, under the leadership of Mahatma Gandhi (1869-1948), India obtained its independence from Britain.

China

China was ruled by the Qing (Ch'ing in the old spelling) or Manchu dynasty from 1644 until 1911. Since the Manchus came from Manchuria in the North, many ethnic

Chinese considered these invaders as foreigners. This made it harder for the imperial family to govern China. By the nineteenth century, the dynasty had become increasingly corrupt and was having trouble in defending its extensive borders. The Mandate of Heaven was slipping away from them. Nonetheless, the Chinese considered themselves to be the "middle kingdom" in the center of the civilized world. A sense of cultural superiority was deeply engrained in Chinese civilization. Neighboring peoples were considered to be inferior and were expected to pay tribute to China. The Confucian belief system was based on mutual obligations between superiors and inferiors: father–son; husband–wife; older brother–younger brother, emperor and people.

When the Europeans first approached China, they were viewed as foreign barbarians and there was almost nothing that the Europeans had that interested the Chinese. On the other hand, there were many goods, like silk, jade, and porcelain, which interested the Europeans. The high level of Chinese civilization and their centralized imperial government prevented Europeans from making much of an impression on China until the Industrial Revolution gave Europeans technological superiority.

From their base in India, the British were particularly active as traders. They found that the Chinese had little desire for British manufactured goods. To buy desired Chinese goods, the English were forced to pay in gold or silver. The British learned that they could gain a more favorable balance of trade by selling opium produced in India to the Chinese. The Chinese government, however, interfered in this "free trade" by prohibiting the importation of opium, much as the United States seeks to prohibit the importation of addictive drugs today. The British

What was the Chinese attitude towards the West?

Compare Britain's Opium War with the U.S. war on drugs.

What was the outcome of the Opium War?

decided to go to war to force "free trade" on the Chinese. In 1839, when the Chinese government stepped up anti-opium enforcement efforts, Britain went to war. What the Chinese call their Century of Humiliation was about to begin.

The Chinese were no match for the firepower of the British navy and were forced into signing the Treaty of Nanjing (Nanking) in 1842. By terms of the treaty, the Chinese ceded the island of Hong Kong to Britain, opened up five ports to foreign trade, and limited duties on British imports to five percent. A supplementary treaty granted extraterritoriality, by which the English (and later other Westerners) in China were subject only to the jurisdiction of their own consular courts. Other Western powers negotiated similar trading arrangements with China.

What were some of the reasons found by Britain and France to fight with China?

In 1856, Britain went to war again with China. The occasion this time was China's seizure of a Chinese crew on board a ship that was flying the British flag. France joined in over the death of a Catholic missionary. When the Chinese failed to honor terms of treaties signed at Tianjin (Tientsin) in 1858, the war was renewed. Beijing (Peking), the capital, was captured and the emperor's Summer Palace was burned. A new set of agreements was signed in Beijing in 1860. The treaties of 1858 and 1860 opened more ports to foreign trade, expanded extraterritoriality, allowed foreigners to travel in the interior of the country, legalized the opium trade, permitted Christian missionary activity throughout the country, and established foreign legations in Beijing. Not only the French and British, who did the fighting, profited from these treaties, but the Americans and the Russians also signed advantageous treaties with the Chinese.

Foreign powers began to nibble at the peripheries of the Chinese empire. The French gained Indochina and the Russians acquired territory in the north. The newly industrialized Japanese fought the Chinese in 1894-1895 over Korea. China was defeated and forced to recognize Korean independence (really Japanese predominance), cede Taiwan to Japan, and open up still more ports to foreign commerce.

The United States became concerned that China might be divided entirely into exclusive spheres of influence. To prevent this and to preserve its own interests, the United States Secretary of State, John Hay, in 1899 and 1900 exchanged notes with other foreign powers seeking to preserve China intact and to guarantee the same trading terms (including the five percent tariff) to all nations who traded with China. This became known as the OPEN DOOR POLICY.

There were periodic internal revolts against Qing rule in the nineteenth century. The dynasty came to depend on the support of the foreigners, who wanted a weak central government to stay in power. A turnabout came when the Empress Cixi (Ts'u-hsi, 1835-1908) became convinced that the foreigners would demand her retirement. She sided with secret societies organized to resist foreign inroads. The most important of these societies was that of the "Righteous Harmonious Fists," so the violent resistance movement of 1898-1900 became known as the BOXER REBELLION. The Boxers killed many foreigners, as well as Chinese with ties to foreigners, such as the Chinese Christians. The foreign legations in Beijing were besieged. An international army relieved the siege and forced still more humiliating terms upon the Chinese, who had to pay an indemnity of $333 million and agree to permit the stationing of foreign troops in Beijing.

What was the Open Door Policy?

Describe the events and results of the Boxer Rebellion.

Who was Sun Yat-Sen?

The Qing dynasty was overthrown in 1911, and a Chinese republic under Sun Yat-Sen was established in 1912. Unfortunately, this was not the end of China's political instability, which continued until the Communist takeover in 1949.

Japan

What were some of the political and social features of Japan under the Tokugawa shogunate?

Since 1640, Japan had excluded all Westerners except for a few Dutch traders who were restricted to a small island near Nagasaki. The Japanese were resisting foreign influence, especially Christianity. The Dutch traders were allowed as a means of getting information about what was going on in the West.

In the mid-nineteenth century, Japan was under the rule of a member of the Tokugawa family. The Tokugawas, who had been ruling since 1603, were shoguns or generals who ruled with the help of local military leaders or daimyo. The shogun and the daimyo were supported by a warrior class known as samurai. There was an emperor, but he was a remote, politically uninvolved, figure in Kyoto, whereas the political capital of the Tokugawas was Edo (present-day Tokyo). There were a number of social problems and economic development had not kept pace with population growth. There had been peasant uprisings. Many daimyo and samurai were indebted to the merchant classes, who were their social inferiors. The shogunate was both extravagant and inefficient.

This was the setting when U.S. Commodore Matthew Perry (1794-1858) arrived in Edo bay, in July 1853, to deliver a letter from President Fillmore asking for trading rights and protection for shipwrecked Americans. He returned in February 1854 and made it clear that the alternative to signing a treaty would be war. The Japanese reluctantly signed a treaty at the end of March, opening up the ports of Shimoda and Hakodate to American traders, offering protection for shipwrecked U.S. sailors, and permitting the provisioning of U.S. ships.

Later in the decade, the Japanese expanded the number of ports open to Americans, and signed similar treaties with Holland, Russia, Britain, and France. These treaties provided for extraterritoriality, meaning Western citizens would not be tried in Japanese courts, and other provisions indicative of Japanese inferiority in western eyes. There was a reaction against the treaties in Japan. Some westerners were killed, and the Tokugawa leaders were not able to control the situation. Western powers took matters into their own hands, leading to the further loss of face for the shogunate. In 1867, the last Tokugawa shogun was forced to resign.

In 1868 a new emperor adopted the name Meiji, which means enlightened rule. The period of his reign, 1868-1912, is known as the Meiji Restoration. Henceforth, the government would act in the name of the emperor, whose imperial palace was moved to Edo, renamed Tokyo. This was the period of the westernization of Japan. The Japanese sought to industrialize and to modernize their military forces so that they could deal with western nations on equal terms. A new army was established, modeled after the Prussian example. The British served as the model for the navy. Shintoism with its reverence for the emperor was given preference over Buddhism. A constitution was promulgated in 1889 with a two-chamber parliament as a gift from the emperor. The emperor never really ruled, nor were political leaders truly responsible to the parliament. Rather

Was the expansion of trade by the Japanese a matter of choice? Explain.

What was the Meiji Restoration?

What happened in the Russo-Japanese War of 1904-1905?

What message did Russian defeat send to the victims of imperialism?

they governed in what they understood to be the best interests of the state. There was slow evolution towards representative government.

The military and industrial growth of Japan was much more rapid. This growth was seen during the Sino-Japanese War (the war with China) of 1894-95 which was mentioned above. Japanese strength was evidenced even more strikingly in the Russo-Japanese War of 1904-1905. Japan and Russia clashed over conflicting interests in Korea and Manchuria. The Russians suffered a series of defeats. On land they were defeated in the Battle of Mukden in March 1905, losing 97,000 out of a force of 310,000. The Japanese losses were half that. The Russian fleet was destroyed in the Battle of Tsushima Straits in May 1905. The humiliated Russians were forced to accept the mediation of U.S. President Theodore Roosevelt. The peace resulted in Russian acknowledgment of Japanese interests in Korea and enabled the Japanese to replace the Russians in Manchuria and gain the southern half of the island of Sakhalin.

This was the first defeat of a European country by an Asian nation. It assured that western powers would have to treat Japan on a more equal basis in commercial and military relations. It inspired many other peoples under imperial domination to seek their independence. Many would do so, using the Japanese model; that is, industrializing while retaining cultural traditions. In the second half of the twentieth century, western imperial dominance would be broken and western economic supremacy challenged.

INTERNATIONAL RIVALRY

What was the Three Emperors' League?

After the Franco-Prussian War of 1870-71, Bismarck was chancellor of a united Germany. He realized that France wanted revenge for defeat and for the loss of Alsace-Lorraine. A major objective of his foreign policy was to keep France isolated. Without reliable allies, France was less likely to go to war with Germany or to succeed in the event that war was initiated. Bismarck tried to reassure other European nations that Germany did not want additional territories. He also sought to deprive France of potential allies by forming alliances between Germany and the major continental powers. In 1873, he established the Three Emperors' League, linking the Russian and Austro-Hungarian Empires with the German Empire. This League was renewed in 1881.

Explain the conflict of interest in the Balkan Peninsula.

The problem with the Three Emperors' League was the fundamental conflict of interest between Russia and Austria over the Balkan Peninsula, which had been dominated by the declining Ottoman Empire. The Russians wanted to support the independence movements of the Slavic peoples in the region, as part of Pan-Slavism (a movement to bring together all Slavic peoples under the protection of Russia). Russia also wanted to make geo-political gains of its own at the expense of Turkey. Austria-Hungary, with substantial numbers of Slavic peoples within its empire, felt threatened. A new south Slavic (Yugoslavian) state might be created at the expense of Austria, as well as Turkey. Such a state did, in fact, emerge after World War I.

What was the Dual Alliance?

How did Germany antagonize Britain?

Because of the weakness of the League, Bismarck sought alternate alliances. In 1879, the Dual Alliance was formed between Germany and Austria. Each side agreed to go to the aid of the other, should Russia attack one of them. If some other party attacked, at least neutrality would be maintained. Italy, in conflict with France over Tunis, joined Germany and Austria in the Triple Alliance of 1882. This was a defensive alliance providing that, if France attacked one of these countries, the other two would come to the aid of the country attacked. In 1887, Bismarck negotiated a Reinsurance Treaty with Russia, whereby both powers pledged neutrality if either one were attacked by a third party. The point of this last treaty was to keep Russia separated from France, even if Russia would no longer agree to be an ally of Austria.

William II came to the German throne in 1888 and dismissed Bismarck in 1890. One of the issues leading to Bismarck's dismissal was his desire to renew the Reinsurance Treaty with Russia. The next chancellor refused to renew the treaty. In response, monarchical Russia formed an unexpected alliance with republican France. The Franco-Russian Alliance of 1894 provided that if France were attacked by Germany, or by Italy supported by Germany, the Russians would use their forces against Germany. Similarly, if Russia were attacked by Germany, or by Austria supported by Germany, France would use its military forces against Germany.

England had traditionally maintained a distance from entangling continental alliances. In 1898, Germany antagonized the British by starting to build a navy designed to lessen English control of the seas. England considered naval dominance necessary for the island's defense and for maintaining the lines to the British Empire. The English had been antagonized already by the Kaiser's pro-Afrikaner sympathies during the Boer War. Britain also found the now industrialized Germany a formidable commercial competitor. In 1904 the English reached an understanding, the Entente Cordiale, with the French which settled all outstanding colonial differences. It was not an actual military alliance, since there was no commitment to use military force if one of the parties was attacked by a third party. France was anxious to reconcile the British with the Russians, who were already French allies. In 1907, a chastened Russia, having suffered defeat in the Russo-Japanese War (1904-05), agreed to an Anglo-Russian Entente. The agreement settled a major difference between the two countries by dividing Persia into separate spheres of influence. The Iranian north was to be a Russian sphere, and the south would be the British sphere. A neutral zone was to be established between these two spheres. The ententes taken together comprise the TRIPLE ENTENTE aligning Britain, France, and Russia against Germany, Austria, and Italy, who were members of the TRIPLE ALLIANCE.

Explain the origins of the Triple Alliance and the Triple Entente.

The Moroccan Crises

The Entente Cordiale between Britain and France did not commit either to military cooperation. Given the historical antagonism between the two countries, it might not have developed into a wartime alliance, except for the clumsy diplomacy of the Germans. The Germans sought to test the Entente Cordiale. They provoked the First Moroccan Crisis to prove to the French that Britain was not a

What did Germany hope to gain by provoking the First Moroccan Crisis?

What were the events and the results of the First and Second Moroccan Crises?

reliable ally. France had imperial ambitions in Morocco in the north of Africa. So in March 1905, William II made a speech in Tangier, saying that Morocco should be independent and open to all, effectively challenging France's protectorate over Morocco. The French tried to negotiate a deal with the Germans by making colonial concessions elsewhere. But the Germans insisted on an international conference, which met at Algeciras, Spain in 1906. At the conference, only the Austrians supported Germany. The other states, including Britain, Russia, Spain, Italy, and the United States sided with France. Morocco remained formally independent and open to all, but in reality the French hand was strengthened, and the French were given control over the Moroccan state bank. More importantly, the French and British military staffs began consulting with one another regarding communications they would take in time of war. The unintended consequence of German pressure was to make the Entente Cordiale take on aspects of a military alliance!

The Second Moroccan Crisis, which occurred in 1911, further reinforced the ties between France and Britain. In response to revolts in Morocco, France had proceeded to take over all of the country. The Germans protested and began to negotiate with France for colonial compensation elsewhere in Africa. To strengthen their hand, the Germans sent a gunboat, the *Panther,* to Agadir on the Moroccan coast. Though Germany did gain some minor concessions in the Congo, in exchange for giving the French a free hand in Morocco, the British were greatly agitated. They tried to negotiate with Germany on limits to the naval arms race, but the Germans would not modify their plans to build three large battleships (dreadnoughts).

The English began to make serious preparations for war.

The Balkan Crises

How did Serbian and Austro-Hungarian interests conflict?

Mention was made of the conflicting interests of Russia and Austria-Hungary in the Balkan area. The Austro-Hungarian Empire was similarly in conflict with the small Balkan state of Serbia, which had gained its independence from the Ottoman Empire in the nineteenth century. Serbia was interested in the nominally Ottoman provinces of Bosnia and Herzegovina which the 1878 Congress of Berlin had permitted the Austrians to administer. Serbian claims were supported by Russia. In 1908 Austria annexed Bosnia-Herzegovina outright. The Serbs were very angry because they believed that they had a right to rule these provinces which had a large south Slav population. The Russians backed the Serbs. But when Germany demanded Russian acquiescence in the annexation, the Russians felt obliged to back down. They were still weak after the Russo-Japanese War.

What happened during the First and Second Balkan Wars?

In 1911, after the Second Moroccan Crisis, Italy went to war with the Ottoman Empire in order to seize Libya before the French took it. This made the Ottomans especially vulnerable. To take advantage of the situation, Serbia, Bulgaria, Greece, and Montenegro joined together in the First Balkan War against Turkey, which began in October 1912. The war ended, with great Turkish losses, in May 1913. Bulgaria, dissatisfied with its share of the spoils, attacked its former allies a month later, in the Second Balkan War. Romania and Turkey joined the others against the Bulgarians, who were

Why was Serbia's resentment towards Austria, who wasn't a combatant in the Balkan Wars, increased?

easily defeated. Fresh from these victories, land-locked Serbia invaded newly independent Albania, which had a coastline along the Adriatic Sea. The Austrians insisted on maintaining the independence of Albania, and thereby blocking Serbia's access to the sea. Most of the other great powers, with the notable exception of Russia, supported Austria, and Austria prevailed. Serb nationalists, who envisioned a Greater Serbia including all south Slav peoples, became increasingly resentful toward Austria. The stage was set for a violent conflict between Serbia and Austria. Few, if any, could predict that such a conflict would lead to World War I.

NOTES

[1]Otto von Bismarck, FROM: A SPEECH IN THE PRUSSIAN BUDGET COMMISSION, ed. Eugen Weber, vol. II: The Western Tradition. (Lexington, Mass.: D.C. Heath, 1990), p. 703.

[2]As quoted in Correct Quotes for Windows, a software package (Novato, Cal.: WordStar International, 1992), Topic: History.

[3]Edmund Burke as quoted in William Ebenstein, Great Political Thinkers: Plato to the Present, 3rd ed. (New York: Holt Rinehart and Winston, 1965), p. 481.

[4] McClure's Magazine (Feb. 1899).

Figure 3.4 **African Primitive Belt Mask**. This sixteenth century carving is made of ivory. Note the delicate design surrounding the mask. (Courtesy of The Metropolitan Museum of Art, The Michael C. Rockefeller Memorial Collection, Gift of Nelson A. Rockefeller, 1972)

Figure 3.5 **Charles Darwin** (1809-1882). From his findings on his voyage around the coasts of Central and South America, British naturalist Charles Darwin advanced a theory of evolution that forever changed man's view of the biological processes of nature. (Courtesy of The Library of Congress)

CHARLES DARWIN

*On the Origin of Species**

A meticulously thorough scientist, Charles Darwin (1809-1882) started his university career as a medical student. Hating the sight of blood, he soon turned to theological studies and had an undistinguished four years at Cambridge University. Because of his avid interest in geology, botany, and zoology and his friendships with some of the greatest scientific minds of his time at Cambridge, he was invited aboard the *Beagle* for a five-year journey (1831 to 1836) as an unpaid naturalist. The *Beagle*'s task was to chart the coastline of Central and South America, establish longitudinal measurements, and to collect specimens. This voyage changed Charles Darwin's life as well as scientific theories of evolution for the nineteenth and twentieth centuries.

On his voyage to the isolated Galapagos Islands off the coast of Ecuador, Darwin observed many species of birds, plants, animals that were unlike the ones on the mainland. He noticed finches had developed different beaks for the purpose of gathering appropriate food on the different islands. He ever so precisely described, labeled, drew his findings. As a result, he theorized that both plants and animals in their struggle for survival adapt to their environment and that those species that possess favorable adaptations have a better chance of surviving and thereby passing these adaptations on to their offspring. Due to this process which Darwin called Natural Selection, all living organisms have been and are continually evolving. Although Darwin did not have the sophisticated understanding of the laws of genetics and mutations that we have today, he was able to document the variations in species that enabled their survival in his monumental work, *On the Origin of Species*, published in 1859.

STRUGGLE FOR EXISTENCE.

BEFORE entering on the subject of this chapter, I must make a few preliminary remarks, to show how the struggle for existence bears on

---

*From Charles Darwin, *On the Origin of Species by Means of Natural Selection* (London: John Murray, 1859).

Adaptations occur in every living organism in both the plant and animal kingdoms throughout the world.

Due to the struggle for life, those individuals who have better adapted to their environment survive. Any given species will produce many more offspring than can possibly survive; however, those who do survive will pass on their adaptive characteristics to their offspring. Darwin calls this process by which useful characteristics are preserved "natural selection."

Natural Selection. ...amongst organic beings in a state of nature there is some individual variability; indeed I am not aware that this has ever been disputed...But the mere existence of individual variability and of some few well-marked varieties, though necessary as the foundation for the work, helps us but little in understanding how species arise in nature. How have all those exquisite adaptations of one part of the organisation to another part, and to the conditions of life, and of one distinct organic being to another being been perfected? We see these beautiful co-adaptations most plainly in the woodpecker and missletoe; and only a little less plainly in the humblest parasite which clings to the hairs of a quadruped or feathers of a bird; in the structure of the beetle which dives through the water; in the plumed seed which is wafted by the gentlest breeze; in short, we see beautiful adaptations everywhere and in every part of the organic world.

Again, it may be asked, how is it that varieties, which I have called incipient species, become ultimately converted into good and distinct species, which in most cases obviously differ from each other far more than do the varieties of the same species? How do those groups of species, which constitute what are called distinct genera, and which differ from each other more than do the species of the same genus, arise? All these results, as we shall more fully see in the next chapter, follow inevitably from the struggle for life. Owing to this struggle for life, any variation, however slight and from whatever cause proceeding, if it be in any degree profitable to an individual of any species, in its infinitely complex relations to other organic beings and to external nature, will tend to the preservation of that individual, and will generally be inherited by its offspring. The offspring, also, will thus have a better chance of surviving, for, of the many individuals of any species which are periodically born, but a small number can survive. I have called this principle, by which each slight variation, if useful, is preserved, by the term of Natural Selection, in order to mark its relation to man's power of selection. We have seen that man by selection can certainly produce great results, and can adapt organic beings to his own uses, through the accumulation of slight but useful variations, given to him by the hand of Nature. But Natural Selection, as we shall hereafter see, is a power incessantly ready for action, and is as immeasurably superior to man's feeble efforts, as the works of Nature are to those of Art.

NATURAL SELECTION.

How will the struggle for existence, discussed too briefly in the last chapter, act in regard to variation? Can the principle of selection, which we have seen is so potent in the hands of man, apply in nature? I think we shall see that it can act most effectually. Let it be borne in mind in what an endless number of strange peculiarities our domestic productions, and, in a lesser degree, those under nature, vary; and how strong the hereditary tendency is. Under domestication, it may be truly said that the whole organisation becomes in some degree plastic. Let it be borne in mind how infinitely complex and close-fitting are the mutual relations of all organic beings to each other and to their physical conditions of life. Can it, then, be thought improbable, seeing that variations useful to man have undoubtedly occurred, that other variations useful in some way to each being in the great and complex battle of life, should sometimes occur in the course of thousands of generations? If such do occur, can we doubt (remembering that many more individuals are born than can possibly survive) that individuals having any advantage, however slight, over others, would have the best chance of surviving and of procreating their kind? On the other hand, we may feel sure that any variation in the least degree injurious would be rigidly destroyed. This preservation of favourable variations and the rejection of injurious variations, I call Natural Selection.

We shall best understand the probable course of natural selection by taking the case of a country undergoing some physical change, for instance, of climate. The proportional numbers of its inhabitants would almost immediately undergo a change, and some species might

Living organisms are mutually dependent on each other and on their environment.

Those individuals that possess favorable adaptations to their environment have a better chance of surviving and thereby passing these adaptations on to their offspring than those individuals that have disadvantageous or unfavorable characteristics.

Natural selection is ever so slowly, gradually occurring so that individuals of species which hav better adapted to their environment survive, thereby preserving the favorable variations.

become extinct. We may conclude, from what we have seen of the intimate and complex manner in which the inhabitants of each country are bound together, that any change in the numerical proportions of some of the inhabitants, independently of the change of climate itself, would most seriously affect many of the others. If the country were open on its borders, new forms would certainly immigrate, and this also would seriously disturb the relations of some of the former inhabitants. Let it be remembered how powerful the influence of a single introduced tree or mammal has been shown to be. But in the case of an island, or of a country partly surrounded by barriers, into which new and better adapted forms could not freely enter, we should then have places in the economy of nature which would assuredly be better filled up, if some of the original inhabitants were in some manner modified; for, had the area been open to immigration, these same places would have been seized on by intruders. In such case, every slight modification, which in the course of ages chanced to arise, and which in any way favoured the individuals of any of the species, by better adapting them to their altered conditions, would tend to be preserved; and natural selection would thus have free scope for the work of improvement.

As man can produce and certainly has produced a great result by his methodical and unconscious means of selection, what may not nature effect? Man can act only on external and visible characters: nature cares nothing for appearances, except in so far as they may be useful to any being. She can act on every internal organ, on every shade of constitutional difference, on the whole machinery of life. Man selects only for his own good; Nature only for that of the being which she tends. Every selected character is fully exercised by her; and the being is placed under well-suited conditions of life.

It may be said that natural selection is daily and hourly scrutinising, throughout the world, every variation, even the slightest; rejecting that which is bad, preserving and adding up all that is good; silently and insensibly working, whenever and wherever opportunity offers, at the improvement of each organic being in relation to its organic and inorganic conditions of life. We see nothing of these slow changes in progress, until the hand of time has marked the long lapse of ages, and then so imperfect is our view into long past geological ages, that we only see that the forms of life are now different from what they formerly were.

> Because these changes occur over long periods of geological time, we only see the present forms of life, not the extinct ones.

In looking at many small points of difference between species, which, as far as our ignorance permits us to judge, seem to be quite unimportant, we must not forget that climate, food, &c., probably produce some slight and direct effect. It is, however, far more necessary to bear in mind that there are many unknown laws of correlation of growth, which, when one part of the organisation is modified through variation, and the modifications are accumulated by natural selection for the good of the being, will cause other modifications, often of the most unexpected nature.

> Other factors, such as climate and food, play a role in the modification of life forms.

Illustrations of the action of Natural Selection.—In order to make it clear how, as I believe, natural selection acts, I must beg permission to give one or two imaginary illustrations. Let us take the case of a wolf, which preys on various animals, securing some by craft, some by strength, and some by fleetness; and let us suppose that the fleetest prey, a deer for instance, had from any change in the country increased in numbers, or that other prey had decreased in numbers, during that season of the year when the wolf is hardest pressed for food. I can under such circumstances see no reason to doubt that the swiftest and slimmest wolves would have the best chance of surviving, and so be preserved or selected,—provided always that they retained strength to master their prey at this or at some other period of the year, when they might be compelled to prey on other animals. I can see no more reason to doubt this, than that man can improve the fleetness of his greyhounds by careful and methodical selection, or by that unconscious selection which results from each man trying to keep the best dogs without any thought of modifying the breed.

> Darwin illustrates his natural selection theory with an example of a wolf whose characteristics of swiftness and ability to capture available prey give the wolf the best chance of surviving.

Domestic animals inherit tendencies to hunt distinctive types of prey, that is, one cat will prefer to catch mice, another cat–rats.

Even without any change in the proportional numbers of the animals on which our wolf preyed, a cub might be born with an innate tendency to pursue certain kinds of prey. Nor can this be thought very improbable; for we often observe great differences in the natural tendencies of our domestic animals; one cat, for instance, taking to catch rats, another mice; one cat, according to Mr. St. John, bringing home winged game, another hares or rabbits, and another hunting on marshy ground and almost nightly catching woodcocks or snipes. The tendency to catch rats rather than mice is known to be inherited. Now, if any slight innate change of habit or of structure benefited an individual wolf, it would have the best chance of surviving and of leaving offspring. Some of its young would probably inherit the same habits or structure, and by the repetition of this process, a new variety might be formed which would either supplant or coexist with the parent-form of wolf Or, again, the wolves inhabiting a mountainous district, and those frequenting the lowlands, would naturally be forced to hunt different prey; and from the continued preservation of the individuals best fitted for the two sites, two varieties might slowly be formed.

Summary of Chapter.—If during the long course of ages and under varying conditions of life, organic beings vary at all in the several parts of their organisation, and I think this cannot be disputed; if there be, owing to the high geometrical powers of increase of each species, at some age, season, or year, a severe struggle for life, and this certainly cannot be disputed; then, considering the infinite complexity of the relations of all organic beings to each other and to their conditions of existence, causing an infinite diversity in structure, constitution, and habits, to be advantageous to them, I think it would be a most extraordinary fact if no variation ever had occurred useful to each being's own welfare, in the same way as so many variations have occurred useful to man. But if variations useful to any organic being do occur, assuredly individuals thus characterised will have the best chance of being preserved in the struggle for life; and from the strong principle of inheritance they will tend to produce offspring similarly characterised. This principle of preservation, I have called, for the sake of brevity, Natural Selection. Natural selection, on the principle of qualities being inherited at corresponding ages, can modify the egg, seed, or young, as easily as the adult. Amongst many animals, sexual selection will give its aid to ordinary selection, by assuring to the most vigorous and best adapted males the greatest number of offspring. Sexual selection will also give characters useful to the males alone, in their struggles with other males.

Whether natural selection has really thus acted in nature, in modifying and adapting the various forms of life to their several conditions and stations, must be judged of by the general tenour and balance of evidence given in the following chapters. But we already see how it entails extinction; and how largely extinction has acted in the world's history, geology plainly declares. Natural selection, also, leads to divergence of character; for more living beings can be supported on the same area the more they diverge in structure, habits, and constitution, of which we see proof by looking at the inhabitants of any small spot or at naturalised productions. Therefore during the modification of the descendants of any one species, and during the incessant struggle of all species to increase in numbers, the more diversified these descendants become, the better will be their chance of succeeding in the battle of life. Thus the small differences distinguishing varieties of the same species, will steadily tend to increase till they come to equal the greater differences between species of the same genus, or even of distinct genera.

We have seen that it is the common, the widely-diffused, and widely-ranging species, belonging to the larger genera, which vary most; and these will tend to transmit to their modified offspring that superiority which now makes them dominant in their own countries. Natural selection, as has just been remarked, leads to divergence of character and to much extinction of the less improved and intermediate forms of life. On these principles, I believe, the nature of the affinities of all organic beings may be ex-

Sexual selection will also give those animals who have inherited favorable variations a distinctive advantage. The most vigorous and best adapted males will have the most descendants.

The more diverse the descendants of any species become, the better their chance of survival in the battle for life. Small differences tend to increase over time until distinct species or even distinct genera are formed.

All animals and plants are closely related to one another, starting with varieties of the same species and branching out to distinct genera, families, orders, and classes.

No one species has been independently created.

plained. It is a truly wonderful fact—the wonder of which we are apt to overlook from familiarity—that all animals and all plants throughout all time and space should be related to each other in group subordinate to group, in the manner which we everywhere behold—namely, varieties of the same species most closely related together, species of the same genus less closely and unequally related together, forming sections and sub-genera, species of distinct genera much less closely related, and genera related in different degrees, forming sub-families, families, orders, sub-classes, and classes. The several subordinate groups in any class cannot be ranked in a single file, but seem rather to be clustered round points, and these round other points, and so on in almost endless cycles. On the view that each species has been independently created, I can see no explanation of this great fact in the classification of all organic beings; but, to the best of my judgment, it is explained through inheritance and the complex action of natural selection, entailing extinction and divergence of character...

The affinities of all the beings of the same class have sometimes been represented by a great tree. I believe this simile largely speaks the truth. The green and budding twigs may represent existing species; and those produced during each former year may represent the long succession of extinct species. At each period of growth all the growing twigs have tried to branch out on all sides, and to overtop and kill the surrounding twigs and branches, in the same manner as species and groups of species have tried to overmaster other species in the great battle for life. The limbs divided into great branches, and these into lesser and lesser branches, were themselves once, when the tree was small, budding twigs; and this connexion of the former and present buds by ramifying branches may well represent the classification of all extinct and living species in groups subordinate to groups. Of the many twigs which flourished when the tree was a mere bush, only two or three, now grown into great branches, yet survive and bear all the other branches; so with the species which lived during long-past geological periods, very few now have living and modified descendants. From the first growth of the tree, many a limb and branch has decayed and dropped off; and these lost branches of various sizes may represent those whole orders, families, and genera which have now no living representatives, and which are known to us only from having been found in a fossil state... As buds give rise by growth to fresh buds, and these, if vigorous, branch out and overtop on all sides many a feebler branch, so by generation I believe it has been with the great Tree of Life, which fills with its dead and broken branches the crust of the earth, and covers the surface with its ever branching and beautiful ramifications.

Darwin uses an analogy of a large tree to illustrate the growth, survival, and extinction of various species as well as different species and genera from a common branch.

RECAPITULATION AND CONCLUSION

The framework of bones being the same in the hand of a man, wing of a bat, fin of the porpoise, and leg of the horse,—the same number of vertebrae forming the neck of the giraffe and of the elephant,—and innumerable other such facts, at once explain themselves on the theory of descent with slow and slight successive modifications. The similarity of pattern in the wing and leg of a bat, though used for such different purpose,—in the jaws and legs of a crab,—in the petals, stamens, and pistils of a flower, is likewise intelligible on the view of the gradual modification of parts or organs, which were alike in the early progenitor of each class. On the principle of successive variations not always supervening at an early age, and being inherited at a corresponding not early period of life, we can clearly see why the embryos of mammals, birds, reptiles, and fishes should be so closely alike, and should be so unlike the adult forms. We may cease marvelling at the embryo of an air-breathing mammal or bird having branchial slits and arteries running in loops, like those in a fish which has to breathe the air dissolved in water, by the aid of well-developed branchiae.

Disuse, aided sometimes by natural selection, will often tend to reduce an organ, when it has become useless by changed habits or under changed conditions of life; and we can

Darwin points out the similarities in the embryos of mammals, birds, reptiles, and fish.

Nature reveals her scheme of modification by the rudimentary organs from long past ages found in the young that fail to develop in the mature animal.

All living beings are but "lineal descendants" of a small number who lived millions of years ago.

clearly understand on this view the meaning of rudimentary organs. But disuse and selection will generally act on each creature, when it has come to maturity and has to play its full part in the struggle for existence, and will thus have little power of acting on an organ during early life; hence the organ will not be much reduced or rendered rudimentary at this early age. The calf, for instance, has inherited teeth, which never cut through the gums of the upper jaw, from an early progenitor having well-developed teeth; and we may believe, that the teeth in the mature animal were reduced, during successive generations, by disuse or by the tongue and palate having been fitted by natural selection to browse without their aid; whereas in the calf, the teeth have been left untouched by selection or disuse, and on the principle of inheritance at corresponding ages have been inherited from a remote period to the present day. On the view of each organic being and each separate organ having been specially created, how utterly inexplicable it is that parts, like the teeth in the embryonic calf or like the shrivelled wings under the soldered wing-covers of some beetles, should thus so frequently bear the plain stamp of inutility! Nature may be said to have taken pains to reveal, by rudimentary organs and by homologous structures, her scheme of modification, which it seems that we wilfully will not understand.

Authors of the highest eminence seem to be fully satisfied with the view that each species has been independently created. To my mind it accords better with what we know of the laws impressed on matter by the Creator, that the production and extinction of the past and present inhabitants of the world should have been due to secondary causes, like those determining the birth and death of the individual. When I view all beings not as special creations, but as the lineal descendants of some few beings which lived long before the first bed of the Silurian system was deposited, they seem to me to become ennobled. Judging from the past, we may safely infer that not one living species will transmit its unaltered likeness to a distant futurity. And of the species now living very few will transmit progeny of any kind to a far distant futurity; for the manner in which all organic beings are grouped, shows that the greater number of species of each genus, and all the species of many genera, have left no descendants, but have become utterly extinct. We can so far take a prophetic glance into futurity as to foretel that it will be the common and widely-spread species, belonging to the larger and dominant groups, which will ultimately prevail and procreate new and dominant species. As all the living forms of life are the lineal descendants of those which lived long before the Silurian epoch, we may feel certain that the ordinary succession by generation has never once been broken, and that no cataclysm has desolated the whole world. Hence we may look with some confidence to a secure future of equally inappreciable length. And as natural selection works solely by and for the good of each being, all corporeal and mental endowments will tend to progress towards perfection.

It is interesting to contemplate an entangled bank, clothed with many plants of many kinds, with birds singing on the bushes, with various insects flitting about, and with worms crawling through the damp earth, and to reflect that these elaborately constructed forms, so different from each other, and dependent on each other in so complex a manner, have all been produced by laws acting around us. These laws, taken in the largest sense, being Growth with Reproduction; Inheritance which is almost implied by reproduction; Variability from the indirect and direct action of the external conditions of life, and from use and disuse; a Ratio of Increase so high as to lead to a Struggle for Life, and as a consequence to Natural Selection, entailing Divergence of Character and the Extinction of less-improved forms. Thus, from the war of nature, from famine and death, the most exalted object which we are capable of conceiving, namely, the production of the higher animals, directly follows. There is grandeur in this view of life, with its several powers, having been originally breathed into a few forms or into one; and that, whilst this planet has gone cycling on according to the fixed law of gravity, from so simple a beginning endless forms most

Each species is not independently created, but rather new species evolve from older, preexisting ones.

The Silurian epoch is a period of geological time around 415 million years ago.

Natural selection works for the good of each organism with a view towards perfection.

Because of the natural selection process, all beings have been, and are, continually evolving.

beautiful and most wonderful have been, and are being, evolved.

Questions for Critical thinking and Discussion

1. How does Darwin apply Malthusian doctrine that human beings multiply faster than their food supply to the plant and animal world?

2. How does Darwin explain the survival of the fittest in the plant and animal world? How does it fit in with natural selection?

3. How does Darwin reconcile natural selection and survival of the fittest with religion? How is it reconciled today?

4. Explain Darwin's analogy of the Great Tree of Life to both extinct and living species.

5. Does Darwin believe that all plants and animals evolved from one prototype?

6. How did businesspersons, geopolitical leaders, and racists in the twentieth century apply Darwinian theories to social, political, and economic problems?

7. Argue for and against extinction of a species from Darwin's point of view and from yours. How are they different? How are they similar?

8. If we became futuristic according to Darwinian theory, how do you imagine man physically, mentally, and emotionally evolving to meet the 22nd century? First state your assumptions, such as genetic engineering, eugenics, destruction of the ecosystem, etc.

9. Explain the objections a fundamentalist Christian finds with Darwinian theory. Are certain religions prohibited from teaching evolution to their believers today?

Self-Test

Part I: Identification

Can you identify each of the following? Tell who, what, when, where, why, and/or how for each term.

1. Nationalism
2. Johann Gottfried von Herder
3. Risorgimento
4. Giuseppe Mazzini
5. Giuseppe Garibaldi
6. Count Camillo di Cavour
7. Count Otto von Bismarck
8. "Blood and iron"
9. Schleswig-Holstein
10. Austro-Prussian War or Seven Weeks' War
11. Franco-Prussian War
12. Ems Dispatch
13. Alsace-Lorraine
14. Dual Monarchy
15. Benjamin Disraeli
16. William Gladstone
17. Parliament Act of 1911
18. Home Rule
19. Baron Georges Haussman
20. Boulanger Crisis
21. Dreyfus Affair
22. Czar Alexander II
23. Russian Revolution of 1905
24. Magyarization
25. Bosnia-Herzegovina
26. *Kulturkampf*
27. Romanticism
28. *The Hunchback of Notre Dame*
29. Franz Schubert
30. "Liberty Leading the People"
31. Conservatism
32. *Reflections on the French Revolution* (1790)
33. Liberalism
34. Thomas Malthus
35. *On Liberty*
36. John Stuart Mill
37. Alexis de Tocqueville
38. *On the Origin of Species by Means of Natural Selection*
39. Social Darwinism
40. Friedrich Nietzsche
41. Sigmund Freud
42. Impressionism
43. Post-Impressionism
44. Henry N. Stanley
45. International Congo Association
46. Boer War
47. Transvaal
48. Orange Free State
49. Sepoy Rebellion
50. Mahatma Gandhi
51. Manchu dynasty
52. Extraterritoriality
53. Open Door Policy
54. Boxer Rebellion
55. Meiji Restoration
56. Three Emperors' League
57. Ottoman Empire
58. Triple Entente
59. Triple Alliance
60. Kaiser or Emperor William II of Germany

Part II: Multiple Choice Questions

Circle the best response from the ones available.

1. Some of the symbols associated with nationalism are:

   a. country's flag.
   b. national anthem.
   c. cultural identity.
   d. all of the above.

2. The following figures were instrumental in the unification of Italy EXCEPT:

   a. Benedetti.   c. Garibaldi.
   b. Cavour.   d. Mazzini.

3. Cavour strengthened the Sardinian economy by:

   a. Building transportation infrastructure.
   b. Reforming the credit system.
   c. Concluding trade treaties to increase commerce.
   d. All of the above.

4. The main thrust of Cavour's policies to unify Italy included all of the following EXCEPT:

   a. Making Sardinia a model state.
   b. Joining the combatants in the Crimean War.
   c. Making a deal with Napoleon III for the compensation of territories.
   d. Restoring the rulers of the central Italian states.

5. In 1860, Giuseppe Garibaldi, at the instigation of Cavour, attacked
   a. France.
   b. Austria.
   c. the Kingdom of the Two Sicilies.
   d. None of the above.

6. All of the following wars furthered the cause of German unification EXCEPT:

    a. Austro-Prussian War.
    b. Austro-Polish War.
    c. Franco-Prussian War.
    d. Danish War

7. Which of the following is NOT true with regard to the process of German unification?

    a. The unification process was directed by the German state of Austria.
    b. The chief architect of the movement was Otto von Bismarck.
    c. As a result of the Chancellor editing the Ems dispatch, France declared war on Prussia.
    d. After the war with France, a new German Empire headed by Emperor William I was proclaimed.

8. As a result of the Franco-Prussian War, all of the following are true EXCEPT:

    a. France reverted to a monarchy.
    b. France ceded Alsace-Lorraine to Germany.
    c. France paid an indemnity of five billion francs.
    d. France sustained a Germany army of occupation.

9. The Zollverein was:

    a. A monetary union.
    b. A customs union.
    c. An Austrian symphony.
    d. A political party devoted to nationalism.

10. The concept of Home Rule was:

    a. the Parliamentary right to evict tenants who did not pay their rent.
    b. the provision of the British Parliament to provide financial relief to Ireland.
    c. the right to have a separate Irish parliament.
    d. the right of reformers to begin a campaign of universal manhood suffrage.

11. Napoleon III's reforms in the Second French Empire included:

    a. Creation of a mortgage bank, the Crédit Mobilier, to encourage economic development.
    b. Lowering of tariff barriers to make French enterprises more competitive.
    c. An extensive public works program, including the building of wide boulevards, in and around Paris.
    d. All of the above.

12. Which one of the following is NOT true of the Dreyfus Affair?

    a. The Catholic Church, the army, the monarchists, and anti-Semites were discredited.
    b. Captain Alfred Dreyfus was falsely accused of spying for Germany.
    c. Major Ferdinand Esterhazy was convicted and imprisoned for the rest of his life.
    d. Émile Zola exposed the cover up in an open letter to the president of the French republic.

13. Czar Alexander II of Russia's greatest accomplishment was:

    a. The winning of the Crimean War.
    b. The introduction of *zemstvos*.
    c. The granting of land to the serfs.
    d. The freeing of the serfs.

14. The greatest problem the Dual Monarchy of Austria-Hungary faced prior to World War I was:

    a. The problem of ethnic minorities desiring independence.
    b. The decision to divide the empire into two separate states with two Parliaments.
    c. The decision to speak two official languages (German and Magyar) within the empire.
    d. The inability to annex Bosnia-Herzegovina.

15. The nineteenth-century Christopher Columbus of the unconscious was:

    a. Sigmund Freud.
    b. Charles Darwin.
    c. Friedrich Nietzsche.
    d. Herbert Spencer.

16. Bismarck's domestic policies included:

    a. Adoption of a protective tariff.
    b. Initiation of extensive social welfare legislation, such as old-age and health benefits, etc.
    c. Outlawing the Social Democratic Party.
    d. All of the above.

17. Which one of the following painters is incorrectly matched with his/her work?

    a. Van Gogh — *Starry Night*.
    b. Cezanne — *Landscape with Olive Trees*.
    c. Monet — *Impression: Sunrise*.
    d. Cassatt — *A Woman in Black at the Opera*.

18. Which one of the following was the proponent of the theory of Social Darwinism?

    a. Sigmund Freud.
    b. Friedrich Nietzsche.
    c. Herbert Spencer.
    d. Alfred Sisley.

19. Which one of the following characteristics is NOT true of the Romantic Movement?:

    a. It rejected the rationalism of the Enlightenment.
    b. It sang the praises of nature.
    c. It rejected revealed religion.
    d. It stressed the uniqueness of the individual.

20. Three musical composers associated with the Romantic movement were:

    a. Wagner, Schubert, Tchaikovsky.
    b. Berlioz, Scott, Wagner.
    c. Schubert, Handel, Smith.
    d. Schubert, Berlioz, Hugo.

21. The following writers were representative of the Romantic movement EXCEPT:

    a. Goethe.   c. Coleridge.
    b. Dickens.   d. Hugo.

22. Which one of the following beliefs was NOT held by nineteenth -century conservatives:

    a. Belief in hereditary aristocracy.
    b. Belief in the status quo.
    c. Belief in established religion.
    d. Belief in democratic institutions.

23. The key figure associated with the conservative ideology of the 18th century was:

    a. John Stuart Mill.   c. John Locke.
    b. Benjamin Franklin.   d. Edmund Burke.

24. Liberalism in the 19th century espoused which of the following:

    a. Bill of rights.
    b. Representative government.
    c. Written constitution.
    d. All of the above.

25. The following authors and their works are correctly matched EXCEPT:

    a. Thomas Malthus — <u>Essay on the Principle of Population</u>.
    b. David Ricardo — <u>Democracy in America</u>.
    c. Adam Smith — <u>Wealth of Nations</u>.
    d. John Stuart Mill — <u>On Liberty</u>.

26. Which one of the following ideas is NOT associated with Thomas Malthus?:

    a. Poor should learn the discipline of sexual abstinence.
    b. Poor should demand government interference for higher wages.
    c. Poor will only have more children if their wages are increased.
    d. Population growth outstrips food supply.

27. Which one of the following factors did NOT contribute to the "new imperialism"?

    a. Economic gain.   c. Isolationism.
    b. Racism.   d. Nationalism.

28. Which one of the following statements is NOT true about the Boer War?

    a. The Boers were originally Dutch colonists who settled around the Cape of Good Hope in Africa.
    b. The Boers created two independent republics: the Transvaal and the Orange Free State.
    c. The Boers used guerrilla warfare against the French.
    d. After the defeat of the Boers, the Transvaal and the Orange Free State joined with the Cape Colony and Natal to form the Union of South Africa.

29. By the terms of the Treaty o Nanking (Nanjing), China:

    a. Ceded the island of Hong Kong to the British.
    b. Opened up ports to foreign trade.
    c. Limited duties on British imports to 5%.
    d. All of the above.

30. Which one of the following statements is NOT true about the Boxer Rebellion?

    a. Boxers besieged foreign legations in Beijing.
    b. Boxers killed many foreigners and Chinese converts to Christianity.
    c. Boxers were a secret society formed to practice fisticuffs.
    d. All of the above.

31. Under the Meiji Restoration,

    a. Japan sought to adopt western ways and modernize its military.
    b. Commodore Perry opened Japan to trade with the West.
    c. The Qing dynasty was overthrown.
    d. Buddhism was given preference over Shintoism.

32. Which one of the following is NOT an explorer?

    a. Livingstone.
    b. Da Gama.
    c. Stanley.
    d. Hobson.

33. During the Age of Imperialism, technical superiority over native peoples was achieved by the following:

    a. Repeating rifles.
    b. Ironclad warships.
    c. Machine guns.
    d. All of the above.

34. The main goal of Bismarck's foreign policy was:

    a. To acquire additional territories for Germany.
    b. To keep France isolated and without allies.
    c. To initiate a general organization dedicated to international peace.
    d. To form an alliance with Serbia.

35. Pan-Slavism is:

    a. A movement to free Turkey from Austrian control.
    b. A movement to bring all ethnic Germans under the protection of Germany.
    c. A movement to bring all Slavic peoples under the protection of Russia.
    d. An agreement with Russia to create a new state north of the Black Sea.

36. The following nations comprised the Triple Entente:

    a. Austria, Germany, Italy.
    b. Russia, France, Britain.
    c. Russia, Austria, France.
    d. Germany, Russia, Britain.

37. The Germans provoked the *First* Moroccan Crisis in 1905 because:

    a. The French and British military staffs were consulting one another regarding war.
    b. Germany wanted a free hand in the Congo as a tradeoff for leaving Morocco to the English.
    c. There was historical antagonism between Germany and Morocco.
    d. Germany wanted to prove to the French that Britain was not a reliable ally.

38. The main source of trouble in the Balkans prior to the outbreak of World War I was:

   a. Serbia wanted its independence from the Ottoman Empire.
   b. Serbia wanted to annex Turkey.
   c. Serbia became increasingly resentful toward Austria because of its annexation of Bosnia-Herzegovina.
   d. Serbia wanted its navy to have ports along the Austrian coastline.

39. The English were antagonized by the Germans prior to World War I for all of the following reasons EXCEPT:

   a. The German buildup of its navy.
   b. Germany's signing the Dual Alliance with France.
   c. The German Kaiser's pro-Afrikaner sympathies during the Boer War.
   d. Germany's commercial success as a fierce competitor to England.

Part III: Review and Thought Questions

1. Explain the divisions of Italy at the middle of the 19th century. What prevented unification?

2. What was Mazzini's strategy to create a unified Italian republic?

3. Why was Cavour more successful than Mazzini or Garibaldi in the *Risorgimento*?

4. What was the main thrust of Cavour's policies in regard to the royal house of Savoy?

5. What strategies did Cavour employ for making Sardinia a model state?

6. What were Emperor Napoleon III and Cavour's schemes for compensation of territories in a war against Austria? What factors led to Napoleon III's unilateral agreement with the Austrian emperor?

7. Explain the role of Garibaldi in the unification of Italy. What made Cavour nervous about Garibaldi's successes?

8. Trace the unification of Germany. Include discussions of Bismarck's wars with Denmark, Austria, and France.

9. What role did the Ems Dispatch have in provoking France to declare war on Prussia?

10. What terms imposed by Bismarck at the conclusion of the Franco-Prussian War made France obsessed with revenge?

11. How did the changes in the Austrian empire from 1867 to 1914 help to set the stage for World War I?

12. Why was the Dreyfus Affair so divisive to the French republic in the early twentieth century?

13. Explain how the Nazis used Nietzsche's theories.

14. Describe Darwin's theory of evolution.

15. Contrast the Impressionists with the Post-Impressionist painters, giving examples of each along with their works.

16. Evaluate the new imperialism of the late nineteenth century. What were its causes? What were its effects?

17. Explain how and why the European powers partitioned Africa.

18. How did Japan cope with its confrontation with the West? How was it possible for the Japanese to retain their cultural traditions and still industrialize? Do you think the Japanese studied what had happened in China?

19. What was the main goal of Bismarck's foreign policy? What steps did he take to achieve this goal?

20. Describe the conflicts of interest in the Balkan Peninsula prior to World War I.

21. Explain how the alliance system operated before Bismarck's dismissal by Emperor William II. How did it work after Bismarck left his post?

Part IV: Full-Length Essays

1. Describe the process of Italian unification step by step.

2. Trace the wars that led to German unification. Describe how each war gave impetus to German unification under Prussian leadership.

3. Compare and contrast liberalism and conservatism as practiced in the nineteenth century with the twentieth century.

4. Discuss the characteristics and personalities of the Romantic Movement. Include three writers, three composers, three artists along with their respective works that best exemplify this movement.

5. Compare and contrast the ideas of Charles Darwin with those of Friedrich Nietzsche.

6. What differences do you find in the domestic politics of Great Britain, France, and Germany prior to World War I?

7. Describe and evaluate the causes for the new imperialism. Give specific examples.

8. Describe imperialism in the nineteenth century in one of the following: the Congo, India, or China.

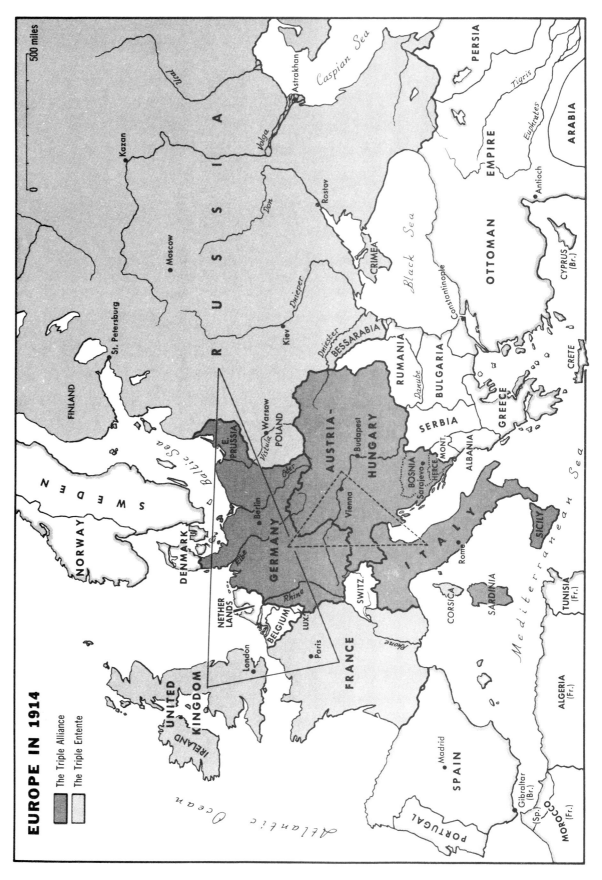

EUROPE IN 1914

The Triple Alliance
The Triple Entente

500 miles

NORWAY

SWEDEN

FINLAND

St. Petersburg

Moscow

Kazan

Ural

Volga

Astrakhan

Caspian Sea

R U S S I A

Don

Rostov

Dnieper

Kiev

Dniester

BESSARABIA

CRIMEA

Black Sea

Baltic Sea

DENMARK

E. PRUSSIA

Warsaw

Vistula

POLAND

Oder

Berlin

GERMANY

Elbe

NETHER-
LANDS

BELGIUM

LUX.

Rhine

Paris

FRANCE

SWITZ.

Rhone

Vienna

AUSTRIA-
HUNGARY

Budapest

Danube

RUMANIA

BULGARIA

SERBIA

BOSNIA

HERCE.

MONT.

Sarajevo

ALBANIA

GREECE

Constantinople

OTTOMAN EMPIRE

PERSIA

Tigris

Euphrates

ARABIA

Antioch

CYPRUS
(Br.)

CRETE

I T A L Y

Rome

SICILY

SARDINIA

CORSICA

Mediterranean Sea

TUNISIA
(Fr.)

ALGERIA
(Fr.)

SPAIN

Madrid

Gibraltar
(Br.)

PORTUGAL

MOROCCO
(Fr.)

UNITED
KINGDOM

IRELAND

London

Atlantic Ocean

From *History of Western Civilization: A Handbook*, 6th edition by William H. McNeill. Copyright 1986 by University of Chicago Press. Reprinted by permission.

Chapter IV

WORLD WAR I
and
WORLD WAR II

Figure 4.2 **Benito Mussolini** (1883-1945). Fashioning a paramilitary organization of Black Shirts, Mussolini became the role model of a right-wing fascist party leader for Adolph Hitler. Mussolini drained the Pontine marshes, built infrastructure, and brought esteem to the Italian people

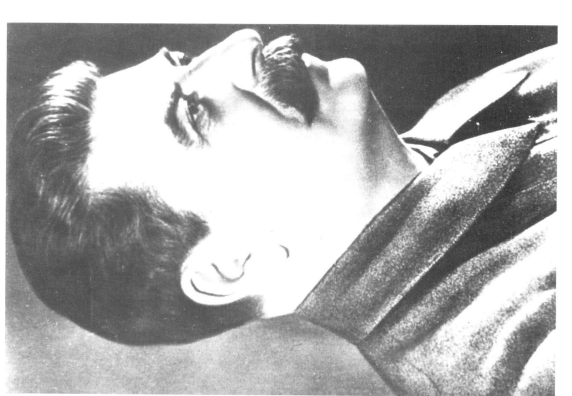

Figure 4.1 **Joseph Stalin** (1879-1953). As Secretary-General of the Communist Party in the former Union of Soviet Socialist Republics, Stalin ruthlessly and brutally consolidated total power in his hands. During his leadership of the USSR from 1928 to 1953, Stalin exiled, imprisoned, or killed between 9 and 11 million of his countrymen in various purges

10

World War I and the Rise of Communism

UNDERSTANDING
The Twentieth Century

This chapter and the next chapter deal with events of the twentieth century. What is most remarkable about the twentieth century is that 1999 is not too dissimilar from 1900. Only at the very end of this century can we make such a statement. In 1900, Europe was at peace, prosperous, and relatively free. If a person had the financial means, he could travel anywhere in Europe and most of the world without even a passport. By 1999, Europeans are at peace, prosperous, and relatively free. The European nations have joined together in the European Union. A single European passport allows them to travel, settle, and work anywhere in the European Union. A single currency is in the works.

While the czar is gone, Russia is again Russia. The Soviet Union, which began in 1917 as a consequence of World War I, had disappeared peacefully by the end of 1991, apparently from internal causes. While the Kaiser is gone, Germany is again the most populous and powerful state in central Europe. Berlin is again the capital of Germany. Two lost world wars, unconditional surrender, division into four zones of mili-

Discuss the similarities between 1999 and 1900.

Look at a map of Europe in 1914. Where are the Balkans? Are the Balkans a part of Europe?

What does the United States have in common with France and England?

tary occupation, creation of two German states within a single nation, East and West Germany, battlefield of the Cold War, all those momentous events which occupied most of this century have dissolved.

Even the Balkans of 1999 show similarities to 1900. Sarajevo re-emerged uncannily in the news like it had in 1914. The beginning and the end of the century are very different from its middle portion.

The focus of this chapter is 1914 to 1945. the period of World War I and World War II. These two wars pitted Germany against France, Russia, and the United Kingdom. The two wars were separated by a twenty-year truce. World War I produced the Russian Revolution and the triumph of Communism in what came to be called the Soviet Union. World War I also produced Mussolini and Fascism in Italy and directly contributed to the rise of Hitler and Nazism in Germany. Totalitarianism of the right and totalitarianism of the left challenged the Franco-Anglo-Saxon liberal, democratic, constitutionalism of what came to be called the West. The United States weighed in on the side of the United Kingdom and France. Our alliance with the Soviet Union in World War II was fortuitous. The enemy of my enemy is my friend. Hitler had attacked Stalin; therefore the U.S. backed Stalin.

World War I

The Assassination of Archduke Francis Ferdinand

On June 28, 1914, Archduke Francis Ferdinand, heir to the Austrian throne, and his wife were visiting Sarajevo in Bosnia, when they were assassinated. The assassin, a Serbian national named Gavrilo Princip (1895-1918), was a member of a secret society called the Black Hand. This terrorist organization was under the influence of the Serbian chief of intelligence. The Austrians supected a Serbian connection and determined to deal with Serbia once and for all. After obtaining assurance of support from Germany, Austria made harsh demands upon Serbia. The intent was to provoke a war. The Austrian ultimatum included demands for the cessation of anti-Austrian propaganda and a demand that Austria be permitted to participate with Serbia in the internal investigation and punishment of those Serbians involved in the assassination. Serbia agreed to most of the demands, but was unwilling to permit Austrian participation in internal judicial proceedings. The Austrians found the Serbian response unacceptable and declared war on Serbia.

Russia mobilized to support Serbia. Since the side that mobilized first would have an advantage, the Germans sent the Russians an ultimatum demanding demobilization. When the Russians did not respond, the Germans declared war on Russia on August 1, 1914. On August 3rd, the Germans declared war on France and began invading Belgium. On August 4th England declared war on Germany. On the following day Austria declared war on Russia. The round robin of war declarations continued. World War I had begun.

The existence of rival alliance systems, the Triple Alliance versus the Triple Entente, was certainly one of the causes of World War I. Nationalism was another important factor. The war started when a Serbian nationalist took revenge on the Austrian heir for Austria's efforts at preventing the crea-

Who was involved in the assassination of Archduke Francis Ferdinand?

Why did Austria reject Serbia's response to the Austrian ultimatum?

How did the major European powers become involved in the war?

What were some of the factors that contributed to the start of the war?

tion of a Greater Serbia. The French need to regain national honor by getting Alsace-Lorraine back is another example of nationalism. Other factors, such as the armaments race and imperial ambitions, also played their roles in setting the stage for World War I. Analysts don't agree on which factor was most important. Lenin, for instance, thought imperialism, as a stage of capitalist development, was the most important cause. What is more certain is that nations drifted into the war without realizing the scope of the war, how long it would last, or how extensive the casualties would be. By 1914, Europe was industrialized, and this was to be a different type of war than those fought previously on European soil.

The Opposing Sides

Who were the Allies and who were the Central Powers?

The war lasted from 1914-1918. Before it ended, there were over fifty declarations of war. The Triple Entente had been transformed into the ALLIES who included Britain, France, Russia, Serbia, Japan, Greece, Portugal, Romania, and even Italy, which joined in 1915. The Italians did not feel bound by the Triple Alliance, since they considered Austria to be an aggressor. The Allied side offered Italy the best deal for joining their side. Turkey and Bulgaria joined Germany and Austria-Hungary to form the opposing side, the CENTRAL POWERS.

The Western Front

The German war strategy, the Schlieffen Plan, which had been worked out long before 1914 by General Alfred von Schlieffen (1833-1913), was aimed at achieving

German success in a matter of weeks. The plan attempted to deal with the probability of a two-front war—one front against France in the west and another front against Russia in the east. As much as ninety percent of the German army was to be used in a move against France from the north, going through Belgium and Holland. The Germans correctly anticipated that the French would concentrate their forces in the east in an effort to retake Alsace-Lorraine. Minimal German forces would be assigned to the east against the slower mobilizing Russians. Once the Germans had defeated the French, they could turn the bulk of their forces eastward to deal with the Russians.

Several things went wrong. The German general, Helmuth Johannes Ludwig von Moltke (1848-1916), did not follow Schlieffen in all its particulars. For example, he diverted some troops to the east. He did not invade Holland. His forces were unable to swing west of Paris as originally planned. The Russians also proved stronger than anticipated.

Despite initial German successes, the French launched a successful counterattack in the First Battle of the Marne, from September 5 to 12, 1914. The German advance, which had reached to within thirty miles of Paris, was stopped. Von Moltke was relieved of his command. In 1916, Emperor William II gave General Paul von Hindenburg (1847-1934) and General Erich Ludendorff (1865-1937) joint operational responsibility for the German supreme command. Very quickly the western front developed into a series of trenches over 400 miles long running from the Belgian coast through France to the Swiss border. The soldiers in the trenches had machine guns and were backed by mortars. Barbed wire was used to protect the trenches and prevent surprise attacks. While

What was the Schlieffen Plan? To what extent was it followed?

Describe the style of warfare on the western front.

Compare German success on the western and eastern fronts.

Why did the Russians do so poorly against the Germans?

tanks and airplanes were used in World War I, they were not used in an effective manner to break the stalemate of trench warfare. The war on the western front became a defensive battle. For most of the four years, commanders on either side tried for the big offensive breakthrough, but the reality was only a little territory was gained here and there at the cost of thousands of lives.

The Eastern Front

The story on the eastern front was different. While the Russians enjoyed some successes against the armies of Austria-Hungary, they enjoyed much less success against the Germans. As early as late August 1914 at Tannenberg, the Russians suffered a major defeat, and about 100,000 Russians were taken prisoner. Nevertheless, the Russians managed to hold on until the end of 1917, thereby forcing the Germans to divert critical resources to the eastern front.

The Russians suffered from poor leadership and from a lack of basic weapons. Russia was not yet fully industrialized, while Germany was. As the war dragged on, the stockpile of guns and weapons available to the Russian army began to disappear. There were instances of Russian soldiers going into battle without rifles. Heavy Russian losses at the front led to the overthrow of the czarist government in March 1917. The provisional government that replaced it continued to fight on the Allied side. In November 1917, in a second revolution, the Bolsheviks, an anti-war party, came to power under Lenin. With the disintegration of the czarist army, which the Bolsheviks had encouraged for their revolutionary purposes, Russia pulled out of the war. The Germans at their furthest line of advance had cut deep into the Russian

Empire, taking all of the Ukraine. The Russians were forced to sign the humiliating Treaty of Brest-Litovsk on March 3, 1918. Under the terms of the treaty, Russia lost control of the Ukraine, Finland, Georgia, Poland, and the Baltic States. Portions of the Caucasus went to Turkey. From the German perspective, gaining access to Ukrainian grain and freeing up armies for transfer to the western front were the most important gains of Brest-Litovsk. This treaty demonstrated the harsh terms the Central Powers would have imposed had they been the victors on all the war fronts. Of course, with the ultimate defeat of the Central Powers, the Treaty of Brest-Litovsk was nullified. The actual territorial arrangements in Eastern Europe after the war are discussed later in the chapter.

Other Fronts

The war brought action on a number of fronts. Italy had joined the Allies in April 1915 because of the Austrian territories it had been promised. Making slow progress against the Austrians, the Italians were attacked by combined German and Austrian forces in 1917 and forced to retreat to a line along the Piave River, inside northern Italy. The Italians had lost over 600,000 men, who either had been taken prisoner or had deserted.

The Central Powers were successful in the Balkans in their assaults against Serbia and Romania. Turkey withstood British and French attempts to take control of the Dardanelles. The Allies sustained some 500,000 casualties in fighting on the Gallipoli peninsula. Eventually, British forces made significant headway against the Ottoman Empire in the Middle East, taking both Baghdad and

What were the major provisions of the Treaty of Brest-Litovsk? What did it demonstrate?

How did the Italians do in World War I?

Where did the Turks succeed?

Describe Allied successes in the Middle East.

Jerusalem. T. E. Lawrence (1888-1935), better known as Lawrence of Arabia, worked among the Arabs to exploit anti-Turkish sentiment. The Armenians needed little inducement to rise up against their Turkish masters. The resulting Turkish massacres cost between 600,000 and one million Armenian lives. German colonies, with the exception of East Africa, were captured early in the war.

Achieving Victory

What was the most important requirement for achieving victory?

Mobilization of the home front was an essential requirement for victory. The armies had to be continuously supplied with ammunition, weapons, and food. Economic controls and press censorship were introduced in most countries. Some countries were more effective than others in their mobilization efforts on the home front. Russia and Austria-Hungary were notably ineffective. Britain and France had credible programs for civilian mobilization by 1915. One of the striking lessons in fighting this industrialized war was the importance of women in industry. The number of women in Great Britain's workforce was 250,000 at the start of the war. When the war concluded, there were five million women in Britain's workforce. It has been estimated that two out of every five workers in Germany's ammunition factories were women. At the Krupp works, in 1914 there were no women workers. By 1917, Krupp employed 12,000 women.

What role did women play on the homefront?

If the war could have been brought to a quick conclusion, as the Schlieffen Plan envisioned, the Central Powers might have won. But as the war dragged on, the Allies had two essential advantages: control of the seas (thanks to the British navy) and a greater population from which to mobilize troops. The total Allied forces mobilized were approximately 42,188,810, compared to the 22,850,000 troops the Central Powers were able to mobilize.

The surface ships of the German navy were easily outgunned by the British fleet. The British defeated the Germans at the battle of Dogger Bank in January 1915 and again in the battle of Jutland on May 31 and June 1, 1916. As a consequence, the German surface fleet spent most of the war holed up in North Sea homeports. The Allies enforced a naval blockade that denied the Central Powers not only weapons of war, but food-stuffs as well. Thus, in the long run starvation might have been the result. Indeed, the civilian population in Germany became more reliant on bark coffee, turnips, and sawdust bread as the war progressed.

The Germans attempted to counter the British advantage in surface ships by using the submarine, or U-boat. This new technology was quite effective. The problem was that submarines could not capture supplies or people; they could only sink the ships with extraordinary loss of life. On May 7, 1915, the Germans sank the *Lusitania*, a British passenger ship that was carrying ammunition. Nearly 1200 people died, including 118 Americans. President Woodrow Wilson vigorously protested to Germany. For a time, the Germans restricted the use of submarine warfare.

As the blockade slowly drained the Central Powers, the Germans reconsidered. In January 1917, they proclaimed the resumption of unrestricted submarine warfare. It has been estimated that the Allies lost six million tons of shipping in 1917 to German U-boats. Eventually, the Allies learned to overcome the German submarines by using

Evaluate the naval strengths of both sides.

Discuss the German use of submarine warfare.

Why did the contents of the Zimmermann Note anger the American public?

Why was the arrival of U.S. troops in Europe important?

depth charges, subchasers, and convoys to protect shipping.

The United States broke off diplomatic relations with Germany after that country's resumption of torpedoing of passenger ships without warning. Then the ZIMMERMANN NOTE became public. The British had intercepted a message between the German foreign minister, Arthur Zimmermann (1859-1940), and the German ambassador to Mexico. The note revealed that Germany was seeking an alliance with Mexico. If the Mexicans would go to war, the Germans would help them regain such territories as Texas, which had been lost in the Mexican-American war. The result of all this was that war fever in the U.S. rose to new highs. Congress declared war against Germany on April 6, 1917.

In March 1918, with Russia out of the war, Germany was in a position to transfer thousands of their troops from the eastern to the western front. The Germans realized that the arrival of fresh American troops would inevitably break the stalemate on the western front in favor of the Allies. So the German general, Erich Ludendorff, launched a new offensive on the western front that lasted into July 1918. The Germans made some progress, once more reaching the Marne River, but the offensive cost them an estimated million men killed, wounded, or captured. This Second Battle of the Marne was met by an Allied counteroffensive on July 18th. The Germans were forced to withdraw completely from the Marne area.

By July 1918, U.S. troops were coming to Europe at the rate of 300,000 a month. There would be two million American troops on hand at the end of the war. This meant that the Allies had reserve forces, whereas the Germans had used up all their reserves. When the Allied forces began a counterattack in July under the now unified command of the French general, Ferdinand Foch (1851-1929), the tide of battle turned. The German forces were forced into a continued retreat in the face of a superior Allied force now equipped with tanks. Their retreat was rapidly taking them back to their own borders. Revolts began to flare inside Germany. Emperor William II abdicated on November 9, 1918. An armistice was signed on November 11th, ending hostilities with the defeat of Germany. As for the other Central Powers, the Bulgarians had surrendered on September 29th, the Turks had capitulated on October 30th, and the Austrians had signed an armistice on November 4th.

Describe the end of World War I.

Terms of the Peace Settlement

The costs of the war were tremendous. It has been estimated that over eight million soldiers died, and more than 21 million troops were wounded. War-related, civilian deaths exceeded six million. The financial costs were more than 180 billion dollars. Many participants experienced huge increases in national debt. In France, for instance, the national debt rose 4.5 times the pre-war level.

Estimate the costs of World War I in human and financial terms.

The peace conference began in Paris on January 18, 1919. Twenty-seven nations sent representatives. The Central Powers were excluded, as was Russia, which was in the hands of the Communists. The actual decisions were made by the Big Four powers: Britain, France, Italy, and the United States.

President Woodrow Wilson (1856-1924) represented the United States. Rather idealistic, he wanted a League of Nations established to preserve peace in the future. He had proposed such an association in the FOURTEEN POINTS of January 1918 as part

What were the aims of each of the Big Four leaders at the Paris Peace Conference?

of a future peace settlement. Other points included such novel arrangements as having open covenants, or agreements, openly arrived at, arms reduction, and popular self-determination.

The French representative, Georges Clemenceau (1841-1929), was a striking contrast to Wilson. Clemenceau put no faith in a League of Nations. As a fervent nationalist, he wanted Germany crippled so that it could not successfully wage war again, and France would be avenged for past wrongs.

The other two members of the Big Four were David Lloyd George (1863-1945), prime minister of Britain, who also distrusted the Fourteen Points, and Vittorio Emanuele Orlando (1860-1952), the premier of Italy, who fought vigorously for adding territory to Italy at the expense of Austria and Yugoslavia.

Describe the organization of the League of Nations.

Woodrow Wilson won acceptance of the LEAGUE OF NATIONS as an integral part of all the peace treaties. The League, headquartered in Geneva, Switzerland, was to have an Assembly in which each member nation was represented. The major political work of the League was to be done by a nine-member Council in which the United States, Great Britain, France, Italy, and Japan would have permanent seats. Many of the decisions of the Assembly and the Council required unanimity. There was also to be a Secretariat for administration, a Permanent Court of International Justice, and an International Labor Organization. A major purpose of the League was to settle disputes among nations without resort to war. Disputes might be settled by arbitration, by judicial decision, or by discussion and recommendation by the Council. Sanctions could be imposed on a party to a dispute that failed to accept League advice. The failure of the United States to join the League, the need for consensus in making decisions, the fact that unhappy members could withdraw from the League, the lack of a permanent military to enforce League decisions—all contributed to the weakness of the League of Nations in practice.

Much of the Fourteen Points was compromised. Popular self-determination was only partially implemented. Separate peace treaties were signed with each of the Central Powers. The first treaty was the Treaty of Versailles with Germany, which provided that Alsace-Lorraine be given back to France, northern Schleswig, after a plebiscite, to Denmark, smaller areas to Belgium, and parts of Posen and West Prussia to a revived Poland, giving the Poles access to the Baltic Sea. The German-speaking city of Danzig (Gdansk) was made a free city under the League of Nations to provide a port at the end of this Polish Corridor. The arrangement separated East Prussia from the rest of Germany and undid German gains going back to the first partition of Poland (1772). World War II would start when Germany invaded Poland in 1939 seeking a new partition of Poland.

France had wanted the Saar Basin with its coal mines, but had to settle for getting the coal mines to exploit. The Saar itself was placed under the League of Nations for 15 years, at the end of which a plebiscite would be held to determine who would possess the area. (In 1935 the Saar region elected to return to Germany.) The Rhineland was to be occupied by Allied forces for a period of 15 years and to be permanently demilitarized. Germany lost all its overseas possessions, which were occupied by Allied nations under League mandates.

German military might was strictly limited. The army could have no more than 100,000 men. An air force was not permitted.

What were some of the reasons for the League's weakness?

What territories did Germany lose as a result of the Versailles Treaty?

What were some of the other provisions affecting Germany? Why was Germany particularly resentful of the War-Guilt Clause?

The navy was greatly reduced and submarines were forbidden.

The most controversial part of the treaty was Article 231, the WAR-GUILT CLAUSE, which required Germany to take responsibility for all losses and damages suffered by the Allies and their supporters as a result of the aggression of Germany and the other Central Powers during the war. The purpose of the clause was to justify imposing reparations upon Germany that were fixed, in 1921, at $33 billion dollars. The Germans felt they were unfairly saddled with responsibility, although other defeated nations were forced to sign similar clauses. In any case, the final sum was quite large and never fully recovered.

When the German delegates, who had not been party to drawing up the treaty were shown the proposal, they denounced it. They had believed that the Fourteen Points were to be the basis of the settlement. It was only when faced with the threat of invasion that a German delegation most reluctantly signed the Treaty of Versailles on June 28, 1919. Though it was the government of the German Empire that had been involved in making war, it was the government of the much more democratic German republic that was forced into making the peace. Since Germany had never actually experienced Allied forces on its soil, it was all too easy for later demagogues to put the blame for Germany's misfortune on treasonous republicans.

What was the German reaction to the treaty?

When Austria signed the Treaty of Saint-Germain on September 10, 1919, its empire had already disintegrated. By the treaty, Austria had to recognize the independence of Hungary, Czechoslovakia, Yugoslavia, and Poland. It had to give up Galicia to Poland; Trieste and South Tyrol to Italy. Austria lost about three-quarters of the area it had as a part of the Dual Monarchy.

Its army was limited to 30,000 men; in addition it had to pay reparations for thirty years. The union of Austria and Germany was forbidden.

Hungary, which signed a separate treaty of Trianon on June 4, 1920, lost approximately two-thirds of its territory. It had to give up territory to Czechoslovakia, Romania, and Yugoslavia. It agreed to pay reparations and limit its army to 35,000 men.

The Bulgarians signed the Treaty of Neuilly on November 27, 1919. They gave up territory to Greece, Romania, and Yugoslavia. Bulgaria had to pay reparations and limit its army to 20,000 men.

The conclusion of peace with Turkey took some unexpected twists. A treaty was signed at Sevres on August 10, 1920. This treaty recognized a Christian Armenia, gave much of Turkey's European territory to Greece and limited Turkey to only a portion of Asia Minor. A group of Turkish nationalists, led by Mustafa Kemal (1881-1938), rose up in revolt. They overthrew the Sultanate, reconquered Armenia, took back territories from Greece, and forced the Allies, as an alternative to renewed fighting, to agree to a new Treaty of Lausanne, on July 24, 1923. At Lausanne the Turks agreed to give up claims to non-Turkish territories, such as Palestine, Syria, Iraq, and Arabia. Turkey retained Asia Minor and the territories it had reconquered. No reparations were imposed. Turkey regained control of the Dardanelles, which were to be open to all in peace time, but which could be closed to an enemy in time of war.

Assessment of the Peace

With the benefit of hindsight, it is easy to criticize the peace settlements concluded

What terms were offered to the Austrians, Hungarians, and Bulgarians?

What happened to Turkey in the peace process?

Was the peace imposed on the Central Powers just? Explain.

after World War I. We know that World War II began September 1, 1939. The contrast has already been made with the ninety-nine year general peace in Europe following the Napoleonic wars. What went wrong?

Aggressors such as Hitler came to power in Germany and Mussolini in Italy. Germany and Italy were among the nations very dissatisfied with the peace settlement. Germany objected to the War Guilt Clause, to the reparations, to the territorial restrictions, such as the loss of west Prussia to Poland. Italy had gained Trieste and other territories, but focused on what was not gained: Fiume and Dalmatia. (In fact, the dispute over Italian claims led to the resignation of Premier Orlando in June 1919.)

There is every reason to believe that, if the Central Powers had won, the peace terms they would have imposed would have been just as harsh or harsher than the terms they received. The evidence is the severe terms of the Brest-Litovsk Treaty imposed by Germany on Russia in March 1918, when Germany had won on the eastern front. The architects of the post-World War I peace settlement failed to create adequate mechanisms to insure the maintenance of peace.

Was Wilson a success as a peace maker?

Wilson had hoped that the League of Nations would serve to maintain the peace. But while he succeeded in calling the League into being, he failed to get the U.S. Senate to accept the League or ratify the treaties discussed above. Indeed the U.S., after signing separate peace treaties with the Central Powers, returned to its traditional policy of isolation from Europe. Nor was an effective balance of power established to keep the peace. France entered into commitments with the newly independent states of Eastern Europe to contain Germany. But, without firm commitments from the U.S. and Britain, the coalition of major powers needed for an effective balance of power was lacking. These newly independent nations of Eastern Europe were in a weak position when Germany and Russia regained their strength. Indeed, it can be argued that the disappearance of the Austro-Hungarian Empire from Eastern Europe was another factor working against the establishment of a stable balance of power.

Describe the prospects for the newly independent nations of Eastern Europe.

The Rise of Communism in Russia

Lenin

The first nation to embrace Communism was Russia in November 1917. The man most responsible for the November Revolution was V. I. Lenin, born Vladimir Ilich Ulyanov (1870-1924). Lenin came from a middle-class background and might have been a successful lawyer. Instead, he joined a revolutionary Marxist party known as the Social Democratic party. Perhaps he was influenced by the hanging in 1887 of his older brother, who had been convicted of plotting against the Czar.

Lenin was not merely a follower of Marxist ideas. He was a theoretician who reshaped Marxism so radically that many write about a new ideology: Marxist-Leninism. One contribution of Lenin was to stress the important role of a dedicated, disciplined revolutionary party as the vanguard of the proletariat. In Russia, which was not fully industrialized, the workers and peasants (the great bulk of the population) did not have a sufficiently revolutionary mind-set. Lenin thought the solution was to have a small, centralized, revolutionary party act for the masses. Eventually, he came to

Who was Lenin? How did he reshape the ideas of Marx?

Distinguish the Bolsheviks from the Mensheviks.

believe that such a party could lead the proletarian revolution envisioned by Marx, even though Russia had not yet had a bourgeois revolution to establish the dominance of middle-class capitalists in the society. In 1903, at a party congress, the Social Democrats split over the issue of what type of party to have. Those who followed Lenin's design of a small centralized party became known as the Bolsheviks or majority, since they temporarily dominated the congress. The others, who favored a more loosely organized mass party, became known as the Mensheviks or minority, even though after 1903 the Mensheviks were usually the majority of Social Democrats in Russia.

What brought about the Czar's fall?

The Russian Revolutions

Lenin did not actually cause the overthrow of Czar Nicholas II in March 1917. The March Revolution that toppled the Czar was the final outcome of a deteriorating situation. Russia did not have adequate supplies to fight in industrialized warfare, and the war effort was poorly organized. There were a series of defeats at the hands of the Germans. After the Czar took personal command of the army, he became identified with these failures. On the home front, the influence on the royal family, especially the Czarina, of a licentious monk, Grigory Rasputin (1872-1916), increased the number of incompetents elevated to high places.

Rasputin was finally removed in December 1916 by a group of noble conspirators who poisoned (unsuccessfully), shot, and drowned him. In March 1917, demonstrations broke out over food shortages on the streets of Petrograd (this was the new, non-German name for St. Petersburg). The army refused to suppress the demonstrators and refused to let the Czar, who was at the front, reach Petrograd. Lacking reliable soldiers, Nicholas II abdicated.

The imperial government was replaced by a Provisional Government favoring liberal democracy. First led by Prince George Lvov (1861-1925) and later by Alexander Kerensky (1881-1970), the new government had to contend with a number of political parties, in addition to the Bolsheviks and Mensheviks. Lvov was a member of a moderate party known as the Constitutional Democrats or Cadets. Kerensky, himself a moderate democrat, was a member of the Social Revolutionary party, which had a large peasant following. The Provisional Government not only had to accommodate different parties, but it had to contend with rival institutions for the allegiance of the masses. There existed, in many of the large cities, soviets or councils made up of soldiers, workers, and intellectuals who generally favored some form of socialism. The most important of these councils was the Petrograd Soviet.

The greatest mistake of the Provisional Government was to attempt to remain in the war on the Allied side. This not only increased the discontent of the masses, but it also led the Germans to look for alternate Russian leaders more disposed toward taking Russia out of the war. Thus the Germans permitted Lenin, who had been living in Switzerland when the Czar was overthrown, to cross their lines in a sealed boxcar (so he wouldn't ideologically contaminate German soil) and return to Petrograd on April 16, 1917.

Lenin prepared carefully for the overthrow of the Provisional Government. He first agitated against the policies of the Provisional Government by advocating im-

Who led the Provisional Government?

What was the most important rival of the Provisional Government?

What was its most important mistake?

How and when did Lenin's followers seize power?

mediate peace and the redistribution of land to the peasants and factories to workers' committees. His slogan was "peace, land, and bread." After Bolshevik loyalists had gained control of the Petrograd Soviet, he advocated "All power to the Soviets."[1] Lenin and his followers seized power on the night of November 6-7. They met little resistance in Petrograd. Kerensky fled abroad and eventually lived out his days in New York City. Thus there were two revolutions in Russia in 1917. One in March overthrew the Czar. The other in November installed Lenin and his Bolsheviks in power. At the time, Russia was still using an old style calendar, so some called these separate events the February Revolution and the October Revolution.

The Civil War

Retaining power was more difficult than gaining power. Elections for choosing a Constituent Assembly to write a Russian constitution had already been scheduled for November 25, 1917. Lenin allowed the elections to be held. The results were that the Social Revolutionaries won the majority of seats, winning almost 21 million votes, compared to the 9 million garnered by the Bolsheviks. When the Constituent Assembly met in January, Lenin dissolved it at gun point. The ousted deputies and their followers formed one of the core groups in the Civil War struggle that lasted from 1918 to 1922.

How did Lenin treat the Constituent Assembly?

On March 3, 1918, the disastrous Treaty of Brest-Litovsk was signed with Germany, taking Russia out of the war. One of the best organized fighting forces in Russia at the time was the Czech Legion, which had been fighting on the Russian side against the Austro-Hungarian forces. The Czechs decided to leave Russia by way of Siberia and get by sea to the Western Front, where they could resume fighting the Central Powers. Fighting broke out when some Bolsheviks tried to disarm them, and the Czech Legion joined the anti-Bolshevik forces.

There were many groups that formed the anti-Bolshevik or White opposition. Some were Social Revolutionaries, some were right-wing Czarists, many were peasants whose crops had been requisitioned, or members of independence-minded nationalities such as the Ukrainians and Georgians. The Allies even joined the anti-Bolshevik forces by landing troops at Archangel and Vladivostock and supplying elements of the White armies.

The Bolsheviks, also called the Reds, had renamed their party the Communist Party in March of 1918. They had several advantages. The Whites were never sufficiently in agreement to present a united front against the Reds. Leon Trotsky (1879-1940) organized the Red Army, which became a superb fighting force. A political police, known as the Cheka (which eventually became the KGB), was used to unleash a RED TERROR to exterminate all opposition. Large farmers, people with middle-class backgrounds, as well as the former nobility, automatically were deemed enemies to be hunted down. By 1922, the Communists had gained control of most of what had been imperial Russia, with the notable exceptions of the Baltic states and lands along the Polish frontier.

The NEP and the USSR

The hardships of the Civil War and the Terror had antagonized many elements of society. After a mutiny in February and March of sailors at Kronstadt, who had once

What factors contributed to the start of the Civil War?

Who were the Reds and the Whites?

Who won the Civil War?

What was the NEP?

been among the most loyal of Communist supporters, Lenin instituted the New Economic Policy (NEP). The NEP permitted some forms of capitalism in Russia. Light industry and some retailing were opened to private individuals. The peasants were permitted to sell produce on the market, rather than meet state requisitions. Overall control of the economy remained in state hands. The NEP lasted from 1921 to 1927.

Another concession was made to the diverse nationalities within Russia. In 1922, the country was renamed the Union of Soviet Socialist Republics (USSR). The word Russia was properly reserved for the Russian Soviet Socialist Republic, which was the largest republic within the Union. Attempts were made to offer varying degrees of cultural autonomy to the fifty distinct nationalities eventually recognized. The USSR was not dissolved until the collapse of Communism in 1991.

Why was the USSR created?

Stalin

Who was Stalin?

Lenin was wounded in an attempted assassination in 1918. He suffered complications and strokes, leading to his death on January 21, 1924, at the age of 53. The man who succeeded him was Joseph Stalin (born Joseph Vissarionovich Djugashvili, 1879-1953). Stalin had been appointed general secretary of the Communist Party's Central Committee in 1922. He used that post to crush opponents of the left, including Trotsky who many considered the heir apparent, and of the right. By 1929, with all power in his hands, Stalin established a blood-thirsty totalitarian regime.

Stalin introduced new economic policies. He ended the NEP and set about collectivizing agriculture and industrializing the

USSR. He expropriated the lands of five million of the wealthier farmers, called "kulaks," who were killed or deported. The nation was industrialized in a series of five-year plans, beginning in 1928. Great deprivation accompanied industrialization, since immediate consumption was sacrificed to the creation of heavy industry and increased industrial capacity.

In the 1930's, Stalin instituted a series of purges to eliminate all opposition. The old Bolshevik leadership was a prime target. By 1939, Stalin had arrested over half (1,108) of the delegates to the seventeenth party congress, held in 1934. Millions died through execution or in concentration camps. It was indeed a totalitarian government; that is, all levers of power were at the disposal of one person. There is some question as to Stalin's sanity, at least in later years. Just before he died in 1953, he appears to have been preparing yet another purge, this time against physicians!

What were Stalin's economic and political policies?

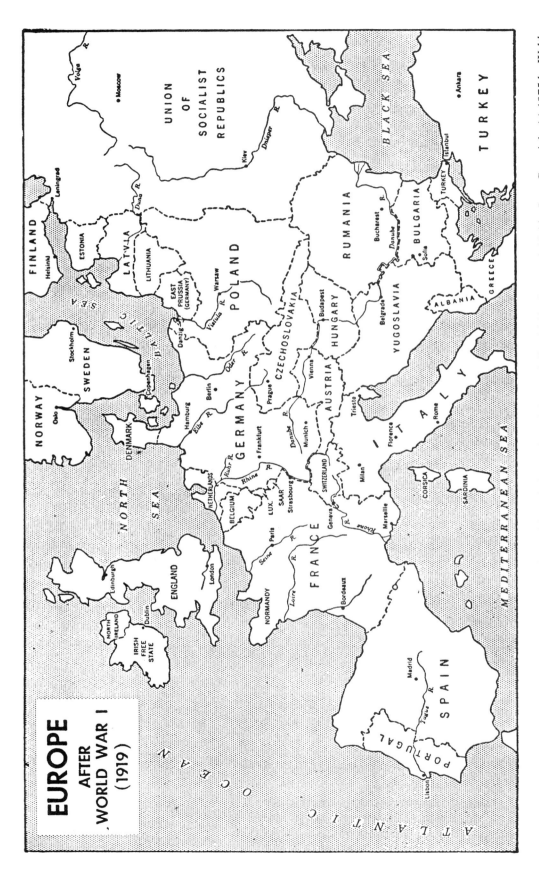

EUROPE
AFTER
WORLD WAR I
(1919)

From *Western Civilization Since 1500*, Second Edition by Walther Kirchner. Copyright (c) 1958, 1966 by Barnes & Noble, Inc. Copyright (c) 1975 by Walther Kirchner. Reprinted by permission of HarperCollins Publishers, Inc.

11

Between the Wars

The Rise of Fascism in Italy

What is fascism?

Mussolini

Communism is an ideology of the extreme left. In Italy and Germany, during the period between the world wars, communism was opposed by fascism, an ideology of the extreme right. It developed as justification for the activities of men like Benito Mussolini and Adolf Hitler. Fascism permits capitalism, or the private ownership of the means of production, but it subordinates economic activity and all other social activities to the regulation of the state, which is dominated by one leader and one party. Fascism may be compatible with capitalism, whereas communism is not. But fascism is incompatible with the kind of liberal democracy that Woodrow Wilson championed when he brought the United States into World War I.

Benito Mussolini (1883-1945) created the prototype of the fascist state. Before World War I, Mussolini was editor of a socialist newspaper in Milan. He broke with the socialists to urge Italy's entry into the war on the Allied side in hopes of nationalist expansion. Mussolini served in the war and was wounded. After the war, in 1919, he founded a highly nationalistic group of war veterans known as the *Fasci di Combattimento*, or Band of Combat. The Fasces, a

Who created the first fascist state? Who were the Fasci?

Why did the March on Rome succeed?

What political changes did Mussolini inaugurate on coming to power?

bundle of rods bound around an ax, had been an ancient Roman symbol of authority. At this time in Italy, the atmosphere was one of great discontent. Italy had expected more rewards for supporting the victorious allies. Inflation, strikes, and street violence prevailed. Mussolini was an opportunist. With support from rightist landlords and factory owners, the blackshirted Fasci carried on a campaign of terrorist aggression against socialists, communists, liberals, and Catholics. By 1922, the Fascists controlled governments in several cities in northern Italy.

Achieving Power

On October 27, 1922, the Fascists, eager to be included in the national government, began a MARCH ON ROME from Milan. When the fearful king, Victor Emmanuel III, refused to call out the army, Mussolini went for broke and demanded that he be made prime minister. The king capitulated, and on October 30th Mussolini arrived by train from Milan to greet his marching followers and to take over the Italian government.

Mussolini formed a coalition government and was granted emergency powers for a year. He forced through parliament a new election law providing that the party who won the most votes (but not necessarily a majority) would get two thirds of the seats in the Chamber of Deputies. When elections were held in 1924, the Fascists received better than three-fifths of the total vote, but there was widespread election fraud and intimidation in the elections. When the socialist deputy Giacomo Matteotti exposed the frauds and bullying, he was murdered. High-ranking Fascists were implicated in the murder. The opposition withdrew from the

Chamber of Deputies. When Mussolini was not dismissed, he moved to consolidate his power. Opposition parties were outlawed, parliamentary and royal powers were limited, and censorship was established.

The Lateran Treaty of 1929

Perhaps Mussolini's greatest diplomatic achievement was the signing of the Lateran Treaty in 1929, whereby the Catholic Church and the Italian state were at last reconciled. Ever since the seizure of Rome from the papacy in 1870, popes had resented their status as "prisoners" in the Vatican. The new agreement recognized the pope as the head of a tiny (0.17 square miles), independent state within Rome called Vatican City. The Catholic Church also received compensation for the property seized in 1870. Roman Catholicism was recognized as the official state religion and religious education was provided in the public schools. What Mussolini gained was new prestige and support of the church for his dictatorship. Pope Pius XI declared Mussolini to be a leader sent by Providence. At last, the hostilities between church and state were ended.

The Corporate State

Mussolini established state control of industry by bringing workers, employers, and government officials together in corporations organized according to industry. These corporations determined wages, prices, and industrial production. Strikes were forbidden, and only Fascist labor unions were permitted. A National Council of Corporations was established in 1929 to settle disputes and to set industrial policy for the

What were the chief provisions of the Lateran Treaty? Why did Mussolini cooperate with the Pope?

Discuss Mussolini's economic policies.

What was Hitler's background?

How did the Weimar Republic originate?

whole nation. In 1938, the Chamber of Deputies was actually abolished, and a new Chamber of Fasces and Corporations was established. Mussolini had succeeded in establishing a dictatorship with totalitarian trappings.

The Rise of Fascism in Germany

Hitler

Adolf Hitler (1889-1945) was born in Austria. He was an unsuccessful artist who left Vienna for Munich, Germany in 1913. When World War I broke out, Hitler joined the German army. Decorated for bravery, he gloried in the role of warrior and rose to the rank of corporal. Germany's defeat was a severe psychological blow, and Hitler convinced himself that Germany had been betrayed by Jews and Marxists. In 1919, he joined the tiny German Workers' Party and became its leader. He changed the name to the National Socialist German Workers' Party, which in German is *Nationalsozialistische deutsche Arbeiter-Partei*. Nazi is an abbreviation.

The Weimar Republic

Also in 1919, an elected assembly met in Weimar to draw up a constitution for a new German republic. A very democratic constitution was written with many civil liberty protections. However, the constitution provided for an election system of proportional representation, allocating seats for

each political party in the Reichstag or legislature in approximately the same percentage
as the party won in the popular vote. The
result was to encourage many political parties. Unstable coalitions of parties were
formed to create governing majorities in the
Reichstag. It was difficult for any coalition
of parties to command a legislative majority
for long. The chancellor, who functioned as
prime minister and was responsible to the
Reichstag, was appointed by a popularly
elected president. In times of emergency, the
president could rule by decree without getting the Reichstag's approval of his orders.
This was a significant power, easily subject
to misuse by an unscrupulous tyrant.

The problems with the Weimar Republic were more than simply structural. Germany did not have a strong democratic
tradition to support the new republic. Many,
especially in the military, supported the
return of the monarchy. The republic was
associated with the humiliating Versailles
Treaty because its representatives had been
forced to sign that treaty. In 1921, German
officials accepted huge reparation requirements under the treaty for 132 billion marks
(approximately $33 billion dollars). Such
payments placed a huge burden on the country and accelerated inflation. In 1922, Germany suspended reparation payments. The
French response was to occupy the Ruhr area
in January 1923. German workers retaliated
by strikes, which contributed to spreading
unemployment and hyper-inflation as the
German government persisted in meeting its
debts, including unemployment benefits, by
printing paper money. The value of the German mark had been 8.4 to the U.S. dollar in
1919. In November 15, 1923, the mark was
so badly inflated that it took 2.5 billion
marks to equal a dollar; by the end of the
year, it took over 4 trillion marks to equal a

What were the weaknesses of the Weimar Republic?

Why were the reparations payments important?

Describe the events of the Munich Putsch.

dollar. A new currency was introduced in Germany, the Rentenmark, equivalent to a trillion of the old marks. The whole affair badly shook up the ordinary German citizen. If he or she had any life savings, they had been wiped out by hyper-inflation. It was not until April 9, 1924 that the Dawes Plan stabilized reparations payments by giving Germany American loans with which it could repay the reparations owed to the French and others.

The Beer Hall Putsch

It was during the worst of the hyper-inflation, on November 8, 1923, that Hitler attempted a putsch or coup. In a Munich beerhall, he declared a national revolution. The next day, accompanied by World War I hero General Erich Ludendorff, Hitler marched on the Bavarian War Ministry in Munich. The almost farcical putsch was easily crushed. Hitler and Ludendorff were put on trial for treason. The General was acquitted, but Hitler got a five-year prison sentence, of which he actually served only eight months!

What ideas did Hitler put forth in *Mein Kampf?*

The trial was used by Hitler to gain national attention for Nazi ideals. He used the time in prison to dictate *Mein Kampf* ("My Struggle") to his secretary, Rudolf Hess (1894-1987). In a rambling, repetitious manner, the book set forth his political philosophy. According to *Mein Kampf,* the Jews ruined Germany; they must be driven from the country. Other enemies included communism, liberalism, and democracy. Hitler glorified the Aryan race and German nationalism. Germany, he said, could never tolerate two continental powers in Europe. It needed living space for the folk, which was to be gained by expanding into central Europe and Russia.

Mein Kampf laid out the Nazi blueprint. Hitler said much the same thing in his speeches, only much more effectively. Still, Hitler was not taken seriously by most people in the Twenties. Indeed, as long as Germany enjoyed prosperity in the second half of that decade, the Nazis were not a threat. What happened was that the Great Depression hit Germany beginning in the Thirties. The loans and capital investment provided by the Americans then began to leave Germany. The economic and political scene changed drastically.

Hitler Becomes Chancellor

Before the Depression, in the May 1928 elections to the Reichstag, the Nazis had won only 12 seats, based on a popular vote of 800 thousand. In the September 1930 vote, the Nazis won 107 seats, with a popular vote of 6.5 million. The Communists also increased their seats from 54 to 77. The Social Democrats were still the largest party with 143 seats (down from a 1928 high of 152). It was the moderate parties in the middle that lost the most seats while the right and left extremes gained. What followed was violence in the streets, especially between the Communists and the Nazis. Chancellor Heinrich Bruning (1885-1970) was forced to depend on presidential decree to rule, since he could not command reliable majorities in the Reichstag.

In March 1932, Hitler ran against the incumbent president, who was the war hero Paul von Hindenburg. Hitler got 30% of the vote, denying Hindenburg a majority. In the runoff election in April, Hindenburg won with 53% of the vote to Hitler's 37%. Hitler

What gave Hitler the opportunity to gain a mass political following?

Describe the changes in German politics after 1928.

Contrast Hitler's rise to power in Germany with Lenin's coming to power in Russia.

was showing great strength in the competition against the old warrior.

Chancellor Franz von Papen (1879-1969), who replaced Bruning, called for new Reichstag elections in July 1932. The Nazis won 230 of 608 seats, while the Communists won 89 seats. Since the Nazis held over a third of the seats in the Reichstag, the parliament was paralyzed. Von Papen too had to rule by presidential decree. Hitler refused to join the government with any lesser position than that of Chancellor.

New Reichstag elections were held in November 1932, partly to exhaust the Nazi party's resources. While the number of Nazi seats declined to 196 seats, it was still extremely difficult to govern without them. Kurt von Schleicher (1882-1934) became Chancellor in December 1932. He attempted to put together a very broad coalition, including the political left. Hindenburg and his conservative friends decided they preferred a coalition cabinet that would include the Nazis. Rather foolishly, they supposed that they could control Hitler as chancellor, as long as von Papen served as vice-chancellor. Hindenburg offered the office to Hitler, who became chancellor by <u>legal</u> means on January 30, 1933.

Why did Hitler find the Reichstag fire convenient?

Hitler Consolidates Power

Hitler lost no time in consolidating his power and eliminating possible sources of opposition. On February 27, 1933, the Reichstag building burned. A mentally deficient Dutch communist had set the fire. Hitler used the incident as an excuse to suspend civil liberties and arrest communists. It was in this setting that new Reichstag elections were held on March 5th. The Nazis won 43.9% of the popular vote and 288 seats. Together with the Nationalists, who won 8% of the vote, the Nazis could dominate parliament. To make things doubly safe for Hitler, the Communist deputies, who had won 12.25% of the popular vote, were arrested and not permitted to sit in the Reichstag. On March 23rd, the Reichstag passed the Enabling Act, which permitted Hitler to rule by decree for four years without having to get legislative approval.

All political parties were outlawed except for the National Socialists. Independent labor unions were eliminated. By the end of 1933, major sources of opposition had been eliminated or put under Nazi control. Nor did Hitler tolerate potential opposition within the party. On June 30, 1934 he ordered the killing of Ernst Roehm (1887-1934), head of the SA or storm troopers, and other key SA officers. The move had the support of the SS (a rival paramilitary organization) and the regular army. A number of others, including former chancellor von Schleicher and his wife, were purged subsequently in what became known as THE NIGHT OF THE LONG KNIVES.

The Anti-Semitic Campaign

The first concentration camp was opened at Dachau, near Munich, in 1933. The anti-Semitic campaign was stepped up in 1935 with the passage of the Nuremberg Laws, which forbade intermarriage between Jews and Gentiles and deprived Jews of German citizenship. On the night of November 9-10, 1938 (*Kristallnacht* or THE NIGHT OF THE BROKEN GLASS), 267 synagogues were burned and 20 thousand Jews were arrested. The Jews were actually made to pay for the property damage the Nazis inflicted on that night. Mass arrests were made of

What political changes did Hitler initiate?

How did Hitler vent his anti-Semitic sentiments?

What were the political and economic trends of the 1920's in the U.S.?

Jews and other "undesirables." It is estimated that during the period of Nazi control six million Jews were eventually put to death. Millions of others, including Poles, Russians, and Gypsies, shared their fate.

The Western Democracies Between the Wars

The United States

After World War I, the United States returned to its more traditional isolationist policy. Woodrow Wilson was unable to get the Senate to approve the Paris peace accords. The big stumbling block was acceptance of the League of Nations, which was perceived to impinge on U.S. sovereignty. Wilson, a Democrat, who was ill and quite uncompromising, did not get the needed Republican support for ratification of the Versailles accord. In the 1920 election, the Republicans regained the presidency, and politics returned to isolationist normalcy.

In the 1920's, there was much material progress. The use of automobiles, paved roads, airplanes, and the radio brought a sense of vitality and optimism to the decade. Charles Lindbergh (1902-1974) became a hero in 1927 when he made the first solo transatlantic flight. Businessmen were greatly admired. Henry Ford (1863-1947) was recognized worldwide for his contributions to the automobile industry and to the assembly line process.

What social changes came in the 1920's?

Women got the right to vote in 1920, but not all social trends were as positive. There was a Red Scare in reaction to the communist gains in Russia. The Ku Klux Klan enjoyed a revival, especially in the north. Thanks to the Eighteenth Amendment PROHIBITION, which barred the manufacture, sale, or transport of liquor, came into force. The noble experiment, which lasted until 1933, encouraged speakeasies (illegal bars) and bootleggers such as Al Capone (1899-1947).

The stock market crash of October 1929 led to a deep economic DEPRESSION in the 1930's. By 1933, 14 million Americans were unemployed, some 25 percent of the workforce. The Smoot-Hawley Act of 1930 introduced economic nationalism in the form of high protective tariffs. The idea was to provide jobs and opportunities for American manufacturers by making it impossible for foreigners to compete effectively. What actually happened was economic collapse in Europe and the devaluation of currencies in countries, like Great Britain, that wished to sell their goods abroad.

Herbert Hoover (1874-1964) lost the election of 1932 to Franklin D. Roosevelt, who became the first Democratic President since Woodrow Wilson. To deal with the economic crisis Roosevelt introduced the New Deal. It gave government a role in the American economic system that had been previously unthinkable. The Securities and Exchange Commission (1934) was created to regulate the buying and selling of financial securities, such as stocks and bonds. The Social Security Act (1935) provided a system of old-age pensions and unemployment insurance. Minimum wage legislation was passed. The Wagner Act (1935) created the National Labor Relations Board to foster and protect labor unions.

The Public Works Administration (1933) and the Works Progress Administration (1935) sought to provide employment

What economic changes followed the Depression of 1929?

Describe some of the New Deal institutions.

Compare British economic performance with U.S. economic performance in the 1920's and the 1930's.

for those out of work. But in 1939, almost 9.5 million workers were still unemployed. It was World War II that brought the needed level of economic expansion to sustain full employment.

Great Britain

Great Britain did not regain the same level of economic prosperity it had enjoyed before World War I. In 1921, the British suffered a depression. Exports dropped to 50 percent of what they had been in 1920, and over two million were unemployed. Limited economic improvement followed, but Britain's unemployment rate never dropped below one million until the coming of World War II. The DOLE or unemployment benefits became a sustained way of life for many.

What major political changes occurred in Britain after World War I?

Labor unrest grew. In 1926, the coal miners went on strike. Other unions joined in sympathy, and the strike grew to a GENERAL STRIKE supported by approximately two and a half million workers out of a labor force of 15 million. A combination of military personnel and volunteers performed essential services in place of the workers. As a result, the strike failed. The power of organized labor was further restricted by the Trade Disputes Act of 1927, which prohibited new sympathy strikes.

The Great Depression affected adversely an already lackluster economy. By 1932, unemployment had risen to three million, 25 percent of the work force. Two years later, it was still at the two million mark. Britain devalued the pound and raised tariffs. The amount of the dole paid to each laid-off worker was cut to make the unemployment payments less burdensome on the treasury.

There were major political changes in Britain in the interwar period. Women thirty and over got the right to vote in 1918, and full women's suffrage came in 1928.

The Labour Party became one of Britain's two major parties replacing the Liberals. By 1900, labor unions and local labor parties had merged to form the Labour Representation Committee, which was renamed the Labour Party in 1906. The party was heavily influenced by the moderate socialism of the Fabian Society.

James Ramsay MacDonald (1866-1937) was the first Labour Party prime minister. His party formed a coalition with the Liberal Party that held power for nine months in 1924. He was Labour prime minister again from 1928-31. With the deepening Depression, MacDonald adopted retrenchment measures that lost him the support of his own party. Instead, in 1931, MacDonald formed a national government coalition with the Liberals and Conservatives and remained in office until 1935. The Conservatives came to dominate the national coalition and were to dominate the government for the next decade.

The status of Ireland was another major political change in the interwar period. The postponement of home rule at the beginning of World War I led to the 1916 Easter Rising in Dublin. The severity of the English repression of the rebellion and the subsequent execution of those involved created great popular support for Irish independence, particularly in the largely Catholic south. The Irish party favoring independence was SINN FEIN (We Ourselves). Sinn Fein won big in elections to the British Parliament in December 1918. Instead of sitting in that parliament, the Sinn Fein members organized a parliament of their own in January 1919 in Dublin and declared Irish independence. A

What were the origins of the Labour Party?

How did the 1916 Easter Rising change the situation in Ireland?

How successful were the British in suppressing the Irish rebellion?

How did Northern Ireland come to separate from what is now the Republic of Ireland?

guerrilla war ensued. In December of 1920, the British Parliament passed the Government of Ireland Act creating separate parliaments for Northern Ireland and Southern Ireland. (Only the Northern Ireland parliament actually functioned.) This effectively divided Ireland into two parts.

The cause of independence was supported militarily by the Irish Republican Army (the IRA). Their hit-and-run tactics, plus the boycott of the British police (the Royal Irish Constabulary) and courts, proved very effective. The English attempted to regain authority by sending in an auxiliary police force. These non-Irish natives were known as the Black and Tans (after the color of their uniforms). Many in this force had seen service in World War I. Bloody atrocities were committed on both sides before a cease fire was arranged. In December 1921, the British and Sinn Fein representatives agreed to an Irish Free State with dominion status within the British Empire for the 26 southern counties. The six northern counties, with a Protestant majority, were allowed to opt out of the Free State and retain their previously established parliament. The treaty, which retained ties to Britain, was rejected by one faction of the IRA that wanted a fully independent Irish republic.

A civil war resulted which the pro-treaty faction won by mid 1923. The leader of the anti-treaty faction, Eamon de Valera (1882-1975), was elected Irish prime minister in 1932. He was responsible for a new constitution in 1937 that made Ireland effectively independent of Britain. The Republic of Ireland was formally proclaimed in 1949. The United Kingdom now includes Great Britain (England, Scotland, and Wales) and Northern Ireland only.

France

After World War I, the French were preoccupied with rebuilding. They hoped to use reparation payments from the Germans to pay much of the construction expenses. In January 1923, when the Germans dragged their feet on reparations, the French and the Belgians sent troops into the Ruhr Valley, an industrial area of Germany. They hoped to force the Germans to make reparations payments. Eventually, with the help of the international community, a repayment plan (the Dawes Plan of 1924) was worked out. But the French occupation proved very costly. It greatly accelerated inflation within France. It was not until 1926 that a new government that was willing to take drastic measures came into power. New taxes were voted and the budget was balanced. In 1928, the franc was devalued and its exchange rate went from 19.3 cents (U.S.) to 3.92 cents. The franc was worth one-fifth of its prewar value! In the period 1926 to 1929, French industry prospered and unemployment was low. France was affected by the Great Depression, but not as badly as some other countries. In 1935, at its height, perhaps one million were unemployed.

A reason France had difficulty dealing with its financial problems was chronic government instability. During the interwar period, some forty different governments were formed. The Third Republic's use of proportional representation in elections encouraged multiple political parties. The society was ideologically fractured into many groups across the political spectrum. On the right were royalist groups such as the *Action Française,* and fascist groups, imitating their German and Italian counterparts. On the left were communists and socialists.

Why did France occupy the Ruhr Valley?

What political problems confronted France in the interwar period?

What was the Popular Front?

Shaky coalitions of these groups were formed into blocs that governed France in the period between the world wars. One such bloc was the POPULAR FRONT, which included socialists, communists, and liberals. It was led by Leon Blum (1872-1950). Blum, who became premier in 1936, was the first socialist and the first Jew to serve as a French prime minister. His government introduced measures such as the forty-hour week and collective bargaining. These were assiduously resisted by the right. He lost leftist support by refusing to intervene in the Spanish Civil War. After two stints as premier lasting approximately a year and a month, he was replaced by the more conservative government of Edouard Daladier (1884-1970) in April 1938. It was Daladier who would face Hitler's demands on Czechoslovakia and Poland.

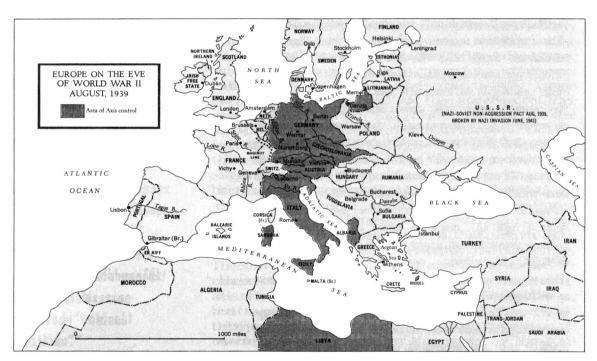

From *The End of the European Era, 1890 to the Present*, Fourth Edition by Felix Gilbert with David Clay Large. Copyright (c) 1991, 1984, 1970 by W.W. Norton & Company, Inc. Reprinted by permission of W.W. Norton & Company, Inc.

12

World War II

The Path to World War II

Dissatisfaction

There were several nations dissatisfied with the Versailles peace which ended World War I. Germany was the most obvious one. It had to accept the War Guilt Clause and enormous reparations. It lost all its colonies and substantial territory. Many Germans were resentful. The creation of the Polish Corridor was a special source of resentment. Land had been taken from what was eastern Germany prior to World War I and given to Poland, so that this recreated country could have access to the Baltic Sea. Strict limits had also been placed on German military forces. But even among the victors there were dissatisfied nations. Italy had wanted more territory along the Adriatic Coast. Japan had wanted more permanent gains in China, but was thwarted by the strenuous opposition of the United States, which continued to foster its Open Door Policy.

Japan and China

The Japanese had gained influence in Manchuria by their success in the Russo-Japanese War of 1904-1905. The impetus for all-out conquest came from the Great Depression. Between 1929 and 1931, Japan's

Mention some of the provisions of the Versailles Treaty resented by Germans.

Why were Italy and Japan discontented?

What was the Mukden Incident?

How did the Japanese government react to the takeover of Manchuria?

How did the League of Nations react?

foreign commerce had dropped almost in half. The solution many army officers favored was the creation of an empire to guarantee markets for Japanese products. In September 1931, Japanese army officers in Manchuria staged the Mukden Incident, an explosion on a railroad they controlled. The incident served as an excuse for the army to rapidly take over all of Manchuria. The Japanese civilian government, unable to control the army, acquiesced in the conquest. In 1932, Manchuria was remade into the puppet state of Manchukuo, dependent upon Japan. In Japan itself, the army began to dominate the government. Friction between Japan and China continued, climaxing in the start of all-out war in July 1937. By 1940, the Japanese controlled the eastern part of China.

After the Mukden Incident, the Chinese sought help from the League of Nations. A commission established by the League eventually brought in a report critical of Japan. The League adopted the report in February 1933. Japan's response was to announce that it would withdraw from the League of Nations. No effective action was taken to stop Japanese aggression. The lesson was not lost on Hitler or Mussolini.

German Rearmament

In October 1933, Hitler took Germany out of disarmament discussions and out of the League of Nations. Germany began vigorous rearmament, contrary to the Versailles Treaty. In March of 1935, Hitler formally denounced the disarmament clauses of Versailles and began military conscription to build up the German army. There was no retaliation from the former Allies. Indeed, Britain signed a naval agreement with Germany in 1935 that permitted an increase in German naval strength. The will to enforce the Versailles peace, through the League of Nations or otherwise, was lacking.

In 1925, Germany had signed the Locarno Pact, committing Germany to the western borders established at Versailles and accepting the demilitarized Rhineland. In March 1936, Hitler denounced the Locarno Pact and sent German troops to occupy the Rhineland, contrary to the Versailles Treaty. A weak French Government made noises about action, but deferred to British reluctance to make the placing of German troops on German soil a war issue. From its new position on the west bank of the Rhine, the German army would be in a better position to invade France and the Low Countries.

The Conquest of Ethiopia

The reluctance of the Western democracies to deal forcefully with the remilitarization of the Rhineland is partly explained by their preoccupation with another crisis. In October 1935, Mussolini had invaded Ethiopia (or Abyssinia) in order to gain glory and to avenge the humiliating defeat of Italian forces in 1896, when they had previously tried to conquer Ethiopia. Emperor Haile Selassie (1930-74) of Ethiopia appealed to the League of Nations. The League approved sanctions against Italy, which went into effect in November 1935. But critical items, especially the oil that Mussolini's forces desperately needed, were left off the sanctions list. The Italian troops, thanks to the ineffective sanctions and overwhelming technological superiority (for example, fighter planes versus spears) were able to enter Addis Ababa, the Ethiopian capital, on

How did Britain and France respond to German rearmament?

Why did Mussolini invade Ethiopia?

What were the Rome-Berlin Axis and the Anti-Comintern Pact?

May 5, 1936. Once more the League was quite ineffective in the face of aggression.

The Axis Agreements

The successful German occupation of the Rhineland and the Italian conquest of Ethiopia encouraged Hitler and Mussolini to form an alliance, the Rome-Berlin Axis. Italy and Germany in October 1936 agreed to support each other in case of war. In November, Japan joined in an Anti-Comintern Pact with Germany, ostensibly against Communism. Italy joined this pact in 1937. The revisionist nations, which had been dissatisfied with the Versailles agreement, were now in an alliance against the satisfied countries, England and France.

The Spanish Civil War

In July 1936, General Francisco Franco (1892-1975) began a revolt against the republican government of Spain. The liberal government side became known as the LOYALISTS, while the more conservative rebels were the NATIONALISTS.

How did Germany and Italy support the Nationalists?

Franco's Nationalists received substantial help from Hitler and Mussolini. The Germans supplied new weapons, which were combat tested in the civil war. German aircraft tried new bombing methods. Regular units of the Italian army fought alongside the Nationalist forces. The cooperation between the German and Italian forces helped to strengthen the Axis alliance.

The Loyalist side received Russian aircraft and Russian volunteers for International Brigades. Idealistic volunteers, who came from Britain, France, and the United States, also joined these International Brigades, which came increasingly under communist influence. But the governments of the Western democracies refused to supply arms on grounds that the Spanish Civil War might escalate to a more general European conflict. This gave the Nationalists a decided advantage.

In 1938, Stalin decided to cut his losses and withdrew his support. By spring of 1939, the Nationalists had won. Franco established a dictatorship that lasted, with some moderation after World War II, until his death in 1975.

Why did Stalin withdraw his support of the Loyalists?

The Annexation of Austria

Hitler was born in Austria. Since becoming Chancellor, he had wanted the union (*Anschluss*) of Austria with Germany. When the Nazi party in Austria had attempted a coup in 1934, Mussolini massed his forces on the border and the Nazis had to back down. However, the Rome-Berlin Axis of 1936 had created increasingly strong ties between Germany and Italy. Hitler felt secure enough to try for *Anschluss* once more in 1938. In February 1938, he demanded a series of concessions from Austrian chancellor Kurt von Schuschnigg (1897-1977). Schuschnigg conceded and admitted Arthur Seyss-Inquart, a Nazi, to the cabinet as minister of the interior. Nazi-inspired disorders broke out in Austria that were difficult to put down without offending the Nazis in Germany. In March, Schuschnigg decided to hold a plebiscite to show that the majority of Austrians favored independence rather than union. Hitler massed his troops on the border, forcing Schuschnigg to resign. The Nazi Seyss-Inquart then became Austrian chancellor. He invited German forces in, at Hitler's telephoned suggestion, to restore order. The

Why was Hitler interested in Austria?

What was *Anschluss*?

How did Hitler achieve the union of Austria and Germany?

How did Hitler justify the taking of Czech territory?

troops marched in. On March 13, 1938, Austria was declared to be a part of Germany. A plebiscite ratifying the annexation was conducted on April 10th in Austria. Union was supported after the fact by 99.75% of the vote. Six million people had been added to Germany. There were no protests from Britain or France about this flagrant violation of the Versailles Treaty, which had become a dead issue.

The Dismemberment of Czechoslovakia

The population of Austria was essentially German. This was not true of the state of Czechoslovakia, which had been created after World War I. While the majority of its population was Slavic, either Czech or Slovak, it had a number of national minorities. There were also significant cultural differences between the Czechs and the Slovaks. The most important group among the non-Slavs were the over three million Germans, who comprised about 22 percent of the population. The Germans were concentrated in the mountainous Sudetenland, along the frontier with Germany. The area had been included in Czechoslovakia to give that country defensible borders.

Hitler had justified the annexation of Austria on the grounds of national self-determination. He played the self-determination card once more in the case of Czechoslovakia. He claimed that the Sudeten Germans were being persecuted and proposed to annex the Sudetenland to Germany.

There were some significant differences between the Austrian and the Czech situations. Czechoslovakia was the most democratic of the East European states with a strong industrial base. The Czechs had entered into security pacts with the French and the Russians, who were supposed to offer military support in the case of German aggression. The Russians made it plain that they were willing to honor their commitments to Czechoslovakia, though this might prove difficult in practice. The Russians would have had to go through Poland to reach Czechoslovakia. The Poles, who in 1920-21 had been at war with the Russians, were quite understandably resistant to permitting any Russian troops on their territory.

How did the Russians and the Poles react to the threats against Czechoslovakia?

Appeasement

The French, and especially the British, were reluctant to become embroiled in a general European war over the Sudetenland. The British prime minister Neville Chamberlain (1869-1940) met with Hitler several times in September 1938. Convinced that Hitler was willing to go to war over the Sudetenland, Chamberlain pressured the Czechs into surrendering the territory. When Hitler found that some of his demands would be met, he made new ones designed to hasten the timetable for German acquisition of the Sudeten region. Czechoslovakia mobilized its army. The French actually called up army reservists. Then, the British and French agreed to meet with the Germans and the Italians at a four-power meeting in Munich, Germany on September 29, 1938 to decide the fate of Czechoslovakia. Chamberlain represented Britain. Edouard Daladier represented France. The Axis powers were represented by Hitler and Mussolini. Conspicuously absent from the negotiations were Czechoslovakia and the Soviet Union, the nations most willing to resist Hitler. A Czech delegation was there, but they were reduced to learning the terms when the negotiations were finished.

What did the British and French do in the face of these threats?

What were the terms of the Munich Agreement?

The Munich terms gave Germany the predominantly German Sudeten areas by October 10th. Additional territories were to be acquired, subject to plebiscites that were never held. Germany wound up with 10 thousand square miles and 3.5 million people. Additional disputed territories were taken by Poland and Hungary. In all, Czechoslovakia lost about 34% or its population and 29% of its land. Within the state, Slovakia gained autonomy in a federated "Czecho-Slovakia."

The Munich Conference has come to be the most famed example of a phenomenon known as APPEASEMENT. Appeasement is making concessions in the face of aggressive demands from a nation threatening war or other grave consequences. The hope is that, if enough concessions are made, the threatening nation will be satisfied and not seek more concessions or actually go to war. When Chamberlain flew back from Munich, he spoke to a crowd gathered in Downing Street, outside his residence, and he said: "I believe it is peace in our time."[2]

Why is Munich frequently associated with appeasement?

The prime minister was wrong. In March 1939, Hitler's troops marched into the Czech capital, Prague. Czechoslovakia disappeared completely, replaced by two German protectorates: (1) Bohemia and Moravia and (2) Slovakia. The March 1939 invasion was significant because it extended Germany's control into areas that were not German but Slavic. The rationale of national self-determination could not readily be applied. Disillusionment came to the western democracies. Appeasement had failed.

The Threat to Poland

The next target for Hitler was Poland. The Versailles Treaty had provided for a

Polish Corridor that cut off East Prussia from the rest of Germany. At the end of March 1939, Germany made a number of demands for gaining control of Danzig, a city whose population was predominantly German, and for auto and rail links through the Polish Corridor. The Poles refused and were bolstered by an Anglo-French guarantee of aid if Polish independence were threatened. For such a guarantee to be meaningful, Russian assistance was needed. The British and French opened negotiations to obtain Russian help for Poland. But the western democracies moved slowly and provided lower level negotiators than the Russians expected. The Russians also had doubts about how meaningful British and French guarantees of help were, given their past record.

The Germans also courted the Russians. Hitler was in quite a hurry. He planned to invade Poland by September 1st at the latest, and wanted a pact with the Russians so that they would not offer aid to the Poles. Joachim von Ribbentrop (1893-1946), the German foreign minister, was sent to Moscow to negotiate the pact. The agreement, which was made on August 23, 1939, shocked the international community. The German Nazis and the Soviet Communists, dedicated enemies, had entered into a non-aggression pact and trade agreements with one another. At least, this was the public announcement. There were secret clauses to the NAZI-SOVIET PACT that provided for the partitioning of Poland between Russia and Germany and gave the Russians a free hand in the Baltic states of Estonia, Latvia, and Lithuania. Hitler was free to enter Poland without Soviet resistance. Stalin gained territory and time and did not have to depend on the dubious pledges of Britain and

Why was Hitler interested in the Polish Corridor?

What motivated the Russians to side with the Germans?

What were the terms of the Nazi-Soviet Pact?

France. Hitler's troops invaded Poland on September 1, 1939. World War II had begun.

WORLD WAR II

What nations attacked Poland in 1939?

1939-1941

Poland

The September 1, 1939 German attack on Poland was a huge success. Within a week the Polish forces had either been destroyed or trapped in pincer movements by German armies. The mopping up of these forces was over by the end of the month. The Poles were the victims of a new military technique called *blitzkrieg* or lightning war. Tanks, motorized vehicles, and dive bombers were coordinated to break through the enemy's front, move rapidly behind the enemy's lines, and encircle the opposing force. The Germans occupied the western portion of Poland, including the Polish Corridor. While Britain and France had declared war on Germany on September 3rd, they were not in a position to give effective aid to Poland. On September 17th, the Russian forces moved in to occupy the eastern portion of Poland.

What was the *blitzkrieg?*

The Baltic States Annexed

In September and October 1939, the Russians demanded and obtained bases in the three Baltic states: Estonia, Latvia, and Lithuania. In August of 1940, the Baltic

States were admitted into the Soviet Union at their "request," after phony, Soviet-controlled elections, in each of the states.

What was the fate of the Baltic states and Finland?

The Russo-Finnish War

The Soviets made demands for Finnish territory. They wanted to extend their border westward to buffer their capital, Leningrad. When the Finns refused Russian demands, the Russians invaded at the end of November 1939. The Finns put up a stiff resistance, but ultimately had to yield to the numerically superior Soviet troops by March of 1940. Russia gained strategic territory, but Finland kept its independence. Britain and France came close to declaring war on the Soviet Union, but ultimately backed off.

German Successes on the Western Front

When and how did the Germans proceed on the western front?

Western Europe had been quiet in the winter of 1939-40. The spring was different. In April, German forces attacked Denmark and Norway, which were fully occupied by early June. In May a German initiative was begun against the Low Countries (Belgium, Luxembourg, and the Netherlands) and France, using *blitzkrieg* tactics. The Low Countries surrendered by the end of May; the French by the end of June. The Germans occupied Paris and all of France bordering on the Atlantic Ocean. A puppet regime, the VICHY GOVERNMENT, was set up under Marshall Petain in the southwestern portion of the country, which was not occupied directly by the Germans until November 1942.

The British remained in the war under new leadership. Winston Churchill replaced Chamberlain on May 10, 1940. The Brits had some particularly difficult, yet heroic mo-

Why is Dunkirk famous?

ments in 1940. When Belgium collapsed, Allied forces were trapped in DUNKIRK, a port city in northern France, seven miles from the Belgian border. Using a fleet of destroyers, commercial vessels, pleasure yachts, and fishing boats, the British managed to evacuate more than 300 thousand Belgian, British, and French troops to safety across the English Channel between May 27 and June 4, 1940.

The Battle of Britain

Describe the Battle of Britain.

Another opportunity for heroism came in the Battle of Britain. Starting in August 1940, when the British refused to come to terms after the fall of France, the Germans launched an air war. Britain was subjected to massive bombing in preparation for an invasion. The German air force, the *Luftwaffe*, attacked ports, airfields and industrial centers. They bombed the city of London for 57 nights without breaking the British will to fight. In October 1940, the plan for invasion (Operation Sea Lion) was given up. The Blitz, the attack on English cities, continued until May 1941, at which time much of the German air force was transferred to the eastern front in preparation for the invasion of Russia. The British Royal Air Force had lost 915 planes, the *Luftwaffe* had lost 1,733. An estimated 20 thousand people were killed in London alone.

The Invasion of Russia

Hitler had intended to launch an attack on the Soviet Union in mid-May, but was temporarily diverted by the need to rescue the floundering Italian invasion of Greece. Instead, the German invasion of Russia was begun on June 22, 1941. The invasion was in accord with long-range plans put forth in *Mein Kampf.* Surprisingly, the attack caught Stalin off guard, and the German army made spectacular progress. In the north, the battle line advanced to within ten miles of Leningrad (St. Petersburg). By late November, they were approaching the Moscow suburbs along the center of the front. In the south, the German forces had less success, but did take the Crimea and advanced to the Don River. The Germans, in the process of this wide advance, had over-stretched their supply lines. They were not adequately dressed for the Russian winter. The German tanks and cannons were not provided with adequate supplies of antifreeze. When the Russians counterattacked in November and December, they were able to halt and even push back the advance in some areas. The Germans did not enjoy on the eastern front the quick victories they had found on the western front.

Pearl Harbor

The Japanese had been engaged in a general war in China since 1937. With the assent of Vichy France, Japan occupied French bases in Indo-China. In September 1940, Japan began to occupy other areas of Indo-China. Japan also concluded the Tripartite Pact renewing and strengthening its ties with Germany and Italy. A major aim of the pact was to provide mutual assistance should any one of these three powers be attacked by the United States.

The United States government had been pro-British from the beginning of the war. In return for the right to garrison British bases on the American side of the Atlantic with American troops, President Franklin Roosevelt had given the British fifty overage de-

How successful were the Germans against the Russians?

What was the Tripartite Pact?

What evidence do we have of Franklin Roosevelt's pro-British sentiments?

Compare American and Japanese losses at Pearl Harbor.

Who were the Allies opposed to the Axis powers?

stroyers. In 1941, Lend-Lease arrangements helped to assure the British of continued American supplies vital to their war effort. The American attitude towards Japanese expansion in Asia was increasingly hostile. In September 1940, the U.S. had placed an embargo on exporting scrap iron and steel to Japan. Japanese ability to import oil was hampered when Japanese assets in the U.S. were frozen in June 1941.

The Japanese sent negotiators to the U.S. But when the Japanese had not obtained the concessions they were seeking by the end of November, they determined to resort to war. On December 7, 1941, 350 Japanese planes struck the U.S. naval fleet stationed at Pearl Harbor in Hawaii. The Americans were unprepared. Though the U.S. was apprised of the likelihood of war, it was believed the first fighting would be closer to the Philippines or Southeast Asia. Almost 2,500 Americans were killed, 200 aircraft were destroyed, and 18 ships were hit. The Japanese lost 29 planes and less than a 100 casualties. The U.S. declared war on Japan on December 8th. On December 11th, Germany and Italy declared war on the U.S.

1942-1944

After Germany attacked the Soviet Union in June 1941, the British and Russians entered a military alliance against Germany. With American entry into the war, a Grand Alliance (the Allies) of some 26 nations, including the Britain, China, the U.S., and the USSR, was formed to defeat the Axis powers. The Axis enjoyed important successes in 1942. The Japanese advanced in

Asia, winning Hong Kong, Guam, Singapore, the Philippines, Malaya, Indonesia, and Burma by midyear. The Germans mounted a major offensive in southern Russia in the summer. By August 23, 1942, the German forces had reached the Volga River, not far from Stalingrad.

Describe some of the successes of the Axis powers.

The Battle at Sea

For the first time in history, aircraft carriers came to rival destroyers in sea battle. In June 1942 a Japanese force of some eighty vessels approached American-held Midway Island in the Pacific. They were intercepted by an American fleet. Both Japan and the U.S. depended heavily on carrier-based aircraft. When the battle ended after four days, the Japanese had lost four aircraft carriers, two cruisers, and three destroyers. The Americans lost a carrier and two other ships. From then on, the Japanese were forced into an essentially defensive posture because they could not replace the ships as fast as the Americans. Between 1942 and 1944, the Japanese added 6 fleet carriers to their navy; the U.S. added 14 fleet carriers, as well as 9 light carriers and 66 escort carriers. The Japanese lacked the resources to keep up with the U.S. in the armaments race. In the Atlantic, the story was similar. At first, German submarines took a heavy toll on Allied shipping, but new types of aircraft, and the development of radar and sonar devices began to change the balance. In October 1942, the first Liberty Ship freighter was launched only ten days after the keel was laid. These mass-produced ships also changed the sea balance in favor of the Allies.

What disadvantage did the Japanese have in their naval effort against the U.S.?

Why is the battle of Stalingrad so important?

Evaluate Allied progress in Africa and Italy.

The Tide Turns in Europe and North Africa

The German advance in southern Russia was halted in October, but only after they had actually conquered some portions of Stalingrad. In November 1942, the Russians counterattacked. The surrounded Germans were forced to surrender in February 1943. A German army of 300 thousand had been lost. The Battle of Stalingrad was a turning point. From then on, with few exceptions, the Russians relentlessly pushed the German forces back towards Berlin.

In North Africa, the Battle of el-Alamein, some sixty miles outside of Alexandria, Egypt, began on October 28, 1942 and lasted into early November. It provided the Allies with another decisive victory. The British commander, Bernard Law Montgomery, halted the advance into Egypt of German and Italian tanks under the command of Erwin Rommel, the "Desert Fox." By May of 1943, the Allies had obtained success over the German forces in North Africa and in the same month they launched an attack against Sicily. In September, U.S. and British forces crossed over to the Italian mainland. Though, Mussolini had been dismissed by the king in July, he was rescued by the Germans and became their puppet in the north. The Germans put up a vigorous defense of Italy, and the narrowness of the Italian peninsula made Allied progress difficult. By December 1944, Allied forces had not yet reached the Po River valley. Such major cities as Bologna and Genoa were still under German control.

The Normandy Invasion

Stalin had long wanted the U.S. and Britain to launch an attack on the western front. An effective second front would relieve the pressure on the Russians. The actual invasion of France began on June 6, 1944 along the Normandy coast. The American general in charge of the invasion was Dwight D. Eisenhower (1890-1969). On the first day, some 5,000 ships landed 150,000 troops. By July 1st, more than a million Allied troops had disembarked. A second invasion was made in southern France in mid-August. In mid-December, the Germans attempted a counterattack known as the BATTLE OF THE BULGE, a German advance that was only short-lived. By the end of 1944, German forces had been cleared out of most of France and Belgium.

Compare the Russian and the American contribution to victory in Europe.

1945

The German Collapse

In February 1945, the tanks of General George Patton (1885-1945) had captured the entire west bank of the Rhine. In March, U.S. forces crossed the Rhine in strength. By April 12th, they had reached the Elbe River. There the Americans halted to give the Russians a chance to take Berlin. The Soviets had taken Warsaw and Krakow in January 1945. By April 20th, the Russians were fighting their way into Berlin. American and Russian troops met at Torgau, on the Elbe, on April 25th. On April 30th, Hitler committed suicide in his Berlin bunker. Two days before, Mussolini had been shot by Italian partisans. On May 7th and 8th, representatives of the German military formally surrendered unconditionally to the Americans and to the Russians.

How did Hitler and Mussolini die?

Describe the various Nazi extermination methods.

The Holocaust

As the Allied armies advanced through Poland and Germany, they found the concentration camps used by the Nazis for slave laborers, medical experiments, and mass exterminations. The most notorious were the extermination camps located in Poland at places like Auschwitz and Treblinka. Other camps, such as Buchenwald and Dachau, were located in Germany. At Auschwitz, victims were sent naked into gas chambers, under the pretense that they were going to take showers. Before their bodies were cremated, gold fillings were extracted from teeth and the female hair, which could be used as mattress stuffing, was cut off. The prisoners' clothing and valuables were also used for economic gain. Two million died at Auschwitz, where the mass killings began in 1942. The Jews particularly were singled out for death, as part of Hitler's FINAL SOLUTION to the Jewish Question. Before the more efficient extermination camps were built, units of the SS rounded up Jews as the German forces advanced through Poland and Russia. These victims would be lined up near large open pits and shot to death. Their bodies were then buried in the pits. Between five and six million Jews died in the Holocaust. They came from all areas of Europe under Axis domination. They were perhaps half of Hitler's victims. Millions of Russians, Poles, Gypsies, and others were also exterminated.

Who and how many were killed in the Holocaust?

The Defeat of Japan

The U.S. began the liberation of the Philippines in October 1944. It was not until July 5, 1945 that General MacArthur an-

WORLD WAR I AND WORLD WAR II

nounced that all the Philippine Islands had been liberated.

In preparation for the actual invasion of Japan, American forces invaded strategic islands. Iwo Jima was invaded on March 19, 1945. The island was secured in mid-March, after some particularly bloody fighting. A photograph of Marines raising the U.S. flag on Mount Suribachi, the highest point on the island, has come to symbolize American valor in the war. The island of Okinawa was captured in June 1945, after a two and a half month struggle. The island's airfields made it possible to bomb Japanese cities.

Based on the stubborn resistance to U.S. advances, it was believed that the Japanese would fight to the bitter end for their home islands at the cost of a million American casualties and even more Japanese losses. President Harry S. Truman (1884-1972) made the decision to use the just-developed ATOMIC BOMB as a means of ending the war in the Pacific quickly. On August 6, 1945, an atomic bomb was dropped on the city of Hiroshima. At least 70 thousand of its 300 thousand citizens were killed outright, and the city was destroyed. Two days later, the Soviet Union declared war on Japan. On August 9th, a second bomb was dropped on Nagasaki, killing 40 thousand out of a population of 250 thousand. The emperor intervened, and the Japanese government was persuaded to surrender on August 14th. The only condition was that the emperor be permitted to remain, under supervision of the occupying authorities. The formal surrender was signed on September 2, 1945.

War Deaths and Costs

The estimates of war dead vary widely. Among the Axis powers, Germany had the

How did the U.S. initially plan to deal with Japan?

How was the atom bomb used in World War II?

Describe the cost of the war in terms of human life and property.

most dead. Combining both military and civilian deaths, the Germans lost between 4 to 6 million. Japan lost 2 to 3.5 million, and Italy lost possibly 350 thousand. The Soviet Union lost the most dead among the Allies: about 20 million. Between 1937 and 1945, the Chinese lost at least 8 million, and possibly 20 million souls. Polish deaths were 6 to 8 million, and 5 to 6 million Jews were lost. France lost 610 thousand, Britain 365 thousand, and the U.S. 300 thousand. Many other countries also suffered losses. Estimates of total war dead range from 40 to 70 million people. Cost in material and property damage exceeded 1 trillion dollars.

A number of war crimes trials were conducted by the Allied victors. The NUREMBERG TRIALS (November 1945-October 1946), conducted by an international tribunal, resulted in sentencing 12 Nazis to death and three to life imprisonment. The Americans held similar trials of Japanese war leaders.

What were the Nuremberg Trials?

Wartime Conferences Shaped the Peace

During the war, the shape of the future peace was discussed in several meetings of the major Allied powers. A November 28-December 1, 1943 meeting of Roosevelt, Churchill, and Stalin at Teheran, Iran was devoted mainly to war strategy. The hard political decisions were put off. Since the strategy left the eastern front to the Russians, it meant that the Russians would have troops in place to dominate Eastern Europe after the war. In October 1944, Churchill and Stalin met in Moscow. and agreed that, after the war, Russia was to have preponderance in

With the defeat of Germany, who was in the best position to dominate Eastern Europe? Why?

Bulgaria and Rumania, Britain in Greece, and influence would be evenly divided in Yugoslavia and Hungary. Roosevelt, at the time in the middle of an election campaign, did not feel bound by the Moscow understandings.

More definitive political arrangements were made in two Big Three conferences held in 1945. Roosevelt, Churchill, and Stalin were in attendance at the Yalta Conference of February 1945 in the Russian Crimea. They agreed to divide Germany into British, French, Russian and U.S. zones of occupation. The capital, Berlin, which was within the Russian zone, was to be similarly divided into four zones. There was no agreement on permanent peace provisions. A United Nations was to be created to replace the League of Nations. Russia agreed to enter the war against Japan 90 days after Germany's surrender. In turn, the Russians would get the southern half of Sakhalin Island, the Kuril Islands, and concessions in Manchuria. The consequences of the Russo-Japanese War of 1905-06 were to be undone! Since the atomic bomb had not been tested, and stubborn resistance was expected from the Japanese, these concessions to Russia made sense at the time. Stalin insisted on keeping the Polish territories annexed in 1939 and suggested giving Poland territory from Germany in compensation. No final settlement was reached. The Polish government was to be drawn from the pro-Soviet Lublin Committee, with a few democratic Polish leaders, who had been in exile in London, added to ease Western consciences.

In July and early August 1945, the Big Three met again in Potsdam, Germany. Truman represented the U.S., since Roosevelt had died. Churchill began the meeting, but was replaced by Clement Attlee (1883-1967), who had just been elected British prime

What was decided at Yalta?

How was Germany affected by the decisions made at Potsdam?

How did the peace process after World War II differ from the process following World War I?

Compare how Germany and Japan were treated after defeat.

minister. Stalin represented the USSR. The four-zone occupation of Germany was confirmed. Russia was to get reparations of $10 billion in kind from Germany. Subject to a final peace treaty, Poland was to get German territory east of the Oder and Neisse rivers, effectively moving Poland's border about 100 miles westward. The former German East Prussia was to be split between Russia and Poland. Russia would keep the Polish territories annexed in 1939, since Poland had been compensated at Germany's expense. The millions of Germans living in these areas were forcibly driven westward. The U.S. and Britain clashed with the Soviet Union on the type of governments to be established in Eastern Europe. Stalin demanded that the Western Allies accept the Soviet puppets he had established.

The rift between the Soviet Union and its Allies meant that no peace treaty would be signed with Germany. Instead, the zones of the Western powers became the Federal Republic of Germany (West Germany) in 1949, while the Soviet zone became the German Democratic Republic (East Germany).

Austria was subject to four-power occupation but was restored to its prewar borders. In 1955, a treaty was signed and the occupation ended. Reparations had to be paid to the Soviet Union.

In 1946, peace treaties were negotiated with Italy, Romania, Bulgaria, and Finland. The treaties were signed in February 1947. All these states had to pay reparations and all, except Bulgaria, had to make some territorial concessions.

Japan was occupied by U.S. troops under the command of General Douglas MacArthur from 1945-1952. A new democratic constitution that renounced the use of force was put into effect in 1947. In 1951,

Japan signed a peace treaty and a mutual defense treaty with the U.S. The Japanese resumed complete sovereignty in April 1952, but continued under U.S. military protection.

NOTES

[1]Palmer, vol. II, p. 749.

[2]Quoted in William L. Shirer, <u>The Rise and Fall of the Third Reich: A History of Nazi Germany</u> (Greenwich, Conn.: Crest Book [Fawcett], 1962), p.567.

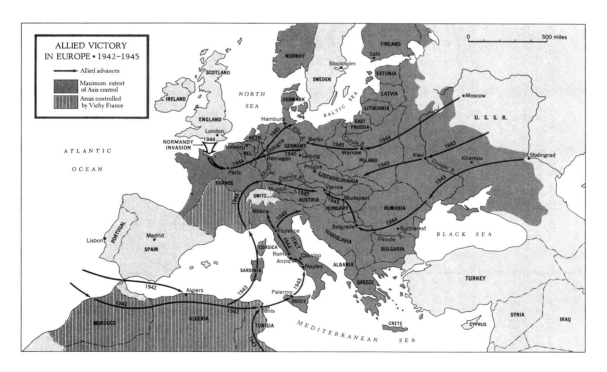

From *The End of the European Era, 1890 to the Present*, Fourth Edition by Felix Gilbert with David Clay Large. Copyright (c) 1991, 1984, 1970 by W.W. Norton & Company, Inc. Reprinted by permission of W.W. Norton & Company, Inc.

Figure 4.3 **Nuremberg Trials** (1945-46). In a German city, Nuremberg, Nazi war criminals were placed on trial for crimes against humanity. Eighteen of the twenty-two high-ranking German leaders were found guilty. The testimony by the defendants provided

Testimony from the Nuremberg Trials

This chapter has discussed the crimes committed by the Nazi's during the Holocaust. The Nazi variation of fascism alleged that Germans were superior to Jews, Slavs, and Gypsies. Those who were labeled "inferior" were treated with a brutality and callousness that denied their basic humanity. Hitler's persecution of the Jews started shortly after he became Chancellor in 1933. Jewish businesses were vandalized and Jews were removed from the universities and local governments. The Nuremberg Laws of 1935 denied Jews citizenship and the right to intermarry with other Germans. *Kristallnacht* or the Night of the Broken Glass on November 9-10, 1938 saw most German synagogues destroyed and over 20 thousand Jews arrested. After this, the persecution escalated rapidly. When the Germans marched into Poland (1939) and Russia (1941), special SS task forces or *Einsatzgruppen* followed. They systematically rounded up Jews and other "undesirables," such as Communist party officials, for extermination. Typically they were shot or gassed in enclosed trucks and then buried in mass graves. By 1942 the Nazi leaders were dissatisfied with the small numbers killed by such methods. Gas chambers and crematoria more suitable for mass executions were installed at places like Auschwitz and Treblinka. Hitler's "final solution" for the Jews, the Holocaust, resulted in the extermination of an estimated 6 million Jews during World War II.

After the war ended, a series of trials were held in Nuremberg, Germany in 1945 and 1946. The International Military Tribunal was established to deal with war crimes and crimes against humanity committed by the former Nazi leaders. These trials produced the eye-witness accounts given below. The first testimony is from Otto Ohlendorf, who was a commander in charge of one of the *Einsatzgruppen*. He was later hanged for his crimes. Another Holocaust witness, Rudolf Hoess, was a commandant at Auschwitz. He was also executed for war crimes. The final witness, Anton Pacholegg, was a prisoner at the Dachau concentration camp.

TESTIMONY OF OTTO OHLENDORF*

COLONEL JOHN HARLAN AMEN (Associate Trial Counsel for the United States): May it please the

---

* From *Trial of the Major War Criminals before the International Military Tribunal* (Nuremberg, 1947) vol. 4, pp. 311-326.

Tribunal, I wish to call as a witness for the Prosecution, Mr. Otto Ohlendorf.

THE PRESIDENT: Will you spell it, please?

COL. AMEN: O-h-l-e-n-d-o-r-f, the first name being Otto. Your Lordship will note that his name appears under Amt III on the chart on the wall.

THE PRESIDENT: What did you say appeared?

COL. AMEN: The name of this witness appears under Amt III of the chart, RSHA, the large square, the third section down.

THE PRESIDENT: Amt III. Oh, yes; I see it.

[Witness Ohlendorf took the stand.]

THE PRESIDENT: Otto Ohlendorf, will you repeat this oath after me: "I swear by God—the Almighty and Omniscient—that I will speak the pure truth—and will withhold and add nothing."

[The witness repeated the oath.]

COL. AMEN: Will you try to speak slowly and pause between each question and answer.

OTTO OHLENDORF (Witness): Yes....

COL. AMEN: How many Einsatz groups were there, and who were their respective leaders?

OHLENDORF: There were four Einsatzgruppen, Group A, B, C and D. Chief of Einsatzgruppe A was Stahlecker; Chief of Einsatzgruppe B was Nebe; Chief of Einsatzgruppe C, Dr. Rasche, and later, Dr. Thomas; Chief of Einsatzgruppe D, I myself, and later Bierkamp.

COL. AMEN: To which army was Group D attached?

OHLENDORF: Group D was not attached to any army group but was attached directly to the 11th Army.

COL. AMEN: Where did Group D operate?

OHLENDORF: Group D operated in the Southern Ukraine.

COL. AMEN: Will you describe in more detail the nature and extent of the area in which Group D originally operated, naming the cities or territories?

OHLENDORF: The northernmost city was Cernauti; then southward through Mohilev-Podolsk, Yampol, then eastward Zuvalje, Czervind, Melitopol, Mariopol, Taganrog, Rostov, and the Crimea.

COL. AMEN: What was the ultimate objective of Group D?

OHLENDORF: Group D was held in reserve for the Caucasus, for an army group which was to operate in the Caucasus.

COL. AMEN: When did Group D commence its move into Soviet Russia

OHLENDORF: Group D left Duegen on 21 June [1941] and reached Pietra Namsk in Romania in 3 days. There the first Einsatzkommandos were already being demanded by the Army, and they immediately set off for the destinations named by the Army. The entire Einsatzgruppe was put into operation at the beginning of July.

COL. AMEN: You are referring to the 11th Army?

OHLENDORF: Yes.

COL. AMEN: In what respects, if any, were the official duties of the Einsatz groups concerned with Jews and Communist commissars?

OHLENDORF: On the question of Jews and Communists, the Einsatzgruppen and the commanders of the Einsatzkommandos were orally instructed before their mission.

COL. AMEN: What were their instructions with respect to the Jews and the Communist functionaries?

OHLENDORF: The instructions were that in the Russian operational areas of the Einsatzgruppen the Jews, as well as the Soviet political commissars, were to be liquidated.

COL. AMEN: And when you say "liquidated" do you mean "killed?"

OHLENDORF: Yes, I mean "killed."

COL. AMEN: Prior to the opening of the Soviet campaign, did you attend a conference at Pretz?

OHLENDORF: Yes, it was a conference at which the Einsatzgruppen and the Einsatzkommandos were informed of their tasks and were given the necessary orders.

COL. AMEN: Who was present at that conference?

OHLENDORF: The chiefs of the Einsatzgruppen and the commanders of the Einsatzkommandos and Streckenbach of the RSHA who transmitted the orders of Heydrich and Himmler.

COL. AMEN: What were those orders?

OHLENDORF: Those were the general orders on the normal work of the Sipo and the SD, and in addition the liquidation order which I have already mentioned.

COL. AMEN: And that conference took place on approximately what date?

OHLENDORF: About 3 or 4 days before the mission.

COL. AMEN: So that before you commenced to march into Soviet Russia, you received orders at this conference to exterminate the Jews and Communist functionaries in addition to the regular professional work of the Security Police and SD; is that correct?

OHLENDORF: Yes.

COL. AMEN: Did you, personally, have any conversation with Himmler respecting any communication from Himmler to the chiefs of army groups and armies concerning this mission?

OHLENDORF: Yes. Himmler told me that before the beginning of the Russian campaign Hitler had spoken of this mission to a conference of the army groups and the army chiefs—no, not the army chiefs but the commanding generals—and had instructed the commanding generals to provide the necessary support.

COL. AMEN: So that you can testify that the chiefs of the army groups and the armies had been similarly informed of these orders for the liquidation of the Jews and Soviet functionaries?

OHLENDORF: I don't think it is quite correct to put it in that form. They had no orders for liquidation; the order for the liquidation was given to Himmler to carry out, but since this liquidation took place in the operational area of the army group or the armies, they had to be ordered to provide support. Moreover, without such instructions to the army, the activities of the Einsatzgruppen would not have been possible.

COL. AMEN: Did you have any other conversation with Himmler concerning this order?

OHLENDORF: Yes, in the late summer of 1941 Himmler was in Nikolaiev. He assembled the leaders and men of the Einsatzkommandos, repeated to them the liquidation order, and pointed out that the leaders and men who were taking part in the liquidation bore no personal responsibility for the execution of this order. The responsibility was his, alone, and the Fuehrer's....

COL. AMEN: Do you know how many persons were liquidated by Einsatz Group D under your direction?

OHLENDORF: In the year between June 1941 to June 1942 the Einsatzkommandos reported 90,000 people liquidated.

COL. AMEN: Did that include men, women, and children?

OHLENDORF: Yes.

COL. AMEN: On what do you base those figures?

OHLENDORF: On reports sent by the Einsatzkommandos to the Einsatzgruppen.

COL. AMEN: Were those reports submitted to you?

OHLENDORF: Yes.

COL. AMEN: And you saw them and read them?

OHLENDORF: I beg your pardon?

COL. AMEN: And you saw and read those reports, personally?

OHLENDORF: Yes.

COL. AMEN: And it is on those reports that you base the figures you have given the Tribunal?

OHLENDORF: Yes.

COL. AMEN: Do you know how those figures compare with the number of persons liquidated by other Einsatz groups?

OHLENDORF: The figures which I saw of other Einsatzgruppen are considerably larger.

COL. AMEN: That was due to what factor?

OHLENDORF: I believe that to a large extent the figures submitted by the other Einsatzgruppen were exaggerated.

COL. AMEN: Did you see reports of liquidations from the other Einsatz groups from time to time?

OHLENDORF: Yes.

COL. AMEN: And those reports showed liquidations exceeding those of Group D; is that correct?

OHLENDORF: Yes.

COL. AMEN: Did you personally supervise mass executions of these individuals?

OHLENDORF: I was present at two mass executions for purposes of inspection.

COL. AMEN: Will you explain to the Tribunal in detail how an individual mass execution was carried out?

OHLENDORF: A local Einsatzkommando attempted to collect all the Jews in its area by registering them. This registration was performed by the Jews themselves.

COL. AMEN: On what pretext, if any, were they rounded up?

OHLENDORF: On the pretext that they were to be resettled.

COL. AMEN: Will you continue?

OHLENDORF: After the registration the Jews were collected at one place; and from there they were later transported to the place of execution, which was, as a rule an antitank ditch or a natural excavation. The executions were carried out in a military manner, by firing squads under command.

COL. AMEN: In what way were they transported to the place of execution?

OHLENDORF: They were transported to the place of execution in trucks, always only as many as could be executed immediately. In this way it was attempted to keep the span of time from the moment in which the victims knew what was about to happen to them until the time of their actual execution as short as possible.

COL. AMEN: Was that your idea?

OHLENDORF: Yes.

COL. AMEN: And after they were shot what was done with the bodies?

OHLENDORF: The bodies were buried in the antitank ditch or excavation.

COL. AMEN: What determination, if any, was made as to whether the persons were actually dead?

OHLENDORF: The unit leaders or the firing-squad commanders had orders to see to this and, if need be, finish them off themselves.

COL. AMEN: And who would do that?

OHLENDORF: Either the unit leader himself or somebody designated by him.

COL. AMEN: In what positions were the victims shot?

OHLENDORF: Standing or kneeling.

COL. AMEN: What was done with the personal property and clothing of the persons executed?

OHLENDORF: All valuables were confiscated at the time of the registration or the rounding up and handed over to the Finance Ministry, either through the RSHA or directly. At first the clothing was given to the population, but in the winter of 1941-1942 it was collected and disposed of by the NSV.

COL. AMEN: All their personal property was registered at the time?

OHLENDORF: No, not all of it, only valuables were registered.

COL. AMEN: What happened to the garments which the victims were wearing when they went to the place of execution?

OHLENDORF: They were obliged to take off their outer garments immediately before the execution.

COL. AMEN: All of them?

OHLENDORF: The outer garments, yes.

COL. AMEN: How about the rest of the garments they were wearing?

OHLENDORF: The other garments remained on the bodies.

COL. AMEN: Was that true of not only your group but of the other Einsatz groups?

OHLENDORF: That was the order in my Einsatzgruppe. I don't know how it was done in other Einsatzgruppen.

COL. AMEN: In what way did they handle it?

OHLENDORF: Some of the unit leaders did not carry out the liqui-

dation in the military manner, but killed the victims singly by shooting them in the back of the neck.

COL. AMEN: And you objected to that procedure?

OHLENDORF: I was against that procedure, yes.

COL. AMEN: For what reason?

OHLENDORF: Because both for the victims and for those who carried out the executions, it was, psychologically, an immense burden to bear.

COL. AMEN: Now, what was done with the property collected by the Einsatzkommandos from these victims?

OHLENDORF: All valuables were sent to Berlin, to the RSHA or to the Reich Ministry of Finance. The articles which could be used in the operational area, were disposed of there.

COL. AMEN: For example, what happened to gold and silver taken from the victims?

OHLENDORF: That was, as I have just said, turned over to Berlin, to the Reich Ministry of Finance.

COL. AMEN: How do you know that?

OHLENDORF: I can remember that it was actually handled in that way from Simferopol.

COL. AMEN: How about watches, for example, taken from the victims?

OHLENDORF: At the request of the Army, watches were made available to the forces at the front.

COL. AMEN: Were all victims, including the men, women, and children, executed in the same manner?

OHLENDORF: Until the spring of 1942, yes. Then an order came from Himmler that in the future women and children were to be killed only in gas vans.

COL. AMEN: How had the women and children been killed previously?

OHLENDORF: In the same way as the men—by shooting.

COL. AMEN: What, if anything, was done about burying the victims after they had been executed?

OHLENDORF: The Kommandos filled the graves to efface the signs of the execution, and then labor units of the population leveled them.

COL. AMEN: Referring to the gas vans which you said you received in the spring of 1942, what order did you receive with respect to the use of these vans?

OHLENDORF: These gas vans were in future to be used for the killing of women and children.

COL. AMEN: Will you explain to the Tribunal the construction of these vans and their appearance?

OHLENDORF: The actual purpose of these vans could not be seen from the outside. They looked like closed trucks, and were so constructed that at the start of the motor, gas was conducted into the van causing death in 10 to 15 minutes.

COL. AMEN: Explain in detail just how one of these vans was used for an execution.

OHLENDORF: The vans were loaded with the victims and driven to the place of burial, which was usually the same as that used for the mass executions. The time needed for transportation was sufficient to insure the death of the victims.

COL. AMEN: How were the victims induced to enter the vans?

OHLENDORF: They were told that they were to be transported to another locality.

COL. AMEN: How was the gas turned on?

OHLENDORF: I am not familiar with the technical details.

COL. AMEN: How long did it take to kill the victims ordinarily?

OHLENDORF: About 10 to 15 minutes; the victims were not conscious of what was happening to them.

COL. AMEN: How many persons could be killed simultaneously one such van?

OHLENDORF: About 15 to 25 persons. The vans varied in size.

COL. AMEN: Did you receive reports from those persons operating these vans from time to time?

OHLENDORF: I didn't understand the question.

COL. AMEN: Did you receive reports from those who were working on the vans?

OHLENDORF: I received the report that the Einsatzkommandos did not willingly use the vans.

COL. AMEN: Why not?

OHLENDORF: Because the burial of the victims was a great ordeal for the members of the Einsatzkommandos....

COL. AMEN:...Referring to your previous testimony, will you explain to the Tribunal why you believe that the type of execution ordered by you, namely, military, was preferable to the shooting-in-the-neck procedure adopted by the other Einsatz groups?

OHLENDORF: On the one hand, the aim was that the individual leaders and men should be able to carry out the executions in a military manner acting on orders and should not have to make a decision of their own; it was, to all intents and purposes, an order which they were to carry out. On the other hand, it was known to me that through the emotional excitement of the executions ill treatment could not be avoided, since the victims discovered too soon that they were to be executed and could not therefore endure prolonged nervous strain. And it seemed intolerable to me that individual leaders and men should in consequence be forced to kill a large number of people on their own decision.

COL. AMEN: In what manner did you determine which were the Jews to be executed?

OHLENDORF: That was not part of my task; but the identification of the Jews was carried out by the Jews themselves, since the registration was handled by a Jewish Council of Elders.

COL. AMEN: Did the amount of Jewish blood have anything to do with it?

OHLENDORF: I can't remember the details, but I believe that half-Jews were also considered as Jews.

COL. AMEN: What organizations furnished most of the officer personnel of the Einsatz groups and Einsatzkommandos?

OHLENDORF: I did not understand the question.

COL. AMEN: What organizations furnished most of the officer personnel of the Einsatz groups?

OHLENDORF: The officer personnel was furnished by the State Police, the Kripo, and, to a lesser extent, by the SD.

COL. AMEN: Kripo?

OHLENDORF: Yes, the State Police, the Criminal Police and, and to a lesser extent, the SD.

COL. AMEN: Were there any other sources of personnel?

OHLENDORF: Yes, most of the men employed were furnished by the Waffen-SS and the Ordnungspo-

lizei. The State Police and the Kripo furnished most of the experts, and the troops were furnished by the Waffen-SS and the Ordnungspolizei....

THE PRESIDENT: The Tribunal would like to know the number of men in your Einsatz group.

OHLENDORF: There were about 500 men in my Einsatzgruppe excluding those who were added to the group as assistants from the country itself.

THE PRESIDENT: Including them, did you say?

OHLENDORF: Excluding those who were added to the group from the country itself....

****

AFFIDAVIT OF RUDOLF HOESS*

I, Rudolf Franz Ferdinand Hoess, being first duly sworn, depose and say as follows:

1. I am forty-six years old, and have been a member of the NSDAP since 1922; a member of the SS since 1934; a member of the Waffen-SS since 1939. I was a member from 1 December 1934 of the SS Guard Unit, the so-called Deathshead Formation [Totenkopf Verband].

2. I have been constantly associated with the administration of concentration camps since 1934, serving at Dachau until 1938; then as Adjutant in Sachenhausen from 1938 to May 1, 1940, when I was

---

*Affidavit Of Rudolf Hoess is a translation of Document 3868-PS from the Office of the U.S. Chief of Counsel for the Prosecution of Axis Criminality, *Nazi Conspiracy and Aggression* (Washington, D.C.: Government Printing Office, 1947) vol. 6, pp. 787-790.

appointed Commandant of Auschwitz. I commanded Auschwitz until 1 December 1943, and estimate that at least 2,500,000 victims were executed and exterminated there by gassing and burning, and at least another half million succumbed to starvation and disease making a total dead of about 3,000,000. This figure represents about 70% or 80% of all persons sent to Auschwitz as prisoners, the remainder having been selected and used for slave labor in the concentration camp industries. Included among the executed and burnt were approximately 20,000 Russian prisoners of war (previously screened out of Prisoner of War cages by the Gestapo) who were delivered at Auschwitz in Wehrmacht transports operated by regular Wehrmacht officers and men. The remainder of the total number of victims included about 100,000 German Jews, and great numbers of citizens. mostly Jewish from Holland, France, Belgium, Poland, Hungary, Czechoslovakia, Greece, or other countries. We executed about 400,000 Hungarian Jews alone at Auschwitz in the summer of 1944.

3. WVHA (SS Main Economic and Administration Office), headed by Obergruppenfuehrer Oswald Pohl, was responsible for all administrative matters such as billeting, feeding and medical care, in the concentration camps. Prior to establishment of the RSHA, Secret State Police Office (Gestapo) and the Reich Office of Criminal Police were responsible for arrests, commitments to concentration camps, punishments and executions therein. After organization of the RSHA, all of these functions were carried on as before, but,

pursuant to orders signed by Heydrich as Chief of the RSHA. While Kaltenbrunner was Chief of RSHA orders for protective custody, commitments, punishment, and individual executions were signed by Kaltenbrunner or by Mueller, Chief of the Gestapo, as Kaltenbrunner's deputy.

4. Mass executions by gassing commenced during the summer 1941 and continued until fall 1944. I personally supervised executions at Auschwitz until the first of December 1943 and know by reason of my continued duties in the Inspectorated [*sic*] of Concentration Camps WVHA that these mass executions continued as stated above. All mass executions by gassing took place under the direct orders, supervisions, and responsibility of RSHA. I received all orders for carrying out these mass executions directly from RSHA.

5. On 1 December 1943 I became Chief of AMT I in AMT Group D of the WVHA and in that office was responsible for coordinating all matters arising between RSHA and concentration camps under the administration of WVHA. I held this position until the end of the war. Pohl, as Chief of WVHA, and Kaltenbrunner, as Chief of RSHA, often conferred personally and frequently communicated orally and in writing concerning concentration camps. On 5 October 1944 I brought a lengthy report regarding Mauthausen Concentration Camp to Kaltenbrunner at his office at RSHA, Berlin. Kaltenbrunner asked me to give him a short oral digest of this report and said he would reserve any decision until he had had an opportunity to study it in complete detail. This

report dealt with the assignment to labor of several hundred prisoners who had been condemned to death-so-called "nameless prisoners."

6. The "final solution" of the Jewish question meant the complete extermination of all Jews in Europe. I was ordered to establish extermination facilities at Auschwitz in June 1941. At that time, there were already in the general government three other extermination camps; Belzek, Treblinka, and Wolzek. These camps were under the Einsatzkommando of the Security Police and SD. I visited Treblinka to find out how they carried out their extermination. The Camp Commandant at Treblinka told me that he had liquidated 80,000 in the course of one-half year. He was principally concerned with liquidating all the Jews from the Warsaw ghetto. He used monoxide gas and I did not think that his methods were very efficient. So when I set up the extermination building at Auschwitz, I used Cyclon B, which was a crystallized prussic acid which we dropped into the death chamber from a small opening. It took from 3 to 15 minutes to kill the people in the death chamber depending upon climatic conditions. We knew when the people were dead because their screaming stopped. We usually waited about one-half hour before we opened the doors and removed the bodies. After the bodies were removed our special commandos took off the rings and extracted the gold from the teeth of the corpses.

7. Another improvement we made over Treblinka was that we built our gas chambers to accommodate 2,000 people at one time.

whereas at Treblinka their 10 gas chambers only accommodated 200 people each. The way we selected our victims was as follows: we had two SS doctors on duty at Auschwitz to examine the incoming transports of prisoners. The prisoners would be marched by one of the doctors who would make spot decisions as they walked by. Those who were fit for work were sent into the Camp. Others were sent immediately to the extermination plants. Children of tender years were invariably exterminated since by reason of their youth they were unable to work. Still another improvement we made over Treblinka was that at Treblinka the victims almost always knew that they were to be exterminated and at Auschwitz we endeavored to fool the victims into thinking that they were to go through a delousing process. Of course, frequently they realized our true intentions and we sometimes had riots and difficulties due to that fact. Very frequently women would hide their children under the clothes but of course when we found them we would send the children in to be exterminated. We were required to carry out these exterminations in secrecy but of course the foul and nauseating stench from the continuous burning of bodies permeated the entire area and all of the people living in the surrounding communities knew that exterminations were going on at Auschwitz.

8. We received from time to time special prisoners; from the local Gestapo office. The SS doctors killed such prisoners by injections of benzine. Doctors had orders to write ordinary death certificates and could put down

any reason at all for the cause of death.

9. From time to time we conducted medical experiments on women inmates, including sterilization and experiments relating to cancer. Most of the people who died under these experiments had been already condemned to death by the Gestapo.

10. Rudolf Mildner was the chief of the Gestapo at Kattowitz and as such was head of the Political Department at Auschwitz which conducted third degree methods of interrogation, from approximately March 1941 until September 1943. As such, he frequently sent prisoners to Auschwitz for incarceration or execution. He visited Auschwitz on several occasions. The Gestapo Court, the SS Standgericht, which tried persons accused of various crimes, such as escaping Prisoners of War, etc., frequently met within Auschwitz, and Mildner often attended the trial of such persons, who usually were executed in Auschwitz following their sentence. I showed Mildner throughout the extermination plant at Auschwitz and he was directly interested in it since he had to send the Jews from his territory for execution at Auschwitz.

I understand English as it is written above. The above statements are true; this declaration is made by me voluntarily and without compulsion; after reading over the statement, I have signed and executed the same at Nurnberg, Germany, on the fifth day of April 1946.

[signed] Rudolf Hoess
RUDOLF FRANZ FERDINAND
        HOESS

Subscribed and sworn to before me this 5th day of April 1946, at Nurnberg, Germany.
[signed] Smith W. Brookhart Jr.
SMITH W. BROOKHART, JR.,
LT. COLONEL, IGD.
****

THE RASCHER EXPERIMENT*

Testimony of Anton Pacholegg at Dachau, Germany, at 13:00 hours on 13 May 1945

Mr. Anton Pacholegg appeared before the Investigator-Examiner and testified as follows:

Q: What is your name?
A. Anton Pacholegg.
Q. What is your address?
A.   Thurndorferstr.   No.   52, Frauenfeld,/Turgan, Switzerland.
Q. We are making an investigation of the alleged atrocities committed by the SS at the Dachau Concentration Camp. Are you willing to be sworn and testify under oath as to what you know of these alleged atrocities at the Dachau Camp?
A. Yes.
Q. Is the address you have given above your permanent address?
A. Yes.
Q. What is your nationality?
A. I am an Austrian.
Q. What was your occupation or profession?
A. I was a patent lawyer.
Q. What has been your education?

---

*"Rascher Experiment" is a translation of Document 2428-PS from the Office of the U.S. Chief Counsel for the Prosecution of Axis Criminality, *Nazi Conspiracy and Aggression* (Washington, D.C.: Government Printing Office, 1947), Supplement A, pp. 414-422.

A. I studied at the University of Gretz from 1912 to 1914 and the University of Paris from 1924 to 1926, having been in the Austrian Army in the interim.

Q. What degrees do you hold?

A. Doctor of Science which authorizes me to practice as a patent lawyer in Switzerland.

Q. How did you come to be in the Dachau Concentration Camp on 2 August 1939?

A. At the request of my business agent in Austria I met him at the Swiss Frontier to discuss personal matters. I was arrested by the Gestapo. I am of the conviction that this meeting was a ruse arranged by the Gestapo in cooperation with my business agent in order to effect my arrest. I actually came to Dachau at the end of the year 1942 and have been here ever since.

Q. Have you been here as a prisoner since that time?

A. Yes.

Q. Why were you kept as a prisoner?

A. I was kept as a prisoner under suspicion of having been in connection with English secret service organizations. The Gestapo could not produce any evidence for this accusation. I was also accused of having dealings with Jewish people and also for violations of Reich Monetary Restrictions.

Q. What was your job in Camp, if any?

A. In the 1st year from 1942 to 1943 I spent my time in the punishment company doing different manual labor such as sweeping the streets or in conjunction with seven other men pulling the street roller, digging in the gravel pit and then I managed somehow to be transferred into Station No. 5 which is the office of the Experimental Station. I received a job as a clerk in cases concerning patients of that station.

Q. What sort of Experimental Station was this?

A. The sole purpose of this experimental station was to compile lists of all German education installations and to get them completely listed and classified in our office so that the SS with this information could use further means of their own to get German educational scientific education completely under SS control.

Q. What was the name of this Experimental Station and was it located in Dachau?

A. Yes, it was located in Dachau and was called the First Experimental Station of the Luftwaffe and then only "Experimental Station" and in 1944 changed to Heritage. They were all cover up names for the true purpose of what was actually accomplished here in an experimental way. I want to add that in the beginning of March 1945 the name again was changed to "Experimental Station" experimenting on living humans for the benefit of mankind.

Q. What was your function in this experimental station?

A. I was a clerk.

Q. In light of your being at this investigation what would you say of interest to this proceeding as to what you know of this experimental station?

A. First I want to talk about experiments about air pressure in connection with the Luftwaffe. The Luftwaffe delivered here at the Concentration Camp at Dachau a cabinet constructed of wood and metal measuring one meter square and two meters high. It was possible in this cabinet to either decrease or increase the air pressure. You could observe through a little window the reaction of the subject inside the chamber. The purpose of these experiments in the cabinet was to test human energy and the subject's capacity and ability to take large amounts of pure oxygen and then to test his reaction to a gradual decrease of oxygen — almost approaching infinity. This amounted to a vacuum chamber in what had been a pressure chamber at the beginning of the experiment. Such prisoners were chosen for these experiments upon written request which was sent to Berlin. Suggested names of prisoners in this camp were sent and authorization was received here in camp. Then the experiment was begun. Dr. Sigmund RASCHER actually picked the physical subjects and sent the names to Berlin. He chose those persons from the group in camp within the punishment company, which group was made up of political prisoners and, so, a few convicts were killed along with the others.

Q. What do you know of the so-called "Rascher Process"?

A. The process so-called is more or less a slang term. It was simply a method of testing a person's ability to withstand extreme air pressure. Some experiments would have no visual physical effect on a person but would only be indicated by meter recordings. There were extremes, however, in those experiments. I have personally seen through the observation window of the chamber when a prisoner inside would stand a vacuum until

his lungs ruptured. Some experiments gave men such pressure in their heads that they would go mad and pull their hair in an effort to relieve the pressure. They would tear their hands and face with their fingers and nails in an attempt to maim themselves in their madness. They would beat the walls with their hands and head and scream in an effort to relieve pressure on their eardrums. These cases of extremes of vacuums generally ended in the death of the subject. An extreme experiment was so certain to result in death that in many instances the chamber was used for routine execution purposes rather than an experiment. I have known RASCHER's experiment to subject a prisoner to vacuum conditions or extreme pressure conditions or combinations of both for as long as thirty minutes. The experiments were generally classified into two groups, one known as the living experiments and the other simply as the X experiment which was a way of saying execution experiment.

* * *

CROSS-EXAMINATION by Captain Clyde Walker, Cross-Examiner:

Q. What were the other tests, if any?

A. There was one to test flight clothing for the Luftwaffe. The victims for this were dressed in various types of flight suits with life jackets and were thrown into vats of water, too deep for a man to stand in and the rim of which was too high to grab into so that a man would have to remain as he was thrown. His hands were always chained together. The water was the temperature of the North Atlantic Ocean or of the North Sea in middle winter. The temperature was important to the experiment. The victim would be left floating for about four hours, or sooner if he fainted, but he would not be removed until the heart beat went down to a certain minimum. After that tests for revivals would be made. I would like to state that on all these experiments, pictures, both still and moving, were taken. Charts and graphs were drawn and all sent to Berlin. At the headquarters of the Luftwaffe and upon decisions by the experts of the Luftwaffe all of the aforementioned experiments were declared scientifically worthless with the result that Dr. RASCHER was fired from his position and reduced to the rank of SS Hauptsturmfuehrer.

Q. Was this in punishment or a feeling of humanitarianism?

A. It was deemed punishment for inefficiency and inexperience and a waste of time when he did so much without knowing first what he was doing.

Q. What else did RASCHER do?

A. Next Dr. RASCHER, in his capacity of SS Hauptsturmfuehrer, conducted experiments to find a remedy to stop bleeding from all causes. He would extract about an eighth of a liter of blood from a prisoner who previously had to swallow certain tablets for the single purpose of causing blood to coagulate in case of an open wound. They would then examine this blood and check the time of coagulation from the time it was extracted.

Q. Did Dr. RASCHER have any assistant that you remember in this work?

A. Yes, there was a prisoner by the name of WALTER NEFF who was the doctor's constant aid. He was discharged from Dachau on 5 April 1944 to accept an appointment in Munich in the office of "Reichsfuehrer SS Personal Staff", which was the bureau in charge of our experiments in this vicinity.

Q. What was the average daily toll from this experiment?

A. I counted daily from one to as many as sixteen bodies left from a day's work. I would say the weekly average was about twenty. These experiments were conducted until September 1943 beginning in 1941.

Q. Was Dr. RASCHER in charge of this work for this whole period?

A. Yes. RASCHER told me that he had been put on this work by HIMMLER personally and he was there until it was abandoned. I forgot to mention that in the early part of the work in 1942 Russian civilians, prisoners of war and Jews of all nationalities were used. Particular attention was paid in being sure that the man was a Russian commissar or some sort of intellectual.

Q. Is there anything else that you would like to add about this experiment?

A. Yes, I can never forget the way RASCHER acted. RASCHER used to go for the prisoners personally and would bring them in at pistol point. He would casually shoot any who tried to make a break or any who did not move fast enough. Once herded into the room he would sneer and tell them that they had fifteen minutes to live and he would relax the prohibition of no smoking among prisoners and that they could have a smoke. The most disgusting part was that when the prisoners lined up, RASCHER would go along and make what he called a leather inspection. He would grab a man by the buttocks and/or thighs and say "good." After the group had been killed, the skin from these bodies would be removed from those thighs and buttocks. I was in the office many times when human skin with blood still on it was brought in to RASCHER. After the bodies had been carted away, RASCHER would inspect them carefully, holding them up to the light for flaws, and would pass on them before they were tanned. They were always stretched over small wooden frames when they came to RASCHER. I saw the finished leather later made into a handbag that Mrs. RASCHER was carrying. Most of it went for driving gloves for the SS officers of the camp.

Q. Was this so-called "Doctor" a doctor of medicine or science?

A. He was a doctor of medicine, I do know that. He was about thirty-four years of age. I have been told that RASCHER was killed by the SS before the Americans got here but I have no proof of that.

Q. Were there any other experiments conducted other than those you have mentioned?

A. Yes.

Q. What were they?

A. The "cold test" was one. RASCHER conducted this one also with the help, of course, of his personal assistant NEFF. The test was to determine the degree of cold temperature that a human being

could stand and still have his faculties. This was for the Luftwaffe also. As well as determining what a man could stand the experiment would usually go on until the man passed out completely. Then there was an experiment to find a way to revive a prisoner who had so collapsed.

Q. Where were these experiments performed?

A. They were performed in the outdoors during the winter time. It was always at night as a rule because the weather was coldest at that time. Men would be put outdoors naked, lying in metal carts from two to twelve hours depending upon the individual's constitution. Some fainted sooner than others. Examinations or written tests were made constantly to record pulses, temperatures and general physical reactions. When a man fainted he was wrapped in a life preserver and thrown into a tank of water at room temperature. He was kept there until he revived or until he was pronounced dead. In addition to this, there was the testing of the heart, blood count, respiratory system, etc. Another experiment conducted with these half-frozen, unconscious people was to take a man and throw him in boiling water of varying temperatures and take readings on his physical reactions from extreme cold to extreme heat. The victims came out looking like lobsters. Some lived but most of them died. Scientifically, I cannot understand how they lived. Still another method was to revive a half-frozen man by the warmth of another body. For this test healthy, normal women were brought from Ravensbruck and two women would be undressed and the half-frozen body of a prisoner placed between the two warm, nude bodies of the women. The three bodies were kept this way until the warmth of the women's bodies revived a man, or until he was declared dead.

Q. Who was present at such an experiment?

A. HEINRICH HIMMLER and his staff generally witnessed these important experiments here at Dachau or any new experiment. Standartenfuehrer SIEVERS was always present with HIMMLER. Another experiment as told to me by NEFF personally was done in the following manner: The prisoner would be taken into the gas chamber at the new crematorium and extremities of the body amputated without the use of anesthetics, i.e., living bodies were used to simulate battle field condition wounds and shell fire wounds. The coagulation tests were being conducted during this time. Dr. RASCHER conducted this experiment and would later dictate his findings for the official report.

Q. Were there any other things of this nature that went on?

A. I remember in particular any report I made out almost always ended with the remark "Experiment successful but the patient died." This may sound like a joke as I have heard it before but I have never had to write it before and realize it was true....

Testimony adjourned at 1600 hours on 13 May 1945.

Anton Pacholegg.

Attest:

signed} David Chavez, Jr.

DAVID CHAVEZ, JR.

Colonel, I.A.G.D.

Investigator-Examiner

Questions for Critical Thinking and Discussion

1. Were Otto Ohlendorf and those under his command responsible for the mass executions that he described? Explain.

2. Why was Ohlendorf so concerned about the manner in which the executions were carried out?

3. Why did no one know about the enormity of the mass executions taking place at the Holocaust death camps in the Allied nations? Weren't these atrocities reported? Why weren't the death camps bombed sometime during the 1941 to 1945 period? Hypothesize your responses.

4. What were some of the more efficient methods of mass execution employed at the death camps as reported by Rudolf Hoess? Based on his testimony, did Hoess perceive his actions to be moral? Do you? Explain.

5. In your opinion did the medical experiments performed, as recounted in Anton Pacholegg's testimony, have any medical validity? Why were these experiments performed according to the deposition of Pacholegg? Upon whose orders?

6. Under what circumstances, if any, are medical experiments on humans ethically justified? Who are appropriate subjects of such experiments? Is the informed consent of the subjects of such experiments always needed? Do medical experiments on animals raise some of the same ethical questions?

7. You have read about the atrocities of the Holocaust. Were the firebombing of Dresden or the atomic bomb vaporization of Hiroshima and Nagasaki also examples of atrocities?

8. Where in the world, in the more recent past, have you seen examples of atrocities or genocide?

9 Can you think of crimes against humanity that have occurred within the United States? Assess the chances of mass exterminations on the scale of the Holocaust occurring in the United States or in foreign areas occupied by U.S. forces.

Self-Test

Part I: Identification

Can you identify each of the following? Tell who, what, when, where, why, and/or how for each term.

1. Archduke Francis Ferdinand
2. Black Hand
3. Allies
4. Central Powers
5. Schlieffen Plan
6. Bolsheviks
7. Treaty of Brest-Litovsk
8. *Lusitania*
9. Zimmermann Note
10. League of Nations
11. Fourteen Points
12. "Big Four"
13. Self-determination
14. Treaty of Versailles
15. War Guilt Clause
16. Lenin
17. Marxist-Leninism
18. Bolsheviks
19. Mensheviks
20. Alexander Kerensky
21. Soviets or Workers' Councils
22. "Peace, land, and bread"
23. February Revolution
24. October Revolution
25. Treaty of Brest-Litovsk
26. New Economic Policy
27. Cheka
28. Red Terror
29. Joseph Stalin
30. "kulaks"
31. Fascism
32. Benito Mussolini
33. The Corporate State
34. Adolf Hitler
35. The Weimar Republic
36. Hyperinflation
37. Dawes Plan
38. Munich Putsch
39. *Mein Kampf*
40. Nuremberg Laws (1935)
41. Great Depression
42. Nazi--Soviet Pact
43. Appeasement
44. *Blitzkrieg*
45. Vichy government
46. Winston Churchill
47. Dunkirk
48. Battle of Britain
49. *Luftwaffe*
50. Tripartite Pact
51. Pearl Harbor
52. Lend—Lease Act
53. Normandy Invasion
54. Holocaust
55. Hiroshima
56. Nagasaki
57. Nuremberg Trials
58. Yalta Conference
59. United Nations

Circle the best response from the ones given.

1. Which one of the following was NOT a cause of World War I?

    a. Disarmament agreements
    b. System of alliances
    c. Imperialism
    d. Nationalism

2. The assassination of Archduke Francis Ferdinand and his wife in 1914 was performed by:

    a. a psychopathic "sicko" who wanted to become Emperor.
    b. an Austrian anarchist.
    c. a Serbian nationalist.
    d. a member of the "The Invisible Hand" society.

3. The chief feature of World War I on the western front was:

    a. its use of carrier pigeons to warn against poison gas attacks.
    b. the lightening strikes and quick gains of territory by the Germans.
    c. a series of German victories at Tannenberg, Masurian Lakes, and the Marne.
    d. a stalemate of trench warfare, costing thousands of lives.

4. The principal strategist for German war plans prior to World War I was:

    a. Hitler.
    b. von Schlieffen.
    c. von Moltke.
    d. Ludendorff.

5. To which of the following alliance systems did Italy belong prior to World War I?

    a. Reinsurance Treaty
    b. Triple Alliance
    c. Pan-Slavic Treaty
    d. Triple Entente

6. Woodrow Wilson's Fourteen Point proposal included:

    a. A League of Nations.
    b. Arms Reduction.
    c. Popular self-determination
    d. All of the above.

7. All of the following nations were founding members of the League of Nations EXCEPT:

    a. Great Britain.
    b. United States.
    c. France.
    d. Italy.

8. All of the following events precipitated America's entry into World War I EXCEPT:

    a. Public announcement of the contents of the Zimmermann note.
    b. United States Senate's refusal to ratify the League of Nations.
    c. American sympathy with the Allies.
    d. Unrestricted submarine warfare.

9. Communism became a reality in which one of the following countries in 1917:

    a. Cuba.
    b. China.
    c. Russia.
    d. Poland

10. The Treaty of Brest-Litovsk signed March 3, 1918:

    a. Took Russia out of World War I.
    b. Placed the czar back on the throne of Russia.
    c. Stopped a mutiny of sailors at Kronstadt.
    d. Dissolved the Union of Soviet Socialist Republics.

11. Fascism is an ideology which:

    a. Permits a multi-party system.
    b. Is compatible with liberal democratic ideals.
    c. Demands that the state own the means of production, i.e., factories, coal mines, etc.
    d. Permits the private ownership of the means of production, but gives ultimate authority over the economy to the state.

12. The totalitarian states that emerged prior to World War II sought to control the lives of their citizens by:

    a. Censorship of the press.
    b. Regulating economic activity.
    c. Outlawing all opposition parties.
    d. All of the above.

13. Which one of the following was NOT included in Lenin's policies?

    a. Redistribution of land to the peasants.
    b. Proposed peace with the White army.
    c. Proposed peace with Germany.
    d. Keeping small the membership of the revolutionary party that would act for the masses.

14. Which one of the following methods was NOT used by Stalin?

    a. He began a series of purges, one of which was the elimination of the "kulaks."
    b. He industrialized the USSR beginning in 1928 with a series of five-year plans.
    c. He used his post as General Secretary of the Communist to crush his opponents.
    d. He initiated the NEP.

15. All of the following were political parties in Russia prior to the Revolution of 1917 EXCEPT:

    a. Mensheviks.
    b. Bolsheviks.
    c. Luddeviks.
    d. Social Revolutionaries.

16. Which one of the following problems did NOT plague the Weimar Republic after World War I?

    a. Low unemployment.
    b. Inability to pay war damages owed to France and others.
    c. Workers' strikes.
    d. Hyperinflation.

17. In 1923 the Ruhr Valley was occupied by _____ because of Germany's inability to make reparations payments.

    a. the Netherlands
    b. Italy
    c. France
    d. Great Britain

18. Which one of the following contributed to the defeat of the Central Powers?

    a. Entry of U.S. troops in 1917.
    b. Allies' use of depth charges, subchasers, convoys to overcome submarine warfare.
    c. Slow starvation of German people due to Allied naval blockade of German ports.
    d. All of the above.

19. Hitler came to power in Germany by:

    a. His decision to rearm Germany in violation of the Versailles Treaty.
    b. Mussolini's recommendation to the Reichstag to have a fellow fascist in power.
    c. His beer hall putsch in Munich.
    d. Being legally appointed as chancellor.

20. Which of these sets were NOT legislatively created during the New Deal?

    a. Securities and Exchange Commission, Social Security, Medicare.
    b. Public Works Administration, Minimum Wage, Works Progress Administration.
    c. Social Security, Works Progress Administration, Securities and Exchange Commission.
    d. Minimum Wage, Public Works Administration, Social Security.

21. The following supported Irish independence EXCEPT:

    a. Irish Republican Army.
    b. Sinn Fein.
    c. Eamon de Valera.
    d. Black and Tans.

22. As a result of the Mukden Incident, what country withdrew from the League of Nations?

    a. Italy.
    b. Japan.
    c. China.
    d. USSR

23. The military technique that the Germans used successfully in attacking Poland, the Low Countries, and France was:

    a. *Sitzkreig.*
    b. *Blitzkrieg.*
    c. Operation Sea Lion.
    d. Operation Overlord.

24. The Vichy government was set up under Marshall Petain in:

    a. Belgium.
    b. the Netherlands.
    c. France.
    d. Luxembourg.

25. Which one of the following statements is true?

    a. Hitler's army inflicted heavy damage and casualties on the Russians at the Battle of the Bulge.
    b. The Battle of Midway took place mid-way between Iceland and Great Britain.
    c. The Tripartite Pact renewed and strengthened a military alliance among France, Great Britain, and the Soviet Union.
    d. The Battle of Britain was a massive air war launched by Germany in preparation for the invasion of Britain.

26. The following developments of the Allies tilted the military balance in their favor during World War II:

    a. radar and sonar.
    b. new types of aircraft.
    c. mass production of ships.
    d. all of the above.

27. The battle in the Pacific that turned the tide against the Japanese was:

    a. Guam.
    b. Pearl Harbor.
    c. Midway.
    d. Saipan.

28. The Germans delayed their surprise invasion of Russia due to:

    a. the fact that the *Luftwaffe* did not win the Battle of Britain.
    b. the Germans were waiting for an Allied invasion of Normandy.
    c. Hitler's need to rescue the Italian invasion of Greece.
    d. Hitler's need to supply additional weapons and warm clothing to his troops.

29. The Japanese surrendered on September 2, 1945 because of:

    a. The dropping of atomic bombs on Hiroshima and Nagasaki.
    b. The invasion of the Philippines and Iwo Jima.
    c. The defeat of Germany on May 7, 1945.
    d. Russia's entry into the war against the Japanese.

30. Most of the actual fighting against Germany on land in World War II was done by:

    a. Russia.
    b. France.
    c. The United States.
    d. Great Britain.

Part III: Review and Thought Questions

1. Explain how and why the assassination of Archduke Francis Ferdinand ignited World War I.

2. How and why were the Germans able to defeat the Russians on the eastern front?

3. What were the territorial arrangements of the Treaty of Brest-Litovsk?

4. What advantages did the Allies have over the Central Powers?

5. Why did resumption of unrestricted submarine warfare and the revelation of the contents of the Zimmermann note incense the American public? Explain how U.S. entry into World War I turned the tide for an Allied victory.

6. Explain Wilson's program for world peace. Was he idealistic?

7. Describe the organization of the League of Nations. Was it an effective international body? Give some reasons for the League's shortcomings.

8. Evaluate the terms of the Treaty of Versailles. Why was Germany particularly resentful of the war-guilt clause? Why would Hitler and other demagogues later say that Germany had been "stabbed in the back" by treasonous politicians?

9. Evaluate some of the problems of the Provisional Government in 1917. What was its biggest mistake?

10. Why were there two revolutions (February and October) in 1917 in Russia?

11. How did Lenin's New Economic Policy operate?

12. By what means did Stalin establish a totalitarian regime?

13. What means did Mussolini use to achieve power?

14. Why did the Pope declare Mussolini to be a leader sent by Providence? How did Mussolini gain favor with the Catholic Church?

15. Evaluate the causes of Hitler's rise to power.

16. How did the Smoot-Hawley Tariff Act operate? What happened to European economies between the wars?

17. Name four pieces of legislation enacted as a result of the New Deal.

18. Why did the dole become a way of life for many of Great Britain's unemployed? How did the Great Depression affect British politics?

19. Trace the process of Irish independence.

20. What caused France and Belgium to occupy the Ruhr?

21. Examine the French government's instability during the inter-war period.

22. Evaluate Germany's dissatisfaction with the terms of the Treaty of Versailles.

23. Explain how the Japanese used the Mukden Incident.

24. When, how, and why did Hitler and Mussolini form an alliance? Why did the Japanese join forces with Germany and Italy?

25. Why and how did the Civil War in Spain prepare the Germans and the Italians for World War II?

26. Trace the relationship between Hitler and Stalin from 1939 to 1942.

27. Explain how and why the Battles of Midway and Stalingrad were turning points in World War II.

28. What was "The Final Solution"? Could it ever happen again?

Part IV: Full-Length Essays

1. Discuss the causes of World War I. Give examples of each cause.

2. Compare and contrast the western and eastern fronts in World War I.

3. Describe the rise and evolution of communism in Russian from 1917 to 1939.

4. Do you think the League of Nations was an effective international body? Explain fully. Give examples to support your point of view.

5. Describe Hitler's path to power in Germany from 1920.

6. Describe the economic and political situations in the United States, France, and Great Britain between the wars.

7. Compare and contrast Stalin's, Mussolini's, and Hitler's regimes prior to World War II.

8. Trace Hitler's path to World War II. Include Germany's dissatisfaction with the terms of the Treaty of Versailles.

9. Compare World War I to World War II.

Figure 4.4 **Holocaust** (1941-1945). Between five and six million Jews, as well as millions of Slavs, Gypsies, and other "undesirables" were executed. Holocaust Concentration Camp, Sachsenhausen, Austrian-Czech border. (Courtesy of The Library of Congress)

Figure 5.1 **25th Infantrymen Walking Through Jungle Near Pleiku, Vietnam.** 1966. One of the most unpopula
wars, the Vietnam conflict led to an erosion in U.S. public confidence as it increasingly seemed impossible to wir
(Courtesy of The Library of Congress, USN & WR Collection)

Chapter V

THE COLD WAR

AND

AFTER

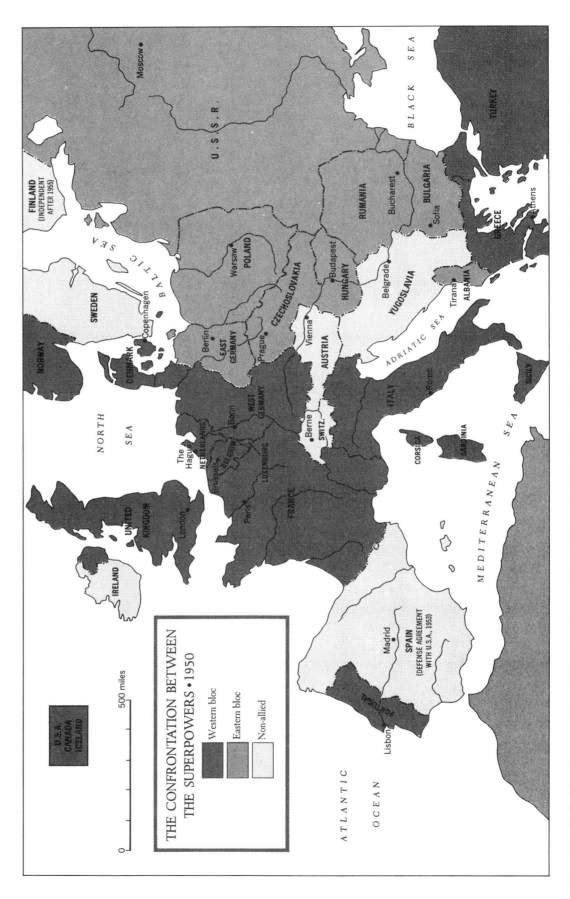

THE CONFRONTATION BETWEEN
THE SUPERPOWERS • 1950

U.S.A.
CANADA
ICELAND

Western bloc

Eastern bloc

Non-allied

0   500 miles

FINLAND
(INDEPENDENT
AFTER 1955)

Moscow

U. S. S. R.

BALTIC SEA

SWEDEN

Copenhagen

NORWAY

DENMARK

Berlin
EAST
GERMANY

Prague

Warsaw
POLAND

CZECHOSLOVAKIA

Vienna

AUSTRIA

Budapest
HUNGARY

RUMANIA

Bucharest

BULGARIA

Sofia

BLACK SEA

TURKEY

Belgrade

YUGOSLAVIA

Tirana
ALBANIA

GREECE

Athens

NORTH
SEA

The Hague

NETHERLANDS

Brussels
BELGIUM

Bonn
WEST
GERMANY

Berne
SWITZ.

Vienna

ADRIATIC SEA

ATLANTIC
OCEAN

IRELAND

UNITED
KINGDOM

London

Paris

LUXEMBURG

FRANCE

ITALY

Rome

CORSICA

SARDINIA

MEDITERRANEAN SEA

SICILY

Madrid
SPAIN
(DEFENSE AGREEMENT
WITH U.S.A., 1953)

PORTUGAL

Lisbon

From *The End of the European Era, 1890 to the Present*, Fourth Edition by Felix Gilbert with David Clay Large. Copyright (c) 1991, 1984, 1970 by W.W. Norton &
Company, Inc. Reprinted by permission of W.W. Norton & Company, Inc.

13

The Cold War

UNDERSTANDING
The Cold War and Its Aftermath

The COLD WAR is a term used to describe the struggle that began after World War II between two rival power blocs. The conflict was "cold" in the sense that, at least in Europe, one side did not attempt to destroy the other with live bullets or bombs. The period of the Cold War was from 1946 to 1991. The United States and its allies organized through the North Atlantic Treaty Organization faced the Soviet Union and its satellites organized through the Warsaw Pact. An "iron curtain" divided Europe between communist and democratic countries.

The United Kingdom and France, while victors in World War II, emerged in 1945 much weaker. They were overshadowed economically and militarily by the United States. Without American economic aid in the form of the Marshall Plan and American military aid through NATO, these countries might have fallen to the Soviet Union. The United Kingdom and France were no longer able to play a global role. Their overseas colonies demanded independence.

European imperialism came to an end during the period of the Cold War. The United Kingdom granted independence to its

What was the Cold War?

Identify the leading powers in each bloc and the alliance to which each belonged.

What happened to the pre-World War II colonial empires?

How did the Soviet Empire collapse?

What event marked the end of the Cold War?

colonies relatively gracefully. First India and Pakistan, then Israel, then one by one the colonies in Africa. The French granted independence bitterly, grudgingly, and after they suffered military defeats in Indo-China and in Algeria. Spain and Portugal surrendered their remaining colonial empires last of all in the 1970s.

And yet, out of the ashes of defeat like the mythical Phoenix bird, the countries of Western Europe forged the basis of a new union. First the European Coal and Steel Community, then the Common Market, then the European Community, and now the European Union are the steps whereby Europe has integrated itself. Will the twenty-first century see the formation of the United States of Europe?

Beginning in 1989, the Soviet Union and its Empire collapsed. Communist regimes were replaced by democratically elected ones in Hungary, Poland, and Czechoslovakia. The East Germans staged their "quiet revolution" against the most Stalinist of the satellite regimes. Erich Honecker was ousted, the wall was torn down, and East and West Germany were united as the enlarged German Federal Republic. Helmut Kohl assumed the role of a new Bismarck. Only this time, unification occurred peacefully and democratically. When Boris Yeltsin, as President of Russia, replaced Michael Gorbachev, who was the head of the former Soviet Union, by the end of 1991, a new age had indeed begun. The Cold War was over, the iron curtain had disappeared, and the European continent was reunited. We were back, almost to where we were at the start of the century.

Still, much had changed. The kings are long gone now, or as in the United Kingdom remain only as Presidential figureheads within a Parliamentary system. Europe has at last fulfilled Woodrow Wilson's hope of "becoming safe for democracy." By the end of the century, democracy has finally won as the preferred form of government in almost every nation of the world. Even dictators pay lip service to the ideals of democracy. Governments depend on the consent of the governed. Another Wilsonian ideal, that of national self-determination, has also triumphed in Europe and in the world. Everywhere, national majorities claim the right to form their own government. Unfortunately, minority groups within these national states still face discrimination and even ethnic cleansing. While human rights are everywhere invoked, they are still violated systematically in too many places.

To what extent have Woodrow Wilson's dreams been realized?

The Start of the Cold War

Tensions between the United States and the Soviet Union increased rapidly after World War II. Truman wanted free elections for those countries in Eastern Europe occupied by Soviet troops. Stalin resisted such elections, since he was convinced that the puppet pro-Soviet governments established in nations, such as Poland, would not survive popular choice. The United States wanted to accelerate the economic recovery of Western Europe, a major trading area. This meant rebuilding Germany economically. The USSR was much more interested in getting reparations from Germany than in seeing its former enemy's economy strengthened. The Soviets were outraged when the Americans and the British refused, in May 1946, to continue shipping goods from their occupation zones to Russia as reparations. Neither

Describe the start of the Cold War.

Discuss the reach of Soviet ambitions after World War II.

the Russians nor the French would agree to the economic unification of Germany as part of the rebuilding process.

Soviet ambitions went beyond the occupied Eastern European countries. Russia, since Czarist days, had wanted to control the Bosphorus, a vital sea link between the Black Sea and the Mediterranean Sea. It pressured Turkey in 1946 and 1947 for joint Russian-Turkish management of the Bosphorus. In the same period Greece's government was faced with a civil war with communist guerrillas, who were aided by neighboring Balkan communist countries. The British had traditionally thwarted Russian ambitions in the area and had been helping the Greek government. But, for economic reasons, the English decided they could not support these Mediterranean countries and asked the U.S. to serve in their place. President Truman not only agreed to assist Greece and Turkey, but in a message to Congress, in March 1947, announced a broad commitment to resist communist aggression wherever it occurred. The TRUMAN DOCTRINE stated:

What was the Truman Doctrine?

> The peoples of a number of countries of the world have recently had totalitarian regimes forced upon them against their will...I believe that it must be the policy of the United States to support free peoples who are resisting attempted subjugation by armed minorities or by outside pressures.[1]

The U.S. Congress responded with a grant of $400 million in aid to Turkey and Greece, which helped both countries not to fall under Soviet domination.

Containment

What was the policy of containment?

Resistance to perceived Soviet aggression became part of a new U.S. foreign policy known as CONTAINMENT. According to George Kennan (1904-), a U.S. diplomat who had served in Russia, the Russians saw the world as divided into two hostile camps: the capitalists and the communists. No conciliatory gestures on the part of the Americans would remove their hostility. The best that the U.S. could do was to consistently apply counter-force to contain the hostile probes of the Soviets. The Russians were psychologically more capable of accepting capitalist strength than capitalist friendship. The adoption of the Truman Doctrine and containment after World War II was a marked contrast with U.S. policy after World War I, which was isolationist and avoided foreign entanglements.

Why did the U.S. begin the Marshall Plan?

The Marshall Plan

Eastern Europe had fallen, in the elegant phrase of Winston Churchill, under an "IRON CURTAIN" of Soviet domination. The U. S. was determined that a similar fate should not await Western Europe. To ensure prosperity and political stability in the West, the U.S. sought rapid reconstruction of the West European economy. On June 5, 1947, Secretary of State George C. Marshall (1880-1959) announced a massive American aid plan for European economic reconstruction that became known as the Marshall Plan.

What was the Common Market?

Sixteen European countries formed a Committee for European Economic Cooperation to coordinate the aid program. Between 1948 and 1952, the U.S. provided over 13 billion dollars in assistance. The plan was wildly successful. By 1951, the productive capacity of the participating members exceeded pre-war capacities.

In 1951, six of these nations formed the European Coal and Steel Community. This was the forerunner to the European Economic Community or COMMON MARKET, which was created by the Treaty of Rome in 1957. This barrier-free trading area has been enlarged through the years to include fifteen Western European nations. The Common Market, now more properly called the European Union, has been a phenomenal success story—eliminating customs duties, establishing a common currency, and making progress toward community-wide citizenship among member nations.

Explain Comecon.

The Soviet Response

The Soviet Union and its allies were given the opportunity to participate in the Marshall Plan, but Russian suspicion of capitalism precluded participation from the start. The Soviets actually tightened their hold on Eastern Europe with a coup in Czechoslovakia in February 1948 that eliminated non-communists from that country's government. The satellite states were drawn into formalized economic dependency on Russia by the creation of the Council for Mutual Economic Aid or Comecon in 1949.

In June 1948, Britain, France, and the U.S. introduced currency reforms in the sectors of Germany they occupied. They had earlier agreed to create a separate constitution for these sectors. The angered Soviets responded with the BERLIN BLOCKADE. Berlin, while occupied by all four powers, was within the Russian sector of Germany. The Russians cut off all rail and road access to Berlin from the other sectors of Germany. The U.S., Britain, and France responded with the Berlin airlift. Could a city of 2.5 million people be fed and supplied purely by air? And if not, what was the alternative? Operation Vittles began on June 26, 1948. It succeeded in keeping West Berlin free from Soviet domination. Perhaps more than anything else, the Berlin Airlift reconciled Germans with the West. Three years after bombing Germany to rubble, the same airplanes were flying coal and wheat to feed starving Germans. On May 12, 1949, the Soviets called off their blockade. It had failed. In September 1949, the pro-American Federal Republic of Germany, or West Germany, became a reality. The pro-Soviet German Democratic Republic, or East Germany, followed in October 1949.

NATO and the Warsaw Pact

Europe had been effectively split into two blocs. This was reflected militarily by the creation of two rival alliance systems. In April 1949, twelve nations agreed to form the North Atlantic Treaty Organization, or NATO. Among its original members were Belgium, Britain, Canada, Denmark, France, Iceland, Italy, Luxembourg, the Netherlands, Norway, Portugal, and the U.S. Greece and Turkey were added in 1952, and West Germany in 1955. Spain joined in 1982. A key provision of the Treaty was that an armed attack against one member was to be consid-

Discuss the Berlin Airlift.

Who were the members of NATO? What commitment did members of NATO have?

Why was the Warsaw Treaty Organization formed?

ered an armed attack against all. A NATO military force with a Supreme Allied Commander was established.

In 1955, when West Germany was admitted to NATO, the Soviets and their East European allies established the rival Warsaw Treaty Organization, or WTO. Originally included in the Warsaw Pact were Albania, Bulgaria, Czechoslovakia, East Germany, Hungary, Poland, Romania, and the USSR. The military structure was more highly centralized than NATO's, with tight Soviet control. With the breakup of the Soviet Union's East European empire, the WTO ceased to exist in 1991.

What advantages did the Chinese communists have in their struggle with the nationalists?

China Goes Communist

After World War II the struggle between the communist revolutionaries under Mao Zedong and the Kuomintang government under Chiang Kai-shek was rapidly concluded in favor of the communists. The communists had attracted support by their energetic defense of the nation against the Japanese. Mao Zedong had adopted communism to Chinese conditions, making the oppressed peasants rather than the oppressed proletariat his central concern. The Kuomintang nationalists, on the other hand, had found their strongest support among landlords and businessmen. Much of Chiang's strength was in the cities, which were associated with the hated foreign traders. The nationalists were aided in their struggle against the communists by the Americans. Given China's history of resentment against foreign domination, the U.S. aid was definitely a mixed blessing. When China fell to the Reds, some Americans thought that communists in the U.S. State Department had betrayed the Chinese. In fact, the often-corrupt nationalists lacked the popular support to withstand their determined and disciplined enemy.

A major Chinese Red Army offensive began in 1947. By the middle of 1948, the communists were numerically on a par with the nationalists. Many nationalist troops, with their American weapons, came over to the communist side. By October 1, 1949, the Reds had taken over the mainland and Mao was able to proclaim the People's Republic of China. Chiang Kai-shek and his nationalist followers fled to the island of Taiwan (Formosa), from which they continued to claim the right to rule the Chinese masses.

The Korean War

The Korean Peninsula had been occupied by the Japanese from 1905 to 1945. At the close of World War II, the U.S. and the USSR agreed to have the Soviet army occupy Korea north of the 38th parallel and the American forces occupy the southern part of Korea. A joint commission was to establish a provisional government for the whole peninsula. The Americans and the Soviets soon disagreed on the particulars of a government. The result was a divided Korea. In the south, after a UN-sponsored election, the Republic of Korea was established in August 1948. Syngman Rhee (1875-1965) was the first president. In the north, the Democratic People's Republic of Korea was formed in September 1948 with Kim Il Sung (1912-1994) as premier. Each state claimed to be the legitimate government for the entire peninsula.

Could the U.S. have prevented the fall of China to communism?

How did Korea come to be permanently divided along the 38th parallel?

Why do you think President Truman sought the approval of the UN rather than the U.S. Congress for U.S. intervention?

Both the USSR and the U.S. had withdrawn their troops when the two Korean governments were formed. But the Russians had left behind a much better trained Korean military force in the north. The U.S. did not demonstrate a firm resolve to defend the south militarily. In fact, U.S. Secretary of State, Dean Acheson did not mention South Korea in a January 1950 speech defining the U.S. defensive perimeter in Asia. On June 25, 1950 North Korea suddenly invaded South Korea.

The U.S. decided to defend South Korea. The matter of the invasion was taken to the United Nations Security Council, where the U.S. and its allies were able to find international support. Since the USSR was boycotting the Security Council to protest the exclusion of Red China from China's UN seat, the Council could act without having to contend with a Soviet veto. The Security Council recommended to the UN members that they furnish military assistance to South Korea, and the U.S. entered the Korean War under the auspices of the UN. Truman proceeded to have U.S. military forces repel the North Koreans. The American forces were commanded by General Douglas MacArthur, who also was named overall commander of UN forces in Korea. Though the UN effort included 17 nations, the bulk of the troops were supplied by the U.S. and South Korea. Truman never asked the U.S. Congress for a formal declaration of war.

Describe the initial course of the Korean War.

The North Korean forces advanced rapidly in the initial phases of the invasion. They overran most of South Korea, except for an area around Pusan near the southern tip. MacArthur halted the advance of the North Korean military, then outflanked their forces by making an amphibious landing at Inchon, 50 miles below the 38th parallel and well behind enemy lines. The successful maneuver forced the North Koreans to retreat north of the 38th parallel. The American objectives now changed. With UN approval on October 7, 1950, the U.S. sought to unify all of Korea under Rhee's government. MacArthur assured Truman of an early victory over North Korea.

In late September, the Chinese communists had threatened intervention if UN forces crossed into North Korea. By November 1, approximately 180,000 Chinese "volunteers" had crossed the Yalu River, which divided Korea from China. They drove UN forces back from the Yalu to below the 38th parallel. The Reds even captured the South Korean capital of Seoul once more. By the spring of 1951, UN forces had slowly pushed their way back over the 38th parallel.

The surprise Chinese intervention brought about a reassessment of U.S. war aims. When the conflict had first started, Truman had seen the North Korean attack in the context of containment. Without distinguishing between Soviet aims and North Korean aims, the communist offensive was perceived as a probe of Western defenses, and it had to be stopped. When UN forces enjoyed huge success after the Inchon invasion, the aim changed, as we saw, to unifying all of Korea under a government friendly to the West. The Chinese forced Truman into yet another rethinking of war aims. He decided that preserving a pro-Western South Korea with borders roughly along the 38th parallel would be enough. To continue to seek the unification of Korea would risk a much larger war, possibly involving China and the Soviet Union and the use of nuclear weapons. Truman decided to move towards a cease-fire.

General MacArthur disagreed with the new policy. He preferred to step up the pressure on Red China by bombing Chinese

How did the Chinese intervention change the situation in Korea?

Analyze the changing U.S. objectives in Korea.

What was the disagreement between Truman and MacArthur? What was the outcome?

facilities and using Chinese Nationalist troops against the Reds. When the General could not persuade Truman, he publicly criticized the administration, even going so far as to correspond with the Congressional opposition. Truman dismissed MacArthur on April 11, 1951. When the General returned to the U.S., he received a hero's welcome, but it was the President's policy that prevailed.

By June, a military stalemate existed with opposing forces balanced in the vicinity of the 38th parallel. Armistice negotiations began in July 1951. An armistice was not signed until July 27, 1953. Dwight D. Eisenhower, who was President then, is said to have threatened the use of nuclear weapons to finally bring the Chinese to the point where they were willing to support an armistice.

How was the Korean War ended? Who won?

When the war ended, the boundaries separating North and South Korea were only slightly different than what they were before it began. Each side had suffered about a million civilian casualties. The Chinese and North Korean military suffered from one and a half to two million casualties. Total UN military casualties were almost 500 thousand, of these 300 thousand were South Korean. The U.S. dead exceeded 23 thousand. America became convinced that containment was a global policy that was to be applied to Asia as well as Europe.

Cuban Missile Crisis

Fidel Castro (1927-) came to power in January 1959 when he overthrew the dictator Fulgencio Batista (1901-1973). The new regime soon demonstrated a profound aversion towards the United States. The Russians became major supporters of Castro. During Eisenhower's Presidency, as Cuban-American relations deteriorated, the CIA began to organize for an invasion of Cuba by Cuban exiles. When Kennedy succeeded Eisenhower, the new President approved the invasion plans. On April 17, 1961, about 1,400 Cuban exiles invaded the BAY OF PIGS on the southwest coast of Cuba in an attempt to overthrow Castro. The invasion went very poorly. The invaders did not have needed U.S. air support, and the anticipated general uprising within Cuba failed to occur. The invasion collapsed on April 19th, and Castro's forces captured 1,189 prisoners. These were later (December 1962) exchanged for $53 million in food and medical supplies.

The disaster was an acute embarrassment to the Kennedy administration. Castro apparently feared that Americans would redress the setback by an invasion of Cuba using U.S. troops. At least this was the idea he sold to the Russians. While Kennedy was capable of planning to assassinate Castro, there is no evidence that JFK planned any direct U.S. invasion of Cuba.

The Russians and Cubans conceived of their own plan to protect against a possible U.S. invasion. They would secretly install medium-range and intermediate-range nuclear missiles in Cuba capable of hitting targets within a radius of two thousand miles. The Russian premier, Nikita Khrushchev (1894-1971), made sure the missiles would be under the control of Russian troops who were to be stationed in Cuba. The Russians hoped not only to deter a U.S. invasion of Cuba, but also to gain a new missile base that would be outside the established U.S. radar early warning system.

What happened at the Bay of Pigs?

What did Cuba and Russia do to deter a U.S. invasion of Cuba?

What was the U.S. response to the introduction of missiles into Cuba?

In late August of 1962, the Russians began transporting the missiles to Cuba. Intelligence reports of the missiles reached Washington in September. Kennedy was persuaded by U-2 spy plane photographs in mid-October that the missiles were indeed being installed in Cuba. The U.S. was unwilling to accept the installation of the missiles, which would have increased Russian power and lowered U.S. prestige throughout Latin America. While Kennedy put in place the necessary force for an actual U.S. invasion of Cuba, he decided on a less risky option. On October 22, 1962, JFK announced a naval "quarantine" (really a blockade) of Cuba to prevent additional missiles from reaching Cuba and demanded that all bombers and missiles already in Cuba be withdrawn. Kennedy made clear that while the U.S. opposed nuclear war, it was willing to risk a nuclear engagement, if necessary.

What was the gravest danger in the Cuban Missile Crisis?

Undoubtedly, the Cuban Missile Crisis was the closest the world has come to actual nuclear warfare. A U-2 spy plane was shot down over Cuba on October 27th. The U.S. warned Russia that it would take further military action unless the crisis was resolved. Khrushchev agreed to dismantle the missiles and return them to Russia in exchange for a U.S. promise not to invade Cuba. The Russian premier lost a great deal of face by the retreat, which contributed to the decision of his colleagues to force him out of office in October 1964. Castro had become a mere onlooker once the two superpowers were directly engaged. There is substantial evidence that he would have preferred a preemptive nuclear strike against the U.S., rather than see the Russian missiles ignominiously pulled off his island. It was only Kennedy who came away with increased international stature.

Whose stature was most enhanced by the outcome? Why?

The Vietnam War

What agreements were reached at the Geneva Conference of 1954?

Vietnam has a long history of struggle against foreign domination. The Vietnamese struggled for centuries to become and remain independent of China. In the latter part of the nineteenth century, the French incorporated Vietnam into the Union of Indochina, which also included Laos and Cambodia. The Japanese occupied Indochina during World War II. Ho Chi Minh, who had seized power briefly at the end of World War II, ran afoul of French ambitions to reestablish their empire. These French efforts resulted in what is often called the First Indochinese War, which began in 1946.

The defeat of the French at Dien Bien Phu (May 1954) led to the conclusion of the First Indochina War in July 1954 at the Geneva Conference. Cambodia, Laos and Vietnam received their full independence. Vietnam was to be partitioned temporarily along the 17th parallel. Ho Chi Minh's Viet Minh would occupy the northern portion of the country, with the French-backed forces confined to the south. An international control commission was established to supervise the armistice. Elections to unify the country were to be held within two years.

Why was the U.S. opposed to Ho Chi Minh?

The United States was present at the Geneva Conference. The Americans did not sign the Geneva Accords, but did commit themselves not to interfere with their implementation. The U.S. had increasingly supported the French effort to overcome the Viet Minh forces. By 1953, America paid 80% of France's war costs. The Americans opposed Ho Chi Minh because he was a communist. The experience of the Korean War had

What was the Domino Theory?

heightened U.S. anxiety. President Eisenhower explained it in terms of the DOMINO THEORY. He feared that if Indochina fell to communism, states such as Burma or Thailand might also be pushed over as if these states were a row of dominoes. There was also a desire that the states of Southeast Asia should be available as free market trading partners of Japan, which was the American counterweight in Asia to Communist China. An awareness of possible conflicting interests among communist states was absent from the statements of American leaders of the time.

The U.S. and Diem

Why was SEATO formed?

The United States was determined to stop Ho Chi Minh from gaining Vietnamese territory south of the 17th parallel and the rest of Indochina. As part of this effort, John Foster Dulles (1888-1959), the American Secretary of State, established the Southeast Asia Treaty Organization (SEATO) in September 1954. This was a collective security arrangement, modeled after NATO, which committed the states signing the agreement to defensive action in case of aggression from outside or subversion from within. Australia, France, Great Britain, New Zealand, Pakistan, the Philippines, Thailand, and the U.S. signed the treaty. The Geneva Accords did not permit the states of the former French Indochina to sign the SEATO treaty, but Laos, Cambodia, and "free" Vietnam were protected by SEATO under a special protocol to the treaty.

The U.S. backed Ngo Dinh Diem in the southern portion of Vietnam. Diem, with American support, refused to participate in the election contemplated at the Geneva

Conference. The fear was that Ho Chi Minh was too popular a revolutionary leader and any election would lead to a unified Vietnam under communist leadership. Instead, the U.S. supported the creation of separate north and south Vietnamese states and replaced the French as the supporter of anti-communist Vietnamese forces.

In the south, Diem became the president of the Republic of Vietnam (or South Vietnam); in the north, Ho Chi Minh headed the Democratic Republic of Vietnam (or North Vietnam). The North Vietnamese government was communist dominated. The South Vietnamese government was anti-communist. Both governments set about eliminating their enemies from the areas under their control. Diem focused on killing off former Viet Minh in the Mekong delta. Ho's efforts were particularly aimed at trying so-called "landlords" in the north.

The Viet Cong

The resistance in the south became known as the VIET CONG, which stood for Vietnamese Communists. Actually, the term is misleading since from the beginning there were non-communist elements in the groups resisting the Diem regime. Isolated acts of rebellion began in 1957. The insurrection broadened in 1960 with the establishment of the National Liberation Front of South Vietnam (NLF).

Diem's problems came to a head in 1963. In January, the numerically superior forces (ten to one) of the South Vietnamese army took heavy casualties and let the Viet Cong slip through their fingers in the battle of Ap Bac. Their reluctance to engage in

How did separate North and South Vietnams develop?

Who were the Viet Cong?

Why was Ngo Dinh Diem removed in a coup?

combat was obvious to the American advisors present.

Diem was a devout Roman Catholic in a largely Buddhist nation. Police shot at Buddhist demonstrators in Hué in May. Buddhist monks, believing they were the victims of religious persecution, resorted to self-immolation as a form of protest. The Diem regime proved incapable of effective suppression or reconciliation of the Buddhists.

With American support, South Vietnamese generals staged a coup against Diem on November 1, 1963. The following day, Diem and his brother were murdered by the plotters. On November 22, the American President, John F, Kennedy, was himself assassinated in Dallas.

The Johnson Administration

Was Vietnam an issue in the 1964 U.S. election campaign? Explain.

Lyndon Baines Johnson (1908-1973) succeeded the assassinated Kennedy as president of the United States. Johnson (or LBJ) faced several difficulties. The South Vietnamese leadership was unstable, and there were a series of coups. 1964 was a Presidential election year. Johnson was running against Senator Barry M. Goldwater (1909-1998), a fervent conservative who advocated aggressive military action. In these circumstances, Johnson did not want to appear too belligerent about Vietnam. He publicly shied away from sending American boys to fight in Asian wars. He preferred that Goldwater be seen as the candidate most likely to get the U. S. into an Asian war or an atomic holocaust. Nevertheless, LBJ did get Congress to approve the GULF OF TONKIN RESOLUTION in August 1964. The resolution gave him the equivalent of a blank check "to take all necessary measures to repel any armed attack against the forces of the United States" and "to take all necessary steps, including the use of armed force, to assist" any SEATO member or protocol state.[2]

The Gulf of Tonkin Resolution resulted from an alleged attack by North Vietnamese torpedo boats on two U.S. destroyers. An attack certainly occurred on one of the destroyers, the *Maddox*, on August 2, 1964. A reported second attack on the two ships, two days later, appears to have been the result of misinformation. Neither the Congress nor the U.S. public were informed that the *Maddox* was monitoring North Vietnam's positions while South Vietnamese gunboats were carrying out a covert mission against North Vietnam.

At year-end 1963, just after Johnson took office, there were 15 thousand American advisors in Vietnam. A year later there were 25 thousand advisors. In March 1965, the first American combat troops were introduced to Vietnam. By December 1965, there were 200 thousand American troops in Vietnam. Two years later, the number had risen to 500 thousand.

The continued escalation of American involvement did not bring the victory President Johnson wished. The Viet Cong dug tunnels to protect against U.S. bombing. The North Vietnamese increased the numbers of their troops fighting in the south, infiltrating troops and supplies along the Ho Chi Minh Trail, which ran through Laos and Cambodia.

The U.S. chose to fight a war of attrition rather than an all-out war that might drag in the USSR or China. The problem was that the North Vietnamese and the Viet Cong had more staying power in such a war. The anti-war movement in the U.S. increased, especially as the number of draftees in Viet-

What was the Gulf of Tonkin Resolution?

What happened in the Gulf of Tonkin?

Describe the escalation of American troop strength in Vietnam.

What was the Tet Offensive?

nam rose. The U.S. government cited "body counts" to convince the public that it was winning. However, the events of the TET OFFENSIVE of January 1968 forced a reassessment of U.S. policy.

The North Vietnamese and Viet Cong chose the lunar New Year or Tet (January 30) to launch a major offensive against the cities, including Saigon and the ancient capital, Hué. During the attack, Hué and other cities were captured, and the American embassy in Saigon actually came under fire. The communists made only temporary military gains and suffered heavy losses. Perhaps as many as 50 thousand of their troops were killed. But it was in the propaganda arena that a major victory was won. The Viet Cong had proved to be a significant force in the supposedly safe urban areas of South Vietnam. The U.S. public became fed up with an evident lack of progress. 1968 was another presidential election year. In March, the anti-war candidate Eugene McCarthy (1916-) won 42 percent of the vote in the New Hampshire democratic primary against Johnson, the incumbent presidential candidate. At the end of the month, Johnson announced that he was no longer seeking reelection; in addition, he was ending the bombing of North Vietnam in hopes of attaining a negotiated peace.

Why didn't President Johnson seek reelection?

The Nixon Administration

The Vietnam War cost the Democrats the presidency. Richard M. Nixon, the Republican candidate, won in 1968. During the campaign, Nixon had promised to end the war in Vietnam. As president, he followed several policies designed to get the Americans out of Vietnam with honor. He hoped to get the USSR and China to pressure Hanoi to be more flexible at the bargaining table. Nixon embraced a policy of DÉTENTE towards Russia and China. Détente was a relaxation or easing of cold war tensions. Détente towards the USSR resulted in the Strategic Arms Limitations Talks (SALT) to curb nuclear weapons and increased trade. In the case of China, détente took the form of a dramatic reversal of American policy. Nixon visited mainland China in 1972 and full diplomatic relations were reestablished by 1979 (after Nixon had left office). No startling breakthroughs were made in the Vietnam peace talks in Nixon's first years. It is doubtful that China or Russia could have forced Hanoi into major concessions, even if they had wished to do so. Also, South Vietnam was not ready to negotiate its own demise.

In South Vietnam itself, Nixon's strategy placed emphasis on the VIETNAMIZATION of the war. This meant turning the fighting over to the South Vietnamese and gradually withdrawing American troops. He attempted to build up the South Vietnamese forces and to bring greater pressure on Hanoi, especially by massive and sometimes secret bombing not only in Vietnam, but also in Laos and Cambodia. There were also troop incursions into Laos and Cambodia.

By the end of 1970, American troop strength in Vietnam was down to 280 thousand; by December of 1971, U.S. forces had been reduced to 140 thousand. The troop cutback helped to reduce protests back in the U.S., but did not noticeably improve the American position at the bargaining table.

The stalemate was broken in March 1972, when North Vietnam launched a conventional invasion of the south across the 17th parallel. The North Vietnamese used 120 thousand of their regular troops and

Describe some of the policies embraced by the President Richard Nixon.

What did Nixon gain by reducing U.S. forces in Vietnam?

What was Nixon's response to the conventional invasion launched by North Vietnam?

Who were the chief negotiators in the peace talks?

How did Nixon break the negotiating deadlock?

thousands of Vietcong. The assault did not collapse the South Vietnamese army, which outnumbered the enemy by about five to one, but it did show its weakness and its dependence on American advisors and bombers. The communists made significant gains in the Mekong Delta region.

Nixon's response included a massive bombing of North Vietnam and a mining of Haiphong Harbor. Negotiations between Henry Kissinger (1923-), representing the United States, and Le Duc Tho (1911-1990), representing North Vietnam, intensified in September and October 1972. A preliminary agreement was reached by mid-October, but Nguyen Van Thieu (1923-), the South Vietnamese leader, would not accept the agreement, which permitted communist forces from the north as well as from the south to stay in place in the south.

Negotiations were once more deadlocked. Nixon was reelected president in a landslide in November. In December, he ordered a massive bombing of the Hanoi-Haiphong area of North Vietnam. Approximately forty thousand tons of bombs were dropped. The North Vietnamese indicated their willingness to resume talks as soon as the bombing was halted. Talks resumed on January 8, 1973, and a peace agreement was signed in Paris at the end of the month. Thieu did not sign the agreement, but did not energetically oppose it. Thieu's acquiescence was the price for continued U.S. aid to South Vietnam. Nixon, in a separate letter, had assured Thieu that the U.S. would respond with full force should North Vietnam violate the peace settlement.

The Paris Accords provided for the withdrawal of American forces and the dismantling of U.S. bases in Indochina. U.S. prisoners of war were to be returned. North Vietnamese and Viet Cong troops remained in place (unlike the 1954 Geneva Accords when the Viet Minh forces withdrew to the north). The South Vietnamese government also remained in power, pending an election to be held by a national council composed of the various Vietnamese factions. A cease-fire was declared, with an international commission created to supervise the cease-fire.

The last American troops left Vietnam on March 29, 1973. Supposedly, the last U.S. prisoners of war were released in Hanoi on April 1st. In November, the Congress limited the President's power to deploy U.S. troops abroad by the War Powers Act. In August of 1974, Richard Nixon resigned the presidency because of his implication in the Watergate election scandal.

The End of the War and After

None of the Vietnamese parties appear to have accepted the cease-fire as the end of the fighting. The North Vietnamese regrouped and, in January 1975, captured Phuoc Long province as part of a planned two-year campaign to take the south. South Vietnamese resistance collapsed much more quickly than anyone expected. President Thieu resigned and fled Saigon on April 25, 1975. Saigon fell to North Vietnamese forces by the end of April.

The rest of Indochina also became communist. The communist Pathet Lao had been part of a coalition government in Laos. After the fall of South Vietnam, the Pathet Lao took complete control of Laos. In Cambodia, the communist Khmer Rouge captured the capital Phnom Penh in April 1975. The radical regime, in power from 1975-1979, emptied many of the cities and launched a bloodbath that took perhaps 1.5 million lives in a population of 7.5 million. The Khmer

What were the provisions of the Paris Peace Accords?

How did the war finally end?

Did the aftermath of the war verify the Domino Theory? Explain.

Rouge were overthrown by Vietnamese army forces, which remained in the country from 1979-1989. After extended guerrilla fighting, a freely elected government that did not include the Khmer Rouge was formed in 1993.

Though the fate of Indochina tended to support the Domino Theory, the theory was not true for the rest of Southeast Asia and no other country in that region turned communist. An estimated 2 to 3 million Indochinese were killed in the course of the war. In Vietnam itself, the feared bloodbath after the war did not occur. The northerners did dominate the united country and pursue socialist policies that failed to bring national prosperity. With the fall of the Soviet Union, there is a new openness to foreign investment and controlled capitalism in Vietnam.

The war had cost the U.S. 58 thousand American dead and over $150 billion. Americans debated among themselves why the U.S. lost the war and what lessons were to be learned from the Vietnam War. The left stressed the failure to recognize that the Viet Cong and North Vietnamese were fighting for national independence, whereas the U.S. leaders thought particularly in terms of containing communism. For many Vietnamese, the Americans were simply the new imperialists replacing the French. The right stressed the corroding effect of the media, particularly TV, on the will to sustain the war and the "treachery" of the Antiwar Movement. It is certainly true that the media insisted on exposing negative aspects of the American military effort, such as the My Lai Massacre (March 16, 1968), in which over 300 unarmed Vietnamese civilians in a rural hamlet were killed by U.S. infantrymen. More important may have been a basic failure of policy analysis. American leaders overstressed the significance of conventional

Why do you think the Viet Cong and North Vietnamese fought so well?

military success, while failing to understand the political and psychological consequences of events. The Tet Offensive resulted in a military defeat for the communists, but in a political victory for them because of the American public's diminished confidence in Johnson's war policy. Indeed, the American military won the military battles they engaged in. What was lacking was U.S. staying power and a willingness to apply all available resources to the war effort for fear that China or the Soviet Union might intervene directly. Many would also question the commitment of our Vietnamese allies.

For some Americans, the lesson of the war was "No More Vietnams." It is certainly true that American presidents, congresspersons, and generals have felt constrained to pull out of places like Lebanon and Somalia at the first hint that "success" would require sustained involvement of U.S. ground forces and continuing casualties. The Gulf War against Iraq in 1991 may have overcome some of the reluctance in circumstances where the U.S. can advantageously deploy massive military power. The favorable reaction to the dedication of the Vietnam Veterans Memorial in Washington, D.C. in 1982 suggests that the public acrimony over Vietnam has faded. The United States had proven reluctant to establish normal relations with Vietnam. Presidents avoided recognizing Vietnam because of dissatisfaction with the Vietnamese accounting for American soldiers still missing-in-action and bitterness within the U.S. over the war. But in February 1994, there was no significant public outcry when the U.S. lifted its economic embargo of Vietnam. In 1997, the U.S. finally fully revived relations with the appointment of Douglas Peterson, a former prisoner of war, as ambassador to Vietnam.

Were there lessons for the U.S. in the Vietnam experience? Explain.

What do you think was the most important reason for the failure of American policy in Vietnam?

Describe some of the occasions for unrest in Eastern Europe after World War II.

Upheavals in Eastern Europe

After a communist coup in Czechoslovakia in February 1948, most of Eastern Europe was under the domination of the Soviet Union. A notable exception was Marshall Tito's (1892-1980) Yugoslavia, which had won its freedom from Hitler's control without significant Soviet help.

With Stalin's death (March 1953), there were some stirrings in Eastern Europe. Riots occurred in East Germany in June 1953. More serious unrest followed Khrushchev's denunciation of Stalin in 1956. Agitation in Poland brought an end to farm collectivization and some relaxation of other controls. In Hungary, the changes under Imre Nagy (1896-1958) were more sweeping. They included loosening ties to the Soviet Union's Warsaw Pact. The Soviets sent in tanks to reestablish their control. Nagy was later executed.

How did the Soviets react to events in Hungary in 1956 and Czechoslovakia in 1968?

The Soviets again demonstrated their determination to maintain their hold on Eastern Europe in 1968. In January of that year, Alexander Dubcek (1921-1992) became the leader of Czechoslovakia during a relaxation of hard-line rule known as the PRAGUE SPRING. He promised "communism with a human face."[3] He permitted freedom of the press and non-communist political organizations. Warsaw Treaty Organization troops, mostly from the Soviet Union, crushed the liberalization in August and reimposed the monopoly of the communist party. Unlike Nagy, Dubcek was merely deposed; he died of injuries received in an auto accident in 1992. Leonid Brezhnev (1906-1982) was the Soviet leader at the time of the Czech intervention. He announced the BREZHNEV DOCTRINE, which gave the USSR the right to intervene any-where in the Soviet bloc when Russian-style socialism was threatened.

The years of détente in the 1970's had brought wider East European contact with Western nations and economies. Poland owed an especially large debt to Western banks. Efforts at economic austerity that included a rise in food prices led to strikes and the rise of the Solidarity labor union. Its leader was an electrician, Lech Walesa (1943-), at the Lenin shipyards in Gdansk. Solidarity, which was independent of the communist party, soon claimed a membership of 10 million. Talk of free elections alarmed the Soviets, who threatened to intervene. To avoid Russian intervention, the Polish general Wojciech Jaruzelski (1923-) was made prime minister in 1981. He declared martial law, outlawed Solidarity, and jailed Walesa.

The situation in Eastern Europe changed radically when Mikhail Gorbachev (1931-) came to power in the Soviet Union, first as general secretary of the communist party (1985-91), then as president of the USSR (1988-91). Gorbachev embraced political and economic restructuring (*perestroika*) and the free flow of information and open discussion of problems in the media (*glasnost*). This example put pressure on the less liberal East European regimes. Above all, Gorbachev indicated that the Soviet Union would no longer intervene to halt the liberalization of governments in Warsaw Pact countries and formally renounced the Brezhnev Doctrine in 1989.

The first East European country to hold free elections was Poland, which was experiencing continued economic problems. There were several strikes in 1988. Poland had a tradition of opposition to Russia, a strong and independent Roman Catholic Church that was then under a Polish Pope, John Paul II

Explain the Brezhnev Doctrine.

Why was Solidarity such a threat to the Polish government?

How did Mikhail Gorbachev change the East European situation?

How did Poland exit the Soviet Block?

What occurred in Hungary?

(1920-), and a prestigious opposition leader in the person of Lech Walesa. Walesa participated in talks with the communist government in early 1989. An agreement emerged to legalize Solidarity and to hold open elections in June. The communist party was guaranteed some seats in the new parliament. Solidarity won a landslide victory. The communist party, which became a minority in a new coalition government, quickly transformed itself into a West European-style socialist party. Jaruzelski served as president of Poland until December 1990, when Walesa won in the first direct presidential elections in Polish history.

The example of Poland and the new-found commitment to non-intervention in the Soviet Union set loose irrepressible forces in the rest of Eastern Europe. In Hungary, Janos Kadar (1912-1989) had replaced Imre Nagy after the Russians put down the 1956 revolt. Kadar, while loyal to the Soviets, had followed relatively liberal economic policies that permitted a degree of private enterprise. However, the economy faltered in the 1980's and popular dissatisfaction increased. The communist party replaced Kadar in 1988 with reform-minded communists. In 1989, the reformers permitted opposition parties and elections. The communists transformed themselves into Western-style socialists, and Nagy was reburied with honor. The pace of change even swept the communists out of office in 1990.

The events in Hungary helped to precipitate change in East Germany. East Germans had long been attracted by the wealth and freedom of their fellow Germans in the west. But the concrete Berlin Wall, with its minefields and guard towers, had for over 28 years (1961-1989) reminded them of their inability to flee to West Germany without great risk. East Germans traveled to Hungary in mid-1989 and found they could easily get across the border to Austria and freedom. Tens of thousands did so.

Mass protests arose in Leipzig, Dresden, and other East German cities. The East German leader, Erich Honecker (1912-1994), attempted to use force against demonstrators in Leipzig in October. But his orders were countermanded, and he was removed from office later in the month. Events moved rapidly. On November 9, 1989, the Berlin Wall was opened up to allow East Germans to cross into West Germany. An estimated 350,00 East Germans did so in 1989.

Honecker was arrested in January 1990, though ultimately he was allowed to go into exile in Chile. West German Chancellor Helmut Kohl took the lead in reuniting the two countries. On October 3, 1990, Germany was once more reunited as the enlarged Federal Republic of Germany with its capital in Berlin. Germany has confirmed the yielding of territory to Russia and Poland that occurred after World War II and has pledged to respect the Polish border.

The examples of Poland, Hungary, and East Germany affected Czechoslovakia. Large-scale protests were begun by students on November 17, 1989. A brutal police crackdown led to popular revulsion and even more massive protests. An opposition group called Civic Forum was formed with the support of Vaclav Havel (1936-), a playwright whose human rights activities had frequently landed him in jail. The communist government was forced to resign on November 24th. In December, the VELVET REVOLUTION (smooth and non-violent) was completed when Havel became president of an interim government.

Like other East European countries, the end of communism brought a renewal of nationalist tensions to Czechoslovakia.

What happened to East Germany?

What was the Velvet Revolution?

How did distinct Czech and Slovak Republics come about?

Describe the pace of change in Bulgaria.

What was different about the revolution in Romania?

Elections in June 1992 brought to power as premiers Czech and Slovak leaders who favored the dissolution of the Czechoslovak union. Havel resigned from the office of president. On January 1, 1993, the two independent states of the Czech Republic and the Slovak Republic came into existence. Havel was once more chosen president by the Czech Republic's parliament on January 26th of that year.

Bulgaria also underwent a change of government in 1989. At first it appeared to be a revolution from above. The communists changed the party name to socialist and ousted the head of the party who had been in power for 35 years. But they kept control of the government. In elections in June 1990, the former communists kept their majority. However, in October 1991, the ex-communists lost their majority in parliament to an opposition party, the Union of Democratic Forces. By 1992, the parliament, and the offices of president and prime minister were controlled by non-communists.

Romania's 1989 revolution differed from the others we have described because it was particularly violent. Nicolae Ceausescu (1918-1989) had dominated Romanian politics since 1965. He was a communist dictator whose regime was highly centralized and quite repressive. Nevertheless, he received loans for industrialization from the West, where he was looked upon favorably because his foreign policy often differed from the Soviet Union's.

Unrest arose in the regional capital of Timisoara, which had a large Hungarian minority. There hundreds were killed. Protests spread to the national capital, Bucharest. In December, Ceausescu fled after hearing chants of opposition at a pro-government rally. Fighting raged between the security forces, which supported

Ceausescu, and the regular army. The dictator was captured by the army, given a hasty trial, and executed, along with his wife. An estimated 900 people were killed and over two thousand injured. The National Salvation Front, which took over after Ceausescu, contained many former communists.

The Breakup of the Soviet Union

It was suggested that the rise of *perestroika* (restructuring) and *glasnost* (openness) in the USSR and the renunciation of the Brezhnev Doctrine were important factors in freeing the East European satellites from communism and Russian domination. The liberation of Eastern Europe, along with *glasnost* and *perestroika*, in turn had profound effects upon the USSR itself.

Perestroika moved the economy towards privatization and a free market, while moving the political system towards democratization. Mikhail Gorbachev had hoped to reform communism in order to preserve it. Ultimately, he unleashed forces of change that he could not control and which, if brought to their logical conclusion, meant breaking the communist party's monopoly on political power. The poorly implemented economic reforms brought an actual decline in the average Russian's standard of living. The ironic result was that Gorbachev was more popular with his former enemies abroad than with his own people at home.

The armed forces felt threatened as the Soviets retreated not only from Eastern Europe but also, in 1988 and 1989, from Afghanistan where they had fought a Vietnam-like war against Islamic resistance forces. There was inadequate housing to

What were *perestroika* and *glasnost*?

What unanticipated problems did Gorbachev encounter?

Why did the Baltic states take the lead in breaking up the Soviet Union?

meet the needs of the returning soldiers and their families.

These conditions unleashed nationalistic feelings among Russians and among other peoples who made up the USSR. *Glasnost* provided the setting for the freer expression of these sentiments. The desire for national independence was particularly strong in the Baltic states of Estonia, Latvia, and Lithuania, which had enjoyed independence in the period 1918-1940 and had been forcibly incorporated into the Soviet Union as a result of the Hitler-Stalin Pact of 1939. Lithuania declared its independence on March 11, 1990. The USSR initially refused to recognize Lithuanian independence. The impetus to seek independence spread to other Soviet states as well. In a move to appease the nationalistic sentiments, Gorbachev agreed to a Treaty of Union that would have shifted vast political power from the central government to the constituent republics. The treaty was scheduled to be signed on August 20, 1991.

Why was a coup against Gorbachev organized?

These changes were too much for more conservative members of the party, the secret police (the KGB), the military, and the government-run industries. A coup was organized and Gorbachev, on vacation in the Crimea, was offered the opportunity on the afternoon of August 18, 1991 to join the coup. When he refused to do so, he was placed under house arrest. It may seem strange that the leader of the USSR would be given an opportunity to join a coup against the established government of the USSR. But among the plotters were many Gorbachev himself had appointed in hopes of moderating the pace of reform and saving a role for the party.

The effective opposition to the coup did not come from Gorbachev, but from an archrival of Gorbachev: Boris Yeltsin

(1931-), the President of the Russian Republic. He and crowds of his supporters gathered at the Russian parliament building, called the White House. Yeltsin, standing on top of a tank, bellowed his defiance while the TV cameras rolled. Increasingly, troops and their commanders refused to accept the orders of the Emergency Committee formed by the coup leaders. The coup leaders lost their nerve and the revolt collapsed. On August 22nd, Gorbachev returned to Moscow, asserting that he was again in full control of the USSR.

The reality was something different. Yeltsin's prestige, not Gorbachev's, had been enhanced by the August coup's failure. The communist party was dissolved in the wake of the coup. In the fall of 1991, Yeltsin outmaneuvered Gorbachev as power slipped from the central Soviet government to republics that announced their independence. The USSR recognized the independence of the three Baltic republics, Estonia, Latvia, and Lithuania, in September. By early December, a Commonwealth of Independent States was formed, which came to include eleven of the former republics of the USSR. Bowing to the new reality, Gorbachev resigned on December 25, 1991. He was the last president of a now defunct Union of Soviet Socialist Republics. With the breakup of the Soviet Union the Cold War was over. An economically and politically stressed Russia, the largest of the successor states to the old USSR, could no longer maintain the Cold War challenge to the United States.

Who led the opposition to the coup?

What were the consequences of the coup's collapse?

Figure 5.2 **"Pasiphae"** by Jackson Pollock (1912-1956). This abstract expressionist painter poured and dripped paints on large canvases, setting a trend for other twentieth-century artists. (Courtesy of The Metropolitan Museum of Art, Purchase, Rogers, Fletcher and Harris Brisbane Dick Funds and Joseph Pulitzer Bequest, 1982)

14

Decolonization and Other Twentieth Century Trends

DECOLONIZATION

How did the decolonization movement affect Africa?

Africa

The mad scramble between 1870 and 1914 to colonize Africa has already been discussed. A similarly rapid movement to decolonize Africa followed World War II. Before World War II, only four states on the whole continent of Africa could be considered independent. Today, there are some 53 independent African nations. We trace here the struggles for nationhood of a few of these peoples whose efforts have attracted worldwide attention.

The emphasis here is on Africa south of the Sahara, or Black Africa. Native Africans found themselves on the lowest rung of the socio-economic ladder in their own homelands. Under colonialism, Europeans and Asians occupied the higher rungs of the ladder. The suspicion was that profits and opportunities would continue to be reserved

What complaints did Africans have about colonial rule?

What did Kwame Nkrumah accomplish?

Who were the Mau Mau?

for these non-African groups, unless independence was achieved.

The British Colonies

In 1948, small farmers in the British Gold Coast were discontented with the availability and price of consumer goods. They suspected that the source of their problem was the profiteering of European merchants. They organized a boycott that expanded and progressed to violent riots. The ferment was led by Kwame Nkrumah (1909-1972) who organized a mass political party to gain self-governance for the Gold Coast. Nkrumah was arrested in 1950, but his party won the first general election in the colony held in 1951. He was allowed by the British to lead a government that was increasingly Africanized. By 1957, the Gold Coast became the fully independent state of GHANA, the first newly independent African state after World War II. Nkrumah himself became increasingly autocratic and was overthrown in 1966 by the army.

In East Africa, Jomo Kenyatta (c.1891-1978) returned to KENYA in 1946 to fight for independence. Previously, he had been in London representing the interests of the Kikuyu tribe at the Colonial Office. In the early fifties, the Mau Mau movement of anti-European terrorists gained force among the Kikuyus. Kenyatta, accused of leading the movement, was arrested in 1952. He was released in 1961. His Kenya African Nationalist Union won electoral victory in 1963, which was followed shortly by the granting of full independence to Kenya. Kenyatta became president of the republic in 1964 and continued as the nation's leader until his death in 1978. He was an example of a successful African ruler. While Kenya remained troubled by tribal divisions and corruption charges, in Kenyatta's lifetime it enjoyed a fairly stable government and free press, with a prosperous mixed economy benefiting from private foreign investment.

SOUTH AFRICA is another story of effective native African leadership. Since 1994, Nelson Rolihala Mandela (1918-) has led the Republic of South Africa as its President after that county's first multiracial elections. Mandela, the son of a Xhosa chief, has shown concern to better the lot of the majority black population. But he has been careful to be conciliatory to all, seeking to retain the support of whites and other groups that are needed if South Africa is to be an economic success. Given the past history of the nation, such a stance revealed true statesmanship.

The formation of the Union of South Africa in 1910 has already been mentioned. The Union, a dominion within the British Empire, adopted a parliamentary style of government. South Africa had a prime minister and political parties that vied with each other for seats in a parliament. But voting rights were largely restricted to whites, except for a few blacks and mixed-race (coloured) people in the Cape Colony. Politics most often involved the clash of interests between the Boers of Dutch descent, called Afrikaners, and the English settlers. The majority blacks faced economic, as well as voting restrictions. For example, they could purchase land only in certain areas that constituted less than eight percent of the whole country.

Conditions for blacks worsened considerably when the Afrikaner-dominated National Party came to power in 1948. A system of apartheid or separation was instituted. Black access to white areas was re-

Discuss the leadership role of Nelson Mandela.

What were some of the restrictions placed on blacks after the formation of the Union of South Africa in 1910?

What was the ANC?

What were the consequences of the Sharpeville Massacre?

stricted by pass laws. Marriage between these races was forbidden. Eventually, the notion was adopted that blacks would be given political freedom only in their own homelands or bantustans—a mere thirteen percent of the land. These underdeveloped territories were incapable of sustaining 75 percent of the population.

A number of groups fought against these repressive laws. The organization Mandela was active in was the African National Congress (ANC). While most members of the ANC were black, it was a multiracial organization that also included whites and Indians. Originally, the ANC was dedicated to non-violent struggle. The Sharpeville Massacre of March 21, 1960, in which police killed 69 black protesters and wounded more than 180 others, brought the ANC to adopt more militant tactics. Mandela became the commander-in-chief of its armed resistance. He was arrested in 1962 and eventually sentenced to life imprisonment. He was not released until 1990.

It was after the Sharpeville Massacre that the government held a referendum to decide if the country should become a republic. In 1961 South Africa became a republic and left the British Commonwealth. If it had stayed, it might well have been forced to leave because of opposition to its repressive segregationist policies. Outside pressures from the United Nations and newly-independent African states mounted against the government. Economic sanctions against South Africa were instituted in the United States and other countries. Banks refused to roll over loans and the value of the Rand, the national currency, plummeted. The South African economy could not move ahead without foreign investment.

Political instability also increased. Student protests in Soweto township in 1976 led to confrontations between police and students. Over 500 people were killed. Protests spread throughout the country. Repressive police measures were simply leading to more determined opposition. Some white South Africans left the country in fear of what the future held.

It was under these circumstances that F. W. de Klerk (1936-) became President of South Africa in 1989. Although he was an Afrikaner and leader of the Nationalist Party, he recognized that dramatic change was necessary. De Klerk found in Nelson Mandela, a black leader willing to work towards a peaceful transition to majority rule. Intense negotiations followed Mandela's 1990 release from prison. In November 1993 agreement was reached for a transitional government. In elections held in April 1994, in which all races could participate, the ANC received 63 percent of the vote for candidates to the National Assembly. Subsequently Nelson Mandela was elected president by this Assembly. A new constitution, approved in 1996, prohibits race, gender, and age discrimination. Instead of demanding vengeance for past wrongs, the government has fostered a Truth and Reconciliation Commission to expose past atrocities and offer amnesty to perpetrators who acknowledge past wrongdoing.

Tribal divisions troubled many new African nations. When the Europeans cut up Africa into colonies, they disregarded tribal territorial divisions. The result was that after independence the new nations often contained many antagonistic tribes, making political stability difficult. NIGERIA, Africa's most populous nation, is an example of the unhappy consequences of tribal diversity. Nigeria gained its independence from Britain in 1960 as a federation of three different regions: northern, western, and eastern. The

Why were the Soweto protests important?

What happened after F. W. de Klerk became president in 1989?

Do you think that the reconciliation of the different races and ethnic groups of South Africa is likely?

How does the treatment of the Ibos illustrate the problem with European-made national boundaries in Africa?

What appear to be the causes of the problems in Somalia?

Were the UN and the U.S. successful in resolving these problems?

north with its larger population was able to dominate the country politically. Tensions developed between the Hausa in the north and the Ibo in the southeast. In 1967, the Ibos attempted to establish the independent republic of Biafra. After a bloody civil war, with hundreds of thousands of casualties, the Ibo were defeated and Biafra was forcibly dissolved. The military has continued to have a role in the political process in tribally-divided Nigeria.

SOMALIA has had a particularly unfortunate post-colonial experience. Located in eastern Africa, between the Indian Ocean and Ethiopia, the northern part had been under the control of the British and the southern, larger portion under the control of the Italians. In 1960, it received independence as one country. A military coup brought Mohammed Siad Barre (1919-1995) to power in 1969. After he was overthrown in 1991, the various clans could not reach a lasting agreement on how to govern Somalia. They had plenty of weapons with which to fight one another since both the United States and the Soviet Union had served as military supporters of Somalia during phases of the Cold War. The uncontrolled factional fighting led to efforts to have a United Nations peacekeeping force restore order. The United States took a leading role, landing Marines near Mogadishu, the Somalian capital, in December 1992. While the mission at first seemed successful, the U.S. suffered 18 dead and 77 wounded on October 3, 1993 when its forces tried to capture a notably uncooperative clan leader, Mohammed Farrah Aidid (1934-1996). The adverse publicity at home led President Clinton to pull out U.S. troops in March 1994. The whole UN peacekeeping force was pulled out in February 1995. Since then, no central government has been reestablished (though there is a diplomatically unrecognized Republic of Somaliland in the north), and Somalia remains a particularly lawless and unpredictable place.

The French Colonies

Algeria, Morocco, and Tunisia were France's North African colonies. These colonies were largely populated by Arabs and Berbers (descendants of pre-Arab North African peoples). There had been a significant influx of French settlers into these colonies. Algeria had the most Europeans—one million settlers or colons comprising, at one time, about ten percent of the total population. Despite some violent disturbances, the road to independence was relatively easy for Morocco, which gained independence in 1956, and for Tunisia, which gained autonomy in 1954 and full independence in 1956.

In ALGERIA, the story was quite different. Technically, it was an integral part of France rather than a colony. When an armed revolt began in 1954, the French resisted stiffly. The French put 500 thousand troops into Algeria to fight the Muslim-dominated National Liberation Front (FLN). Both sides used terror tactics. The French found that they were spending nearly a billion dollars annually without success. This stalemate led, in turn, to a revolt by French settlers and elements of the army in Algeria. They formed a Committee of Public Safety ready to replace the constitutional government of France. In Paris, the frightened National Assembly gave Charles de Gaulle (1890-1970), the leader of the Free French forces during World War II, emergency powers for six months. De Gaulle created a new constitution for France. The Fifth Republic re-

Name the former French colonies in North Africa.

Why were the French so resistant to granting independence to Algeria?

How did the French handle the demands for independence in West and Equatorial Africa?

placed the Fourth Republic. De Gaulle became its first president under the new constitution. He dealt decisively with the North African crisis, getting the French to accept a plebiscite in Algeria to determine Algeria's future. The Algerian vote was overwhelmingly in favor of independence, which was granted in July 1962.

France's unhappy experience in North Africa helps to explain the very different scenario for the colonies of France in West Africa and in Equatorial Africa. These colonies, with their predominantly black populations, gained independence relatively peacefully. Among the new states created by the end of 1960 were Benin, Burkina Faso, Chad, the Central African Republic, the Congo, Gabon, Guinea, the Ivory Coast, Mali, Mauritania, Niger, and Senegal.

Contrast the independence process in the Belgian and French colonies.

The Belgian Congo and Rwanda

The transition to independence was anything but peaceful for the Belgian Congo, now the DEMOCRATIC REPUBLIC OF THE CONGO. The Belgians had deprived both blacks and white settlers of opportunities to gain political experience. Blacks were used as cheap labor and left uneducated in the belief that they would be easier to manage. When the French colonies across the Congo River made progress towards independence, the Congolese under Belgian rule also demanded independence. Nationalist riots occurred, which shook the Belgians badly. They hastily decided in 1959 to hold elections and permit independence in the hope that their response would protect Belgian economic interests in the long run. Independence came in June 1960, with Patrice

Lumumba (1925-1961) as the first premier. Civil strife followed. The most serious disturbance was in the mineral-rich province of Katanga, where foreign mining interests encouraged secession. Lumumba was dismissed by his nation's president, Joseph Kasavubu (c1913-1969) who was one of his rivals, and later assassinated. United Nations' forces succeeded in putting down the secession by 1964. In 1965, Mobutu Sese Seko (1930-1997), who had been involved in a previous coup, seized control of the government. General Mobutu then used the military to remain in power until overthrown by Laurent Désiré Kabila (1939-) in 1997. Mobutu had the state renamed Zaire in 1971. Kabila changed the name back to the Democratic Republic of the Congo.

Another former Belgian colony, RWANDA, has also been racked by violence. The Hutus and the Tutsis, who have been neighbors there for centuries, have different ethnic origins. Belgian colonial policy, which favored the Tutsis, had exacerbated Hutu resentment. The most notorious bloodletting occurred in 1994 when approximately 800,000 Tutsis and moderate Hutus were systematically slaughtered. The genocide was ended when the Hutu-dominated government that had fostered the genocide was overthrown by Tutsi-led forces.

What roles did Patrice Lumumba, Mobutu Sese Seko, and Laurent Kabila play in the Congo?

Who are the Hutus and the Tutsis?

Asia

The nationalist movement in INDIA had deep roots. The Indian National Congress was founded in 1885. In the early twentieth century, the more radical wing of the Congress demanded independence from

How did Mahatma Gandhi contribute to the Indian independence movement?

Britain. Starting in the 1920's, Mahatma Gandhi (1869-1948) became the leader of an independence movement using tactics of non-violent civil disobedience and passive resistance to the British. During World War II, he and the Congress leaders refused to cooperate with the Allies and demanded total British withdrawal from India.

Gandhi hoped to include all of India's many minorities, especially the Muslims, in a newly independent India. But this was not to be. Muhammad Ali Jinnah (1876-1948), leader of the Muslim League, felt that Muslims should have their own state, separate from the dominant Hindus. When independence came in 1947, the subcontinent was divided into Hindu India and Muslim PAKISTAN. Both Jinnah and Gandhi died in 1948. Gandhi was killed by a Hindu fanatic who thought he was pro-Muslim. There was a mass movement of Muslim refugees from India to Pakistan and of Hindu refugees from Pakistan to India. Many died of mob violence incited by religious differences. Pakistan originally consisted of West and East Pakistan. In 1971, with India's help, East Pakistan became the separate state of Bangladesh.

Why was Pakistan separated from India?

The Japanese had driven the Europeans out of southeast Asia during World War II. The PHILIPPINES were recaptured by the United States in 1944 and granted independence in 1946. The Dutch had ruled INDONESIA before the Japanese occupation. They attempted to regain control after the Japanese defeat, but were faced by armed resistance from Indonesian nationalists in 1945. The Dutch formally recognized the independence of Indonesia in 1949.

Before the French could return to Indochina after the Japanese surrender, the communist Ho Chi Minh (1890-1969) had declared an independent republic of

VIETNAM. His Viet Minh fought the French from 1946 to 1954, when the French were defeated at Dien Bien Phu. After the French defeat, Ho Chi Minh controlled the northern part of Vietnam and the Americans sponsored the government of Ngo Dinh Diem (1901-1963) in the south to prevent all of Vietnam falling under communist control. This led to the Vietnamese War, which was discussed earlier.

How did the Japanese contribute to the independence movement in Asia?

The Middle East

The area known as the Middle East may be said to include such predominantly Arab states as Egypt and Libya; the Fertile Crescent countries of Iraq, Jordan, Lebanon and Syria; Saudi Arabia and the other states of the Arabian Peninsula; as well as the non-Arab states of Iran, Israel, and Turkey.

Among the first Arab states to gain independence were Egypt and Iraq. The British protectorate over EGYPT was ended in 1922. British troops were withdrawn in 1937, except for the Suez Canal area. IRAQ ceased to be a British mandate under the League of Nations in 1932, although British influence there remained strong until a 1958 coup. Lebanon and Syria had become French mandates after World War I. LEBANON gained its independence in 1943. SYRIA, after an armed struggle, gained its independence in 1946. LIBYA, which had been an Italian colony before World War II, was granted independence by the UN in 1951.

More intricate and confusing is the history of the British colonies of Palestine and Transjordan. Transjordan (literally "across the Jordan") was the name given an Arab kingdom established, with close British

What Middle Eastern states had gained independence by 1951?

What were the origins of Jordan?

cooperation, on the right bank of the Jordan River (Palestine was on the left bank). Transjordan became autonomous in 1923 and nominally independent in 1928. It was transformed into the Hashemite Kingdom of Transjordan, another British creation, in 1946. This kingdom was renamed JORDAN in 1949 after participating in the Arab-Israeli War of 1947-49 over the fate of Palestine. As a result of this war, Jordan gained some Palestinian territory on the other side of the Jordan River.

PALESTINE was a British mandate under the League of Nations. Before World War I, it had been part of the Ottoman Empire and had a substantial Arab majority. During the interwar period, an increasing number of Jews settled in Palestine, influenced by the Zionist movement, which sought to create a Jewish homeland in the ancient Holy Land. British policy on the matter of a Jewish homeland can charitably be described as contradictory and ambiguous. At least at one point, in the Balfour Declaration of 1917, the British Foreign Secretary endorsed the establishment of a national home in Palestine for the Jewish people.

What gave impetus to the movement to create a Jewish homeland?

Before World War II, as Jewish migration expanded, there had been increasing conflict between Arabs and Jews. Britain attempted to restrict Jewish immigration. The influx of Jewish settlers greatly increased at the end of World War II as a reaction to Hitler's campaign of extermination. When the English tried to block illegal Jewish immigration, some Jewish groups resorted to terrorist tactics. The British announced their intention to withdraw, giving the newly formed United Nations the task of deciding Palestine's future. The UN, in November 1947, approved a plan to divide Palestine into Jewish and Arab sectors that were to be linked economically. The Jews accepted the arrangement; the Arabs did not. The British refused to implement the resolution, since both sides had not agreed. Instead, they simply withdrew their forces in May 1948.

The Jews immediately proclaimed the establishment of the Jewish state of ISRAEL. The Palestinian Arabs took up arms and armies from neighboring Arab states poured across the border to help them. The better organized and led Jewish forces won. When the fighting halted in 1949, Israel had a third more territory than had been allocated to the Jews by the UN partition plan. 750 thousand Palestinian Arabs became refugees in other Arab lands. Arab nations and Israel engaged in a series of other wars in 1956, 1967, 1973, and 1982. Palestinian Arabs organized the Palestine Liberation Front (PLO), which conducted guerrilla warfare and terrorism against Israel. In 1993, Israel and the PLO signed a peace accord, which promised limited Palestinian autonomy in some areas and raised hopes for a more lasting peace in the Middle East. Many think that the eventual outcome will be a separate Palestinian state.

How did Israel come into existence?

What might the prospects be for a permanent Palestinian-Israeli peace?

OTHER TWENTIETH CENTURY TRENDS

Science and Technology

World War II and the Cold War that followed gave a huge boost to the development of new science and technology. The

Explain nuclear deterrence theory.

changes in computers, telecommunications, and other fields may even constitute a new communications revolution or, at the least, a new stage of the industrial revolution.

NUCLEAR ENERGY

Nuclear energy was first harnessed in the form of the atom bomb. In 1939, President Franklin Roosevelt ordered the development of atomic weapons, fearing that the Germans might beat the Americans to the punch. The first atom bombs were dropped on Japan in August of 1945. After 1945, the U.S. built more powerful hydrogen bombs, as well as smaller scale tactical weapons for battlefield applications. Whereas in 1945 only the U.S. possessed the atom bomb, nuclear weapons have since proliferated rapidly. The Soviet Union acquired atomic weapons in 1949, followed by Britain in 1952, France in 1960, China in 1964, and India in 1974. The Cold War period gave birth to nuclear deterrence theory. With atomic weapons both the U.S. and the USSR were able to destroy each other's civilizations. As long as the first one attacked retained the ability to destroy the other side, neither superpower would launch a nuclear attack and risk its own destruction. The efficacy of the theory depended on the maintenance of a nuclear balance of terror between the two sides and an assumption of rationality on the part of those who had the capacity to launch nuclear weapons.

Illustrate the proliferation of nuclear weapons.

Several other nations have since obtained nuclear capabilities, including Israel, Pakistan, and South Africa. Even nations that had signed the 1968 Nuclear Non-Proliferation Treaty as non-nuclear weapons states have since tried to develop them. The efforts of Iraq and North Korea to obtain the capacity to make and launch nuclear weapons have been of particular concern to the U.S. and its allies in recent times. There is always the risk that some madman will acquire nuclear capability.

Nuclear energy also has non-military applications. It has been used to generate electricity. There was a major push to develop nuclear generating plants in the 1950's and 1960's. Some nations, such as Japan, which lacks many natural energy resources, still have substantial nuclear generating programs. But in many nations nuclear energy has become less important as alternate energy sources have become more competitive. Nuclear accidents have particularly discouraged the use of nuclear power facilities. In 1979, at the Three Mile Island reactor in Pennsylvania, U.S., the reactor plant failed, but the containment system prevented the discharge of radioactive particles into the environment. An accident at the Chernobyl reactor in 1986, in what was then the USSR, had more serious consequences. Possibly 30 to 50% of the total radioactive material of the reactor was released into the atmosphere. Over 100,000 people faced long-term evacuation and foodstuffs were polluted in large areas of Europe.

SPACE EXPLORATION

Space exploration has been an area of intense competition between the U.S. and the USSR. Russia launched the first Sputnik satellite on October 4, 1957. The first probe to go past the moon was the *Luna 1* launched by the Soviets on January 2, 1959. They also launched the first manned spacecraft on April 12, 1961. Soviet space success greatly alarmed the U.S. On May 25, 1961, President John F. Kennedy (1917-1963) set a goal for

Discuss the non-military applications of nuclear energy.

Why was the U.S. afraid of Russian advances in their space program?

Discuss the U.S. space program.

the U.S. to land a man on the moon by the end of the decade. That goal was achieved when the *Apollo 11* landed on the moon on July 20, 1969.

The U.S. has also considered a space station program. As a preliminary step toward a permanent space station, the U.S. developed a reusable space shuttle. There have been a number of space shuttle flights, including the tragic tenth flight of the *Challenger*, which exploded just two minutes after lift-off on January 28, 1986. In terms of actual space stations, the Soviets have been ahead of the U.S. While the Americans launched the relatively small Skylab in May 1973, the Russians have had a series of *Salyut* space stations and in February 1986 launched the first element of the *Mir* space station into orbit. To save costs the U.S. and Russia agreed in 1994 to a joint space station development program known as the International Space Station.

What was the ENIAC?

COMPUTERS and TELECOMMUNICATIONS

Humans have used mechanical devices, such as the abacus, to assist them in mathematical computations for over two thousand years. Computers using electronic vacuum tubes or transistors are products of the twentieth century. The first successful electronic digital computer was the ENIAC, built during World War II under contract from the U.S. Army. Its original task was to calculate trajectories for weapons systems. It contained 17,468 vacuum tubes, took up 18 thousand square feet of floor space, and could perform five thousand additions per second.

The 1950's and 1960's saw important advances in computer technology. Transistors and integrated circuits on small silicon chips replaced vacuum tubes connected together with bulky external wires. The newer computer systems gave off much less heat, were less bulky, and were much more reliable. The Remington Rand Corporation's UNIVAC was delivered to the Census Bureau in March 1951. International Business Machines (IBM) came out with large computers, or mainframes, which appealed to corporations. IBM built the model 701 in 1953 and the System/360 series in the 1960's. By the middle of the 1960's, IBM had two-thirds of the world computer market.

The first microcomputers designed to sit on desktops made their appearance as do-it-yourself kits in 1974. In June 1977, the Apple II microcomputer was introduced. IBM finally responded with its own version of the microcomputer, the IBM PC in 1981. IBM's PC (personal computer) had 640 kilobytes (roughly 64,000 words) of random access memory (RAM), which is readily accessible, transient information. This was equivalent to the amount of RAM that many early 1960's mainframe computers had. The power and variety of PC's have continued to increase. By 1999 home PCs with 128 megabytes (131,072 kilobytes) were commonplace. In IBM's rush to get into the PC market, it used hardware and software developed elsewhere that were not protected by IBM patents or copyrights. This meant that the standard IBM set could easily be copied or cloned by others, and these clones could be sold at commodity prices. IBM lost control of the market. At the end of the twentieth century the two most powerful corporate players in the PC market were Intel, in hardware, which made the most widely used microprocessors for PCs and Microsoft, in software, which licensed the ubiquitous Windows operating system.

How did IBM lose its dominance in the computer industry?

How do today's PC's compare to mainframes of the 1960's?

At the end of the twentieth century, who dominates the PC market?

Why is the Internet important?

How might computers change the workplace?

What is telecommunications?

Another surprise was the phenomenal growth of the Internet. The Internet developed after World War II as a tool for communicating among computers used by the military and universities in the US. In 1989 Timothy Berners-Lee, an Englishman, introduced an easy-to-use graphical interface for the Internet, the World Wide Web (WWW). Its original purpose was to facilitate communications for physicists working for the European Laboratory for Particle Physics. Others quickly adopted the new standard and the use of the Web spread to many corporations and individuals. In the US there were some 53.5 million adults (27 percent of the population) with access to the Internet in late 1998. Worldwide Internet access is projected to be 206 million by the year 2005.[4]

A computer revolution was born. Affordable computing power became available not just to large corporations and to big government, but also to small business and ordinary citizens. The industrial revolution of the nineteenth century changed the way work was performed and centralized the workplace in the factory. When the powerful desktop or laptop PC is combined with communications equipment, such as networks, faxes or modems, there is the potential for radical change of comparable magnitude in the way work is performed and where it is performed.

TELECOMMUNICATIONS refers to communication over long distances by electrical or electronic means. The telephone and telegraph are examples of telecommunications technology that came into wide use in the nineteenth century. The radio broadcast industry was developed after World War I and television broadcasting after World War II. What is most striking in the late twentieth century is the marriage or merger of diverse technologies. Telephones, computers, and broadcasting were once considered very separate businesses. Then telephony became increasingly computerized. Computers replaced electromechanical telephone switches. Telephone lines ceased to be hard-wired and came increasingly to depend on the airwaves through microwave towers, communications satellites, and cellular phone technologies. The telephone lines are used by facsimile machines (faxes) and computers equipped with modems to send mail, bypassing hand-delivery systems. Cable companies using fiber optics not only provide multiple channels for TV programming, but also send voice and data messages. Governments, whether democratic or dictatorial, have great difficulty determining appropriate regulations for these intertwined technologies. In the United States, the country's largest telephone company, the American Telephone and Telegraph Company, actually consented in 1982 to its breakup so that it could escape regulations that prevented it from getting into non-telephone businesses. Information technology contributed to the political upheavals in 1989 in several Chinese cities, including Beijing, threatening the domination of the Chinese communists. Many have argued that the new telecommunications technology was important in bringing an end to the Soviet empire in 1991.

The Environment

The story of science and technology in the twentieth century is not one of unrelenting progress. The contemporary environmental movement owes much to the publication of Rachel Carson's (1907-1964) *Silent Spring* in 1962. Carson warned about the dangers that pesticides, such as DDT, posed for the environment. Others followed

Discuss some of the changes in telecommunications in the second half of the twentieth century.

Who was Rachel Carson?

What are some of the concerns that led to the rise of the environmental movement?

her lead. An Environmental Protection Agency was created in the U.S. in 1970 to deal with pollution and other concerns. So-called "green parties," political parties concerned with the environment, arose in several countries. The Greens in West Germany were the best known. But similar parties could be found in Austria, Belgium, Denmark, Finland, and Switzerland. Greenpeace, an environmental group of Canadian origin, advocated direct nonviolent confrontation to stop harm to the environment. They attempted to block ships engaged in whaling, transportation of nuclear wastes, etc. In 1985, one of their ships was actually blown up in New Zealand by French agents as a deterrent to nuclear protest activities!

Art and Architecture in the Twentieth Century

Modern Art

Distinguish between the Greens and Greenpeace.

History is heading not only to the end of the century but also to the end of a millenium. The third millenium is about to begin. How do we approach this third millenium? Do we look to the past or to the future? Great events, wars and peace, are often less indicative of the times than are the arts. The arts offer up a symbolic mirror to an age. The pyramids have symbolized ancient Egypt long after detailed knowledge of that age has become an obscure specialization of historians. What is the symbol of our own age: the Empire State Building and the World Trade Center? Picasso? Warhol? Woody Allen?

The twentieth century has been a time of Modern Art. Beginning with Impressionism, art has become less and less representational and more and more abstract and symbolic. Just as physics has discovered the realities of nuclear particles and quantum mechanics, so art is delving into shape, color, and planes.

The twentieth century has witnessed movement away from the objective representation of reality, as in the works of such painters as Russian-born Wassily Kandinsky (1866-1944), who was an originator of abstract art. His swirling blots of color and diverse lines did not represent particular objects found in nature. Abstract art has taken many forms. In the U.S., there developed a school of abstract expressionism, non-representational paintings with vivid colors and striking, swirling masses. Jackson Pollock (1912-1956) adopted such techniques as dripping paint from cans and pouring paint on canvases lying on the floor.

Cubism and surrealism are important styles of modern painting. Spanish-born Pablo Picasso (1881-1973), whose work has reflected several styles, is one of the founders of cubism. Early cubism probed the representation of three-dimensional objects on two-dimensional surfaces using overlapping planes. Later, cubism made use of materials, such as chairs and other objects, to create collages, which brought new dimensions to the art, linking painting with sculpture. Surrealism, which uses imaginary forms from fantasy and dreams, was influenced by Freudian interest in the subconscious. Salvador Dali (1904-1989), another artist of Spanish origin, is noted for his contributions to surrealism. Among his works are *The Sacrament of the Last Supper* and *The Persistence of Memory*, better known as *Soft Watches*.

Pop art of the 1960s turned common commercial products, like Coke bottles or

What techniques did Wassily Kandinsky and Jackson Pollock use?

What is cubism and surrealism?

Give examples of pop art.

What is postmodernism?

Name some painters and sculptors associated with postmodernism.

Brillo pads, into the subjects for paintings. Andy Warhol's (1928-1987) *Brillo Boxes (1964)* is a prime example. Minimalist artists created large canvasses of a single color edged by a single stripe of another color. Barnett Newman's (1905-1970) *Who's Afraid of Red, Yellow, and Blue II (1966-7)* offers a striking example of this style.

Minimalism may be considered the end of Modern Art. It is difficult to see what further abstraction could be developed than a flat surface painted in a single color with a black edge. All the experimentation of abstract art has reached its logical conclusion. Modern art is at an end.

Postmodernism

This is why we are now in the Postmodern Period, according to some commentators. Postmodernism was recognized in the 1980's although its antecedents go back to the 1960's and 1970's. Postmodernism is an eclectic movement in that it deliberately borrows from all sorts of previous styles of art. Eric Fischl (1948-), Francesco Clemente (1952-), David Salle (1952-), A. R. Penck (1939-), Nancy Spero (1926-), Sigmar Polke (1941-) and Mark Tansey (1949-) are painters who represent the post-modern ethos. Julian Schnabel (1951-) is both a painter and a sculptor. Among other post-modernist sculptors are Louise Bourgeois (1911-), Kiki Smith (1954-) and Jeff Koons (1955-) What unifies these various borrowings, provocatively juxtaposed against each other, is the philosophical intent motivating the work. A critic has explained:

> [P]ostmodernism is marked by an abiding skepticism that rejects modernism as an ideal defining twentieth-century culture as we have known it. In challenging tra-

dition, however, postmodernism resolutely refuses to provide a new meaning or impose an alternative order in its place. It represents a generation consciously not in search of identity. Hence it is not a coherent movement at all, but a loose collection of tendencies which, all told, reflect a new sensibility."[5]

Architecture

Modern architecture was the result of our modern, industrial society: it is the product of steel-reinforced concrete. Older architectural techniques based on columns with proper bases and capitals, arches, and vaults could be replaced with steel I-beams and poured concrete. The Crystal Palace (1851), designed by Sir Joseph Paxton (1801-65), may be viewed as an early forerunner of modern architecture since it was built entirely of iron and glass. It looks like a giant green house, which is what Sir Joseph had previously designed.

Louis Sullivan (1856-1924) designed the Wainwright Building (1890-91) in St. Louis, Missouri, which is one of the first modern skyscrapers. Sullivan propounded the modern idea that form should follow function. His famous student, Frank Lloyd Wright (1867-1933) followed up on this idea in his famous Prairie Houses. In Europe, Walter Gropius (1883-1969) designed a number of buildings for the Bauhaus at Dessau. He exemplified the International School of Architecture of the 1920s. In France, Le Corbusier (1887-1965) designed *machines à habiter*, machines to live in, that is modern buildings.

Other famous buildings in the United States which define modern architecture include the Chrysler Building (1930),

What are some of the materials used in modern buildings?

Name some modern architects and discuss their works.

What are the characteristics of postmodern architecture?

the Empire State Building (1931), Rockefeller Center (1940), the United Nations Secretariat Building (1949), the Lever House (1952), the Seagram Building (1958), the Pan Am Building (1963), and the World Trade Center (1970)—all in New York City.

Postmodernism, as the name implies, is a reaction to the modern. Postmodern architecture often mixed many different architectural styles in unexpected ways in the same building. In postmodernism there is often a search for new rules and a rejection of the homogeneity thought to have characterized modern architecture. The Piazza d'Italia in New Orleans (1978) by Charles Moore (1925-1993), the Portland Public Service Building in Oregon (1980) by Michael Graves (1934-), the Neue Staatsgalerie in Stuttgart (1983) by James Stirling (1926-1992), and the Guggenheim Museum in Bilbao, Spain (1997) by Frank O. Gehry (1929-) are notable examples of postmodernism.

identify several post modern architects and give examples

Philosophy

Existentialism

What is existentialism?

The best known philosophical movement of the twentieth century is existentialism. Existentialist thinkers have no common set of dogmas. They reject the adequacy of reason or theology to give meaning to life. A common existentialist theme has been that existence itself is absurd. Those existentialists who are atheists often see Christianity and other organized religions as crutches for the weak, who seek to avoid responsibility for determining their own values.

This atheistic approach is reflected in the writing of the Frenchman, Jean Paul Sartre (1905-1980). He wrote philosophical works such as *Being and Nothingness* and literary works such as the one-act play, *No Exit*. According to Sartre, the human being stands alone, without any God to help him. Life is essentially meaningless, absurd. But the human being through his or her actions has the freedom to decide what meaning to give to life. In this sense, existence or the fact of being precedes essence, what I choose to be or what meaning I give to life. If I allow someone else to choose my role in life or my values, I have still made a choice. I have chosen to act irresponsibly. In this sense, the human is always faced with choice or is "condemned to be free."

There are theistic (as opposed to atheistic) existentialists. Gabriel Marcel (1889-1973), who converted to Catholicism in 1929, stressed the importance of belief in God's existence. Marcel urged that we stop looking at other persons as objects to be analyzed egocentrically in terms of function and usefulness to ourselves. Rather, we should treat the other person as someone who matters, a "thou" who is worthy of our love. This kind of relationship with another gives us insight into the transcendent love of God.

Analytic and Linguistic Philosophy

Bertrand Russell (1872-1970), G.E. Moore (1873-1958), and Ludwig Wittgenstein (1889-1951) are the founders of analytic and linguistic philosophy, which, in the English-speaking world, has predominated within the philosophy departments of most major universities in the period after 1945. The logical analysis of ordinary language is the starting point of this approach to phi-

How did Jean Paul Sartre contribute to the existentialist movement?

How did the approach of Gabriel Marcel differ from Sartre's?

Explain the difference between normative prescription and empirical description.

losophy. Words are symbolic abstractions. While some words refer to sense data and objects that can be empirically verified, not all words do. Words that describe feelings and beliefs are different from words that refer to what we might call facts. Clarifying the differences between words that contain normative prescriptions (ought statements) from words that make empirical descriptions (is statements) proves to be an important task. Indeed, some words may simply be sounds that have no meaning whatsoever. There is a difference between the grammatical structure of a sentence and its logical meaning. "Who is the current king of the United States?" sounds like a reasonable question until it is realized that there have never been kings in the United States. Some analytic philosophers would argue that words like "God," when fully analyzed, have no meaning at all. Metaphysics, these philosophers would argue, is no more significant that a bunch of hens clucking. Statements about ethics are nothing more than emotive ejaculations. The only meaningful statements are logical, mathematical, or empirically verifiable statements. Many of those who hold these radical views are called Logical Positivists.

What are human rights?

Human Rights

Human rights are basic freedoms all persons have from arbitrary or discriminatory treatment by other individuals or by government. The horrors of World War II brought revulsion at crimes against humanity and renewed for many a fresh commitment to human rights.

The Civil Rights Movement

In the United States in the 1950's and 1960's, the focus of the civil rights struggle was to obtain equal rights for Afro-Americans who were often discriminated against and segregated from the white population in places such as public schools and transportation vehicles. The U.S. Supreme Court in May 1954 declared that segregation in public schools was inherently contrary to the equal protection of the laws guaranteed by the Fourteenth Amendment to the Constitution. Not only were schools segregated, but many other facets of American life were also segregated, particularly in southern states.

The Reverend Martin Luther King, Jr. (1929-1968) led a successful boycott of the segregated Montgomery, Alabama public bus system in 1956. He went on to participate in a number of civil rights activities before he was assassinated in April of 1968. King led demonstrations against segregation in Birmingham, Alabama in April and May 1963. The sight of the marchers being attacked by police dogs helped to raise national sympathy for the civil rights movement. In August 1963, the Reverend King led a March on Washington. There, over 200 thousand people listened to him plead for an end to discrimination so that all Americans might be "free at last." These efforts bore fruit in the passage of the Civil Rights Act of 1964. The Act's provisions prohibited discrimination in public accommodations that affect interstate commerce, such as hotels and restaurants, and permitted the federal government to withhold funds to programs which practiced discrimination. The Voting Rights Act of 1965 had the effect of dramatically increasing Afro-American registration in the South.

What was the focus of the civil rights movement of the 1950's and the 1960's?

What role did the Rev. Martin Luther King, Jr. play in this movement?

Discuss Simone de Beauvoir's ideas about gender roles.

While other gains were made as well, the civil rights movement did not solve the problems of racial and ethnic minorities in America. Proof can be found in the continuance of urban riots such as Watts in 1965, Detroit and Newark in 1967, and Los Angeles in 1992.

The Women's Rights Movement

Women's rights have been an issue for a considerable time. The 1792 publication of Mary Wollstonecraft's *Vindication of the Rights of Women* was mentioned earlier. After World War I, women in Britain and the U.S. obtained the right to vote as a result of the work of suffragettes. Two important works that influenced the women's rights movement were published after World War II. Simone de Beauvoir's (1908-1986) *The Second Sex* was published in French in 1949. De Beauvoir, who was a companion of Jean Paul Sartre, argued that man treats woman as the Other. Man defines woman not in herself but in relation to him. He expects her to be submissive, and she is often complicit. Women have been confined to a secondary position in history, similar to the way Americans have exploited Blacks. Her hope was that modern women would move towards liberation—true equality with men. This would require changes in law, economies, customs, and the whole social context.

How did Betty Friedan contribute to the women's movement in the U.S.?

An American, Betty Friedan (1921-) published *The Feminine Mystique* in 1963. In this work, she said that psychologists, educators, and advertisers had conspired to emphasize the role of woman as housewife, as if the role promised total fulfillment. She advocated providing women with opportunities in the workplace and elsewhere for fulfillment beyond those provided in marriage and child rearing. Friedan was one of the founders of the National Organization for Women (NOW) in 1966.

The record of success for the women's rights movement is mixed. In highly developed countries, including the U.S., Canada, France, and England, women compose 40 percent or more of the labor force. In Third World countries, particularly Muslim countries, women's participation in the workforce is much less, often 10 to 30 percent. Women are still concentrated in low-status, low-paying jobs, such as teaching, sales, and clerical work. In the U.S., attempts to ratify an Equal Rights Amendment, first introduced in Congress in 1923, failed again in 1982. Yet, recent court decisions have been sympathetic to efforts to compensate for the kind of sexual harassment that was given wide publicity by the allegations raised in the Anita Hill-Clarence Thomas hearings of 1991.

Human rights efforts have gone beyond minority rights and women's rights. In 1948, the United Nations General Assembly adopted a Universal Declaration of Human Rights. In 1975, the Helsinki Accords were signed in Finland by 33 European countries, as well as by Canada and the United States. These accords committed governments to respect such human rights as freedom of thought, conscience, and belief. Organizations like Amnesty International and Human Rights Watch have sought to hold governments accountable for gross violations of human rights.

The United Nations in 1993 and 1994 established war crimes tribunals for the victims of genocide in Bosnia and in Rwanda. While there have been a few indictments, many of the perpetrators of these crimes remain unpunished.

Evaluate the success of the women's rights movement.

What remains to be done to better protect human rights?

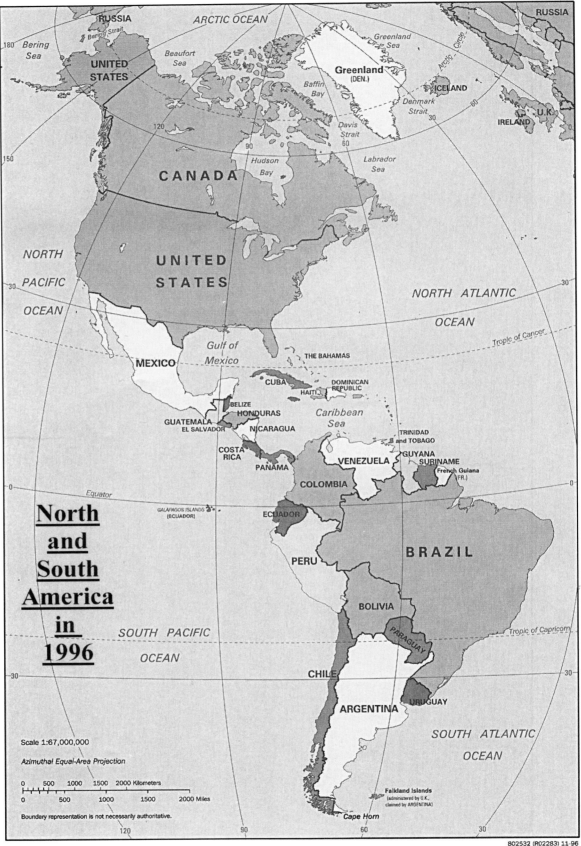

RUSSIA
ARCTIC OCEAN
Greenland
Sea
RUSSIA

Bering
Strait
Bering
Sea

Beaufort
Sea

UNITED
STATES

Greenland
(DEN.)

ICELAND

U.K.

IRELAND

Baffin
Bay

Denmark
Strait

Davis
Strait

Hudson
Bay

Labrador
Sea

CANADA

NORTH

PACIFIC

OCEAN

UNITED

STATES

NORTH ATLANTIC

OCEAN

Tropic of Cancer

Gulf of
Mexico

THE BAHAMAS

MEXICO

CUBA

DOMINICAN
REPUBLIC

HAITI

BELIZE

HONDURAS

Caribbean
Sea

GUATEMALA
EL SALVADOR

NICARAGUA

TRINIDAD
and TOBAGO

COSTA
RICA

GUYANA
SURINAME

VENEZUELA

French Guiana
(FR.)

PANAMA

COLOMBIA

Equator

North
and
South
America
in
1996

GALAPAGOS ISLANDS
[ECUADOR]

ECUADOR

BRAZIL

PERU

BOLIVIA

SOUTH PACIFIC

PARAGUAY

Tropic of Capricorn

OCEAN

CHILE

URUGUAY

ARGENTINA

SOUTH ATLANTIC

OCEAN

Scale 1:67,000,000

Azimuthal Equal-Area Projection

0   500   1000   1500   2000 Kilometers

0   500   1000   1500   2000 Miles

Boundary representation is not necessarily authoritative.

Falkland Islands
(administered by U.K.,
claimed by ARGENTINA)

Cape Horn

15

Beyond the Cold War

Between 1989 and 1991, the Cold War came to an end. The West had won. The Gulf War may be viewed as the first event of the post-Cold War era. In early 1991 the U.S. attacked a former Soviet client, Iraq, without any interference from Russia. Ever since, U.S. presidents have supported the established leaders of their one-time enemy. President George Bush (1924-) supported Gorbachev and President Bill Clinton (1946-) has supported Yeltsin. In January of 1994, Russia and the U.S. agreed to stop aiming nuclear weapons at each other.

While the end of the Cold War has erased some world tensions, predictably not only do other tensions remain, but many new problems have arisen. Economic rivalry among Asia, Europe, and America continues in an increasingly interdependent global economy.

When did the Cold War end?

What has been the subsequent U.S. attitude towards Russian leaders?

The United States

The collapse of the Soviet Union in 1991 came suddenly, unexpectedly, and, perhaps to almost everyone's pleasant surprise, peacefully. The United States won the Cold War by default. Since 1991, the United States has been the world's only remaining superpower. Only the United States has the military capacity to deploy troops anywhere

What nation or nations are considered to be superpowers today?

Do you agree that Richard Nixon was a "flawed" President? Explain.

What were the failings of Jimmy Carter?

in the world within days. Our technological superiority to all other armed forces gives the U.S. and each American soldier incredible firepower. To date, the U.S. has used its military predominance carefully and with great restraint.

The American triumph is all the more remarkable because it took place under a series of flawed Presidents from Richard Nixon to Bill Clinton. Richard Nixon was forced to resign in 1973 as a result of Watergate. His vice president, Gerald Ford, pardoned Nixon, lost the Vietnam War, and failed to be elected President in 1976.

Jimmy Carter (1924-) was a decent person, but a weak President. His advocacy of human rights, while laudable, alienated the Soviet Union. His moralizing without taking decisive action contributed to the success of a Muslim revolution in Iran. The pro-American shah was overthrown by the Muslim fundamentalist Ayatollah Khomeini (c1900-1989). When the exiled shah was allowed to come to the United States for cancer treatment, radical Muslim "students" stormed the American embassy in Teheran and took the diplomats hostage. They held our diplomats prisoner for 444 days in blatant violation of international law. A rescue attempt failed dismally. The Soviet Union invaded Afghanistan and, at home, inflation hit double digits. Carter was not re-elected. On the last day of his Presidency, as his successor Ronald Reagan was about to be sworn in, the American hostages in Iran were released, perhaps in fear of what Reagan might do if they were not.

Ronald Reagan (1911-) was elected to two terms and served as President from 1981 to 1989. He was a conservative Republican, heir to the Goldwater legacy, twice Governor of California, an actor, and the oldest person so far to be elected President. Reagan has been described as the Teflon President because his critics could never dent his popularity with the American people even when his failings were obvious. Persistent rumors that he was senile and literally asleep during much of his Presidency had little effect. His "ahw shucks" or "there you go again" responses deflected all opposition. He was also extremely lucky in that he survived an assassination attempt early in his Presidency.

Reagan presided over the biggest military buildup in American peacetime history. Many have suggested that by outspending the Soviet Union in a high technology arms race, he brought about the collapse of the Soviet empire. The Soviet Union, so the argument goes, simply could not match the new technologies being developed and placed on line in the American military. Reagan's advocacy of Star Wars, a space-based anti-ballistic missile system using laser weapons, was the most spectacular example of the application of high technology to the Cold War.

Reagan was an outspoken anti-communist. He was one of the few American politicians who were not traumatized by the Vietnam War and staunchly defended that war as having been winnable. He referred to the Soviet Union as the "evil empire"; yet he held successful summit meetings with both Leonid Brezhnev and Mikhail Gorbachev when they ran that empire.

Reagan provided secret aid for the Afghan rebels fighting the Soviet occupation of Afghanistan. That war became a major drain on Soviet resources, much like Vietnam had been for the U.S. He bitterly opposed Cuban communism and acted vigorously to invade Grenada, where Cubans were building a military airbase. He supported the Contras who were seeking to topple the communistic Sandanista government of Nicaragua.

What were the accomplishments of Ronald Reagan?

Discuss any weaknesses in the Reagan presidency.

What was the Iran-Contra scandal?

When Congress refused to fund the Contras, the White House found illegal ways to funnel money to them. This included an incredible scheme whereby the U.S. sold arms to Iran and used the profits from the sale to finance the Nicaraguan rebels. Selling arms to Iran was in violation of Reagan's own policies of not dealing with terrorist states. The arms sale was motivated apparently by the desire to gain freedom for several hostages taken prisoner in Lebanon. Even the Iran-Contra scandal did not seriously diminish Reagan's popularity and his vice president, George Bush, was elected President in 1988 in what, in effect, amounted to a third term for Reagan.

What did George Bush accomplish?

George Bush was a Republican Brahmin, a member of the upper class who turned out to be much less conservative in practice than his mentor. Bush had, after all, once called Reagan's domestic agenda "voodoo economics." Bush was President when the Cold War ended. He watched the unfolding of the "Velvet Revolution" in Czechoslovakia, the ending of the division of Germany symbolized by the dismantling of the Berlin Wall, the liberation of all of Eastern Europe from communist governments maintained through at least implicit Soviet military force, and the end of the Soviet Union itself.

Why do you think we fought to restore the independence of Kuwait?

In 1991, with Soviet acquiescence, the United States engaged in the Gulf War against Saddam Hussein of Iraq. Iraq had invaded Kuwait and was threatening the oilfields of Saudi Arabia. Bush put together carefully and skillfully a coalition of Western and Arab countries to fight Hussein and to restore the independence of Kuwait. After an extensive air bombardment, Kuwait was liberated after 100 hours of fighting. American arms proved spectacularly their superiority over the Soviet-made weapons used by the Iraqis. It has been suggested that the

Gulf War was a dry run for what would have been had the U.S. and the Soviet Union ever engaged in earnest – a dry run except for the use of missiles and nuclear weapons. After the Gulf War, George Bush had a popular approval rating of over 90 percent.

It is mind boggling that one year later George Bush lost his bid to be re-elected President to an obscure Governor from Arkansas, Bill Clinton (1946-). The domestic economy appears to have been the primary reason for Clinton's victory. Many Americans felt that the economy was passing them by, taxes were too high, and Bush was insensitive to "real" Americans. Throughout the Reagan-Bush years, the Federal government's budget deficit had skyrocketed. The national debt had increased from $1 trillion to $3 trillion.

Bill Clinton was the first Democrat to be elected to two terms since Franklin Delano Roosevelt. From the very beginning, his Presidency had been haunted by allegations of personal improprieties: womanizing, shady land deals in Arkansas, cronyism in appointing a new White House travel agency, and looking for dirt in FBI files on prominent Republicans. Special Prosecutor Kenneth Starr had been investigating most of these issues for most of the Clinton Presidency. In September 1998 he reported to the House of Representatives that Clinton had perjured himself and obstructed justice to avoid admitting a sexual relationship with a White House intern, Monica Lewinsky. On December 19, 1998, the House impeached Clinton on a largely party-line vote. On January 7, 1999, the U.S. Senate began only its second presidential impeachment trial. It ended on February 12, 1999 with an acquittal. Neither count received a majority of the votes, much less the two-thirds required to remove a president from office. Clinton's

Why did George Bush lose his bid for election to Bill Clinton?

Describe the events that later historians will most probably associate with Bill Clinton.

What have been the accomplishments of Bill Clinton?

major achievements include a robust national economy, a federal budget balanced for the first time since 1968, deficit reduction, and continued peace in most of the world. Times had indeed been good.

Russia

Is Russia still an important country? Explain.

The old Soviet Union collapsed during the course of the year 1991. The fifteen union republics, somewhat similar to the American states, which made up the Soviet Union, have each become sovereign, independent states and members of the United Nations.

Russia is the largest and most important of these successor states. It has inherited the Soviet Union's veto power in the Security Council of the United Nations and most of that country's nuclear arsenal. With more than 147 million people and the largest landmass of any country on earth, Russia remains a major power and the most populous country in Europe.

In August 1991, hard-line Communists sought to oust Gorbachev and to reverse the course of liberalization. It was Boris Yeltsin's defiance in Moscow of the coup, which led to its failure. Gorbachev never recovered from this attack on his leadership. Russia declared its independence from the Soviet Union on August 24, 1991. The Soviet Union ceased to exist legally as a sovereign entity on December 25, 1991.

Boris Yeltsin was born in 1931, became a member of the Communist Party in 1961, reached the Central Committee of the Communist Party in 1981, and was ousted from all high party offices in 1987 in a power struggle with Gorbachev. Yeltsin shifted his focus to the politics of the Russian republic. In 1990, he became President of the Russian Parliament and quit the Communist Party. In June 1991, Boris Yeltsin was popularly elected as President of the Russian Republic within the Soviet Union. That election was an historic first.

Russia's history has been tumultuous since 1991. The job of restructuring the centrally planned Soviet economy into a free market economy has been much more difficult than anticipated. In many instances, privatization of State-owned enterprises has meant simply that the same Communist Party bureaucrats who ran the State-owned factories are now the corporate managers of the joint stock companies, which they themselves helped to set up legally in the waning days of communism. Their management attitudes have not changed. Many of these Soviet functionaries granted themselves stocks in the new corporations. Poor Russians could not afford to buy stocks so they were left out in the cold. The wealth and assets of Russia are being looted by a small elite of mobsters with ties to the state bureaucracy. The strong and powerful under communism are becoming the rich under capitalism. Cradle to grave socialism is being replaced with cutthroat capitalism where the devil takes the poor, the weak, the sick, and the elderly. No wonder that Russia is near bankruptcy and in social turmoil. Whether democracy can survive under such conditions remains to be seen.

Against all these odds, Yeltsin hung on to power and has continued to pursue a, more or less, democratic policy. He was re-elected to a second five-year term in June 1996. During the reelection campaign, Yeltsin was deathly sick with heart disease, facts that were kept from the Russian electorate. Shortly after his reelection on the second

Discuss the career of Boris Yeltsin.

Why has Russia had difficulties adapting to capitalism?

Do you think Russia will succeed in becoming a Western-style democracy?

ballot, Yeltsin underwent triple heart by-pass surgery, which he survived. After being incapacitated for more than seven months, Yeltsin resumed the duties of his office in March 1997. He has remained President since, reshuffling his cabinet periodically, borrowing billions of dollars from the World Bank to keep the Russian ruble afloat, and maintaining a tenuous democracy.

However tenuous, the Yeltsin era is the first time in Russian history that Russia has been governed by a democratically elected President and a separately elected legislature. It would be a decisive turning point in Russian history if this experiment in democracy were to become permanent.

The United Kingdom

How did Margaret Thatcher change Britain?

Tony Blair (1953-) was elected Prime Minister on May 1, 1997. The Labour Party gained control of Parliament for the first time in eighteen years. Labour won 419 seats to 165 for the Conservative Party in the 659 member House of Commons.

The Conservatives had been in power since 1979 when Margaret Thatcher (1925-) was elected as the first woman Prime Minister in British history. Thatcher was a conservative, free-market, British nationalist. Under her leadership, a major restructuring of the British economy was begun. State-owned enterprises were sold to the private sector. Labor union power was curtailed. Social welfare programs were scaled back. While revitalizing the British economy, these measures increased unemployment and brought very uneven social benefits. Thatcherism, as her policies came to be called, was greatly admired by Ronald Reagan.

On April 2, 1982, the brutal military regime of Argentina invaded the Falkland Islands, a British possession just 300 miles off the coast of Argentina. Argentina has claimed these islands, which it calls the Malvinas, for a long time. Most of the inhabitants of the Falklands are, however, English-speaking sheepherders. Thatcher decided to respond militarily. It took the British almost two months to bring their navy into position. On May 21, they launched a counteroffensive and by June 14, 1982 had rewon the islands. The fact that two allies of the United States had fought a war against each other was deeply embarrassing to the U.S., which had, nonetheless, favored the British side. The military junta ruling Argentina was overthrown shortly after their defeat and a more democratic regime took its place. In Britain, a surge of patriotism led to Thatcher's reelection. What needs to be emphasized about the Falklands-Malvinas Islands War, and what makes it interesting, was its anachronistic nature. This was an old-fashioned, nineteenth-century, colonial war. Britain may have won, but it did so the old-fashioned way. Britain is simply no longer in the same league, militarily, as the United States.

Margaret Thatcher won three consecutive parliamentary elections, but by 1990 Britain faced renewed inflationary pressures and her conservative party was increasingly divided about her leadership. She resigned in November 1990 and was replaced by her Chancellor of the Exchequer John Major (1943-). In April 1992, the Conservative Party won a fourth consecutive parliamentary election victory under John Major.

Electoral victories in democratic countries depend on the mood of the voters and are often decided by choosing the person perceived as the lesser of two evils. Another

Explain the events in the Falkland Islands in 1982.

Who was the prime minister following Margaret Thatcher?

How did Tony Blair succeed in bringing Labour into power?

Have Blair's policies been friendly to English nationalism?

political truism is that power corrupts. Eighteen years of power is a long time; and eighteen years in opposition is an even longer time.

When Margaret Thatcher gained power in 1979, the Labour Party was deeply split between its moderate, pragmatic wing and its doctrinaire, socialist wing. Not until Tony Blair became its leader did Labour finally get its act together. It got rid of its socialist rhetoric and, under Blair's charismatic leadership, presented itself as the voice of a new, Europe-centered Britain. The Conservatives, on the other hand, were worn out, divided, and embroiled in various sex scandals. Tory nationalists were opposed fundamentally to the further integration of Great Britain into the European Union.

Since becoming Prime Minister, Tony Blair has followed up on many of his campaign themes including increased regionalization within the United Kingdom. In September 1997, the Scots voted in a referendum to establish a separate Scottish legislature, the first since 1707. A similar arrangement is planned for Wales. And perhaps most importantly, in 1998, a power sharing agreement was reached in Northern Ireland between Catholics and Protestants that may bring about an end to the "troubles."

A final paragraph may also be in order about the British monarchy. Queen Elizabeth II continues to reign as she has since 1952. The monarchy seems to have weathered the divorce of Crown Prince Charles from his wife, Princess Diana. The tragic death of Diana in a car accident in Paris on August 31, 1997 stirred the entire world but it also removed a major source of negative publicity from the monarchy.

France

The contemporary history of France was shaped by Charles de Gaulle, who created the Fifth French Republic in 1958. The Constitution of the Fifth Republic established a hybrid Presidential-Parliamentary System. In a Presidential System a chief executive is elected separately from the legislature and has independent power as in the U.S. In a Parliamentary System the prime minister is the head of the government. The prime minister and his cabinet are all elected members of Parliament. The executive is, therefore, a committee of the legislature. The political party with a majority of delegates in the lower house of the legislature forms the government. Great Britain is the oldest and best example for a Parliamentary System.

Under the French Fifth Republic, the President of France is popularly elected for a seven-year term and has real political power. But there is also a Parliament, the National Assembly, which chooses the Prime Minister, or Premier. A French Premier has two masters: the National Assembly and the President of France. As long as both are in the hands of the same political party, conflict is minimized. But if the majority of the National Assembly is of a different political party than the President, then serious conflicts can arise.

De Gaulle was President of France from 1958 to 1969, when he resigned. De Gaulle had created not only a new constitution and political regime, but also a new political movement: Gaullism. The Gaullists are a conservative, nationalistic party committed to European unity under French leadership and to modernization. After de

Discuss the constitutional system of the Fifth French Republic.

Who are the Gaullists?

How does the present French political party system compare to the two-party system in the United States?

Gaulle, the next two Presidents of France, Georges Pompidou (1969-1974) and Valery Giscard d'Estaing (1974-1981) were conservatives.

In 1981, the leader of the Socialist Party, Francois Mitterand (1981-1995), was elected. This was an important shift in power and established acceptance by the left of the new constitution.

The French have had, historically, a multi-party system. In a Parliamentary System when no single political party has a majority, then an alliance of parties must be worked out to form a coalition government. Coalition governments are often unstable. It was the instability of coalition governments that had led to the creation of the Fifth Republic. A strong Presidency was meant to compensate for a divided National Assembly.

This shift in power has also resulted in a change in the French political party system. Since only one person can be president, the system established by de Gaulle has ended up producing a two-person, two-party race in the second round of Presidential voting. All political parties run their Presidential candidates in the first round of balloting; but in the second run-off, only the top two vote getters square off. This has meant usually that a candidate of the right faced the candidate of the left. A multi-party system has, in effect, been turned into a two-party system. Mitterand was the first candidate of the left to win the French presidency.

Identify the parties of the French left.

The French left includes the Radical Republicans, Socialists, and Communists. The French Socialists are much more doctrinaire than the British Labour Party or the German Social Democrats. The French Socialists continue to believe in state ownership of banking and heavy industry.

In the Presidential elections of 1995, Jacques Chirac was the candidate of the right and Lionel Jospin of the left. Chirac won. But in the Parliamentary elections of 1997, the Socialists made a surprising come back by gaining a majority of the National Assembly. Jospin became Premier. The French call it "cohabitation" when the Presidency and the Premiership are in different party hands.

Regardless of which political party controls the government, France faces many problems that are similar to those of the rest of Europe. It has an unacceptably high unemployment rate—11.7% in 1995. It also has an aging population, which is producing a crisis in social welfare costs. The working population is highly unionized and values security over efficiency. France is finding it hard to adjust to the global economy. Its workers are resisting the efforts to outsource manufacturing enterprises to third world countries with underpaid workers and weak environmental regulations. Calling national strikes is a long tradition in France.

Given its economic difficulties, it is not surprising that a significant neo-fascist movement exists in France which is led by Jean-Marie Le Pen's National Front. France has a significant minority population of North African Moslems and Indo-Chinese, a legacy from the days of French colonialism. These groups are the subjects of Le Pen's poisonously anti-immigrant venom.

Germany

On May 7, 1945, Nazi Germany surrendered unconditionally to the victorious allies. Most of Germany was a pile of rubble. The Allies divided Germany into four zones of military occupation; Berlin, the capital of

Describe some of the economic and political problems facing French leaders.

Who has led the neo-fascists in France?

Discuss the post-Cold War history of Germany.

the Reich, was similarly divided into four pieces. When the wartime alliance broke down into the Cold War, Germany was divided into two separate states. The Soviet zone of occupation became the German Democratic Republic, East Germany. The American, British, and French zones of occupation were merged and became the Federal Republic of Germany, West Germany. This split was complete by 1949.

On October 3, 1990, East and West Germany were reunited as a single country of 82 million people. This reunion was not so much a merger as it was a take-over. West Germany absorbed East Germany; the Federal Republic's Basic Law became the Constitution for a united Germany. The West German Chancellor Helmut Kohl remained the chancellor of the united country. Only the West German capital city of Bonn has been given up in favor of Berlin. Thus the post-war history of Germany is essentially the history of West Germany with merely a footnote to call attention to the defunct East.

How is the German government structured?

Germany is a federal republic. It is composed of sixteen states or Laender. Each Land has its own state government. On the national level, Germany is a parliamentary system, made up of a two-house legislature: the Bundesrat and the Bundestag. The Bundestag is the lower house, which like the House of Commons in Britain, predominates. Helmut Kohl had been chancellor, the equivalent of a prime minister, since 1982. Under Kohl's leadership his political party, the Christian Democratic Union (CDU), had won four consecutive elections. On September 27, 1998, the main opposition party, the Social Democratic Party (SPD), whose candidate for the chancellorship was Gerhard Schroeder, won. Kohl's long-lasting government. a coalition of the CDU, its sister party in Bavaria, the Christian Social Union

(CSU), and the liberal Free Democratic Party (FDP) had been defeated. Schroeder, the former Minister-President of Lower Saxony, became the new Chancellor of Germany. He formed a government in coalition with the Green Party—a first in German history.

It is now more than fifty years since the end of World War II. Germany has become the economic powerhouse of Europe. Politically, Germany is still haunted by its Nazi legacy and the holocaust. In recent years, unemployed youths, many of them skinheads, have shouted Nazi slogans and beat up foreigners, especially those coming from Turkey and Eastern Europe. Such expressions of hatred are more frightening when they take place in Germany, given its history.

German unification has proven to be much more expensive than anticipated. West Germans have had to shoulder higher taxes to pay for the rebuilding of the entire infrastructure of the six, formerly East German Laender. Unemployment in the former East continues to be higher than in the former West. Considerable resentment exists between Wessies, who feel their prosperity is being sapped by the East, and Ossies, who resent the overbearing condescension of Westerners. It should also be noted that East Germans moved directly from Nazism to Communism. Until reunification in 1990, they have had no experience with the give and take of democracy, market economies, and fundamental freedoms.

In many ways, Germany continues to be a country in search of itself. Germans are most proud of their economic recovery and the soundness of their currency, the Deutsche Mark or D-Mark, which was introduced in 1948. There is considerable concern about the coming of the Euro. The Euro is the name for a common currency for all of the coun-

Name some recent German chancellors and give their party affiliations.

What are the major concerns facing Germany today?

Name the independent states that have emerged in Eastern Europe after the fall of Communism.

Contrast the differing fates of Czechoslovakia and of Yugoslavia in the post-Cold War period. What do you think accounts for the differences?

tries of the European Union, whose introduction began on January 1, 1999.

Eastern Europe

The Iron Curtain has fallen. The countries of Eastern Europe have thrown off the yoke of Soviet Communism and are exploring their separate national destinies. Poland, the Czech Republic, Slovakia, Hungary, Romania, Slovenia, Croatia, Bosnia and Herzegovina, Yugoslavia, Macedonia, and Bulgaria are the list of countries once aligned with the Soviet Union. To these should be added the list of former Soviet republics that have gained their independence: Estonia, Latvia, Lithuania, Belarus, Ukraine, and Modova.

Independence does not guarantee success. Whether all these countries will survive, will split into even smaller fractions, or become reabsorbed by more powerful neighbors remains to be seen. The former state of Czechoslovakia divided peacefully into the Czech Republic and Slovakia on January 1, 1993. The former state of Yugoslavia has broken apart into five separate states so far: Slovenia, Croatia, Bosnia and Herzegovina, Yugoslavia, and Macedonia. These divisions have provoked bloody wars and ethnic cleansing. What in 1998 is called Yugoslavia is actually made up of Serbia and Montenegro. These are the two remaining provinces of the old Socialist Federal Republic of Yugoslavia. The Serbians are the most discontented by this break up. Their nationalistic excesses have caused most of the bloodshed in the region. Since December 1995, 60,000 NATO troops, including 20,000

Americans, have been stationed in Bosnia-Herzegovina to implement the Dayton Peace Accords signed on November 21, 1995. By 1998, the ethnic war had been brought to a halt but the goal of recreating a peaceful, multi-ethnic community has not been achieved. Serbs, Moslems, and ethnic Croats remain hostile toward each other. The NATO troops have been reduced in number but remain to guard the peace.

By 1998 a new conflict had broken out in Serbia itself, whose Kosovo region is home to ethnic Albanians. The Serbs are determined to keep these ethnic Albanians under their domination even though they make up 90% of the population in Kosovo. This conflict could easily become a major Balkan war involving Serbia, Albania, Macedonia, and Greece. What is at work here in the Balkans is a conflict among three civilizations as represented by three great religions: Orthodox Christianity, Catholic Christianity, and Islam.

Many see a more positive sign in the expansion of the North Atlantic Treaty Organization (NATO). Poland, the Czech Republic, and Hungary were allowed to join that organization as of 1999. This eastward expansion of NATO into an area previously dominated by the Soviet Union was strongly opposed by Russia. It is a sign of Russia's weakened condition that it ultimately accepted this expansion. Russia was able to extract some face-saving concessions in that NATO agreed not to place nuclear missiles in these three countries, not to place significant numbers of combat troops in these states, and to grant Russia itself a special relationship with NATO. Russia was reassured that the purpose of NATO is no longer to plan war against Russia but to maintain peace in the region.

How do you explain the conflicts in Bosnia-Herzegovina and in Kosovo?

Assess the significance of NATO's expansion into Eastern Europe.

Why have Poland, the Czech Republic, and Hungary been anxious to join NATO?

Poland, the Czech Republic, and Hungary gain greater security by being members of NATO. However benign Russia may be at the moment, there is always the fear of what a resurgent Russia might do. NATO membership also has financial advantages in that the armed forces of the three new members must be brought up to NATO standards. It should also be noted that these three countries are the most "Western" of the former Warsaw Pact countries. Roman Catholicism is the religion of the dominant majority in all three. Finally, by giving a new purpose to NATO, rather than dissolving it, two other purposes are being served. The United States is a member of NATO and through NATO remains linked to the future of Europe. Secondly, the military potential of reunited Germany is kept under international control by keeping NATO alive. The Poles, Czech, and Hungarians are at least as concerned about Germany as they are about Russia. NATO is a good deal for all concerned.

What is the European Union?

European Union

Who are its members?

The European Union (EU) is a transnational organization of 15 member states who have agreed to form a single economic union with the ultimate goal of forming a political union. A United States of Europe may be the final result.

The current members of the EU are: Belgium, France, Germany, Italy, Luxembourg, and Netherlands (original members joined 1957); Denmark, Ireland, and the United Kingdom (joined 1973); Greece (1981); Spain and Portugal (1986); and Austria, Finland, and Sweden (1995). Norway has twice been admitted to the European

Union and each time the Norwegian voters have rejected the proposal. Nine additional countries have petitioned for membership. These are: Bulgaria, Cyprus, Czech Republic, Hungary, Malta, Poland, Romania, Slovakia, and Turkey.

The European Union has its roots in the post-war reconstruction period, the Benelux agreement, the U.S. Marshall Plan, and the European Coal and Steel Community (ECSC). In 1957, six countries signed the Treaty of Rome and founded the European Atomic Energy Commission (Euratom) and the European Economic Community (EEC). The EEC had as its main purpose the creation of a common market for industrial products among its six member states. In 1962, a common agricultural policy was added. In 1965, the Treaty of Brussels, which is often called the second Treaty of Rome, created the European Community (EC). ECSC, Euratom, and EEC were merged into the European Community. The EC was provided with a governing body made up of four parts: the Commission, the Council of Ministers, the European Parliament, and the European Court of Justice. A "Europe without frontiers" was proposed in the Single European Act of 1987. In December 1991, the Treaty of Maastricht created the European Union and set the goal of a common European currency to be implemented in 1999. By 1992, the EU had created a single European passport and all customs barriers within the EU have been abolished.

This ideal of a common currency for the entire European Union became reality in January 1999 when a new currency, the "euro" was introduced in all electronic bank transactions. By 2002, this conversion will be complete with the "euro" replacing all national currencies. The current currencies of the EU countries—the drachma, escudo,

What other countries have recently sought membership in the European Union?

What is the history of the European Union?

**Why is the "euro" impor-
tant—even for the United
States?**

franc, guilder, krone, lire, mark, peseta, pound, and schilling—will be replaced with the "euro." A European Central Bank has already been established headed by Wim Duisenberg. This bank was created in the image of the German Bundesbank and is intended to have the same political independence. Monetary policies for the EU will be set by the European Central Bank. Once fully implemented this will be a major transfer of sovereignty from the national level to the European level. The European Monetary Union is a giant step in the direction of the United States of Europe.

The Broader Picture

**Name some of the Third World's
known nuclear powers**

As we head toward the end of the century, it is time to take stock and look at the broader world picture. What used to be called the "Third World" is growing up. China is clearly emerging as a superpower of the 21st century. In May 1998, India and Pakistan each exploded nuclear weapons despite universal condemnation from the other nuclear powers. Other countries like Iran, Iraq, and North Korea are likely to build their own weapons within five to ten years regardless of what the United States and Europe think about it.

More and more states are industrializing. Industrialization creates the infrastructure for the development of a modern military. Nuclear weapons and intercontinental missiles are the status symbols of a modern military and of great national power. It is doubtful that the Nuclear Non-Proliferation Treaty will prevent countries from developing "the bomb" if their leadership is determined to do so. After condemning India and

Pakistan and slapping comprehensive trade embargoes on them, the United States by July 1998 was already reconsidering its position. Sale of agricultural products was taken off the embargo list.

Europe is again prosperous and free. It has survived and overcome the consequences of two world wars. The European Union forms the largest aggregation of economic strength in the world. With 370 million people, it is larger than the North American market.

Eastern Europe and the Balkans are in social turmoil. Several civil wars are roiling. But even that instability is an improvement over the oppression exercised by the former totalitarian regimes under Soviet hegemony. There is a real chance that things will sort themselves out. New state boundaries based on national self-determination, with governments providing some degree of participatory democracy, and a stable free market economy providing for a reasonable standard of living are likely to emerge in the near future. Europe as an entire continent seems to be moving in the right direction.

Even within Europe, it is the United States that provides the cornerstone of their security. The North Atlantic Treaty Organization (NATO) was the American-led alliance against the Soviet Union and its Warsaw Pact. Even with the demise of the Soviet Union, Europe still needs NATO and American leadership. The prime example illustrating this fact is the situation in Bosnia-Herzegovina. The Europeans failed dismally to deal with the war and ethnic cleansing going on in Bosnia. The situation was stabilized only after President Bill Clinton took an active leadership role and convened the Dayton Peace Conference.

American leadership remains critical for European stability. The Atlantic Alliance

Explain the nuclear non-proliferation problem.

Contrast the political stability of Western and Eastern Europe.

Discuss how essential the United States might be to European and global stability.

between Europe and North America is the keystone for peace and prosperity in the world. But even the Atlantic Alliance is no longer the whole picture. Since World War II, a truly global balance of power has emerged. The world has divided into various regional balances and various regional states have emerged. Instead of one global picture, one must analyze several regions separately. The Middle East, South Asia, East Asia, Pacific Rim, South America, Central American and the Caribbean, North Africa, and Sub-Saharan Africa are parts of the world which function independently of Europe and North America. In each of these regions, the United States is an active participant as the world's only remaining superpower. American influence is generally directed toward the maintenance of stability. But however beneficial America's intentions may be, there are very real limits on how much influence the U.S. or "the West" might have on events in a region. One need only look at the Middle East to see how complex these regional balances of power have become.

What Europe has lost, which it had at the beginning of the century, is that it is no longer at the center of the world. European colonialism is a thing of the past. Witness the reversion of the British Crown Colony of Hong Kong back to Chinese rule on July 1, 1997 after a 99-year lease. The broader picture is that Europe is a prosperous piece within a larger global puzzle. If there is a global center, then it is the United States which conducts the cacophony of nations.

NOTES

[1]U.S. Congress, *Congressional Record*, 80th Congress, 1st Session, 1947, XCIII, p. 1981.

[2]William Appleman Williams, Thomas McCormick, Lloyd Gardner, and Walter La-Feber, eds., <u>America In Vietnam: A Documentary History</u> (Garden City, NY: Anchor Press, 1985), p. 237.

[3]Palmer, <u>A History of the World Since 1815</u>, p. 913.

[4]These statistics are from the the <u>CyberAtlas</u> (Internet, <http://www.cyberatlas.com /highlights/numbers.html> and <http://www.cyberatlas.com/big_picture/demographics /ovum.html>, 11 January 1999).

[5] H. W. Janson and Anthony F. Janson, <u>History of Art</u>, 5th ed., revised (New York: Harry N. Abrams, Inc., 1997), p. 914.

Reprinted by permission of the publisher from *A History of the World in the Twentieth Century* by J.A.S. Grenville, Cambridge, Mass.: The Belknap Press of Harvard University Press, Copyright (c) 1994 by the President and Fellows of Harvard College.

Europe in 1998

Serbia and Montenegro have asserted the formation of a joint independent state, but this entity has not been formally recognized as a state by the United States.

F.Y.R.O.M. - The Former Yugoslav Republic of Macedonia

Scale 1: 19,500,000

Lambert Conformal Conic Projection, standard parallels 40°N and 56°N

US Central Intelligence Agency

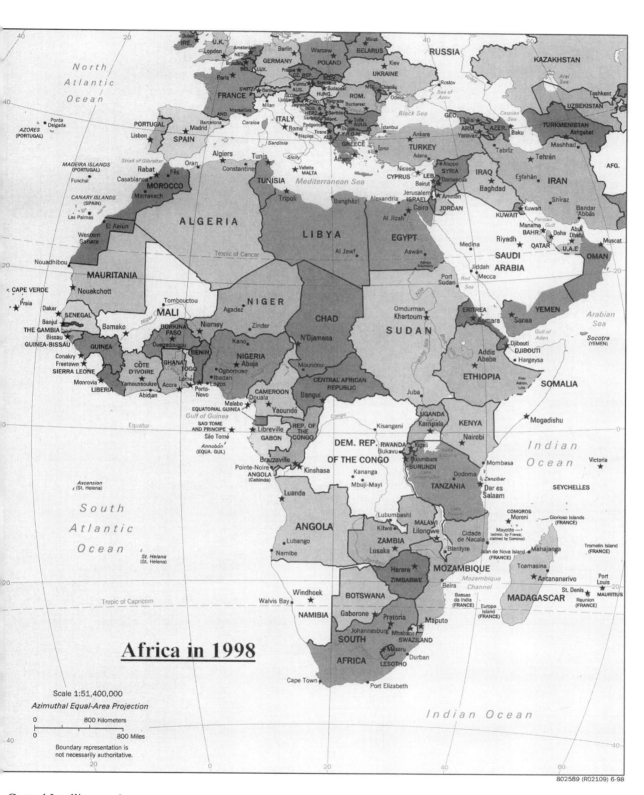

Africa in 1998

Scale 1:51,400,000
Azimuthal Equal-Area Projection

0   800 Kilometers
0   800 Miles

Boundary representation is
not necessarily authoritative.

802589 (R02109) 6-98

Central Intelligence Agency

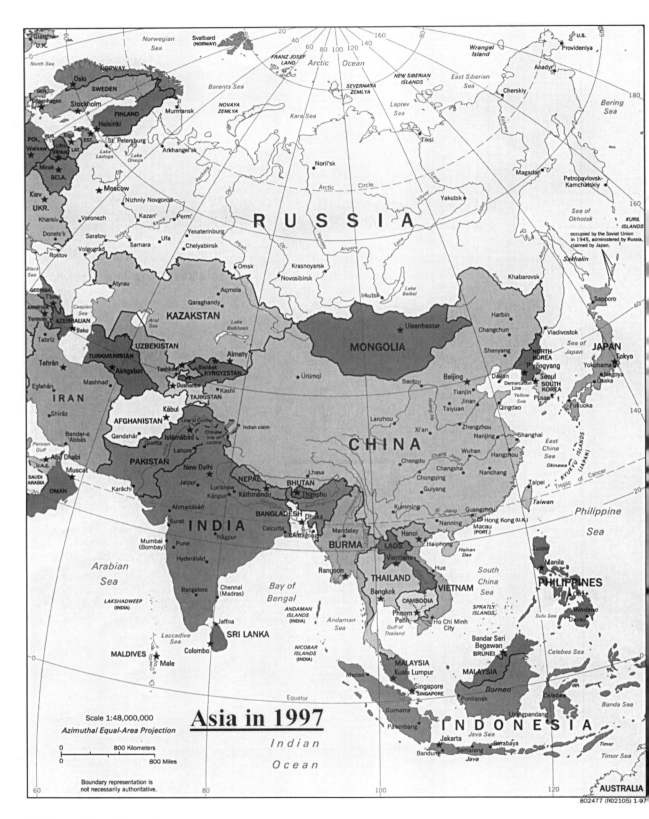

Asia in 1997

Scale 1:48,000,000

Azimuthal Equal-Area Projection

800 Kilometers

800 Miles

Boundary representation is
not necessarily authoritative.

802477 (R02105) 1-97

US Central Intelligence Agency

SIMONE DE BEAUVOIR

The Second Sex

An extremely well-educated French intellectual with a doctorate from the Sorbonne, Simone de Beauvoir (1908-1986) expresses the frustration and inner feelings of many Western women in her seminal work, *The Second Sex*. Her treatise, published in 1949, exerted a powerful influence in the development of the women's liberation movement in the 1960s.

De Beauvoir feels women throughout history have been treated as inferiors (the Other) and subordinate to men because they allow themselves to be. In line with her existentialist philosophy, she urges women to become independent, freed from their oppressors, able to make choices to give meaning to their lives. Because of the traditional roles of wives and mothers thrust upon them, women need to gain equality with men, capable of exercising their independence.

These passages from *The Second Sex* that you are about to read give you a glimpse of de Beauvoir's range of thought and research about topics, including marriage, prostitution, and traditional values, that both men and women should be familiar with.

If her functioning as a female is not enough to define woman, if we decline also to explain her through "the eternal feminine," and if nevertheless we admit, provisionally, that women do exist, then we must face the question: what is a woman?[1]

To state the question is, to me, to suggest, at once, a preliminary answer. The fact that I ask it is in itself significant. A man would never get the notion of writing a book on the peculiar situation of the human male.[2] But if I wish to define myself, I must first of all say: "I am a woman"; on this truth must be based all further discussion. A man never begins by presenting himself as an individual of a certain sex; it goes without saying that he is a man. The terms masculine and feminine are used symmetrically only as a matter of form, as on legal papers.

[1]From Simone De Beauvoir, *The Second Sex*, translated and edited by H. M. Parshley (New York: Vintage Books, 1989 [first published in 1949]).

[2]The Kinsey Report [Alfred C. Kinsey and others: Sexual Behavior in the Human Male (W. B. Saunders Co., 1948)] is no exception, for it is limited to describing the sexual characteristics of American men, which is quite a different matter.

In actuality the relation of the two sexes is not quite like that of two electrical poles, for man represents both the positive and the neutral, as is indicated by the common use of man to designate human beings in general; whereas woman represents only the negative, defined by limiting criteria, without reciprocity. In the midst of an abstract discussion it is vexing to hear a man say: "You think thus and so because you are a woman"; but I know that my only defense is to reply: "I think thus and so because it is true," thereby removing my subjective self from the argument. It would be out of the question to reply: "And you think the contrary because you are a man," for it is understood that the fact of being a man is no peculiarity. A man is in the right in being a man; it is the woman who is in the wrong. It amounts to this: just as for the ancients there was an absolute vertical with reference to which the oblique was defined, so there is an absolute human type, the masculine. Woman has ovaries, a uterus; these peculiarities imprison her in her subjectivity, circumscribe her within the limits of her own nature. It is often said that she thinks with her glands. Man superbly ignores the fact that his anatomy also includes glands, such as the testicles, and that they secrete hormones. He thinks of his body as a direct and normal connection with the world, which he believes he apprehends objectively, whereas he regards the body of woman as a hindrance, a prison, weighed down by everything peculiar to it. "The female is a female by virtue of a certain lack of qualities," said Aristotle; "we should regard the female nature as afflicted with a natural defectiveness." And St. Thomas for his part pronounced woman to be an "imperfect man," an "incidental" being. This is symbolized in Genesis where Eve is depicted as made from what Bossuet called "a supernumerary bone" of Adam.

Thus humanity is male and man defines woman not in herself but as relative to him; she is not regarded as an autonomous being. ...For him she is sex—absolute sex, no less. She is defined and differentiated with reference to man and not he with reference to her; she is the incidental, the inessential as opposed to the essential. He is the Subject, he is the Absolute—she is the Other.

...If woman seems to be the inessential which never becomes the essential, it is because she herself fails to bring about this change. Proletarians say "We"; Negroes also. Regarding themselves as subjects, they transform the bourgeois, the whites, into "others." But women do not say "We," except at some congress of feminists or similar formal demonstration; men say "women," and women use the same word in referring to themselves. They do not authentically assume a subjective attitude. The proletarians have accomplished the revolution in Russia, the Negroes in Haiti, the Indo-Chinese are battling for it in Indo-China; but the women's effort has never been anything more than a symbolic agitation. They have gained only what men have been willing to grant; they have taken nothing, they have only received.

The reason for this is that women lack concrete means for organizing themselves into a unit which can stand face to face with the correlative unit. They have no past, no history, no religion of their own; and they have no such solidarity of work and interest as that of the proletariat. They are not even promiscuously herded together in the way that creates community feeling among the American Negroes, the ghetto Jews, the workers of Saint-Denis, or the factory hands of Renault. They live dispersed among the males, attached through residence, housework, economic condition, and social standing to certain men—fathers or husbands—more firmly than they are to other women. If they belong to the bourgeoisie, they feel solidarity with men of that class, not with proletarian women; if they are white, their allegiance is to white men, not to Negro women. The proletariat can propose to massacre the ruling class, and a sufficiently fanatical Jew or Negro might dream of getting sole possession of the atomic bomb and making humanity wholly Jewish or black; but woman cannot even dream of exterminating the males. The bond that unites her to her oppressors is not comparable to any other. The division of the sexes is a biological fact, not an event in human history. Male and female stand opposed within a primordial *Mitsein*, and woman has not broken it. The couple is a fundamental unity with its two halves riveted together, and the cleavage of society along the line of sex is impossible. Here is to be found the basic trait of woman: she is the Other in a totality of which the two components are necessary to one another.

Now, woman has always been man's dependent, if not his slave; the two sexes have never shared the world in equality. And even today woman is heavily handicapped, though her situation is beginning to change. Almost nowhere is her legal status the same as man's, and frequently it is much to her disadvantage. Even when her rights are legally recognized in the abstract, long-standing custom prevents their full expression in the mores. In the economic sphere men and women can almost be said to make up two castes; other things being equal, the former hold the better jobs, get higher wages, and have more opportunity for success than their new competitors. In industry and politics men have a great many more positions and they monopolize the most important posts. In addition to all this, they enjoy a traditional prestige that the education of children tends in every way to support, for the present enshrines the past—and in the past all history has been made by men. At the present time, when women are beginning to take part in the affairs of the world, it is still a world that belongs to men—they have no doubt of it at all and women have scarcely any. To decline to be the Other, to refuse to be a party to the deal—this would be for women to renounce all the advantages conferred upon them by their alliance with the superior caste. Man-the-sovereign will provide woman-the-liege with material protection and will undertake the moral justification of her existence; thus she can evade at once both economic risk and the metaphysical risk of a liberty in which ends and aims must be contrived without assistance. Indeed, along with the ethical urge of each individual to affirm his subjective existence, there is also the temptation to forgo liberty and become a thing. This is an inauspicious road, for he who takes it—passive, lost, ruined—becomes henceforth the creature of another's will, frustrated in his transcendence and deprived of every value. But it is an easy road; on it one avoids the strain involved in undertaking an authentic existence. When man makes of woman the *Other*, he may, then, expect her to manifest deep-seated tendencies toward complicity. Thus, woman may fail to lay claim to the status of subject because she lacks definite resources, because she feels the necessary bond that ties her to man regardless of reciprocity, and because she is often very well pleased with her role as the *Other*.

Legislators, priests, philosophers, writers, and scientists have striven to show that the subordinate position of woman is willed in heaven and advantageous on earth. The religions invented by men reflect this wish for domination. In the legends of Eve and Pandora men have taken up arms against women. They have made use of philosophy and theology, as the quotations from Aristotle and St. Thomas have shown. Since ancient times satirists and moralists have delighted in showing up the weaknesses of women. ...Sometimes what is going on is clear enough. For instance, the Roman law limiting the rights of woman cited "the imbecility, the instability of the sex" just when the weakening of family ties seemed to threaten the interests of male heirs. And in the effort to keep the married woman

under guardianship, appeal was made in the sixteenth century to the authority of St. Augustine, who declared that "woman is a creature neither decisive nor constant," at a time when the single woman was thought capable of managing her property. Montaigne understood clearly how arbitrary and unjust was woman's appointed lot: "Women are not in the wrong when they decline to accept the rules laid down for them, since the men make these rules without consulting them. No wonder intrigue and strife abound." But he did not go so far as to champion their cause.

It was only later, in the eighteenth century, that genuinely democratic men began to view the matter objectively. Diderot, among others, strove to show that woman is, like man, a human being. Later John Stuart Mill came fervently to her defense. But these philosophers displayed unusual impartiality. In the nineteenth century the feminist quarrel became again a quarrel of partisans. One of the consequences of the industrial revolution was the entrance of women into productive labor, and it was just here that the claims of the feminists emerged from the realm of theory and acquired an economic basis, while their opponents became the more aggressive. Although landed property lost power to some extent, the bourgeoisie clung to the old morality that found the guarantee of private property in the solidity of the family. Woman was ordered back into the home the more harshly as her emancipation became a real menace. Even within the working class the men endeavored to restrain woman's liberation, because they began to see the women as dangerous competitors—the more so because they were accustomed to work for lower wages.

In proving woman's inferiority, the antifeminists then began to draw not only upon religion, philosophy, and theology, as before, but also upon science—biology, experimental psychology, etc. At most they were willing to grant "equality in difference" to the other sex. That profitable formula is most significant; it is precisely like the "equal but separate" formula of the Jim Crow laws aimed at the North American Negroes. As is well known, this so-called equalitarian segregation has resulted only in the most extreme discrimination. The similarity just noted is in no way due to chance, for whether it is a race, a caste, a class, or a sex that is reduced to a position of inferiority, the methods of justification are the same. "The eternal feminine" corresponds to "the black soul" and to "the Jewish character." True, the Jewish problem is on the whole very different from the other two —to the anti-Semite the Jew is not so much an inferior as he is an enemy for whom there is to be granted no place on earth, for whom annihilation is the fate desired. But there are deep similarities between the situation of woman and that of the Negro. Both are being emancipated today from a like paternalism, and the former master class wishes to "keep them in their place"—that is, the place chosen for them. In both cases the former masters lavish more or less sincere eulogies, either on the virtues of "the good Negro" with his dormant, childish, merry soul—the submissive Negro—or on the merits of the woman who is "truly feminine"—that is, frivolous, infantile, irresponsible—the submissive woman.

In particular those who are condemned to stagnation are often pronounced happy on the pretext that happiness consists in being at rest. This notion we reject, for our perspective is that of existentialist ethics. Every subject plays his part as such specifically through exploits or projects that serve as a mode of transcendence; he achieves liberty only through a continual reaching out toward other liberties. There is no justification for present existence other than its expansion into an indefinitely open future. Every time transcendence falls back into immanence, stagnation, there is a degradation of existence into the "en-soi"—the brutish life of subjection to given conditions—and of liberty into constraint and contingence. This downfall represents a moral fault if the subject consents to it; if it is inflicted upon him, it spells frustration and oppression. In both cases it is an absolute evil. Every individual concerned to justify his existence feels that his existence involves an undefined need to transcend himself, to engage in freely chosen projects.

Now, what peculiarly signalizes the situation of woman is that she—a free and autonomous being like all human creatures—nevertheless finds herself living in a world where men compel her to assume the status of the Other. They propose to stabilize her as object and to doom her to immanence since her transcendence is to be overshadowed and forever transcended by another ego (*conscience*) which is essential and sovereign. The drama of woman lies in this conflict between the fundamental aspirations of every subject (ego)—who always regards the self as the essential—and the compulsions of a situation in which she is the inessential. How can a human being in woman's situation attain fulfillment? What roads are open to her? Which are blocked? How can independence be recovered in a state of dependency? What circumstances limit woman's liberty and how can they be overcome? These are the fundamental questions on which I would fain throw some light. This means that I am interested in the fortunes of the individual as defined not in terms of happiness but in terms of liberty.

The Married Woman

MARRIAGE is the destiny traditionally offered to women by society It is still true that most women are married, or have been, or plan to be, or suffer from not being. The celibate woman is to be explained and defined with reference to marriage, whether she is frustrated, rebellious, or even indifferent in regard to that institution. We must therefore continue this study by analyzing marriage.

Economic evolution in woman's situation is in process of upsetting the institution of marriage: it is becoming a union freely entered upon by the consent of two independent persons; the obligations of the two contracting parties are personal and reciprocal; adultery is for both a breach of contract; divorce is obtainable by the one or the other on the same conditions. Woman is no longer limited to the reproductive func-

tion, which has lost in large part its character as natural servitude and has come to be regarded as a function to be voluntarily assumed; and it is compatible with productive labor, since, in many cases, the time off required by a pregnancy is taken by the mother at the expense of the State or the employer. In the Soviet Union marriage was for some years a contract between individuals based upon the complete liberty of the husband and wife; but it would seem that it is now a duty that the State imposes upon them both. Which of these tendencies will prevail in the world of tomorrow will depend upon the general structure of society, but in any case male guardianship of woman is disappearing. Nevertheless, the epoch in which we are living is still, from the feminist point of view, a period of transition. Only a part of the female population is engaged in production, and even those who are belong to a society in which ancient forms and antique values survive. Modern marriage can be understood only in the light of a past that it tends to perpetuate in part.

Marriage has always been a very different thing for man and for woman. The two sexes are necessary to each other, but this necessity has never brought about a condition of reciprocity between them; women, as we have seen, have never constituted a caste making exchanges and contracts with the male caste upon a footing of equality. A man is socially an independent and complete individual; he is regarded first of all as a producer whose existence is justified by the work he does for the group; we have seen why it is that the reproductive and domestic role to which woman is confined has not guaranteed her an equal dignity. Certainly the male needs her; in some primitive groups it may happen that the bachelor, unable to manage his existence by himself, becomes a kind of outcast; in agricultural societies a woman coworker is essential to the peasant; and for most men it is of advantage to unload certain drudgery upon a mate; the individual wants a regular sexual life and posterity, and the State requires him to contribute to its perpetuation. ...The young girl's freedom of choice has always been much restricted; and celibacy—apart from the rare cases in which it bears a sacred character—reduced her to the rank of parasite and pariah; marriage is her only means of support and the sole justification of her existence. It is enjoined upon her for two reasons.

The first reason is that she must provide the society with children; only rarely—as in Sparta and to some extent under the Nazi regime—does the State take woman under direct guardianship and ask only that she be a mother. But even the primitive societies that are not aware of the paternal generative role demand that woman have a husband, for the second reason why marriage is enjoined is that woman's function is also to satisfy a male's sexual needs and to take care of his household. These duties placed upon woman by society are regarded as a *service* rendered to her spouse: in return he is supposed to give her presents, or a marriage settlement, and to support her. Through him as intermediary, society discharges its debt to the woman it turns over

to him. The rights obtained by the wife in fulfilling her duties are represented in obligations that the male must assume. He cannot break the conjugal bond at his pleasure; he can repudiate or divorce his wife only when the public authorities so decide, and even then the husband sometimes owes her compensation in money: the practice even becomes an abuse in Egypt under Bocchoris or, as the demand for alimony, in the United States today. Polygamy has always been more or less openly tolerated: man may bed with slaves, concubines, mistresses, prostitutes, but he is required to respect certain privileges of his legitimate wife. If she is maltreated or wronged, she has the right—more or less definitely guaranteed—of going back to her family and herself obtaining a separation or divorce.

In marrying, woman gets some share in the world as her own; legal guarantees protect her against capricious action by man; but she becomes his vassal. He is the economic head of the joint enterprise, and hence he represents it in the view of society. She takes his name; she belongs to his religion, his class, his circle; she joins his family, she becomes his "half." She follows wherever his work calls him and determines their place of residence; she breaks more or less decisively with her past, becoming attached to her husband's universe; she gives him her person, virginity and a rigorous fidelity being required. She loses some of the rights legally belonging to the unmarried woman. Roman law placed the wife in the husband's hands *loco filiae*, in the position of a daughter; early in the nineteenth century the conservative writer Bonald pronounced the wife to be to her husband as the child is to its mother; before 1942 French law demanded the wife's obedience to her husband; law and custom still give him great authority, as implied in the conjugal situation itself.

It is still agreed that the act of love is, as we have seen, a *service* rendered to the man; he *takes* his pleasure and owes her some payment. The woman's body is something he buys; to her he represents capital she is authorized to exploit. Sometimes she may bring a dowry, or, often, she undertakes to do certain domestic work: keeping house, rearing children. In any case she has the right to accept support and is even urged to do so by traditional morality. She is naturally tempted by this relatively easy way, the more so because occupations open to women are often disagreeable and poorly paid; marriage, in a word, is a more advantageous career than many others.

The attainment of sexual freedom by the unmarried woman, further, is still made difficult by social customs. In France adultery committed by a wife has been considered, up to the present time, to be a legal offense, whereas no law forbids a woman free love; nevertheless, if she wishes to take a lover, she must first get married. Even at the present time many young middle-class women of strict behavior marry "so as to be free." A good many American young women have gained sexual freedom; but their actual experiences are rather like those of the young girls described by Malinowski in *The Sexual Life of Savages*, who practice inconsequential love-making in the "bachelors' house"; it is understood that they will marry later, when they will be regarded as fully adult. A single woman in America, still more than in France, is a socially incomplete being even if she makes her own living; if she is to attain the whole dignity of a person and gain her full rights, she must wear a wedding ring. Maternity in particular is respectable only for a married woman; the unwed mother remains an offense to public opinion, and her child is a severe handicap for her in life.

Prostitutes and Hetairas

MARRIAGE as we have seen, is directly correlated with prostitution, which, it has been said, follows humanity from ancient to modern times like a dark shadow over the family. Man, for reasons of prudence, vows his wife to chastity, but he is not himself satisfied with the regime imposed upon her. Montaigne tells us with approval:

The kings of Persia were wont to invite their wives to join them in their banquets; but when the wine began to excite them in good earnest and they felt impelled to give the reins to sensuality, they sent them away to their private apartments, that they might not make them partake of their immoderate lust, and caused other women to come in their stead, toward whom they did not feel such an obligation of respect.

Sewers are necessary to guarantee the wholesomeness of palaces, according to the Fathers of the Church. And it has often been remarked that the necessity exists of sacrificing one part of the female sex in order to save the other and prevent worse troubles. One of the arguments in support of slavery, advanced by the American supporters of the institution, was that the Southern whites, being all freed from servile duties, could maintain the most democratic and refined relations among themselves; in the same way, a caste of shameless women" allows the "honest woman" to be treated with the most chivalrous respect. The prostitute is a scapegoat; man vents his turpitude upon her, and he rejects her. Whether she is put legally under police supervision or works illegally in secret, she is in any case treated as a pariah.

Viewed from the standpoint of economics, her position corresponds with that of the married woman. In *La Puberté* Marro says: "The only difference between women who sell themselves in prostitution and those who sell themselves in marriage is in the price and the length of time the contract runs." For both the sexual act is a service; the one is hired for life by one man; the other has several clients who pay her by the piece. The one is protected by one male against all others; the other is defended by all against the exclusive tyranny of each. In any case the benefits received in return for the giving of their bodies are limited by existing competition; the husband knows that he could have secured a different wife; the performing of "conjugal duties" is not a personal favor, it is the fulfilling of a contract. In prostitution, male desire can be satisfied on no matter what body, such desire being specific but not individualized as to object. Neither wife nor hetaira succeeds in exploiting a man un-

less she achieves an individual ascendancy over him. The great difference between them is that the legal wife, oppressed as a married woman, is respected as a human being; this respect is beginning definitely to check the oppression. So long as the prostitute is denied the rights of a person, she sums up all the forms of feminine slavery at once.

Conclusion

It must be admitted that the males find in woman more complicity than the oppressor usually finds in the oppressed. And in bad faith they take authorization from this to declare that she has desired the destiny they have imposed on her. We have seen that all the main features of her training combine to bar her from the roads of revolt and adventure. Society in general—beginning with her respected parents—lies to her by praising the lofty values of love, devotion, the gift of herself, and then concealing from her the fact that neither lover nor husband nor yet her children will be inclined to accept the burdensome charge of all that. She cheerfully believes these lies because they invite her to follow the easy slope: in this others commit their worst crime against her; throughout her life from childhood on, they damage and corrupt her by designating as her true vocation this submission, which is the temptation of every existent in the anxiety of liberty. If a child is taught idleness by being amused all day long and never being led to study, or shown its usefulness, it will hardly be said, when he grows up, that he chose to be incapable and ignorant; yet this is how woman is brought up, without ever being impressed with the necessity of taking charge of her own existence. So she readily lets herself come to count on the protection, love, assistance, and supervision of others, she lets herself be fascinated with the hope of self-realization without doing anything. She does wrong in yielding to the temptation; but man is in no position to blame her, since he has led her into the temptation.

If the little girl were brought up from the first with the same demands and rewards, the same severity and the same freedom, as her brothers, taking part in the same studies, the same games, promised the same future, surrounded with women and men who seemed to her undoubted equals, the meanings of the castration complex and of the Oedipus complex would be profoundly modified. Assuming on the same basis as the father the material and moral responsibility of the couple, the mother would enjoy the same lasting prestige; the child would perceive around her an androgynous world and not a masculine world. Were she emotionally more attracted to her father—which is not even sure—her love for him would be tinged with a will to emulation and not a feeling of powerlessness; she would not be oriented toward passivity. Authorized to test her powers in work and sports, competing actively with the boys, she would not find the absence of the penis—compensated by the promise of a child—enough to give rise to an inferiority complex; correlatively, the boy would not have a superiority complex if it

were not instilled into him and if he looked up to women with as much respect as to men. The little girl would not seek sterile compensation in narcissism and dreaming, she would not take her fate for granted; she would be interested in what she was *doing*, she would throw herself without reserve into undertakings.

Woman is the victim of no mysterious fatality; the peculiarities that identify her as specifically a woman get their importance from the significance placed upon them. They can be surmounted, in the future, when they are regarded in new perspectives. Thus, as we have seen, through her erotic experience woman feels—and often detests—the domination of the male; but this is no reason to conclude that her ovaries condemn her to live forever on her knees. Virile aggressiveness seems like a lordly privilege only within a system that in its entirety conspires to affirm masculine sovereignty; and woman *feels* herself profoundly passive in the sexual act only because she already *thinks* of herself as such.

As a matter of fact, man, like woman, is flesh, therefore passive, the plaything of his hormones and of the species, the restless prey of his desires. And she, like him, in the midst of the carnal fever, is a consenting, a voluntary gift, an activity; they live out in their several fashions the strange ambiguity of existence made body. In those combats where they think they confront one another, it is really against the self that each one struggles, projecting into the partner that part of the self which is repudiated; instead of living out the ambiguities of their situation, each tries to make the other bear the abjection and tries to reserve the honor for the self. If, however, both should assume the ambiguity with a clear-sighted modesty, correlative of an authentic pride, they would see each other as equals and would live out their erotic drama in amity. The fact that we are human beings is infinitely more important than all the peculiarities that distinguish human beings from one another...

To begin with, there will always be certain differences between man and woman; her eroticism, and therefore her sexual world, have a special form of their own and therefore cannot fail to engender a sensuality, a sensitivity, of a special nature. This means that her relations to her own body, to that of the male, to the child, will never be identical with those the male bears to his own body, to that of the female, and to the child; those who make much of "equality in difference" could not with good grace refuse to grant me the possible existence of differences in equality. Then again, it is institutions that create uniformity. Young and pretty, the slaves of the harem are always the same in the sultan's embrace; Christianity gave eroticism its savor of sin and legend when it endowed the human female with a soul; if society restores her sovereign individuality to woman, it will not thereby destroy the power of love's embrace to move the heart.

It is nonsense to assert that revelry, vice, ecstasy, passion, would become impossible if man and woman were equal in concrete matters; the contradictions that put the flesh in opposition to the spirit, the instant to time, the swoon of immanence to the challenge of transcendence, the absolute of pleasure to the nothingness of forgetting, will never be resolved; in sexuality will always be materialized the tension, the anguish, the joy, the frustration, and the triumph of existence. To emancipate woman is to refuse to confine her to the relations she bears to man, not to deny them to her; let her have her independent existence and she will continue none the less to exist for him *also*: mutually recognizing each other as subject, each will yet remain for the other an *other*. The reciprocity of their relations will not do away with the miracles—desire, possession, love, dream, adventure—worked by the division of human beings into two separate categories; and the words that move us—giving, conquering, uniting—will not lose their meaning. On the contrary, when we abolish the slavery of half of humanity, together with the whole system of hypocrisy that it implies, then the "division" of humanity will reveal its genuine significance and the human couple will find its true form.

Questions for Critical Thinking and Discussion

1. What is de Beauvoir's definition of a woman? How does this definition fit in with her title?

2. How have men traditionally defined women?

3. According to de Beauvoir, are women pleased with their inferiority? Explain her position. What is your position?

4. Summarize the past history of women's subordination to men as presented by the author.

5. How does de Beauvoir analyze marriage for a man? — for a woman?

6. "The only difference between women who sell themselves in prostitution and those who sell themselves in marriage is in the price and the length of time the contract runs." Do you agree with Marro's quote? Why or why not?

7. Even if women achieved parity with men in the marketplace, would the "new woman" appear?

8. What changes in the educational system would de Beauvoir make?

9. How should the female emancipate herself?

Self-Test

Part I: Identification

Can you identify each of the following? Tell who, what, when, where, why, and/or how for each term.

1. The Cold War
2. The Truman Doctrine
3. Containment policy
4. Marshall Plan
5. "Iron Curtain"
6. Common Market
7. Berlin Blockade
8. North Atlantic Treaty Organization
9. Warsaw Treaty Organization
10. Mao Zedong
11. The Korean War
12. Cuban Missile Crisis
13. Bay of Pigs invasion
14. Domino theory
15. South East Asia Treaty Organization (SEATO)
16. Gulf of Tonkin Resolution
17. Tet Offensive
18. Detente
19. Strategic Arms Limitation Talks
20. Prague Spring
21. Brezhnev Doctrine
22. Solidarity
23. *Perestroika*
24. *Glasnost*
25. Kwame Nkrumah
26. Jomo Kenyatta
27. Democratic Republic of the Congo
28. Nelson Mandela
29. Mahatma Gandhi
30. Indian National Congress
31. Ho Chi Minh
32. Viet Minh
33. Zionist movement
34. Balfour Declaration (1917)
35. Palestine Liberation Front (PLO)
36. Nuclear Non-Proliferation Treaty (1968)
37. Chernobyl
38. *Sputnik*
39. Silent Spring
40. Greenpeace
41. Existentialism
42. The Civil Rights Movement
43. The Second Sex
44. National Organization for Women
45. Helsinki Accords
46. Amnesty International
47. Post-Modernism
48. Logical Positivists
49. European Union
50. Brezhev Doctrine
51. Velvet Revolution
52. Somalia
53. World Wide Web (WWW)
54. Bosnia
55. Kosovo
56. Iran-Contra scandal
57. Gaullism
58. Dayton Peace Accords
59. Third World
60. Hutus—Tutsis

Part II: Multiple Choice Questions

Circle the best response from the ones given.

1. Containment was:

   a. a new way of shipping manufactured goods.
   b. a U.S. foreign policy that attempted to limit communist expansion.
   c. an attempt by the U.S. Congress to check an out-of-control Presidency.
   d. None of the above.

2. Not among the military alliances forged after World War II was:

   a. SEATO.
   b. NOW.
   c. NATO.
   d. WTO.

3. Which of the following was an opposition leader elected to head a new, non-communist government in what is now the Czech Republic:

   a. Nicolae Ceausescu.
   b. Charles de Gaulle.
   c. Lech Walesa.
   d. Vaclav Havel.

4. The Korean War began when:

   a. UN forces were driven back from the Yalu River to below the 38th parallel.
   b. North Korea successfully made an amphibious landing at Inchon, south of the 38th parallel.
   c. North Korea suddenly invaded South Korea.
   d. South Korea suddenly invaded North Korea.

5. *Perestroika*, a restructuring of the Soviet economy, was proposed by:

    a. Leonid Brezhnev.
    b. Boris Yeltsin.
    c. Mikhail Gorbachev.
    d. Nikita Khrushchev.

6. The following were used to thwart the growth of communism after World War II in Europe:

    a. NATO alliance.
    b. Truman Doctrine.
    c. Marshall Plan.
    d. All of the above.

7. Which *one* of the following incidents during the Cold War brought the world closest to nuclear destruction?

    a. Berlin airlift.
    b. Bay of Pigs invasion.
    c. Cuban Missile crisis.
    d. Invasion of Afghanistan by the Russians.

8. The Gulf of Tonkin Resolution gave President Lyndon Baines Johnson the following:

    a. Approval to proceed with the Vietnamization of South Vietnamese forces.
    b. The equivalent of a blank check to repel any armed attack against U.S. forces in southeast Asia.
    c. The legislation to have an official "body count" in order to convince the public the United States was winning the war.
    d. The legislation to limit the power of the President to send troops abroad without Congressional approval.

9. One example of a successful modern African ruler was:

    a. Jinnah.
    b. Lumumba.
    c. Nkrumah.
    d. Kenyatta.

10. The former Belgian Congo officially changed its name first to Zaire, then to
    _____ in 1997.

    a. Ghana.
    b. Liberia.
    c. The Democratic Republic of the Congo.
    d. Chad.

11. In order to gain independence from Great Britain, Mahatma Gandhi used the
    following tactics:

    a. Passive resistance.
    b. Non-violent civil disobedience.
    c. Refusal to cooperate with the Allies.
    d. All of the above.

12. Not among the modern art forms is:

    a. Abstract expressionism.
    b. Surrealism.
    c. Existentialism.
    d. Cubism.

13. The Greenpeace Movement is a movement:

    a. To grow plants hydroponically in greenhouses.
    b. Advocating non-violent confrontation to help protect the environment.
    c. To blow up ships in New Zealand that threaten peace.
    d. None of the above.

14. A famous surrealist who painted *The Persistence of Memory*, better known as
    Soft Watches, was:

    a. Picasso.
    b. Jones.
    c. Kandinsky.
    d. Dali.

15. If you are an existentialist, you may believe in which one of the following statements:

    a. Exercise regularly at least three times per week.
    b. Organized religion helps to provide an explanation for belief in a Supreme Being.
    c. Life is essentially without meaning; it is absurd.
    d. Dogma should be avoided; instead believe in a final authority.

16. Which one of the following areas was NOT a locale of an urban riot in the 1960's

    a. Minneapolis.   c. Watts.
    b. Newark.   d. Detroit.

17. Gabriel Marcel was a (an):

    a. "Free spirit."
    b. Dogmatic egocentric.
    c. Theistic existentialist.
    d. Atheist existentialist.

18. Simone de Beauvoir in The Second Sex argues that:

    a. Man expects woman to be submissive.
    b. Man defines woman not in terms of herself but in relation to him.
    c. Woman should move toward true equality with men.
    d. All of the above.

19. The Civil Rights Movement achieved all of the following EXCEPT:

    a. Desegregation of the nation's public schools.
    b. Prohibition of discrimination in public accommodations.
    c. Equal funding for all public schools.
    d. Voting rights legislation.

20. The following organizations have made governments accountable for gross violations of human rights EXCEPT:

    a. Amnesty International.
    b. Human Rights Watch.
    c. United Nations.
    d. Greenpeace.

21. The Cold War era took place from:

    a. 1946-1989.
    b. 1946-1991.
    c. 1979-1989.
    d. 1949-1999.

22. Which one of the following groups was most reponsible for ending the Diem regime in South Vietnam?

    a. South Vietnamese military.
    b. Roman Catholics.
    c. Viet Cong.
    d. Zoroastrians.

23. Detente can be defined as:

    a. A policy to get American troops out of Vietnam.
    b. A gradual withdrawal of French forces in Vietnam.
    c. A policy focused on easing or relaxing Cold War tensions.
    d. The right of the Soviets to intervene in any socialist country.

24. The Paris Accords signed in January 1973 at the conclusion of the Vietnam War provided:

    a. U.S. prisoners of war were to be repatriated.
    b. A cease-fire was to take place.
    c. The withdrawal of US forces in Vietnam.
    d. All of the above.

25. The first East European country to experience free democratic elections in the post-Cold War era was:

    a. Hungary.
    b. Czechoslovakia.
    c. Poland.
    d. Romania.

26. Which one of the following reasons is the most accurate for the breakup of the Soviet Union?

    a. Inadequate food, housing, and clothing made life miserable for the average Russian citizen.
    b. Lithuania, Latvia, and Estonia demanded increased economic support.
    c. The Brezhev Doctrine shifted political power to Boris Yeltsin, the President of the Russian Republic.
    d. Gorbachev unleashed forces of change, which in turn promoted nationalism.

27. Tribal and/or clan tensions have caused killings and political instability in which of the following African countries:

    a. Rwanda.   c. Somalia.
    b. Nigeria.   d. All of these.

28. At Potsdam in 1945, Germany was divided into four zones occupied by the following powers:

    a. Great Britain, France, Russia, and East Germany.
    b. Russia, France, U.S., and West Germany.
    c. Great Britain, France, Belgium. and West Germany.
    d. Great Britain, Russia, France, and the U.S.

29. Who was appointed Commander of UN forces in Korea in 1951?

    a. Dwight Eisenhower.   b. George Patton.
    c. Douglas MacArthur.   d. George Marshall.

30. All of the following reasons validated for the Soviets the installation of missiles in Cuba in 1961 **except**:

    a. The Russians wished to gain prestige throughout Latin America.
    b. The Russians wished to negotiate an exchange of Cuban exiles captured during the Bay of Pigs invasion.
    c. The Russians hoped to gain a new missile base outside the United States radar early warning system.
    d. The Russians hoped to deter an U.S. invasion of Cuba.

Part III: Review and Thought Questions

1. What stopped The Cold War from becoming a "hot war"?

2. What events started the Cold War?

3. Explain the purpose of both the Truman Doctrine and the Marshall Plan. Did they achieve their goals?

4. What were the causes and the effects of the Berlin Blockade?

5. Contrast the two rival military alliances that were formed in Europe in 1949 and 1955 respectively.

6. Where and with what groups did the Nationalist Chinese under Chiang Kai-shek establish a base of support? Why was Mao able to turn China into a communist state?

7. How and why was President Harry S. Truman able to place U.S. troops in combat without a declaration of war from Congress against North Korea?

8. Why was the Cuban Missile Crisis so alarming to the United States? What was its final resolution?

9. How did SEATO protect the independence of Laos, Cambodia, and Vietnam?

10. Explain the Domino Theory in relation to Indochina before and after the Vietnam War.

11. Describe three lessons the United States learned from its involvement in the Vietnam War.

12. Describe the breakup of the former Soviet Union. Do you think the Russian republic can survive under democracy? Explain why or why not.

13. What has happened in the Kosovo region of Serbia with the ethnic Albanians?

14. What trouble did the French have with the Algerians before independence in 1962? Did they have similar problems with their other colonies in North Africa?

15. What are the pros and cons of nuclear energy?

16. What strides have been made in the telecommunications industry in the past decade? What do you foresee in the third millenium?

17. Why was Somalia a disappointing post-colonial experience? Is Somalia unified in 1999?

18. How integrated is Europe under the European Union?

Part IV: Full-length Essays

1. Describe the policy of containment toward the Soviet Union after World War II. Give examples of policy, such as the Truman Doctrine, the Marshall Plan, the Berlin Blockade, NATO alliance, etc.

2. Compare and contrast the Korean and Vietnam Wars. Did either war illustrate the "domino" theory?

3. Describe and evaluate the recent breakup of the Soviet Union and the former satellite states of Eastern Europe.

4. Trace the course of the Vietnam War. Would you have been a pro or an anti-war demonstrator? Give reasons for your selection.

5. Describe the decolonization movement in four African, Asian, and Middle Eastern countries after World II.

6. Compare and contrast the movement for national independence in India with China.

7. Describe and evaluate the successes and failures of the Civil Rights Movement in the United States. In your opinion, what remains to be done?

8. What strides have been made in the area of human rights in the 70's, 80's, and the 90's? Give examples.

Figure 5.3 **"Standing Nude with Seated Musketeer"** by Pablo Picasso (1881-1973). This role model of modern art used geometric designs in unconventional ways so that the viewer is forced to reconstruct some semblance of reality in his/her own mind. (Courtesy of The Metropolitan Museum of Art. Jointly owned by The Metropolitan Museum of Art and A. L. Blanche Levine, 1981.)

TIPS FOR STUDENTS:

HOW TO ANSWER MULTIPLE CHOICE QUESTIONS

Imagine you enter a 120-seat capacity lecture hall filled with other students for a computer scored 80-question multiple-choice exam. After a quick survey of the exam, you panic, for you feel no one has prepared you for the range of questions or the degree of complexity this type of test presents. (No, you are not having a nightmare!) Be assured, however, you can train yourself to develop the necessary skills to become a proficient test taker. **It's all in knowing how.**

Here are some tips:

1. When you receive your multiple-choice test, read the directions carefully. Will you be penalized for incorrect responses; that is, will one point be deducted for each incorrect response? If there is no penalty for wrong answers (guessing included), be sure to respond to each question. Are you to mark **all** correct responses or only **the one** that best answers the question? Look closely.

2. Multiple-choice questions consist of two parts: (a) **the stem**, which identifies the question (it may itself be a question or it may be an incomplete statement); (b) **the response options**. The alternatives or options usually number four or five in college or university tests. Begin by reading the stem in its entirety; then treat each option as a true—false statement. Eliminate the statements you consider to be false. For many responses, there is no absolute truth; recognize you are selecting the best response from the alternatives given.

3. Most multiple-choice questions have one option that is far-fetched, silly, or without a doubt absolutely incorrect. You usually can eliminate it. If you have two or more correct responses in the group out of four or five alternatives given, consider the possibility that your response may be correct if you select "all of the above" as your choice. What about "none of the above"? Similarly, if two or more of the group are incorrect, consider the possibility that your choice should be "none of the above."

4. Watch out for words, such as *never, none, not, always, all, every, except.* These qualifiers are called **absolute** words. Be very suspicious of them, either in the stems or in the response. Responses containing these words can usually be eliminated, whereas statements containing words such as **most, usually,**

some, many tend to be true. Practice circling these qualifiers in your multiple-choice tests.

5. Most times multiple-choice tests have two alternatives that are extremely close, perhaps by only one word or a different phrase. Concentrate on the difference in meaning or content between the two similar ones. Look closely at the concept the stem is asking. Which option best answers the question?

6. Look for information in questions as you read the exam that may trigger a response to another question. You never can tell what will jog your memory when you are covering a large volume of material.

7. Place a check mark next to each question you are having difficulty with. Leave sufficient time to go back over each question where you have placed a mark. Some psychologists will tell you your first answer is usually the correct one; however, the latest studies have produced controversy and disagreement whether or not your first response is the correct one. So now you are free to review carefully and cautiously; then record your response!

8. Now check that you have answered every question and that you are not out of synchronization with the alignment of your responses on a computer scored or marksensed exam.

| Here are a few examples | of Multiple Choice Questions from Chapter 4 an 5 of this Worktext that illustrate the above tips.

---

3. Which one of the following statements is true?

   a. Hitler's army inflicted heavy damage and casualities on the Russians at the Battle of the Bulge.
   b. The Battle of Midway took place mid-way between Iceland and Great Britain.
   c. The Tripartite Pact renewed and strenghtened a military alliance among France, Great Britain, and the Soviet Union.
   d. The Battle of Britain was a massive air war launched by Germany in preparation for the invasion of Britain.

You are asked to determine which one of the statements is true; as a consequence, you have to treat each one as a true—false statement. Your choice should be "d" since this statement is the only factually correct one from the ones given. Choice "a" is incorrect. Although a counterattack by the Germans occurred in the Battle of the Bulge, the battle was won by the Allies, not the Germans. Choice "b" is incorrect as Midway is an island in the Pacific Ocean, not in the Atlantic. Choice "c" is incorrect because the Triparte Pact was concluded by Japan with Germany and Italy as signatories, not France, Great Britain, and the Soviet Union.

4. The following developments of the Allies during World War II tilted the military balance in their favor:

    a. radar and sonar.
    b. new types of aircraft.
    c. mass production of ships.
    d. all of the above.

In the response section you have two correct responses out of the three alternatives given; therefore, you would be wise to select choice "d" all of the above.

11. Not among the modern art forms is:

    a. Abstract expressionism.
    b. Surrealism.
    c. Existentialism.
    d. Cubism.

The question reads: "**Not** among the modern art forms is:" For this question you know in advance that one of the four alternatives as given is incorrect. You would select choice "c" as the correct response, for you know existentialism is a 20th-century philosophy, not an art form as are: abstract expressionism, surrealism, and cubism.

7. The Japanese officially surrendered on September 2, 1945 because of:

    a. The dropping of atomic bombs on Hiroshima and Nagasaki.
    b. The invasion of the Philippines and Iwo Jima.
    c. The defeat of Germany on May 7, 1945.
    d. Russia's entry into the war against the Japanese.
    e. The firebombing of Tokyo and other Japanese cities.

The correct response to this question is choice "a". Although the other alternatives have some validity attached to them, the dropping of atomic bombs on Hiroshima and Nagaski was the deciding factor of the unconditional surrender of the Japanese.

Be aware that there are multiple-choice questions in most of the parts of this book for you to practice. Also avail yourself of the opportunity to create your own multiple-choice questions as you prepare for exams. Good luck!

TIPS FOR STUDENTS:

HOW TO ANSWER ESSAY QUESTIONS

In the college game, there are winners and losers. In order to place yourself in a win-win game strategy, you have to decide, plan, and then activate a mode of study well in advance of the actual hourly, midterm, or final examination. Take the offensive position, for there is no substitute for careful preparation. Here are some suggestions:

1. Practice forming essay questions from the lecture material, text, and readings from the start of the course. For example, practice the essay questions given in this book, chapter by chapter as given in the side bars, as you go through the semester.

2. Consider simulating or pretending to take an examination perhaps a week or ten days before the actual exam. Buy yourself a kitchen timer or use the timer on your digital watch set for 60 minutes to see how long it takes to answer two practice-extended essay questions. It usually takes longer than you think it will! That is why I strongly urge you to practice in advance what the actual exam will force you to do.

3. Form study groups with your peers; pose questions; discuss the material; analyze it from all points of view. Let your peers read your practice responses for comments and constructive criticism.

4. Review your notes on at least three to four separate occasions for a complete depth of understanding. Many times, professors ask you to recombine and reconstruct material in a novel or different way in order for you to illustrate mastery of the material and depth of understanding. For example, assume you have read and heard a lecture on the French Revolution. Several weeks later when you arrive at the exam, the instructor asks you to take on the role of a twenty-year old female/male *sans-culotte* living in Paris during Year One of the Revolution. You are then asked to describe your situation and explain how the events in your life up to this point in time have influenced you and your loved ones. Obviously you have to have a firm grasp of the events that have already occurred in their correct chronological sequence in order to respond.

5. Budget your time. On the day of the examination, arrive early to your designated lecture hall or exam room fully equipped with writing instruments. Find out in advance the time allotted to your exam as well as the type (identification, multiple choice, matching, essay) questions that may be asked. After you have read the exam in its entirety once, estimate the minutes available to you versus the point count of each ques-

tion. Next to each question roughly pencil in the number of minutes you plan to spend on that question. Allow at least ten to fifteen minutes to proofread as well as to revise your exam. When you have two extended essays to answer on a 60-minute midterm along with five identification questions, obviously spending the bulk of your time on the one essay question you know very well will not give you a passing grade. What should you do if your time on the second essay response runs out? I suggest outlining or listing the main points you plan to cover; however, recognize that if you allocate your time at the exam's onset, then you should not find yourself in this dilemma.

6. Do not start to write immediately. Analyze the questions you plan to answer. After you have assigned a time quota for each response, reread your test. Many more students than you think hastily misinterpret questions. Identify the buzz or key words that will set up your response. Some examples of these descriptors are:

Define Means to explain what it is or what it means within an historical context.

Example: Define mercantilism as it was practiced in France during the seventeenth century.

Describe Means to write a detailed account using illustration, details, and a logical sequence (chronological or from the least to the most important).

Example: Describe trench warfare during World War I.

Discuss Means to describe using details, sometimes explaining the pros and the cons. Consider from various points of view.

Example: Discuss Marx's historical influence.

Compare Means to show both the similarities and the differences.

Example: Compare the imperialism of the 19th century to the new imperialism of the 20th century, using specific examples of each.

Contrast Means to show only the differences.

Example: Contrast the League of Nations with the United Nations' actions in a twenty-year post-war period.

Evaluate Means to discuss pros and cons (advantages versus disadvantages); give your opinion.

Example: Evaluate the legacy of the Vietnam War.

Trace Means to describe the progress or the history of a subject.

Example: Trace the rise of Adolph Hitler to power.

7. Now **outline** your proposed responses. The outline will help you stay focused. After you have made your outline or listed the main points you wish to include, stick to these

points; do not get sidetracked. Readers look for clear, concise, well-organized responses. A "blue shadow" (B.S.), fuzzy, padded response will annoy the reader most of the time to the point of an "F". Think positively. Be confident that you will prove to the reader you know the material and can organize it.

Below is an example of an actual student outline written as part of a final exam. Question: Contrast World War II with the Vietnam War. (30 points)

World War II
Global
Pearl Harbor— surprise attack
Fought Japanese in Pacific; Germans in N. Africa and Europe.
A-bombs on Hiroshima & Nagasaki
Island hopping
Germans surrounded USSR; Russians fought back valiantly at Stalingrad.
Bombardment of Ger. destroyed transportation network, canals, rr, factories; terror bombing killed civilians.
Popular war — all-out effort.
Unconditional surrender of Ger. & Japan.

The Vietnam War
Limited struggle; began as anti-colonial struggle between North Vietnam and France.
N. Vietnam (Communist) supported by Russia, China. S. Vietnam (Non-communist)
US faced disadvantage of S. Vietnamese not identifying with them.
US could not engage in certain strategies; could not shoot at Vietnamese who was standing still—rules of engagement.
Guerilla warfare — jungle warfare.
Napalm; agent orange as a defoliant.
US lost war; unpopular war at home.
US agreed to pull out.

8. Use a general statement first, supported by details or examples in your extended essay. It is a good idea to repeat some of the words of the question in your first sentence to demonstrate that you have grasped its meaning. Support your generalizations with details, illustrations, and examples from the beginning to the end of your essay. Use transitions to move your reader along: *for example, first, additionally, similarly, for these reasons, second, more important, finally,* etc. In addition, be sure to have a summary or concluding paragraph to reinforce your previous discussion or arguments.

9. Watch your mechanical errors and handwriting. Studies have shown that mechanics do count in your grade. An exam that is virtually illegible, riddled with mechanical (grammar, spelling, sentence structure) errors will, without a doubt, receive a lower score.

SAMPLE EXTENDED ESSAY

Here is a sample community college student essay, unedited, written in a constrained time period of approximately 50 minutes. Other questions were also given. What grade would you assign to this essay? Question: Compare and contrast World War I and World War II in terms of causes, events, and outcomes. (40 points; 50 minutes)

Both WW I and WW II were total wars, involving many nations and continents in both the Eastern and Western hemispheres. Yet the two wars have amazing similarities and differences. The causes of World War I were many. The main reasons were great feelings of nationalism, the militarization of Europe and the arms race, secret alliances, as well as internal revolt in many nations. World War II, in contrast to World War I, probably had one main cause. Authoritarian nationalistic leaders. After both Adolf Hitler and Benito Mussolini came to power in Germany and Italy respectively, they created authoritarian governments and instilled a great feeling of nationalism in their people. The steps that Hitler took before the war almost forced other nations into it. His first move was to take back the Rhineland, he militarized his army and naval forces (all in violation of the Versailles Treaty), and then took over Austria and Czechoslovika. He did all this with complete authorization of the Western powers, such as France and England. The other leaders did not see the evil intent and aggression in Hitler. They felt that he was just getting back what Germany lost in the last war.

The outbreak of war in World War I and World War II differed greatly. In WW I it was the Serbia-Austrian conflict that led Russia and Germany to war, with England, France, and later American joining in. In contrast to WW I, the United States entered the war as a result of a Far East offensive (Pearl Harbor) whereas in WW I it was Germany. Both resulted in total war across the globe. The greatest example of this total war can be seen on the homefronts of the battling nations. During WWI, nations took many approaches toward dealing with economic and social changes on the homefront. As war broke out, nations concentrated all their efforts toward the war, instituting the draft as well as imposing economic sanctions on their people. They had to ration food as well as natural resources to support the war effort. Some nations were better prepared for this than others, such as Germany versus France. Women also played a key role on the homefront and did many of the jobs which men used to do. Propaganda was also instituted to boost the morale of the people and help them in supporting the war. The homefronts were very similar in World War I and II, except they had to

deal with another problem -- the mass bombing and destruction of civilians and civilian cities. This, as well as the lessons of WW I made morale very low among the people, and more propaganda was used, especially among the Axis powers. Government interference in the economy and the work of women also played a key role in WW II.

Probably the major key difference in the events of WW I and WW II was the methods of warfare. WW I proved to mainly be an immobile war, as exemplified in the battles in the trenches on the Western front. These battles were slow and indecisive, and many lives were lost. In WW II there were major changes. Hitler's Blitzkreig, where he would overcome a nation in one swift swoop of bombing and tank invasion with air support proved to be extremely effective in reaching his goals of gaining land (lebensraum) for the Aryan race of Germany. Mass bombings of civilian cities by planes proved to be effective in lowering morale in many nations.

There were "many inventions of war" that also made killing more efficient. In addition to firebombing, WW II added chemical warfare, improved machine guns, faster tanks, improved submarine technology, and eventually nuclear warfare.

There were many key battles in both wars. The trench battles of WW I proved to be a loss on both sides. But a turn of events came about in 1917. The largest of these being the withdrawal of Russia because of the civil war and the entrance of the United States. In WW II, the key battles were fought in Britain, Stalingrad, and El Alamein in Africa. At all three battles in the European theatre, the Germans were driven back, but not without great casualities to both soldiers and civilians. In contrast to the 30,000,000 (?) who died in WW I, over 50,000,000 (?) died in WW II. Most of them were Russians, who were believed to constitute 2/5ths of these people.

Although Hitler never accomplished his goal of the propagation the Aryan race, he caused mass destruction in the process.

After the two wars ended, there were outcomes and effects of both of them. After WW I was over, the allied nations signed the Treaty of Versailles with the losing nations. As a result of this treaty, Germany was forced to pay reparations in excess of $30 billion, admit sole guilt for the war, and were forced to demilitarize and leave the Rhineland. Their army was ordered to keep a maximum of 100,000 people, and they had to lower their air and naval militia. They had to give up Alsace-Lorraine. An uneffective League of Nations was formed to keep the peace, when Germany began breaking the treaty, the League proved ineffective. Another result of WW I was economic distress in both Italy and Germany. This distress helped to get Mussolini and Hitler into power. In a way, the results and treaties of WW I lead to an even greater war in WW II. Although I am not yet learned as to many of the results of WW II, I do know a few of the major ones. Although the United States and Russia were allies during the war, a combination of Russian fear of the West and differing political and economic views led to the Cold War. In addition to this, Russia put up an invisible "Iron Curtain" over Eastern Europe. They began to take isolationist policies and reconstruct all that they had lost. Another result of WW II was the atomic age and race. After seeing the power of the bomb, nations such as Russia began to build them. This race also aided in forming the Cold War. The United Nations was formed as a result of WW II. Looking back on the failed League of Nations, the countries of the world felt they needed a stronger organization to maintain peace and prevent what had happened again. The UN proved to be effective, and nations are still joining today.

Here is a checklist of questions to ask about this essay as well as other essays.

1. Are explanations given in sufficient detail to show knowledge and mastery of the material?
2. Is the content factually correct?
3. Does the writer answer the question?
4. Is the essay well organized? Does it skip it around?
5. Does the writer have adequate examples, illustrations, and details to back up general statements?
6. Are the ideas and concepts presented clearly? Is the reasoning sound in the essay?
7. Does the writer show depth of understanding of the material? Originality of thought?
8. Has grammar, spelling, sentence structure, punctuation, or illegible handwriting interfered with the essay's content or readability?

This in-class essay received an 80 on a scale of 0 to 100. Some of the details of factual content, as given in the professor's lecture presentation, were omitted. There should have been further explanations of the causes, the events, and the outcomes as well as integration with the text. However, I am certain that after appropriate consultation and critiquing with the professor, this student would be able to write a more detailed, comprehensive essay that would receive a 90 or above ("A") grade.

Here is another example of a student response to the same question.

What grade would you give to this one? Can you justify your grade?

During World War I there was a certain excitement of the unknown, going off to war for a few weeks then coming back to tell about it. It was not carefully thought out. Everyone assumed it would be a short war, similar to the ones in the past.

Nations believed only in victory. They prepared their offensive manueveurs. Never preparing themselves for the defensive position. Which they believed meant defeat.

Every nation formed allies, which would support them in any crisis situation. This made it difficult to get together and negotiate.

Woodrow Wilson began creating a committee which would involve all who were participating in the war to try to come together to negotiate. This was called the League of Nations.

He also was involved with the Treaty of Versailles, which concluded that Germany was solely responsible for the war and should pay $33 billion in reparation fees. They should disarm their military to a smaller size.

The United States earned $14 billion dollars in foreign wealth. They loaned Germany money to pay reparations to the British and the French. They loaned military aircraft and ammunition.

While during World War II we realized that we can't afford the luxury of war. The allies avoided any war confrontation, believing we could avoid it as long as we have free trade which was included in the Treaty of Versailles.

The Allies allowed Hitler to take over land as long as he had the pretext that it was living space. Everyone believed he wouldn't try to take over Europe. Yet sure enough he was. In WW I we were quick to jump the gun while in WW II we had to wait to be attacked.

Hitler wanted to take over the world. Once he had his hands on Poland he tried to take Russia (which saw him coming and torched itself). He waited for the perfect moment, which was when China bombed Pearl Harbor.

Hitler's final solution was becoming stronger. Innocent lives were being exterminated and nothing was being done. Finally the United States joined Great Britain, Italy, and Russia.

Many accuse the Treaty of Versailles as being the main culprit in feeding Hitler. He walked out of a meeting and denounced the disarmament movement. He was just wasting time and fooling the rest of the committee into believing he was harmless.

The atomic bomb and the destruction caused by WW II is a luxury the world cannot afford.

Do you think this essay is well organized, or factually correct? Does this essay, as compared to Student No. 1's, show mastery of the material or depth of understanding?

To be specific, what was the Final Solution? Does the Student No. 2 explain in detail? Does the writer support general statements with illustrations, examples, or details? Does the author answer the question as given? Does the writer seem confused with the events as they happened in time order? Does Student No. 2 have a well-developed conclusion? Was the student knowledgeable about the outcomes of each war? the causes? the events?

Using the eight suggested questions as a guide, the above essay shows a negative answer to each question posed. The professor spent four 50-minute lecture hours on material for this question. Do you think the student took good lecture notes? After studying the appropriate material in this Worktext, would you give Student No. 2 a passing grade?

Answers to Multiple Choice Questions

Chapter 1, pp. 76-80.

1. c	9. b	17. c	24. d
2. b	10. b	18. c	25. a
3. c	11. c	19. b	26. b
4. d	12. d	20. d	27. a
5. a	13. a	21. a	28. c
6. a	14. b	22. d	29. d
7. c	15. a	23. b	30. b
8. a	16. d		

Chapter 2, pp. 166-172.

1. b	10. c	19. c	28. b
2. c	11. a	20. d	29. b
3. d	12. d	21. c	30. b
4. d	13. a	22. a	31. a
5. a	14. d	23. d	32. d
6. a	15. d	24. c	33. b
7. b	16. c	25. b	34. a
8. b	17. d	26. d	35. d
9. c	18. a	27. c	

Chapter 3, pp. 264-271.

1. d	11. d	21. b	31. a
2. a	12. c	22. d	32. d.
3. d	13. d	23. d	33. d
4. d	14. a	24. d	34. b
5. c	15. a	25. b	35. c
6. b	16. d	26. b	36. b
7. a	17. b	27. c	37. d
8. a	18. c	28. c	38. c
9. b	19. c	29. d	39. b
10. c	20. a	30. c	

Chapter 4, pp. 358-363.

1. a	9. c	17. c	24. c
2. c	10. a	18. d	25. d
3. d	11. d	19. d	26. d.
4. b	12. d	20. a	27. c
5. b	13. b	21. d	28. c
6. d	14. d	22. b	29. a
7. b	15. c	23. b	30. a
8. b	16. a		

Chapter 5, pp. 474-479.

1. b	9. d	17. c	24. d
2. b	10. c	18. d	25. c
3. d	11. d	19. c	26. d
4. c	12. c	20. d	27. d
5. c	13. b	21. b	28. d
6. d	14. d	22. a	29. c
7. c	15. c	23. c	30. b
8. b	16. a		

Index

Check also the **EXPANDED CONTENTS FOR EACH SUBCHAPTER** *which begins on page v for a detailed outline of the subjects discussed in this worktext.*

Empire State Building, 424, 428
Ems Dispatch, 193
Enabling Act, 309
Encomienda, 32
Encyclopedia (Encyclopédie), 53
Engels, Frederick, 137-138, 141, 151
Enghien, Duke of, 110
England, 5, 11-13, 23-25, 32, 34, 37, 40-48, 51, 52, 56, 90, 108, 112, 114, 116-17, 122, 123-126 129-131, 133-135, 141-144, 192, 197-199, 202, 211, 233, 244, 278-79, 314, 320, 433
ENIAC, 420
Enlightened Despots, 30
Enlightenment, 26, 37, 42, 51-53, 56,-58, 91, 208, 210, 220
Entente Cordiale, 245
Equal Rights Amendment, 433
Equatorial Africa, 412
Esmeralda, 209
Essay Concerning Human Understanding, 49
Estates General, 93, 96
Esterhazy, Ferdinand, 202
Estonia, 325, 326, 402-403, 450
Ethiopia, 230, 319-320, 410
EU, *see* European Union
Euratom, 453
Euro, 449
Europe, 4-8, 11, 12, 16-18, 22-25, 27-30, 32, 33, 35, 36, 39, 90, 106, 112- 114, 116, 118, 121-123, 125, 127, 140-141, 143, 145, 147-48, 182, 194-195, 197, 203, 214, 224, 232-33, 234, 277-278, 280, 283, 286, 292-293, 307, 311, 327, 332-334, 336, 338, 371-373, 375-377, 382, 396-398, 401, 419, 427, 435,

438, 440, 444, 447, 449-456
European Atomic Energy Commission, 453
European Coal and Steel Community, 372, 376, 453
European Community, 372, 453
European Economic Community, 376, 453
European Union, 277, 372, 376, 444, 450, 452-453, 455
Evolution, 215-217
Existentialism, 428
Extraterritoriality, 225, 238, 241
Fabian Society, 313
Falkland Islands, 443
Fasces, 301, 304
Fasci di Combattimento, 301
Fascism, 278, 301, 304
Fascists, 302
Faust, 209
FBI (Federal Bureau of Investigation), 439
FDP (Free Democratic Party), 449
Feminine Mystique, 432
Fenian Brotherhood, 199
Ferdinand of Aragon, 5
Ferdinand II of the Holy Roman Empire (also Ferdinand of Styria), 14-16
Ferdinand II of the Two Sicilies, 143
Ferdinand III of the Holy Roman Empire, 17
Ferdinand VII of Spain, 115
Fichte, Johann Gottlieb, 181
Fillmore, Millard, 240
Final Solution, 334
Finland, 125, 283, 327, 338, 424, 433, 452
First Consul, 89, 106, 108
First Moroccan Crisis, 245
Fischl, Erich, 426
Fiume, 292

FLN (National Liberation Front, Algeria), 411
Florence, 4, 6
Florida, 36
Foch, Ferdinand, 287
Ford, Gerald, 436
Ford, Henry, 310
Formosa, 379
Fouché, Joseph, 110
Fourier, Charles, 136
Fourteen Points, 288, 289, 290
Fourteenth Amendment, 431
France, 5, 10-13, 16-20, 22-25, 28, 30, 31, 34-36, 40, 47, 52, 56, 89, 90-103, 106, 108-09, 111, 113-114, 116-118, 121-126, 132, 141-145, 148, 184-186, 188-189, 191-195, 200-03, 207, 215, 220, 226, 230, 232-234, 238, 241, 243-246, 278-281, 284, 287-289, 292, 315, 319-20, 322-23, 326-329, 333, 336, 371, 376-377, 385-386, 411-412, 418, 427, 433, 445, 447, 452
Francis Ferdinand of Austria, 278, 279
Francis II of Austia, 100
Francis II of the Two Sicilies, 187
Francis Joseph of Austria, 186, 205
Franco, Francisco, 320, 321
Franco-Prussian War, 192, 194, 201, 226, 243
Franco-Russian Alliance, 244
Frankenstein, 209
Frankfurt, 146, 188, 189, 192
Frankfurt Assembly, 146, 188, 189
Franklin, Benjamin, 56
Frederick I of Prussia (also Frederick III, Elector of Brandenburg), 28

Hoover, Herbert, 311
House of Commons, 199,
211, 442, 448
Hudson Bay, 24
Hué, 388, 390
Hugo, Victor, 209
Huguenots, 20, 22, 28
Human Rights, 373, 399,
430-433, 436
Hume, David, 57
Humiliation of Olmütz, 188
Hunchback of Notre Dame,
209
Hundred Days, 118, 124,
125
Hungary, (*see also* Austria-
Hungary), 11, 195, 205-
206, 232, 243, 247, 280,
282, 284, 290-291, 324,
337, 372, 378, 396,
398-399, 438, 450, 451-
453
Hussein, Saddam, 438
Huxley, Thomas, 216
IBM (International
Business Machines),
421
Ibos, 410
Iceland, 377
Il Risorgimento, 184
Illyria, 112
Imperialism, 223-242
Impression: Sunrise, 220
Impressionism, 220, 221,
425
Inca, 5
Inchon, 380, 381
India, 5, 34, 36, 108, 224,
227, 233-237, 372, 414,
418, 454
Indian National Congress,
236, 413
Indochina, 239, 385-386,
392-394, 414
Indonesia, 331, 414
Industrial Revolution, 90,
129-136, 215, 228, 237,
418, 422
Inquisition, 39
Intendants, 21
International Congo
Association, 229-230

International School of
Architecture, 427
Invisible hand, 58
Ionian Islands, 108, 125
IRA (Irish Republican
Army), 314
Iran, 336, 415, 436, 438,
454
Iraq, 233-234, 291, 395,
415, 418, 435, 438, 454
Iraqis, 438
Ireland, 44-45, 47, 130,
197, 199, 313-314, 444,
452
Irish Free State, 314
Irish Republican Army,
314
Iron Curtain, 450
Isabella of Castile, 5
Islam, 232, 451
Israel, 372, 415, 417, 418
Istanbul, 232
Italy, 3, 7, 13, 21, 24, 38,
107-108, 113, 117, 143,
146, 148, 181-183, 185-
188, 191-195, 201, 226,
233-234, 244-247, 278,
280, 283, 287-288, 290,
292, 301, 317, 319-321,
329-332, 336, 338, 377,
452
Ivanhoe, 208
Ivory Coast, 412
Iwo Jima, 335
J'accuse, 202
Jacobins, 99-103, 107
James I of England (James
VI of Scotland), 42, 43
James II of England, 47,
48, 49
Japan, 224, 226, 239-242,
280, 288, 317-318, 320,
329-331, 334-338, 386,
418-419
Jaruzelski, Wojciech, 397-
398
Jefferson, Thomas, 56
Jena, Battle of, 112
Jerusalem, 284
Jesuits, 206
Jews, 5, 304, 306, 309,
334, 336, 416-417

JFK, , *see* Kennedy, John
F.
Jinnah, Muhammad Ali,
414
John Paul II, Pope,
Johnson, Lyndon Baines,
388-390, 395
Jordan, 415-416
Josephine, Empress of
France, 111
Jospin, Lionel,447
Judaism, 218
June Days, 145
Junkers, 188
Justinian, 109
Jutland, Battle of, 285
Kabila, Laurent Désiré, 413
Kadar, Janos, 398
Kandinsky, Wassily, 425
Kasavubu, Joseph, 413
Katanga, 413
Kay, John, 131
*Keelmen Heaving Coals by
Moonligh*t, 210
Kemal, Mustafa, 235, 291
Kennan, George, 375
Kennedy, John F., 383-384,
388, 419
Kenya, 406
Kenya African Nationalist
Union, 406
Kenyatta, Jomo, 406
Kepler, Johann, 38
Kerensky, Alexander, 295-
296
KGB (Soviet intelligence
agency, 297, 402
Khmer Rouge, 393
Khomeini, Ayatollah, 436
Khrushchev, Nikita, 383-
384, 396
Kikuyus, 406
Kim Il Sung, 379
King, Martin Luther, Jr.,
431
Kipling, Rudyard, 227
Kissinger, Henry, 392
Kohl, Helmut, 372, 399,
448
Koons, Jeff, 426
Korea (*see also* North
Korea and South

Marie Antoinette of
France, 100, 103, 211
Marie Louise of France,
111
Marne, Battle of, 281, 286
Marsala, 187
Marseilles, 102
Marshall Plan, 371, 375-
376, 453
Marx, Karl, 50, 137-140,
141, 151, 215, 293, 294,
Marxism, 140, 215, 293
Mary II of England, 48
*Mathematical Principles of
Natural Philosophy*, 39
Matteotti, Giacomo, 302
Mau Mau, 406
Mauritania, 412
Maximilian of Mexico, 201
Mazarin, Cardinal, 20-21
Mazzini, Giuseppe, 118,
182-184
McCarthy, Eugene, 390
Medicis Dynasty, 6
Mediterranean Sea, 374
Meiji Restoration, 241
Mein Kampf, 306-307, 329
Mekong Delta, 387, 392
Mensheviks, 294-295
Mercantilism, 10, 33
Metternich, Prince
Klemens von, 121-123
Metz, 193
Mexico, 5, 31, 201, 286
Midlands, 134
Midway Island, 331
Milan, 56, 301, 302
Mill, James, 213
Mill, John Stuart, 213, 214
Minimalism, 426
Minorca, 24
Mir, 420
Mississippi, 31, 36
Missouri, 427
Mitterand, Francois, 446
Mobutu Sese Seko, 413
Modena, 124, 183, 186
Modern art, 424-426
Modova, 450
Mogadishu, 410
Moltke, Helmuth Johannes
Ludwig von, 281
Monet, Claude, 220

Montagnards, 101
Montenegro, 247, 450
Montesquieu, Charles
Louis de Secondat,
Baron de la Brède et de,
53-54, 91
Montgomery, Bernard Law
332
Montgomery, Alabama, 431
Moore, Charles, 428
Moore, G.E., 429
Moravia, 324
Morocco, 246, 411
Moscow, 25, 116, 232,
325, 329, 336, 403, 440
Moslems, *see* Muslims
Mountain, The see
Montagnards
Mukden, Battle of, 242
Mukden Incident, 318
Munich, 304, 306, 309,
323, 324
Munich Putsch, 306
Muslims, 5, 236, 414, 447,
451
Mussolini, Benito, 195,
278, 292, 301-303, 318-
321, 323, 332-333
My Lai Massacre, 394
Nagasaki, 240, 335
Nagy, Imre, 396, 398
Nanjing (Nanking), Treaty
of, 238
Naples, 102, 113, 126, 187
Napoleon Bonaparte, 10,
89-90, 104, 106-118,
121, 122, 124-125, 145,
181, 203, 224, 233-234
Napoleon I, *see* Napoleon
Bonaparte
Napoleon III, *see* Louis
Napoleon
Nassau, 192
Natal, 231
National Assembly of
France (1789-1791), 89,
94, 95, 96, 97, 98, 99,
122, 212
National Assembly of the
Fifth French Republic,
445, 446, 447

National Convention of
France, 89, 100, 101,
102, 104, 105
National Liberation Front,
387, 411
National Organization for
Women, *see* NOW
National Salvation Front,
401
National Socialist German
Workers' Party (Nazi
Party), 304
National Workshops, 144-
145
Nationalism, 8, 126, 140,
146-148, 177, 181-182,
218, 226, 233-234, 279-
280, 306, 311, 444
Nationalists, 248, 291,
309, 320-321, 378-379,
414, 444
*Nationalsozialistische
deutsche Arbeiter-
Partei* (Nazi Party), 304
NATO (North Atlantic
Treaty Organization),
371, 377-378, 386, 450-
452, 455
Nazi (Party), 304
Nazi-Soviet Pact, 325
Nazis, 217, 218, 307-309,
321, 325, 334, 336
Nazism, 278, 449
Neisse River, 338
Nelson, Lord Horatio, 108,
114
Neo-fascists, 447
NEP (New Economic
Policy), 297-298
Netherlands, 11-12, 23-24,
35, 102, 108, 113, 123-
124, 142, 327, 377, 452
Neue Staatsgalerie, 428
Neuilly, Treaty of, 291
New Deal, 207, 311
New Economic Policy, *see*
NEP
New Granada, 31
New Hampshire, 31, 390
New Harmony, 137
New Organon, 41
New Orleans, 428
New York City, 296, 428